International Energy and Resources Law and Policy Series

Exploitation of Natural Resources in the 21st Century

The titles published in this series are listed at the end of this volume.

International Energy and Resources Law and Policy Series

Exploitation of Natural Resources in the 21st Century

Edited by

Malgosia Fitzmaurice
and
Milena Szuniewicz

KLUWER LAW INTERNATIONAL

THE HAGUE · LONDON · NEW YORK

Published by:
Kluwer Law International
P.O. Box 85889, 2508 CN The Hague, The Netherlands
sales@kluwerlaw.com
http://www.kluwerlaw.com

Sold and Distributed in North, Central and South America by:
Aspen Publishers, Inc.
7201 McKinney Circle, Frederick, MD 21704, USA

Sold and distributed in all other countries by:
Turpin Distribution Services Limited
Blackhorse Road, Letchworth, Herts.,
SG6 1HN, United Kingdom

A C.I.P. Catalogue record for this book is available from the Library of Congress.

Printed on acid-free paper

ISBN 90-411-2063-7

Printed and bound in Great Britain by Antony Rowe Limited.

Table of Contents

Foreword
Professor T. Wälde   vii

Preface   ix

Sustainable Development in the European Union Treaties and
in National Legislation: Some conclusions
Nigel Haigh   1

The International Dimension of EU Energy Law and Policy
Thomas Wälde   9

General Principles of Sustainable Development: From Soft Law
to Hard Law
Gerhard Hafner   53

Sustainable Development, War Reparations and Environmental
Damage
Olufemi Elias   67

Incorporating Sustainable Development Concerns into the
Development and Investment Process – the World Bank
Experience
David Freestone   91

The Progressive Integration of Environmental Protections
within Offshore Joint Development Agreements
David M. Ong   113

The Customary International Law of Transboundary Fresh Waters
Joseph W. Dellapenna   143

New Era in Luso-Spanish relations in the Management of
Shared Basins? The Challenge of Sustainability
Paulo Canelas de Castro   191

Finnish–Swedish Frontier River Commission – Effective Water
Co-operation
Professor Malgosia Fitzmaurice   235

Legal and Institutional Aspects of Management Arrangements
for Shared Stocks of Marine Fish
Daniel Owen   247

Participants   289

Index   293

Foreword

Sustainable development is the key principle of global civilisation of our time. It is so successful because it combines what to some appears so difficult to reconcile: economic growth and environmental protection. The idea is that these dilemmas are solvable if economic growth is influenced by, guided by and channelled into ways that minimise environmental damage, while appreciating that to a considerable extent environmental protection, its political acceptance, the resources required to fund it and the increase in human expectations to support it requires prosperity. The concept has become the pillar of North–South consensus as it accommodates the objectives of achieving higher prosperity (essential for the aspirations of the South) with the objectives of maintaining and sustaining prosperity in consonance with environmental quality of the North. But to make this principle more than a mantra that is mindlessly repeated over and over, one needs to reflect on the principles and its inherent dilemmas and implications and to work it in the numerous rules that are relevant in the global economy. The principle by itself can only achieve a public relations effect – weaker the more it gets diluted by repetition. Its true impact will emerge to the extent if influences the specific details and operations of the legal regimes for the global economy. Professor Malgosia Fitzmaurice's book makes a welcome contribution to the study on the operational relevance of the principle of sustainable development, mainly, though not exclusively, in the field of natural (in particular) resources. She and her team merit all responsibility and credit for this new book.

Thomas Wälde
St Andrews, June

Preface

The concept for the book originated from the Conference on Exploitation and Management of Natural Resources in the Twenty-First Century: The Challenge of Sustainable Development which was held on 26/27 October 2001. The Conference was organised by the British Institute of International and Comparative Law and the Department of Law at Queen Mary, University of London.

The concept of sustainable development became inexorably connected with the protection of the environment. However, it is almost impossible to define the concept. Therefore the present book adopts a practical approach and deals with particular fields of environmental protection to which the concept of sustainable development is applied.

The essays included in the book cover the following topics:

- Using Treaties to Solve Management Problems;
- New Era in Luso-Spanish Relations in the Management of Shared Basins? – The Challenge of Sustainability;
- The Customary International Law of Transboundary Fresh Waters;
- Sustainable Development, War Reparations and Environmental Damage;
- Finnish-Swedish Frontier River Commission-Effective Water Co-operation;
- Incorporating Sustainable Development Concerns into the Development and Investment Process – the World Bank Experience;
- General Principles of Sustainable Development: From Soft Law to Hard Law

- Sustainable Development in the European Union Treaties and in National Legislation;
- The Progressive Integration of Environmental Protection within Offshore Joint Development Agreements;
- Legal and Institutional Aspects of Management Arrangements for Shared Stocks of Marine Fish;
- International Energy Law: Concepts, Context and Players.

The problem of sustainable development took a prominent place at the Johannesburg meeting in September 2002. Principle 1 of the Johannesburg Declaration on Sustainable Development reaffirms the commitment of the peoples of the world assembled at the World Summit to sustainable development. A collective responsibility is assumed to advance and strengthen the interdependent and mutually reinforcing pillars of sustainable development – economic development, social development and environmental protection – at local, national, regional and global level (Principle 5).

The Johannesburg Declaration acknowledges that the global environment continues to suffer. Loss of biodiversity continues, fish stocks continue to be depleted, desertification claims more and more fertile land, the adverse effects of climate change are already evident, natural disasters are more frequent and more devastating and developing countries more vulnerable, and air, water and marine pollution continue to rob millions of a decent life (Principle 13).

Plan of implementation of sustainable development adopted at Johannesburg reaffirms the importance and the leading role of the 1992 UN Conference on Environment and Development (UNCED) held in Rio and advocates full commitment to the Rio Principles and full implementation of Agenda 21 adopted there. (Principle 1).

In the light of all the above the book which we are presenting is very topical and important in that it outlines the programme of sustainable development in concrete fields of economic and environmental co-operation.

NIGEL HAIGH*

Sustainable Development in the European Union Treaties and in National Legislation: Some Conclusions

Both the European Union (EU) and the European Community (EC), of which it is part, now have the promotion of sustainable development explicitly stated among their objectives. This was achieved, not without a struggle, by a series of treaties which amended and supplemented the original Treaty of Rome that created the European Economic Community in the 1950s. An outline of the struggle has been provided elsewhere,[1] as have some legal analyses.[2, 3] This paper will look at some of the consequences so far. It will also

* Former Director, Institute for European Environmental Policy, London and Honorary Fellow, Department of Laws, University College, London.

[1] N. Haigh 'Introducing the concept of sustainable development into the treaties of the European Union' (1998) in *The Transition to Sustainability: the politics of Agenda 21 in Europe*, eds T. O'Riordan and H. Voisey, Earthscan.
[2] D. Wilkinson, Maastricht and the Environment, *JEL* Vol 4 No 2, 1992.
[3] S. Baer and R. A. Kramer, European Environmental Policy after Amsterdam, *JEL* Vol 10 No 2, 1998

M. Fitzmaurice and M. Szuniewicz (eds.), Exploitation of Natural Resources in the 21st Century, 1–7.
© *2003 Kluwer Law International. Printed in Great Britain.*

take the example of some UK national legislation where references to promoting sustainable development are to be found, and will draw some conclusions.

We will argue that sustainable development suffers from uncertainty as a legal term. It is still best seen as an aspiration which certainly should mould policy and hence the law, and that we are now in need of extra legislation of a certain kind to put the concept to work more effectively. Elsewhere we have called this volume control.[4]

1.   The European Community

The Treaty of Amsterdam did more from an environmental point of view than including sustainable development among the tasks of the Community that are set out in Article 2 of the Rome Treaty. It also lifted the pre-existing 'environmental integration requirement' – the provision that environmental protection requirements must be integrated into other EC policies – out of the Environment Title of the Treaty and put it in a new Article 6 near the front. It is now impossible for other Directorates-General of the European Commission to argue – as they sometimes did – that environmental integration was a matter for DG Environment and not for them.

Even more significantly, Article 6 says that such integration is to promote sustainable development, thus putting some flesh on the bare bones of the new task in Article 2. This formulation is particularly gratifying to my former institute because it was that institute, in the run up to the intergovernmental conference, that put into play the linking of sustainable development in Article 2 with the integration requirement.[5]

The effect has been startling. When the ink on the Treaty was hardly dry, and before it was ratified, the Swedish Prime Minister at the European Summit at Luxembourg in 1997 proposed that there be a strategy on sustainable development and integration. Following a report from the Commission, the Cardiff Summit in 1998 then invited all relevant formations of the Council (initially Agriculture, Transport and Energy) to establish their own strategies for giving effect to sustainable development. The Commission also began preparing an EU sustainable development strategy in addition to a Sixth Action Programme on the Environment.

Subsequent Summit Meetings, or meetings of the European Council as they

---

[4]   N. Haigh, *Space, Time and Volume Control: further reflections on the law for sustainable development,* UKELA Yearbook (forthcoming).

[5]   *The 1996 Intergovernmental Conference: Integrating the Environment into Other EU Policies,* IEEP London, April 1995. A report prepared at the request of the Department of the Environment (UK).

are properly called consisting of heads of State or Government, have continued to pay attention to sustainable development, first by extending the list of subject matter Councils to be covered by the Cardiff process (adding third world development, industry and internal market, and then economic and financial measures, fisheries, and general affairs), then by considering the Commission's Communication on an EU sustainable development strategy and deciding to link it to the strategic goal that the EU set itself at the Lisbon Summit in early 2000: '*to become the most competitive and dynamic knowledge-based economy in the world capable of sustainable economic growth with more and better jobs and greater social cohesion*'. This was to be done by including environmental indicators among the social and economic indicators that each Summit is to review annually at its spring meeting as a way of measuring progress with the Lisbon goal.

The first report presented by the Commission at the Barcelona Summit in spring 2002 was roundly criticised by the European Environment Agency, the Parliament and by the Environment Council for dealing inadequately with environmental matters. The Commission then conceded that the process was a new one where much had yet to be learnt and that subsequent reports would be improved.

There had been some discussion of whether the 'Cardiff process' should be subsumed entirely within the 'Lisbon process' which risked diminishing the attention being paid to the environment in sectoral policies, since sustainable development reports would no longer be prepared for sectors such as agriculture, transport and energy, but the decision was made to continue with the Cardiff process. An analysis of the reports prepared so far has been made and an updated list of the reports is available.[6]

Some of the strategies that have emerged so far have been disappointing as one would expect. But two points of importance should be noted. Firstly, it is the Council and not the Commission that has been preparing the sectoral strategies under the 'Cardiff process'. Secondly, the overall EU strategy is the responsibility of the Commission's Secretariat-General, while the Sixth Action Programme was prepared by DG Environment. This diversification was an objective of the Swedish Government, which wanted sustainable development to get under the skin of the whole EU, rather than just remaining an enthusiasm of DG Environment and some Ministers in the Environment Council.

While it is of course too soon to say that this explosion of strategy writing is moving the EU towards a more sustainable path in any measurable way, it clearly demonstrates a strong political response to the Treaty amendments, a response that is surely more than enough to rule out the possibility of a Member State, or perhaps the Parliament, referring the Commission or

---

[6] *Manual of Environmental Policy: the EU and Britain*, Institute for European Environmental Policy and Maney Publishing, looseleaf (updated every six months), see Chapter 3.

Council to the European Court for failing to fulfill its Treaty obligations. The Parliament had successfully done this in the early 1980s, in connection with the failure of the Council to adopt a Common Transport Policy as called for by the Treaty. But it is possible to imagine, say, Sweden taking legal action if the Council or Commission had failed to move, and one cannot rule out the possibility of legal action if a Member State is outvoted on some specific proposal for legislation that it believes is deeply flawed environmentally.

2. UK legislation

The term 'sustainable development' is now appearing, not just in policy documents and international treaties and conventions, but also in national legislation. In the UK it has appeared in many Acts of Parliament. For example, the Greater London Authority Act 1999 which created this new authority and gave it a general power to do anything to further its principal purposes, also requires it to *'have regard to the effect which the proposed exercise of the power will have on . . . the achievement of sustainable development in the United Kingdom'*. A discussion of all the appearances of the phrase 'sustainable development' in UK legislation has been made elsewhere,[7] and here we will discuss only its appearance in the Environment Act 1995 which created the Environment Agency for England and Wales to carry out, in an integrated way, the duties formerly performed by separate bodies responsible for water, air and waste management.

Section 4(i) of the Act states that: *'It shall be the principal aim of the Agency . . . . In discharging its functions so as to protect or enhance the environment, taken as a whole, as to make the contribution towards attaining the objective of achieving sustainable development mentioned in sub-section (3) below'*.

Sub-section 3 then refers to guidance to be given by Ministers with respect to the contribution which Ministers consider it appropriate for the Agency to make *'towards attaining the objective of achieving sustainable development'*.

What is the reason for this extremely convoluted language? Let us imagine that the Act placed an *unconvoluted* duty to promote sustainable development on the Agency on top of its other statutory functions, and that there had been no cautious Ministerial guidance. Let us also imagine an industrial plant being granted an environmental licence by the Agency in accordance with the requirements of the EC Directive on integrated pollution prevention and control (IPPC), allowing it to emit a quantity – severely limited of course – of toxic and persistent substance x. Let us further imagine this licence being challenged by an environment group. If this is not to stretch our imaginations

[7] W. Upton, *The need for legal limits to sustainable development* (April 2000) in 'The Changing Role of Environmental Law', proceedings of the UKELA conference, London.

too far, the group generously concedes that the licence has been properly given under the IPPC regime and that the Agency has properly interpreted best available technologies (BAT). The group's complaint is instead that the Agency has failed to fulfill its sustainable development duty in that the persistent substance x, while perhaps not causing any harm locally or in the short term, will in the long term build up in the North Sea and then the Atlantic where eventually it will do harm. The court would be faced with asking itself how far ahead it had to look – 10 or 50 or hundreds of years – and with the unenviable task of answering that question and balancing present welfare against the welfare of future generations. More plausibly and dramatically, imagine a challenge to the licence for any fossil fuelled power station on similar grounds. Any lawyer could make a good case.

If we turn to the current convoluted language of Section 4 and to the Ministerial guidance, we will see that the chances of challenges of this kind being mounted successfully, or mounted at all, fade into insignificance. The guidance says that the Government's policy for industrial regulation recognises the principles of sustainable development through the use of the concepts relating to best available technologies (BAT) which are designed to achieve levels of pollution which reconcile society's interests in the environment and in industry, in both the short and the long term.

This is not quite the same as business as usual because the guidance does expect the Agency to apply the concepts in such a way as to respect the principles of sustainable development. But it does not tell it how.

In short, the Government has said to the Agency: think about sustainable development as you fulfill your previous duties, but if you do that properly you are making the contribution to sustainable development that we expect. The Government has in effect reserved to itself the right to interpret 'sustainable development' because the objective of achieving sustainable development that the Act placed on the Agency would otherwise have created legal uncertainty.

Two questions arise. First, how *should* the concept of sustainable development alter existing industrial regulation? Some thoughts on this are presented below. Secondly, has the convoluted aim had *any* effect on the Agency? Briefly the answer is yes, because the aim of sustainable development is the only overarching framework provided by Parliament and the Government to connect the constituent bodies that came together in 1996 to form the Agency. Without that aim, the Agency would not have produced a strategy or 'vision' document which looks much more broadly at environmental issues than its predecessor bodies would have done. The process of producing its strategy is altering the way the Agency thinks which will affect the way it acts.

3. Some conclusions

The embodiment of the concept of sustainable development in the EU treaties has stimulated a process which has begun to confront politicians at the highest level with the need to modify their sectoral policies such as those for agriculture, transport and energy, as well as with their overarching goals such as those set out by the Lisbon Summit. The Lisbon goal of 2000 was essentially concerned with social and economic development and was clearly framed without attention to environmental protection or the management of natural resources. One can say that it was because of the treaty requirement to promote sustainable development that pressure has been successfully applied on the European Council to take account of matters which do not yet come naturally to many politicians at that level. The embodiment of the concept in the treaties has therefore started a process.

The same can be said at the national level where the Environment Agency in the UK is now thinking in a different way as a result of the duty relating to sustainable development in its governing Act. It is still rather difficult to point to specific actions at either EU or national level which are different because of the sustainable development duty. Indeed, the difficulty of using the term to define a line dividing a legal from an illegal action is illustrated by the hypothetical example above of the licence for an industrial plant. The UK Government, foreseeing that sustainable development is too unclear to be used in deciding on specific site related decisions, has carefully ensured that the concept of sustainable development remains only a guiding concept. But does this mean that the concept remains only a concept, albeit a remarkably powerful one? Is there some way that the important new elements of the concept can be given legally binding force, at a level above specific site related decisions while being more precise than a broad concept? The answer is that this is already happening.

Essential elements of sustainable development are that it extends in time and space. It is concerned with future generations (time) and extends to beyond a locality (space). Indeed, one cannot conceive of sustainable development being achievable at all below the level of the global system. No locality, or industry or country can be sustainable on its own, since all are dependent on other parts of the earth for resources or markets, and the most that each can do individually is contribute to the objective of achieving sustainable development (to quote the language of the UK Environment Act 1995).

We know well that some environmental problems are global and so require concerted global action but others are more circumscribed in space. Acidification of surface waters is not experienced in some parts of the world but it is a serious problem in Northern Europe, and laws to tackle the problem over time have been agreed by groupings of countries some of which, such as Spain, hardly experience the problem. The making of sacrifices for someone else's benefit is one of the characteristics of sustainable development, with the beneficiaries being displaced from us in *space*, or *time* or both.

In theory, it is possible to identify the geographical extent of an environmental problem – ranging from the purely local to the truly global – and we try to do so in order to tackle it. But the extent in time is indeterminate and we avoid talking about it. Do we really mean sustainable in eternity? Probably not, because astronomers tell us that one day the earth will fall into the sun. If not forever, then for how many generations? To make a sacrifice for one generation may be quite different from making one for many. Because we cannot answer this question, sustainable development must remain only an aspiration. If one purpose of good law is to provide certainty, then sustainable development as a legal term fails the test resoundingly.

To tackle problems remote in space and time, which are not in our own self interest, we need the concept to justify the laws required for action, and the particular kind of laws that we can call volume control.

An early item of environmental legislation that exhibits 'volume control' is the EC Council Decision of 1980 that placed a production capacity cap on certain ozone depleting substances (CFCs). Subsequently the volume control has been turned to zero for some of the substances.

The ozone layer may be an exceptional global problem calling for exceptional measures, but there are other examples of volume control not entailing total bans. In the early 1980s, the Scandinavian countries formed the '30% Club' of those countries committing themselves to cutting their total national sulphur dioxide emissions by that amount over a given period. In 1985 this was formalised as a Protocol to the convention on long range transboundary air pollution. As the UK refused to sign that Protocol, volume control of SO_2 only applied in the UK with the adoption in 1988 of the EC Directive on large combustion plants.

A similar approach to greenhouse gases is the cornerstone of the Kyoto Protocol, but that is yet to become binding.

So there are indeed precedents for volume control meaning *legislation influencing the total volume of some activity as opposed to controls applied only at site level.* Of course the volume control may need to be translated into controls at site level in which case it provides a strategic level of control over local decisions.

Volume control, then, is a key way in which the concept of sustainable development can be translated into laws which bear on long range and long term environmental problems.

Nor is volume control confined to traditional environmental issues. Think of fishing quotas – certainly a sustainable development issue – and set-aside under the Common Agricultural Policy. Volume control is not therefore a new subject to be frightened of, though it certainly needs developing, and indeed is developing. Recent examples are to be found in the EC landfill Directive (which limits biodegradable waste discharged to landfills), the water framework Directive (which limits abstraction to the rate of recharge), and the emissions ceiling Directive (covering certain gases).

THOMAS WÄLDE*

The International Dimension of EU Energy Law and Policy

1. International dimension of EU Energy Law and Policy

1.1 Players, policy and issues

EU approaches are normally very inward-looking. That is natural for a community of sovereign states engaged in the difficult process of integration and of developing, and accepting, joint institutions. There is little time to look outside, when what happens inside is so absorbing. But the EU is not on a lonely planet nor a 'Fortress Europe', and nowhere less so than in the field of energy. Without energy the EU societies will not function, and most of the energy comes from abroad, and mostly from a difficult, volatile, risky abroad full of problems with human rights, environment and good governance – not

* Professor and Jean Monnet Chair for EU Economic & Energy Law, CEPMLP/Dundee
  Preliminary version of Chapter IX for forthcoming book on EU Energy Law.

M. Fitzmaurice and M. Szuniewicz (eds.), Exploitation of Natural Resources in the 21st Century, 9–52.
© *2003 Kluwer Law International. Printed in Great Britain.*

part of the community of civilised nations one would have said 100 years ago. In the old world of state-ownership and monopoly, energy was a strictly national matter. Companies went out as national champions to find coal and later oil, all sponsored by and supported by their home government. This mercantilistic approach – with governments trying to ensure security of supply by dealing with other governments – has informed the energy policy of most EU countries until fairly recently and is visible in most of the EC external energy actions of the past. It is far from disappearing from the mind-set of most agencies and people involved. If the going gets tough and energy supply anxieties arise, the state is expected to ensure the supply, with all of its forces – the 1991 Gulf War may have had a legitimate cause in the defense of the integrity of an independent state against neighbourly aggression, but it is unlikely to have happened would the Gulf not be of principal importance to the energy security of both the US and the EU. But with the energy markets becoming regional (e.g. electricity and gas) and increasingly global (e.g. in oil, but also LNG and coal), the long-established connection between anxiously observed 'energy dependence' and strategic state, or EU-wide, action, to assure 'security of supply' is no longer automatic. Apart from the cases of world war, no EU country has such has ever suffered a serious disruption of supply, though 'energy dependence' has relentlessly increased. Countries with very high degrees of energy self-sufficiency, e.g. the former Soviet Union, on the other hand, have done rather badly.[1] If markets function, energy will respond to economic rules: It will go to where the prices are highest; its use, substitution and investments will respond to prices. The better the market works – the more liquidity, players, sources of energy, transport networks, instruments facilitating and protecting investment, laws combating predatory behaviour, the less will energy security become an issue and a specific task for high foreign politics of governments. International energy policy means therefore in a market environment less to do costly – and in all cases inefficient – intergovernmental deals than to create a market environment with high liquidity, diversity of supply flows and support for infrastructure investment in high-risk cases where the market may be wary (e.g. pipelines, interconnectors and investment support for high-risk, long pay-off situations). International policy then is no longer interventionist, but rather facilitative, regulatory and in cases of long-term infrastructure investment, supportive.

The EU Green paper on security of energy supply of November 2000[2] reflects this transition from a a 'dirigiste', intergovernmental and mercantilistic view of security of supply to a more market-based one. It details energy dependence of the EU and concludes that the future will bring higher dependence on oil and gas imports, highlights the significant contribution coal

---

[1] J. Mitchell (ed) *The New Economy of Oil*, Earthscan London 2001, 176–207.
[2] EC Communication on the development of Energy Policy for the Enlarged EU, COM(2003) 262 final of 1315/2003.

(with better environmental technology) and nuclear (with no climate effect) can make and identifies the market-oriented steps to take to ensure a functioning market, both through market-facilitative institutions and instruments, and through support for investment in significant physical infrastructure (mainly pipelines and interconnectors). But it is still mired in the self-absorptive perspective not atypical of EU institutions. While it identifies 'dependence' , i.e. where oil and gas come from and are likely to come from in the future, it does not do the necessary next step and ask not only what the EU expects, but what the external parties' interest and constraints are and how to strike deals based on a reciprocal congruity of interest. The external dimension of EU energy policy needs to be understood out of both the internal play and the regional (e.g. eastwards, southwards) and global play of energy production, transport and supply.

Within the EU, DG TREN (ex DG XVII) represents the technocratic energy focus, with greatest concern over energy flows to the EU, also defending its own international turf against more mighty actors in the Commission. Together with DG Competition (ex-IV), it is responsible for implementation of the energy directives. There is a special relation – application of EU energy law to the EEA countries (mainly Norway) to watch over. EEA countries have to incorporate EU internal market law (e.g. competition, internal trade law and the energy directives) as it evolves, with consultation, but no (!) participation. As the largest oil and gas producer in Europe, but outside the EU, Norway is therefore now subject to EU energy and competition law, though there are special procedures to observe.[3] Norwegian energy policy has always been strongly statist and protectionist[4]; its participation in the ECT negotiations focused on maximising Norwegian carve-outs from the ECT liberalisation policies. EU energy law challenged Norwegian's licensing (i.e. its protectionist, pro-STATOIL bent); its emphasis on Norwegian procurement; its former policies to maintain a privileged role of the state in the oil and gas industry and its policy of selling Norwegian gas through a Norwegian syndicate. Enforcement actions, so far, have not been very emphatic,[5] though Norway seems to at least to bend its system to avoid a legal confrontation.

DG I and I A (new DG RELEX) represent the foreign policy interests of the Commission, much concerned with managing accession (and bringing the accession countries in Eastern Europe into the acquis communautaire now including the energy directives). Wider-ranging foreign policy interests include building economic collaboration with Russia and the Central Asian/Caucasus

---

[3]   T. Blanchet et. al., *The Agreement on the European Economic Area*, Oxford 1994; more recently: McGoldrick, 186, 187.

[4]   Anderson, S.; *The Struggle over North Sea Oil and Gas: Government Strategies in Denmark, Britain and Norway*; (Scandinavian Univ. Press, 1993).; Thorsen/Arnesen, Offshore licensing in Norway: a privilege for Norwegian companies, [1995] *JENRL*, 258.

[5]   But settlement of the gas syndicate investigation in 2002, *FT*, 17 July 2002.

countries where energy again is a major factor of both economic growth, growing supply interest and investment interest for the EU, but also a source of internal and external tensions over control of oil&gas wealth. The EU's direct interest in border security also extends to the Mediterranean countries with energy and insecurity both most relevant for Algeria, but also relevant for Tunisia and Morocco (oil transit), Syria and Egypt (oil supply) and Iran as a key country for both regional security, tensions with the US (infra) and oil and gas supply both from Iran direct and in terms of its political and transit leverage over the Caspian oil and gas potential (Azerbaijan, Turkmenistan, Kazakhstan, Uzbekistan).[6] Turkey is a pivot country, both for regional security and transit (from the Caspian, through the Bosphorus). Its relation to the EU is unstable because of the uncertain fate of its accession request; there are serious problems of cultural compatibility, both within the EU against Turkey and in Turkey's internal political make-up. The Middle East's role as major supplier to the EU is likely to grow as North Sea oil and gas supplies fade and to the extent Russian energy production is absorbed domestically if the Russian economy takes off. The Middle Eastern countries are all troublesome. Not one oil&gas producer in the Middle East (or Mediterranean or Caspian region) reflects contemporary Western expectations of good governance, democracy and respect for human rights. Violently divisive and modernised feudal structures predominate. If there is a linkage between these values and political stability, then any of these countries can be thrown into political turmoil and external conflict. If the EU takes serious the current resurgence, under a different label, of the 'civilised nation' concept, then it should not be in close business with any of those countries – which are essential for EU energy supply. It is an interesting question if Islam is a major risk factor for stable energy trade relations with the EU, or a factor which can stabilise the relationship based on mutual respect.[7] While the EU relies, and increasingly with no realistic alternative in the middle-term, on these problem countries as major oil and gas suppliers, one should not forget that these rely as much, and probably more so,[8] on exporting their energy. With growing demands from growing populations and with no realistic industrial alternative, the oil and gas producers – whatever their regime and even during civil war as in Algeria – are in much more desperate straits. They do have to export to the market and if they don't or the price is too low, all the thin fabric of their countries' institutions is immediately and seriously in peril.

[6] For maps and other information, EC May 15, 2003 supra.
[7] Oystein Noreng, *Oil and Islam*, Wiley, 1997; Samuel Huntingdon's clash of culture prediction – Samuel Huntingdon, *The Clash of Civilisation and the Remaking of World Order*, New York: Simon & Schuster, is one way of looking at it, but the modern European way would rather tend towards respect and tolerance for Islam; Islam itself is torn between a need to modernise and fundamentalist tendencies which may in due time lead to a modernisation of Islam incorporating Islam's respect for property, contract and trade.
[8] J. Mitchell, Ed. *New Economy of Oil* (2001) 177, 203.

There are energy relations outside this circle of core interest – both political and energy-based – for the EU. First, the EU maintains through the Cotonou (ex-Lome) Agreement with the 'ACP' (Asia-Caribbean-Pacific) countries the (mainly) French and British post-colonial relationship. There seems to be no particular energy significance here. West African countries (in particular Nigeria and Angola) have acquired a growing role in energy (oil, LNG) supplies which requires nurturing. In Asia, the EU meets a large, growing and competing supply interest (e.g. for Siberian, Central Asian and Middle East oil and gas), but also a market for investment and export of equipment and services. In Latin America, there is both a traditional EU cultural (Spain) and economic (UK, Germany) interest. In both Asia and Latin America, there is a strong, not always clearly visible, counter-interest to balance the over-whelming US position by developing relations with a more economically-focused and less power-oriented EU.

A major energy focus of the EU is, or should be, the US. The US is the major, at times stronger, competitor of the EU companies in terms of investment, capital and services throughout the world, with an equally voracious need for growing energy supplies. Different from the EU, where energy saving has actually worked and where energy use per GNP units is much more modest, the US has not developed the political will to take drastic action to reduce its energy needs, but rather confides in its superior economic and supreme political power to assure sufficient supplies. The US is also, in climate change terms, a major polluter. It is likely that due to – understandable – US opposition on the Kyoto climate change protocol will either not become effective or would require serious revision.[9] US international energy policy is more assertive (e.g. Gulf Wars (91–2003)) and more self-confident i.e. less interested in consensual, multilateral solutions (e.g. the US forced entry and then surprise exit from the Energy Charter Treaty).[10] Throughout the world, EU companies and US companies, often with home-state and EU support, compete for access to oil and gas acreage, investment, and sale of equipment and services, with US companies often hindered by the now widespread use of domestically motivated US economic sanctions, e.g. against Iran and Libya.[11] This competition is not reflected in official EU documents – the US is not mentioned as a distinct actor relevant for EU energy policy in the 2000 Green Paper. This lack of openness over the EU-US relationship in the energy field is compensated, perhaps regrettably, by considerable subcutaneous hostility by EU (and possibly US) officials involved in winning influence in the post-Soviet countries through policy-oriented

[9]   J. Mitchell (2001) 218.
[10] W. Fox, in T. Waelde (1998), *The Energy Charter Treaty.*
[11] T. Waelde, Managing the risk of sanctions in the global oil and gas industry, in: 36 *Texas Intl Law J.* 184–230 (2001).

technical assistance programmes.[12] It might be a much better option to discuss this relationship, one of competition, but also of cooperation, more transparently rather than suppress and camouflage arising tensions. First, competition is no reason for hostility. In the global society, nation states, and identification of 'national interest' with them, is a much diluted and possibly partly obsolete concept. Focusing on competition between nations is another case of being locked in a historical, now obsolete mind-set. Many of the companies, being US or EU, are owned by a community of investors on both sides of the Atlantic. Both the US and the EU have an overarching interest in stability and smooth functioning of the global economy and to safeguard global environmental interest. They, in particular together, also have the means through the control of the largely US-created, but EU-supported international institutions (WTO; World Bank; OECD; IMF; IEA; UN) and their own resources and internal stability. All EU countries have massively benefited from US political and economic leadership in the past, and continue to do so – in spite of continued griping in particular from France. It may be hard for traditional nationalistic pride to have a hegemonic power, but there is also huge benefit from the 'Pax Americana'. It is very difficult to move these two large powers, and they are very few actual agreements between them. Nevertheless, it is necessary that the policy dialogue and the institutional processes involving both (e.g. OECD, IEA, WTO, World Bank, EBRD) are strengthened. EU energy supply will work if there is a functioning global market emitting effective signals to market players – and the global market requires both the US and the EU to work at it.

It would be wrong to portray the relevant actors only within the traditional model of states and their strategies. EU (and US) foreign policy is very much influenced by non-state actors, be it non-governmental organisations (NGOs) which now represent themselves as the truest guardians of Western cultural values, multinational companies – which as well are now forced to present themselves not only as profit machines, but as 'forces for the good',[13] business organisations – which tend to represent the common denominator of corporate interest and the press through which the actions of all actors are filtered and magnified. Not all that is seen by governmental actors as good for business (e.g. the MAI negotiations up to 1998 or the ECT) is so seen by the companies themselves. Close corporate-government relations – e.g. between the former state company Elf and the French government – tend to give way to greater distance as international capital markets exercise more influence on corporate management than their home governments. International organisations in which the EU member states or the EU itself participate develop at times a

---

[12] I refer here to my own experience as EU consultant to CIS governments negotiating with US companies for oil and gas development.
[13] J. Mitchell (2001), 209 et seq.

dynamic of their own, propelled by either the secretariat or the caucus of like-minded and similarly-oriented government delegates.

Within WTO processes, the emphasis is on free trade – now reaching energy; within the OECD, the emphasis is on free movement of capital; within the IEA, the emphasis is on identifying current trends and prospects and recommending governmental action, plus consultation with the producing countries; within the World Bank, the traditional emphasis on good project lending has given way to a much more diffuse effort to leverage lending to influence economic (and energy investment/ privatisation) policies and now 'hard' imposition of 'soft' cultural policies (environment; human rights; participatory democracy; poverty eradication).[14] In UN for a, where the EU participates not in a strong position, the emphasis is rather on defending developing countries against imposition of economic and now cultural policies mainly representing the Western countries, e.g. in particular Unctad.[15] Critical assessment of liberalisation and privatisation in markets which may not be ripe for this and proposal of quid-pro-quo energy trade deals are developed here.[16] The financial institutions (World Bank, mainly under US influence; EBRD – under European, but not EU influence; EIB – under EU influence) have their own policy contribution to make. In the energy field, their role lies in exercising financing leverage to obtain favourable investment terms and in supporting for infrastructure facilities for which private banks are by themselves and without public guarantees not ready. With OPEC, the EU has started a dialogue (but possibly one of the deaf); both OPEC and the EU environmentalist (and tax) interests are in favour of the consumer paying a high oil price, but they differ on who is to collect oil&gas rent (Opec prefers taxes and high prices in favour of producing country, the EU high consumption taxes in favour of EU member states). OPEC, on the other hand, is politically very useful to the EU as, first, it contributes, now perhaps more effectively than in the past, to reasonably high and more stable oil prices by better production control; second, because being outside the jurisdiction of EU law and not vulnerable to internal EU political and public pressure, it can serve as a convenient scapegoat for high energy prices. In a way, it now does the dirty business of consumers and international oil companies which both, for reasons of competition law and public opinion, can not do themselves.

EU international energy policy, and the legal instruments deployed, is therefore not a carefully planned outcome of a political process by a unitary actor, but rather the unplanned, and not plannable, result of many players within and outwith the EU. The particular measures taken will often require consent and involvement by outside actors. In most cases, they will be the

---

[14] Helge Ole Bergesen/Leiv Lunde, *Dinosaurs or Dynamos? The United Nations and the World Bank at the Turn of the Century*, Earthscan Publications, London 1999.

[15] Unctad, 2000, trade agreements, petroleum and energy policies.

[16] Unctad, 10 April 2001, Energy Services in International Trade: Development Implications.

generated by coalitions of like-minded actors in all major players,[17] e.g. climate change policies by officials from DG Environment, environmental ministries, NGOs and executives from climate-change divisions in major energy companies, international energy policy/law assistance by linked groups in DG TREN, DG I/IA, and energy agencies in the accession countries and development aid by the DG VIII officials, aid industry lobbies, NGOs and institutional and individual beneficiaries in the recipient countries. It is not surprising that EU international policy in the energy field can be contradictory, with the transnational environmental coalitions transcending organisational borders producing multilateral environmental agreements (MEA) calling for trade restrictions, while the corporate-Commission trade-focused groups produce treaties and GATT-panel-based trade law aimed at excluding MEAs.[18] In this process certain dominant themes are generally present, though often dominant only in their particular play area, such as energy security for DG TREN, integrated markets for DG Competition (ex-IV), climate change for DG Environment (ex-XI), and building stability by economic and energy investment in the former Soviet Union[19] and the Mediterranean. Development aid plays a role, but EU development aid suffers from lack of focus and the tension between 'selfless' aid on one hand and more 'selfish' aid tied to the donour's interest on the other, with no clear understanding which of both approaches is in the final result more better for donour and recipient. New themes pervading all other activities relate to the current enthusiasm for exporting, and imposing, Western cultural values on countries which do not conform with Western governance concepts – i.e. a revived form of 19th century concepts of missionary colonialism and the civilising mission of the West.

There are also more technical imperatives for external EU energy action: Some issues (e.g. global warming) need global action, though national (e.g. Danish emission trading) and EU-wide policies can serve as a laboratory for global policies (and provide a competitive advantage to EU companies warned earlier of regulations to come). As global energy markets emerge (as already largely the case for oil, to some extent now for gasoline, LNG, uranium, coal and more slowly gas), regulatory solutions have to be sought, and EU external energy policy will then be about creating a global regulatory framework. The harbingers of such developments are the – though unsuccessful – efforts to create a global investment code (MAI) through the

---

[17] Robert D. Putnam, Diplomacy and domestic politics: the logic of two-level games, 42. *International Organization* 427–460 (1988).

[18] T. Waelde, Sustainable development and the 1994 Energy Charter Treaty: between pseudo-action and the management of environmental investment risk: in: Friedl Weiss et.al. (Eds), *International Economic Law with a Human Face*, Kluwer Law, London 1998, 223–271.

[19] T. Waelde, International Good Governance and Civilised Conduct among the Caspian Sea States: Oil and Gas lever for prosperity of conflict, in: W. Ascher/ N. Mirovitskaya, *The Caspian Sea: A Quest for Environmental Security*, Kluwer London 2000, 29–51.

OECD and the now emerging applicability of WTO – but also environmental – rules to cross-border energy trade (infra). The pooling of regulatory powers in the form of EU economic (including energy) law should only be a first step to pooling global regulatory powers in international institutions, though the resistance observable in the EU is likely to be even more intensive on a world scale, and thus progress likely to be very gradual. In the fullness of time, external EU energy law should be nothing but a regional component of international energy law.

1.2 Instruments and legal authority of EU external energy policy

To pursue its energy goals, the EU in the main uses treaties and money: Treaties to create a network of legal, but thereby also political and administrative obligations and procedures with the partner countries. No systematic analysis of the role of energy in such treaties has so far been done[20] While energy is mentioned in most treaties of the economic cooperation type, it is rarely the focus of a treaty. The 1994 Energy Charter Treaty seems to be the only energy-dedicated treaty the EC has acceded to. It would not be surprising if over 95% of treaty language relates to friendly expressions of good will with respect to trade, investment, environment – in newer treaties (e.g. the 2000 Cotonou agreement) also good governance, civil society and human rights. Specific legal obligations are rare in these treaties, and mostly related to trade. Energy trade is only now becoming a subject of EU treaty negotiations (infra). One can perhaps understand EC treaty-making as, firstly, an effort to develop a significant, and acknowledged, foreign policy role, castrated, though, by the absence of the traditional levers of projecting political and military power abroad; secondly, it is based on the explicit or implicit strategy to develop 'reasons to talk' with governments of interest to the EU. Treaties thus involve a dialogue process, from the negotiations stage to the stage of implementation, which in most cases is rather about discussing with governments the general, adhortatory principles contained in such treaties.

The second major instrument of EU international energy policy is money, mainly funds dedicated for technical assistance projects in the energy field. The EU regularly requires a treaty before committing technical assistance (older term is 'development aid') funds. Treaties and monies thereby complement each other. Technical assistance provided under the manifold and regrettably periodically changing EU-typical acronyms ('Tacis, Phare, Synergie, Altener, Save' 2003) have a multiple function: They are intended to

---

[20] But see the – dated – section in Macleod/Hendry & Hyett., *The External Relations of the European Communities*, Clarendon, Oxford 1996, 386–391. Energy is not mentioned in D. McGoldrick, *International Relations Law of the EU*, Longman 1997.

help the recipients to get expertise they do not have and can not pay themselves; they are a way to influence the partner countries' policies in the EU direction; they provide work for the large EU consultancy industry; they help this industry and larger EU companies to penetrate new markets, typically in competition with US (USAID) technical assistance pursuing a similar strategy. Their main benefit is probably that they facilitate the emergence of knowledge-based networks (consultants; academics; officials; corporate executives; NGO experts; specialised press) privileging the outreach of EU specialists.

Treaties and money never deliver what they promise in their high-sounding preambles and press releases. They are often not taken serious on both sides; their adhortatory language replete of expressions of good will, friendship and morally welcome purposes does not favour direct impact. The same applies to technical assistance projects. The EC has perhaps one of the lowest reputations worldwide for professionalism, organisational efficiency and focus of its development aid and technical assistance. No outside, independent and comprehensive assessment of either the agreements or the technical assistance practice has been carried out[21] focusing on user and stakeholder satisfaction. The combination of friendly treaty language with funding of – almost exclusively EU consulting groups – is perhaps a reflection of the lack of traditional power projection capacity. The EU is not, and can for the time being not be, as is often misunderstood, the mirror image of the US. Nevertheless, it would be wrong to deny the usefulness of these instruments. Deployed in large quantity, they project the EU as a prosperous partner with overwhelmingly cooperative and commercial interest. The net of treaties and the professional networks created by technical assistance are a conduit for channelling EU influence through concepts, methods, models, precedents and best practices to countries who have a need for models and are unable to develop effective approaches to governance on their own. The EU influence on energy policy in partner countries is therefore rarely a matter of power and direct pressure, but a matter of persuasion and intellectual osmosis facilitated by trust and the commonality of a joint search for peace and prosperity. It is not the way of power, but rather the way of collaborative dialogue.

As there is, to the dismay of many, no explicit energy chapter in the Treaty, so there is no explicit authority for EC treaty-making in the energy field. EC external competences[22] are based either on explicit authority of the treaty or they are the external manifestation of internal powers ('external/internal parallelism'). Once the Community has exercised internal powers to harmonise rules in a comprehensive way in a field of mixed competence, it

---

[21] There are regular – usually – critical reports for the European Parliament and the EU Court of Auditors.
[22] McGoldrick, 1997, 40–115; Macleod et.al., 37–75.

has also acquired the corollary of exclusive external powers.[23] With the emergence of more and more detailed and comprehensive specific EU energy law through the recent Energy Directives, there are strong arguments for exclusive Community jurisdiction for treaties with respect to energy. As it appears, the Community has exclusive competence with respect to competition,[24] so that the subject matter of the directives should be covered by exclusive Community jurisdiction. The rule – apart from the exclusive external trade competence under Art. (ex-113) – is shared competence, and most EU international treaties are 'mixed', i.e. both the EC and member states are signatories.[25] Environmental treaties, the very large number of economic cooperation agreements (association; partnership and cooperation; Europe agreements) and most commodity agreements are mixed agreements reflecting shared competence. For issues relating to energy, these authorisations are the most relevant:

- Common commercial policy (Art. 133, ex-113);
- Environmental cooperation (Art. 174, Ex 130r (4)
- Development policy (Art. 131, 130 (y);
- Association (economic cooperation), Art. 310, ex-238;

In principle, the Commission negotiates based on a mandate from the Council and in consultation with a Council committee. The Council, on the basis of a Commission proposal concludes an international agreement after consultation with the EP (Art. 300).[26]

1.3 Technical and financial assistance programmes

With its technical and financial assistance programmes, the EU tries to influence the partner countries' energy policies in the direction of the EU: Liberalisation, opening-up of the energy industries for (preferably EU) investment, greater trade relations (export of EU equipment and services, import of partner state oil and gas), better environmental performance (in particular related to negative climate-change emissions, emissions (e.g. of SO2) with a cross-border effect on EU environmental quality (e.g. air pollution; survival of forests) and nuclear safety. This, sometimes direct, but more often informal underpinning of EU assistance, is not necessarily in

---

[23] The ERTA case: Case 22/70 Commission v. Council of 1970.
[24] McGoldrick, 69; Opinion 1/92 ECR I–2812 paras 40–1.
[25] McGoldrick 1977, 78–88.
[26] For details of qualified majority, unanimity and a greater role for the EP in particular cases: Art. 300; McGoldrick 89–115 (pre-Treaty of Amsterdam) who also discusses the role of an advisory opinion of the ECJ.

conflict with host state overall objectives: Most of the countries with an energy relation with the EU (Eastern Europe; Russia; Central Asia; Mediterranean; Middle East; West Africa) are stuck in systems of economic governance which obstruct development: Inheritance of Communist organisation and attitudes[27] without replacement by a functioning markets and a market-supporting system of institutions and culture.[28] The problem of most of these projects lies not in that they are supposed to preach EU principles and policies (which have proven reasonably successful), but that their duration and impact is typically short, minimal and localised. There seems to be no systematic reflection and strategic planning what the EU wants to achieve and how in the always complex circumstances of post-Communist and developing countries. Here, advice (rather than perquisites of foreign aid) is often not wanted, not by the right people, not professionally rendered, relies rather on re-telling of EU systems than transposing concepts and experience to the often very different host state context and is rarely absorbed with a lasting effect. This problem affects all technical assistance (e.g. World Bank, UN, EBRD, bilateral agencies: Know-How Fund in the UK; GTZ in Germany), but it may be particularly acute in the case of the EC. Here, there is no systematic in-house expertise with policy and legislative reform advice; while there is energy expertise in DG TREN, such expertise seems neither existent nor effectively transferred. An impression of a giant funding system operating with no focused and expert mind watching over such activities, and learning from them is sometimes hard to avoid. Managing administrative challenges seems to prevail over the more relevant challenge of thinking seriously about real, rather than purely formalised, objectives. Much of the expensively purchased and developed expertise lies dormant in Commission archives,[29] while little absorbed and mostly ignored elsewhere. Few companies specialise in policy and legislative advice so that the preferred consultant is either a law or accounting firm using a EU project as a loss-leader to develop contacts and clients or an engineering firm with mainly administrative experience to jump over the hurdles of EU procurement (and payment collection) procedures, but no real interest, longer-term commitment or expertise in the areas of policy and legislative reform.

---

[27] See: Waelde/Gunderson, *Legislative Reform in Transition Economies* and Waelde/Hirschhausen, T. Waelde/ C von Hirschhausen, Legislative Reform in the Energy Industry of Post-Soviet Societies, in: R. Seidman/A.Seidman/ T. Waelde, *Making Development Work: Legislative Reform for Good Governance*, Kluwer, London 1999.

[28] Mancur Olson, *Power and Prosperity*, Basic Books, New York 2000.

[29] It is difficult to understand why almost all of the technical reports of EU assistance projects are not available on the internet. One suspects that they are not available to anybody – apart from being traded between consultants, and therefore likely to be duplicated in new projects.

Synergy[30]*:* (Total Budget:3.5 M E in 2001 SYNERGY is a co-operation programme managed by DG TREN. It finances co-operation activities with non EU countries in the field of the formulation and implementation of energy policy. It follows earlier energy related co-operation projects following the oil crises in the 1980s, with the 'EC International Energy Co-operation Programme', which has evolved into today's SYNERGY' programme. Synergy is the international co-operation component of the 'Energy Framework Programme' which runs from 1998 to 2002. SYNERGY should improve the competitiveness of Community industries, enhance the security of supply, promote sustainable development and improve energy efficiency. According to the new guidelines[31] the implementation of the programme will refocus on activities related to security of supply and implementation of the Kyoto protocol. Unlike other EU programmes that are of a more general nature and include energy as one of several aims, SYNERGY is a specific energy policy programme covering the external dimension of EU actions in the energy policy sector. *Altener II* (supra), the EC's renewable energy programme, now extends to the countries in Eastern Europe.[32]

Phare: Phare is currently the main channel for the European Union's financial and technical cooperation with the countries of central and eastern Europe (CEECs). The current Phare budget is Euro 6.693 billion for the 1995–1999 period.

The Phare Programme is focused on preparing the candidate countries for EU accession. In the energy field, this means review of the regulatory and institutional situation in the CEEC countries to bring them, by legislative reform, institution-building and training into conformity with EU energy law. The EU Energy Directives, the Energy Charter Treaty and EU competition law are the most relevant benchmarks for reform of the energy sector in Eastern Europe. Support for a twinning mechanism between partner institutions is also used. In the end, the programmes are about creating professional networks, explaining the rationale, the methods and the concepts of the Energy Directives and help the accession countries to gradually reach a similar stage, first formally, and then, hopefully, also with proper understanding and absorption. The main weakness of most projects is their short-term nature. Developing a relationship of reciprocal understanding between the EU and the CEEC partner takes a year – by which the project's period has usually come to an end. The very heavy machinery of procurement means that the largest amount of funds and time is not spent on professional communication across often substantial cultural borders, but on dealing with

---

[30] For more information, budgets and types of projects supported: *http://www.europa.eu.int/ external_relations/news*

[31] Official Journal of 5.5. 2001 (L125/24).

[32] Website: *http://www.europa.eu.int*

the Commission services.[33] The need for long-term partnerships between competent institutions, in my view the only effective way of developing a productive professional and intellectual partnership seems not yet to have been properly recognized.

CEEC countries are with respect to energy in a very different situation to Russia and the Central Asian states. They are all dependent on energy imports based on preferential supply of oil and gas from the Soviet Union. There is coal and lignite production (notably in Poland), but it is, as in Western Europe, economically and environmentally not efficient and requires large-scale restructuring, closure and privatization. There is an essential distinction to the EU: While the EU, before embarking on liberalization, had an efficient and reliable energy infrastructure, such situation does not exist in Eastern Europe. There are unsafe nuclear reactors, 100% reliability on Russian gas now charged at full market price and domestic power stations which are often not competitive with Russian electricity produced with cheaper energy and under lax conditions. A simple import of the EU – new – model, embodied in the energy directives, may not work as envisaged. Liberalisation and full competition is often not conducive to building modern new energy facilities, in particular when cross-border competition operates under more favourable conditions. These issues have to our knowledge not been fully appreciated as yet. They may in fact delay the establishment of an efficient energy industry when full competition meets obsolete and unsatisfactory energy infrastructure. The solution here should be to identify, without blind import from the EU, where liberalization and competition will bring benefits, and where time-wise limited special regimes are necessary to encourage large-scale and long-term energy plant investment. Blinded by the precedent effect of the ECT and the energy directives, too much attention may have been paid to competitive markets, and not enough to the conditions for investment, including direct financial support, risk guarantees and viable long-term contracts.

Tacis: The EU programme to provide technical assistance to Russia and other post-Soviet countries. In the former Soviet Union, the situation is again very different from the accession countries. Here, there are usually (except Ukraine) ample national reserves and production. The issue is rather to create a regulatory regime that encourages investment in upstream oil and gas development, fair access to transportation pipelines and market-based incentives for efficient production, transport and consumption. At all levels,

---

[33] Based on quite long consultancy experience, I estimate that about 90% of the time and budget is not spent on what is the real purpose of the project, but on transactions within the project consortia and even more so on tender preparation, project administration and cost collection from the Commission services. This is surely too much. It does not occur with other, more professionally focused, funding organisations. A transaction-cost wastage of 60–70% should therefore be typical for this sort of project.

these quite evident objectives confront Soviet-style obstruction: Extensive resentment against foreign investment in Russia, an opaque, volatile and corrupt culture interposed between investor and the government's licensing system; absence of a culture of trust, commitment and law and a very close mix between business and state which prevents the state to regulate effectively and business to focus on commercial and competitive performance properly. The policy requirements here are very different. The Energy Directives have only a quite limited usefulness as benchmarking models. The Energy Charter Treaty, with its emphasis on introduction of market economy, respect of property, non-discrimination and access to transit and transport facilities is probably more relevant at this stage. Russia does not need to manage the importation and distribution of energy (as the CEEC countries), but rather to produce and distribute more efficiently. Also, Russia is not an accession country and it is very large and with a tradition of supremacy. The EU model must therefore develop its attractiveness not out of the obligation to adopt EU law that comes from accession, but through persuasion as being the right model for Russia's needs. While the Tacis programme's funds are substantial, they are not sufficient to exercise financial leverage on Russia to adopt foreign-imported policies. There is, or rather was, also acute competition between US (or Anglo-Saxon) models that were underpinning Russia's early shock reform efforts, and the EU model which allows to emphasise more liberal (e.g. UK) and more statist (e.g. France) versions. It is likely that Russia will for cultural affinity lean rather to moderate European models with a strong element of state presence, and with real (rather than the past formal) liberalisation perhaps rather a matter for the more distant future.

The situation is again different in the Central Asian/Caucasus countries. Here, Azerbaijan, Kazahkhstan, Turkmenistan and Uzbekistan hold significant oil and gas reserves. Their problem is internal political instability and internal plus external security. They have been used in post-Cold-War rivalry between Russia and the US. Their interest is in depoliticising energy relations and developing (and to some extent sharing with Russia) oil-based prosperity by investment, transit and trade. The EU, and the Tacis' programme's role here must be to help to create an internal culture of law and order, to facilitate depoliticised and more commercially oriented neighbourly relationships and to help create transit corridors for oil and gas to markets, in particular Turkey and Southeastern and Eastern Europe. If such policies succeed, is a long-term matter and depends on matters of political (internal and external) security over which the EU has little influence. The main purpose is, and should be, to contribute towards structures of stable, and ideally also good, governance which will allow the commercial potential of domestic oil and gas reserves to be fully mobilised.[34] The organisational problems of the Tacis programme are

---

[34] T. Waelde, *International Good Governance* (2000).

the same as that of Phare (supra). Administrative overload in lieu of focus on substantive objectives; short-term nature of projects and duplication (e.g. the Tacis Inogate project with the ECT's transit protocol) due to organisational rivalries. The overall direction is right, but requires more orientation at creating lasting professional communities in the energy field.

1.4 Association and economic cooperation agreements

The EU concludes several types of economic cooperation agreements.[35] They differ by the level of economic integration aimed at (good-will discussions only; basis for development aid and trade preferences intention to move to a customs union; customs union plus gradual adoption by the partner state of EU law to prepare for accession.) They have no specific energy focus, though energy may be mentioned as an object of development aid, included in customs union and adoption of EU law. They also tend to formulate good-will declarations concerning foreign investment, but do not have the hard and specific legal obligations such as bilateral investment treaties or the Energy Charter Treaty. It is in fact surprising that bilateral investment treaties (BITs) are still concluded by member states, and not by the EC.[36] These are the main types of agreement:

Association agreements: Provide preferential access to EU markets, often aiming at a later customs union. There is an institutional machinery for dialogue (Council or Committee), increasingly also competent to deal with governance issues, i.e. a way for the EC (never in practice for the partner country) to raise, with some financial, trade and political leverage in the background, governance issues. There is an emphasis, pushed in particular by the Southern EU countries, to closer relations with the Mediterranean countries.[37] Association agreements exist with most Mediterranean countries, with Turkey a customs union is being established based on the agreement of 1995. These agreements are implemented by the MEDA programme which contains a number of TA projects relating to energy.[38] There are no specific 'energy' agreements in the EU-Mediterranean relationship; some of the countries have looked at the ECT (which would be the most appropriate instrument), but felt the 'hard law' obligation and the direct enforcement (by investor arbitration) not acceptable.[39] This situation reflects the internal political status of most

[35] W. Shan, J. World Investment, 2/603.
[36] McGoldrick, 182–192; Macleod; 389–393.
[37] McGoldrick, 190, 201.
[38] EU, 2003, supra.
[39] T. Wälde, *The Emery Charter Treaty*, 1996.

Mediterranean countries: weak governance, religious problems where fundamentalist Islam is challenging governments which provide no significant popular participation; inter-ethnic strife and suppression of minorities (e.g. Turkey, Israel; Algeria; Syria).[40] From an energy perspective, these countries are of great importance, in particular to Southern Europe: oil and gas investment supply from Syria, Egypt and Algeria and through Turkey, Tunisia and Morocco. There are post-colonial linkages (in particular with France), but the often violent responses to the modernisation challenge for Islam both threatens regime stability and at least investment stability (though less trade stability). As in the case of Russia and the Caspian/Caucasus countries, the EU wishes good commercial relations with all of these countries; it can by treaty, dialogue, professional community-building and assistance help positive governance elements to grow, but in essence it can not, on its own and without strong domestic allies, guarantee stable systems of good and democratic governance.

The most important association agreement has been the series of *Yaounde/ Lome Conventions*, now the 2001 *Cotonou agreement*.[41] The ACP countries are most of the former colonies of EU member states (UK, France, Portugal, Belgium and Spain), with some important exceptions (e.g. India and Latin America). It maintains to some extent, and in tension with GATT commitments, former colonial preferences, is the legal basis for substantial development aid. Energy, which used to be a section in the Lome agreement, appears in the new Cotonou agreement only as a series of passing references, mainly to renewable energy. Investment promotion – relevant to the substantial investment of EU companies for example in Nigeria, Trinidad and Angola – is commented positively, with the prospect of unspecific EU investment guarantees and future specific investment protection treaties (Art. 75–79). The Cotonou agreement is long on adhortatory and other general policy declarations in the style of a preamble or UN General Resolutions, but short of specific mechanisms and obligations in the style of a BIT or the ECT. It reflects the revival of neo-missionarism in Western countries[42] by providing for a consultation procedure for human rights, democratic principles, the rule of law and corruption (Art. 96–98), but without the specificity of, for example, the OECD anti-corruption convention.[43] It is hard to assess the effectiveness of both the very open-ended good-will obligations and the massive development aid (including finance) for which the agreement serves as a legal basis. One way is to look at most of the language as a public relations exercised meant to

---

[40] Noreng, *Oil and Islam*, 1997.
[41] EU, 2003, supra: Partnership agreement between the ACP states and the EC and its member states.
[42] Reluctant Missionaries, Marina Ottaway, July–August 2001, Foreign Policy.
[43] *www.oecd.org* – see comment: Giorgio Sacerdoti, Bribery of foreign public officials in international business transactions, *IBL* 1999, 3–17.

placate the EP and NGOs, the other one is to view this as a step towards more effective measures to support good governance. Good governance itself can – if applied and imposed on weaker developing countries – be seen as the right move to make the world a better place, or as the continuation, albeit under different labels, of the economic and cultural dominance over what were formerly colonies, and now are underdeveloped and aid- and finance-dependent countries, i.e. the contemporary format of cultural colonialism with a now revived strong missionary element.

Partnership and cooperation agreements do not envisage accession nor a customs union. They provide a basis for economic and trade policy dialogue as well as for technical assistance. This form has been chosen for the EU relationship with Russia and most post-Soviet states.[44] Given the mutual EU and Russian interest to expand, with European capital, Russian oil and gas production and to acquire a large market share, this agreement would lend itself to energy-specific initiatives.[45] But there has so far not been the willingness, on both sides, to envisage a large joint energy project, create a legal foundation and provide EU finance and risk guarantees. It is not certain this is absolutely necessary, as there exist already large Russian oil and gas flows into the EU. Perhaps there is no readiness on the Russian side to provide the necessary specific legal guarantees (and ratify the ECT) and on the EU side to direct large financial flows eastwards without a credible Russian counter-commitment. Arguably, more and faster pipeline and electricity transmission facilities, interconnectors, transit of Central Asian gas through Russia to the CEEC and EU countries could be established if there were a better legal foundation. The essential deal, though, has as yet not been identified, and possibly due to institutional weaknesses both on the EU and the Russian side.

Europe agreements, finally, are the instrument to prepare Eastern European countries for accession to the EU.[46] With the EU as the dominant partner, they set up a programme for preparing the partner countries for eventual accession. They provide the means whereby the European Union offers the associated countries the trade concessions and other benefits normally associated with full memberships of the EU. The Europe Agreements aim to establish free trade in industrial products and in services, limited freedom of movement, introduction of competition law (including anti-state aids rules) over a gradual, transition period, although the EU opens its markets more

---

[44] McGoldrick, 190–191; EU-Russia PCA at: *http://europa.eu.int/comm/external_relations/russia/pca_legal/annexes.htm*.

[45] Such as the Prodin-Putin energy initiative which, so far, has remained without a tangible result, EC, 2003, supra.

[46] McGoldrick, 188–189; *http://www.europa.eu.int/comm/enlargement/pas/europe_agr.htm*; COM (95) 163.

quickly than the associated country. As a result, industrial products from the associated countries have had virtually free access to the EU since the beginning of 1995. They also contain provisions regarding the free movement of services, payments and capital in respect of trade and investments, and the free movement of workers. When establishing and operating in the territory of the other party, enterprises must receive treatment not less favourable than national enterprises. Under the Agreements, the partner countries also commit themselves to approximating their legislation to that of the European Union, particularly in the areas relevant to the internal market. Energy is mentioned as one of the areas of economic cooperation and nuclear safety is mentioned as a special concern[47] The form of the obligations is not specific; they refer to a general policy in the sector (e.g. opening up of the energy sector), define a best-efforts obligation, enable financial and technical assistance and define full approximation as ultimate target, but without a specific time-table. They have been the basis of several PHARE projects to assist the accession countries to develop regulatory regimes for energy (including competition) in line with the EU law and the energy directives. While such projects and subsequent legislative change does not yet make countries fully prepared, they are the first, more formal, step. If the wholesale adoption of EU energy law is at this stage of development of their energy industries fully appropriate given their need for large-scale modernisation investment has already been questioned (supra). The legal status and direct effect of the 'Europe Agreements' in domestic law is not settled.

1.5 Environmental

Together with security of supply (which in a more modern understanding should be translated as concern to develop a well functioning EU-wide, regional and global energy market), the other dominant paradigm for current EU energy policy is environment, and here mainly climate change obligations assumed enthusiastically by the EU (without US participation and with no specific commitments on CO_2 emissions by developing countries. (supra). The EC and the member states have signed and modfied the Kyoto protocol. The EU commitment will therefore be to stabilise CO_2 emissions at 1990 levels in 2000 and then reduce them, up to 2012, by 8% compared to 1990 levels.[48]

---

[47] Art. 79 and 80 of the EU-Bulgaria Europe Agreement (Europe agreements are virtually identical), the article mentions as areas of cooperation energy efficiency, savings, development, transfer of technology, diversification of supply, transit, environmental impact and opening up of the sector including modernisation. This is a ante-chamber to full accession in the energy area. Art. 81 includes, with a similar intention, environmental including climate change obligations.
[48] EC Security of Energy Supply Green Paper, November 2000, 51–55.

This is the major EU environmental commitment relating to energy; it is very difficult to achieve. To achieve it, the role of nuclear energy would have to be expanded, growth rates in the utilisation of renewable energy would have to be achieved which seem unrealistic (even given much stronger fiscal support in the future) and the role and oil consumption of private transport drastically reduced. It is hard to see how such developments are economically and politically achievable, since the European people are often vehemently opposed to nuclear energy, but also against higher gasoline prices (which would have to include agriculture, trucking and air travel). In addition, achieving the Kyoto targets for the EU would have almost no relevance for the global situation. Europe contributes only 14% to total CO_2 emissions, far behind Asia (25%) and North America (29%), with irresistible growth rates from the large, increasing and increasingly prosperous populations in Asia. The US – not just for temporary, but for solid domestic reasons – unlikely to accept the Kyoto limits.[49] Developing countries have not accepted specific commitments to reduce CO_2 emissions – and it would be hard to persuade or compel them to accept such limits to enable the rich Western countries to be both much more prosperous and environmentally comfortable. The Kyoto protocol also suffers from the fact that the collapse of Communism (with its industrial and thereby emission contraction) is heavily rewarded, though such funds would be much better spent on achieving serious efforts at reducing emissions. Though Kyoto has already spawned a large academic and consultancy cottage industry, it is therefore far from certain that the Kyoto route will lead anywhere, both for global climate protection and for EU targets. It is therefore necessary to re-think the Kyoto approach, both for on-going negotiations and internal EU climate change policies, but also to think creatively about alternatives that would both help to manage the climate challenge, and be politically and economically more viable. There is certainly no harm to try to foster the development of energy-efficient technologies and renewable energies in the EU and worldwide, with an emphasis on properly integrating climate-change external costs into the prices of energy by tax or emission trading. There is also a good rationale to control emissions in the EU and worldwide by agreement and by use of the Kyoto mechanisms (clean development mechanism, Joint Implementation; Emission trading); development of internal EU emission trading would provide experiences ready for more global application. But given the inherent limits of the Kyoto protocol, the likelihood that the major polluters will not sign up (US) or not be much affected (Asia), one needs to go beyond Kyoto.

A first strategy which is generally ignored is that the EU, and the world, have to prepare themselves for global warming, irrespective if it is based on natural cycles or on gas emissions by industrial society. Humanity had to cope with climate changes often in their history, and with modern resources and

---

[49] J. Mitchell, (2001), 227–228.

technologies it should be easier though the heavy sacrifices paid in the past are unlikely to be completely avoidable now. A second strategy is not to rely only on emission control as the Kyoto protocol does, but also to discuss supply measures. John Mitchell[50] questions why the approach followed in the earlier Montreal-protocol of limiting the supply of noxious substances could not be followed for climate change as well. That would not be a substitute for emission control, but rather the opening of a second front. There are explicit and implicit limits on oil and gas production (national parks and reserves; heavy planning-permit requirements), not least in OPEC countries (e.g. production-control to achieve higher prices at a more stable level). Would it not be possible, in concerted action with OPEC, to limit oil and gas production, possibly also impose a global climate-change tax on it? OPEC's argument has been that consumer countries' high (in the EU) excise taxes shift the largest part of the petroleum rent to consumer countries treasuries. Would it not be possible to design, jointly, a climate-change tax mechanism which gives to producing countries a higher and stable share of petroleum rent, while also limiting production and increasing the ultimate price of oil and gas to level which encourage efficiency, reduced use and development of clean energy? All these measures which can be identified by rational analysis are hindered by the political baggage of past, and now realistically obsolete, perceptions and attitudes: of OPEC as the enemy of Western economies; of nuclear energy as the main environmental offender and of markets (rather than state command) as cause, rather than solution to the climate change problem.

While offshore oil pollution (both from engine oil dumped and from tanker accidents) is a serious environmental problem, enhanced by the increase in oil transportation to Europe, it is much more solvable than the more intractable climate challenge. We have already discussed the various measures of increasing strictness the EU has taken to implement IMO and related conventions for offshore oil pollution. The EU is party to the relevant agreements and the IMO[51] an active participant, usually pushing towards more rigour in standards and enforcement. Its self-confidence in using port state leverage to enforce such guidelines is bringing about extraterritorial regulation to compensate for the institutional weakness of flags-of-convenience.

1.6 Trade of energy goods and services

In the good old times of energy monopoly, energy trade was not an issue. State-owned or protected monopolies 'exchanged' electricity at times, but only if they

---

[50] (2001), 216–238.

[51] M. Goranson, *Liability for Damage to the Marine Environment*, 345 and D. Anderson, Port States and Environmental Protection 325, in Boyle/Freestone (*op. cit.* 1999).

both, and the states involved, wanted it – no need to rely on international trade
law to obtain access, reduce tariffs, eliminate non-tariff trade barriers, combat
state aids and participate in procurement of energy by public agencies. Oil trade
was liberalised in the developed countries in the 1980s; since the consuming
countries are mostly dependent on oil, there were no tariffs on imported oil
(excepting some protectionist measures before the first oil price hike in 1972 in
the US). Nor were there any significant non-tariff barriers (e.g. regulation,
standards, import licensing practices).[52] The tariff issue has become only
relevant for petroleum products, the more acute the more value is added outside
the importing country.[53] At first the oil, and now electricity and increasingly gas
are traded across borders, into increasingly competitive markets, issues of tariff
and non-tariff barriers inevitably arise. First, there are sometimes, though
rarely, protectionist sentiments to be translated into trade restrictions against
imports of primary energy sources. This is rare, but has been raised twice in
periods of low oil prices by high-cost US producers against oil imports, arguing
that lower oil prices prevailing in the producer countries (Venezuela, Mexico)
plus the predominant role of the state with no clear distinction between
government and state enterprise budgets indicated either dumping or export
subsidies – to be countered by US anti-dumping duties or other import
restrictions.[54] The German coal subsidy scheme (including direct subsidies and
domestic minimum purchase obligations) can be seen in a similar vein as
protection for German coal against more competitive energy and from coal
imports.[55] – Trade restrictions typically come into play as more value is added
by the producer (thus threatening importer state refining and petrochemical
industries), but also as different regulatory and tax regimes change the elusive
'level playing field'. Under GATT, a US import restriction on Venezuelan and
Brazilian gasoline was held to be discriminatory. While there was a worthwhile
environmental rationale, its application was discriminatory and favoured US
competitors.[56] Under NAFTA Chapter XI, trade restrictions on certain
chemicals and hazardous waste may have had, according to the plaintiff and
at least one arbitral tribunal, an environmental cover for what was in effect a
protectionist discrimination.[57] These cases illustrate the growing importance of

[52] Unctad, 2001.
[53] Unctad, 2001.
[54] But these complaints were not taken up by the US when repeated in 1999: *http://www.ita.doc.gov/import_admin/records/download/oil-term.htm*.
[55] RJB Mining v. Commission ECJ of February 2002.
[56] WTO Appellate Body: Report of Appellate Body in US- Standards for Reformulated and Conventional Gasoline, 35 *ILM* 603 (1996); *http://www.wto.org/wto/dispute/gas1.htm*.
[57] Myers-case (export restriction on hazardous waste to favour a Canadian competitor; Ethyl case, trade restriction on hazardous chemical, but without a similar impact on Canadian competitors, Ethyl Corp v. Government of Canada, 38 *ILM* 700 (1999) (settled in favour of plaintiff before final award); Myers v. Canada, *www.naftaclaims.com*. See now also the Methanex case.

real – and fake – environmental policies used to justify trade restrictions.[58] Within the EU, it has been, in particular, German voices who have called for import restrictions to counter:

- Energy imports from EU countries with a lower level of theoretical liberalisation through the reciprocity principle (Art. 19 (5) of the ED) incorporated into the new German Energy Law;[59]
- Energy imports from EU and non-EU countries with a more lax 'environmental' regime or other hidden or apparent state aids and/or more favourable tax regimes. That would be directed against countries where costs of nuclear decommissioning and waste disposal were not properly 'internalised' (e.g. argument for UK and France), where nuclear power plants were unsafe in any way (design, operation, decommissioning) – an argument applied to power import from Lithuanian Igualina plant to Latvia, from Russian nuclear plants to Baltic countries or from the Kozludui nuclear plant in Bulgaria or the Temelin nuclear plant exports to Germany.[60]
- With state aids being developed on the national level in many forms for renewable and other forms of clean energy and electricity traded at the same time across-border (including Community borders), distortions due to such promotional measures can occur easily, and either advantage energy exports beyond their objective clean-energy character, or disadvantage domestic energy production subject to clean-energy levies and rules.[61]

The Commission itself has now raised the issue of 'unfair competition' when power plants not subject to the stricter EU environmental standards or 'unsafe' nuclear plants export into the EU. It argues that unlimited access would undermine the basis of the EU energy liberalisation process requiring a 'level playing field'. It also refers in this context to the need for political and environmental acceptance if the view were that such imports would help the

---

[58] S. Moreno/ J. Rubin et.al. 'Free trade and the environment: The NAFTA, the NAAEC', 12 *Tulane Intl L J* 405, 458 (1999); P. Mavroides, 'Trade and environment after the shrimps-turtles litigation', 34 *JWT* 73–88 (2000).

[59] *http://www.bmwi.de/Homepage/Politikfelder/Energiepolitik/Liberalisierung*. The main target is France, though the French argument is that German liberalisation is only formal, but has through established practices, relations and oligopolistic practices not led to 'real competition', e.g. statement by ENBW (Figaro June, 2001).

[60] SPD-Bavaria motion in the Bavarian diet, June 2001; Rudolf Steinberg, Gabriele Britz & Andrea Schaub, Die Bedeutung des Rechts der EG fuer eine umweltorientierte Energiepolitik und Energierechtssetzung, in: *Recht der Energie*, 165 (1996); A. Schaub, *op. cit.* 1996.

[61] This is developed in more detail in EC: Second Harmonisation Report, 1998, 9; in more detail: Green Paper on greenhouse emissions trading, COM (2000) 87 final.

continuation of unsafe operations.[62] The question therefore is if countries can invoke the already existing powers (E.g. in the German or Austrian Energy Law) to prevent such imports of allegedly 'dirty' energy. It is very difficult to argue that under EU law this is possible; EU-internal energy trade is covered by the freedom of movement for goods; any limitations on this are now regulated specifically by the Energy Directives, in particular Art. 19 (5) ED. One should assume that the ED provides a specific formulation and set of rules to deal with justification for trade restrictions under Art. (30-ex 36; and 86 (2) ex-90(2)). Lack of reciprocity of eligibility is under the ED a good reason for prohibiting import of electricity, but environmental regulation of a lower or different standard is not. The EU internal trading system is based on either full harmonisation or mutual recognition based on a common minimum standard. It would disrupt the functioning of the internal market if countries – entitled to national diversity under the concept of directives and the legal concept of subsidiarity – would suddenly use trading restrictions against its EU partners. Quite apart from the prohibition on EU-internal trade restrictions, it is usually quite easy to assert from a self-centred perspective of a country that its environmental regulation are superior, but difficult to prove this once a more objective and balanced assessment is done. For example, the much cited higher quality of German environmental legislation for energy contrasts with the fact that Germany has the by far highest CO_2 emissions in the EU and in addition has been for decades actively subsidising, and fighting for EU state aids exemption, for its environmentally most noxious coal production and mandatory use in domestic energy. Arguments against 'dirty' foreign energy, e.g. East European nuclear plants, for example do not look credible at all when assessed from a climate change point of view. The common presumption that energy imports from less regulated countries are by force of necessity more competitive and thus 'dirty' energy will crowd out 'clean energy', a concept much relied upon by environmentalist argument about 'races to the bottom',[63] is far from proven. It is argued by economists that good environmental taxes need to be imposed globally as competition otherwise will handicap companies subject to such environmentally acceptable fiscal and regulatory regimes.[64]

But it is far from proven or universal that higher standards of required quality are undermined by lower standards.[65] Higher standards can encourage technological innovation, lead to better cost control and can lead to products better accepted by the markets. Lower standards may often reflect the level of development of an economy, i.e. be appropriate for the particular country.

---

[62] EC working paper ' Completing the Internal energy market: SEC (2001) 438 of March 2001.

[63] J. Scott, *EU Environmental Law*, 1998, 84.

[64] Also M. Radetzki, *Taxation of Energy* (1998), *op. cit.* 303.

[65] For a review of the discussion: R. Stewart, 'Environmental Regulation and international competitiveness', 102 *Yale LJ* 2039 (1993).

They allow countries which are lower on the level of general prosperity (e.g. transition or developing countries) to secure market share and move upwards in the level of development and therewith level of quality standards, while higher standards tend to foreclose market access to competitors from less developed societies. There is therefore an element of abuse of market power and economic domination if higher-standard societies try to impose their standards against competition from other countries. It is also far from certain that purchase from power plants with a different regulatory regime (sometimes lower-level, but sometimes only different) helps lower standard operations to survive. Buying from East European power plants, for example, may generate cash flow for modernisation and upgrading, while denying such income may focus such power plants on poorer markets and thus contribute to low levels of safety. To sum up: A level playing field is not always necessary, and sometimes a playing field is level when some of the cards are stacked in favour of the weaker players.

Much of the intensity of feeling lies in the convenient combination of both a sentiment of moral superiority combined with protectionism which protects not only better environmental standards, but a comfortable way of living. For these reasons, a proper legal assessment of import restrictions under established principles of international trade – mainly GATT law – is both necessary and practically justified. This is quite clear in the EC papers where the doubtful legality of import restrictions is implicitly acknowledged and were suggestions are made to bypass GATT law as it stands by bilateral agreements, i.e. agreements where the dominance of the EU can be utilised much better than in the more 'level-playing field' of GATT dispute settlement. GATT rules are not only applicable directly between EU member states and non-EU GATT members, but also by way of the reference in the Energy Charter Treaty to GATT rules for relations between EU member states and states which are not (yet) members of the GATT, but members of the Energy Charter Treaty (Art. 29). Furthermore, the free-trade provisions of Europe agreements[66] do not contain exceptions for energy (as there are e.g. for agriculture, fisheries and

---

[66] Eg. Art. 9, EU-Bulgaria Agreement; the EC Commission, recognises that 'environmental dumping' is no justification for trade restrictions under the GATT (Second Harmonisation Report, 23–24. It argues that an import restriction might be justified under the 'reciprocity' concept when an electricity exporting accession country does itself not provide similar access to the EU energy trade. The argument is that the ED are part of the EU energy law which the accession countries, under the Europe agreements, have to adopt. But it is not a persuasive reason: First, the ED do not have an immediate direct effect in accession countries; rather, these countries are obliged to introduce them over a lengthy period until accession. Second, the reciprocity exception under Art 19 (5) of the ED links an energy import restriction to ineligibility of energy consumers in the exporting countries – but that is often not the case in accession countries, and these are rather interested in energy export than (e.g. France) from preventing Western energy imports. Thirdly, the reciprocity exception has nothing to do with different environmental terms.

textiles) nor is there an exception for goods produced in the accession country under technical standards that are different, or lower, than in the EU.[67] The EU has a difficult case to justify energy protectionism against poorer countries in Eastern Europe. An analysis of the applicable GATT rules will make this clear. While anti-dumping and safeguard measures may be allowed, sale of energy produced under a regulatory regime that is different from the environmentally more stricter EU regime does not constitute dumping. To the contrary, it is quite likely that the electricity is exported at a higher price than the domestic price, i.e. rather the opposite of dumping. 'Eco-dumping' is currently not a legal concept under GATT law.[68] There is very little precedent dealing specially with electricity under the GATT/WTO system – as electricity was not competitively traded across borders until recently.[69] Energy trade receives no specific special treatment under the GATT. Energy goods, including electricity, are treated as any other goods. The EC does not apply any duty with regards to electricity imports. The national treatment rule of the GATT (Art. III (4) means that once it has entered the EU, it must be treated as electricity produced in the EU.[70]

Import restrictions are forbidden under Art. XI GATT as a 'quantitative restriction'. There is no doubt that electricity now has to be considered as a 'good' under GATT law.[71] The question is if the exceptions of Art. XX, in particular section (b) ('necessary to protect human .... Life or health' are applicable. The main authorities are the GATT panel reports in the Tuna-Dolphin[72] cases and the WTO panel and Appeal Body report in the

---

[67] The Commission (Completing the internal energy market, 2001, 67–68) makes the point that the Europe agreements oblige the accession countries to gradually adopt EU law (including emission and nuclear standards). That is right, but it is an obligation of best efforts working towards an accession date in the future; it does not mean that EU law is directly applicable in and against the accession countries from the day of signature of the agreement. The Commission, and member countries, would certainly protest if the accession countries would, for example, require immediate effect of free movement of persons. The Commission paper here confuses a policy target to be achieved in the future for both sides with immediately effective legal obligation.

[68] J. Scott, 1998, 104 based on a much more extensive analysis; Vossenaar in Brack/Ward 2000.

[69] For GATT relevance for energy: UNCTAD, trade agreements, petroleum and energy policies, 2001; special issue of 12 *J. Energy & Natural Resources Law* (1994).

[70] EC, Completing the internal energy market, 2001, 67.

[71] Zarilli/Unctad, Energy Services, 7; WTO, Energy Services, Background Notice by the Secretariat, S/C/W/59 of 9 September 1998; ECJ Judgement of October 1997, Case C157–160/94.

[72] Tuna-Dolphin II: 33 *ILM* 839 (1994); for detailed discussion: Mavroides, 2000 *op. cit.*; J. Cameron/K. Gray, Principles of international law in the WTO dispute settlement body, 50 *ICLQ* 248, 264–268 (2001); IDEM, The Shrimp-turtle dispute, in: H. Ward/D. Brack, *Trade, Investment and the Environment*, RIIA-Earthscan, London 2000, 203.

subsequent Shrimp-Turtle case.[73] These cases seem to establish the following sequence of tests for Art. 20: Import restrictions need to be based on legitimate environmental objectives, without discrimination and selecting the least-restrictive measure. The measure must be primarily based on environmental harm coming from the product itself – not the production process. Electricity by itself is not environmentally harmful, so that a product-based justification for an import restriction does not exist. Allowing the import of electricity from, say, France or Poland, but then excluding electricity produced by nuclear plants from the Czech republic would constitute discrimination according to Art. III GATT. The key question is if such restrictions can be based on the 'production process' occurring abroad. If countries were allowed to use trade sanctions based on production processes abroad, they would in essence acquire a trade-sanction based extraterritorial regulation power over conduct in foreign countries.[74] It would mean that strong economies can impose their standards on weaker ones dependent on access. That seems in principle prohibited, except for narrow exceptions, under general international law.[75] WTO law is based on 'regulatory competition' and de facto on mutual recognition of standards.[76] A country can not, under WTO law, impose its standards by extraterritorial reach outside its own territory. But both the Tuna-Dolphin panel reports and the Shrimp-Tuna Appeal Body decision have left an opening: If there is a tangible impact on the importing state, then import restrictions could be justified if there is a good environmental reason, sound scientific evidence and reasonable prior efforts to reach a bilateral or multilateral agreement and if the least restrictive measure necessary for the purpose is chosen.[77] It makes sense to leave decisions on environmental policies to the exporting state if there are no transboundary externalities – while a carefully regulated role of the importing state subject to procedural and

---

[73] See here also the detailed discussion of the problems the EC had in making its import restriction against furs from animals caught by leghold traps GATT-compatible: J. Scott, 1998, 95–96. The internal conclusion was that short of a multilateral agreement or recognised guideline to rely on, such import restrictions based on the production process rather than on the product itself were infringing the GATT obligations of the EU and its member states.

[74] T. Waelde, Sanctions, 2001 *op. cit.*; Andrea Bianchi, Comment, in: Meessen, *Extraterritorial Jurisdiction in theory and practice*, Kluwer Law International, London 1996.

[75] Joseph Weiler, Epilogue: Towards a Common Law of International Trade, in : Weiler (ed) *The EU, the WTO, and the NAFTA*, OUP 2000, 201, 230, 231;.

[76] The first Tuna/Dolphin report – supra – considered it relevant that the US had 'not demonstrated that it had exhausted all options reasonably available to it to pursue its dolophon protection objectives [...] in particular through the negotiations of international cooperative arrangements'.

[77] See: R. Vossenaar, 152, but also J. Cameron, 203 and T. Cottier at 187, from a NGO view C. Arden-Clarke, from a developing point of view M. Shahin in: Ward/Brack, *op. cit.* 2000.

substantive rules makes more sense if the production-process has extraterritorial effects.[78]

Unilateralism combined with extraterritorial reach of such trade sanction tends to indicate incompatibility, while the existence of recognised international standards (best in an environmental treaty to which both countries are parties) and serious effort of finding a consensus-based solution will indicate compatibility with Art. XX GATT. This WTO-specific formulation is not that far from the 'protective' principle which in general international law is often used to justify extraterritorial regulation. Furthermore, reliance on and conformity with environmental agreements that are relevant – i.e. effective between the parties – or universally accepted multilateral guidelines can justify such trade sanctions, again provided that there is no protectionist intention and effect, no discrimination and the least restrictive method necessary for the purpose is chosen.[79] One can perhaps infer from the sequence of WTO decisions that once a country uses trade sanctions to impose its standard on others, it has a heavy burden of proof: legitimacy of principle, solid scientific evidence of risk, conformity with accepted international guidelines or environmental agreements effective between both states and evidence of serous efforts to reach a solution by agreement. This set of tests requires some reasonable assessment of the likely impact of the measure proposed (and alternatives measures with less restrictiveness commensurate with the risk) for the objective. These standards are very reasonable; they take into account that each country (or the EU) will find its own standards superior to others, represent rather the morally superior environmental intention than the more basic protectionist effect and be blind towards environmental damage caused within the country while extra sharp-eyed for the eco-faults of the other country. In short, the WTO standards stand for countervailing the arrogance of economic power blinded by ideology of self-superiority. One needs to realise, though, that the GATT standards may afford legal protection to weaker countries against the compulsion from stronger economies, but the economic pull of standards in a powerful market will, whatever the legal situation, exercise strong pressure for the importing country producers to conform. The instruments of pressure are consumer expectations, increasingly formalised in labelling and other forms of mandatory or voluntary information, importer

---

[78] This is a very short summary of a much more complex and much discussed issue, see: J. Cameron 2001; Mavroides 2000; Joanne Scott, 263 et seq; Weiss, The Second Tuna Gatt Panel Report, 8. *Leiden Journal of International Law*; F. Abott, The North American Integration Regime, in: J. Weiler (ed) 2000, *op. cit.*; 189 and 200; both the second Tuna-Dolphin panel and the AB in the shrimp-turtle case were ready to interpret Art. XX GATT in light of environmental agreements.

[79] There is another parallel to the tuna-dolphin, shrimp-turtle cases: While the US imposed its standards of proper production on other countries, it was of the five countries involved in the shrimp dispute the one with the lowest record of ratification of multilateral environmental treaties, reference by Arden-Clarke in Brack/ Ward 2000, 184.

specifications and many other forms of pressure and conditionalities involved. But that should not lead to imposition of globally harmonised standards on the level of the most powerful import market as such harmonisation would deny to the weaker economies the exploitation of the few comparative advantages left to them.

For the EU, the legitimate environmental objective can not be to compel non-EU countries to adopt their own, better standards to create a level playing field. It must be that the import restriction is the only way to prevent serious environmental harm to the EU – and in this case, given the extraterritorial reach undermining the sovereignty of the export state, serious efforts at reaching a cooperative agreement must have been tried and reliance on accepted guidelines must have been sought. Lower environmental standards in power production may, for example, have an effect through emission of noxious (SO4) gases migrating westwards, basically through low-standard burning of coal and fuel oil. A low-standard nuclear plant may constitute a risk of accident with serious implications (viz. Chernobyl) for the EU country. The question then is if the import restriction is necessary to manage that risk, and if it is the least restrictive method. But it is likely that under the impact of an import restriction the electricity would be sold rather to the lower-tariff-paying customers in Eastern Europe. That would not reduce the EU environmental risk, but possibly even increase it – as less revenue would be available for upgrading. The same applies to the nuclear power plant. Shutting nuclear power off is unlikely to lead a wealthy export market to closure, rather to further deterioration. The Chernobyl accident did not happen because the Soviet plant could export to the EU, but perhaps rather because it could not, and was so not connected to the safety culture (resources) of prosperous energy export markets. The right solution, rather than extraterritorial compulsion by the economically and politically stronger country, would be to seek to develop or rely on common guidelines (for nuclear safety and sequestration of coal-based electricity production) which do not have to be those of the EU, but of a more neutral source and seek to either provide finance, or to maximise electricity imports to raise finance for such upgrading to better environmental quality and nuclear safety. Possibly, the protection of the global climate against CO2 emissions might be a reasonable environmental justification as well, founded on the Kyoto protocol. But here, an importing country such as Germany can not rely on climate change considerations when its own policy and industry is much more damaging to the global environment – climate-dirty energy – than for example nuclear electricity import which in fact reduces substantially German coal or oil-based emissions.[80]

---

[80] UNCTAD, Energy Services, 15; WTO Doc S/CSC/M/15–165–17 and 18.

To sum up: A simple import restriction as now possible under the new German and Austrian energy laws is likely to contravene GATT and can not be justified under Art. XX. Such contravention would also apply if GATT is applied via Art. 29 of the ECT (e.g. to Ukrainian or Russian electricity) and under the free trade provisions of the Europe agreements to the extent they make GATT rules directly applicable. Possibly, energy investors from ECT member countries operating in the import restricting country would also be able to invoke Art. 26 investment arbitration if the import restriction could be seen as a protectionist discrimination, i.e. if domestic companies could import electricity from their established sources, but not the foreign investor. It would make a difference if the trade sanction was primarily used to enforce a multilateral agreement (to which both countries must be parties). Such agreements (ratified, effective) with both the EU and the CEEC countries (plus Russia and Ukraine) which impose minimum safety standards on nuclear plants or minimum environmental standards on power plants do currently not exist.

There are also discussions in the WTO on the idea of creating a specific sector for energy services in which the EU participates.[81] This is meant to develop models for liberalisation commitments. It would probably require a classification of various types of energy services[82] Under the Kyoto protocol, emission trading and execution of CDM and JI projects would constitute a possibly dynamic new services industry for which special GATS regulation might be useful. A US/Norway proposal suggests to use a 'reference paper', i.e. a set of rules concerning free access, transparency, third-party access to energy networks and grids, non-discrimination and control of abusive practices – similar to the successful reference paper annexed to the GATS Agreement on Telecommunications. Easier access might be in the interest of both developing and developed countries as producer countries are currently dependent on such energy services, but tend to obtain them only at a much higher price in view of the many restrictions and lack of transparency. On the other hand, there is clearly a quid-pro-quo to negotiate. Transfer of technology, initial association of local companies for effective learning and better access for producing countries energy products (in particular refined petroleum and petrochemical products) could be part of such a deal. The problem is that it is hard to distinguish the traditional mandatory association with local companies – which have been in the energy field become the perhaps major method for corruption and crony capitalism – from an association that is not only siphoning off rent, but produces actual learning. A further development of the telecommunication

---

[81] They are described extensively in the Unctad, 2001 document, supra.

[82] The Kyoto Mechanisms: Linking Technology to Ratification publication envisaged in Climate Change Policy 2002.

reference paper model for the energy sector might therefore emphasise and introduce anti-corruption measures.

International emission trading as envisaged under the Kyoto protocol opens up, as it will for internal EU trade law, application of GATT/WTO law. There are issues of subsidies (under the WTO subsidies code as under the EU state aids rules) to consider; Benito Mueller has raised the interesting question: if the Kyoto-based trade in emission rights and climate-change equipment and services funded by an international agency of the countries participating in a hypothetical Kyoto climate control programme are subject to GATT non-discrimination rules, or if it is possible to limit trade to the countries participating in the Kyoto programme.[83] It is difficult to argue that business from non-Kyoto countries should benefit from Kyoto-engendered and financed trade. One would here have to look at the parallel to the carve-out of regional economic organisations (such as the EU) under the GATT, at the question if GATT rules apply to procurement from international organisations with a limited membership to see if an exception can be justified. Presumably, countries where such an organisation would be located or with joint liability the members of such a Kyoto organisation would be responsible for the organisation under the GATT. They would rely on an interpretation of Art. XX and argue that keeping free-riders out of a Kyoto programme is necessary to carry out an effective climate change programme. They would also argue that keeping non-Kyoto companies out is not discrimination as it is a distinction with a legitimate environmental, and not protectionist, reason.

The Commission has also raised[84] the issue of market access in general for non-EU countries. It has argued that as market access is only being established gradually throughout the EU with implementation of the Energy Directives, outside countries should at least be subject to the EU reciprocity (Art. 19 (5) rule – i.e. open up as much as they request access, to equivalent market access conditions (third-party access, unbundling, fair transmission fees) and be subject to equivalent environmental standards. But, as the Commission has recognised itself, lack of reciprocity is not a reason under the GATT to refuse access to a good – the proper remedy is to seek recourse from the WTO dispute settlement system. But the Commission has brought up a correct point: Electricity is not as easy to arrange access for as normal imported goods. Theoretical access – as even now EU ED implementation shows – is not enough. Electricity needs to have access to transmission and distribution grids; gas needs to have access to pipelines, storage and local distribution networks. The theoretical non-discriminatory access now available under the GATT resembles the equally theoretical freedom of movement for energy in the EU from 1957 up to very recently – a theoretical concept that did and could not work before a much more comprehensive regulatory restructuring took place

[83] In: 36 *JWT* 57 (2002).
[84] EU Green Paper on Security of Supply, 2001.

in 1996/98. One can probably construct the ancillary obligations of countries to provide access out of the GATT non-discrimination (Art. III) rule and the obligation with respect to state and special-rights enterprises under Art XVII. I have interpreted the non-discrimination rule in Art. 10 (1) ECT in connection with its state enterprise/special enterprise provisions (Art. 22, 23) as making governments responsible for non-discriminatory access to energy infrastructure facilities controlled by dominant enterprises;[85] a similar interpretation could probably be constructed into the comparable GATT articles. But what the EU experience – the most pertinent laboratory for wider GATT situations – demonstrates that it is not enough to be able to rely on legal principles and dispute procedures against governments, but a much more specific set of rules negotiated to ensure electricity transmission is both legally and technically feasible. A reference paper – such as the one for telecommunications – could be elaborated on electricity and gas (i.e. network-bound energy) trade. Such a multilaterally negotiated 'reference paper' would be more likely to create a playing field that is truly 'level' given the differences and disparities of participating countries and prevent truly 'unfair competition' than a set of rules elaborated by the EU based on its own internal experience and by way of economic, political and accession leverage imposed on post-socialist countries.[86]

2.   'Civil society' challenges to external EU energy policy: governance, superior ethics and sanctions

As energy markets internationalise and become part of the global economy, politicisation follows them. Political conflicts once focused on action by national government; in the global economy, the influence of governments is diluted, that of market increases. But political interest does not fade, but moves from an exclusive focus on governmental action to the action of the actors visible in the global economy – mainly multinational companies, international agencies and non-state actors such as NGOs and business organisations.[87] As political parties engage mainly in the competition for formal elections, NGOs have taken over a substantial role in politicising international relations, in particular by focusing on special situations and special value clusters (environment and human rights; wildlife; indigenous

---

[85]   Waelde/Wouters (1996), 27 *Neth. Y.Bk. Int'l Law* 143 (1996).
[86]   Wälde/Gunst in: 36 *JWT* 191 (2002).
[87]   Susan Strange, *The retreat of the state: the diffusion of power in the world economy*, Cambridge University Press Cambridge 1996; Marina Ottaway, Reluctant Missionaries, July-August 2001 in: Foreign Policy; John Mitchell (ed), *Companies in a world of conflict*, RIIA/ London 1998.

people). These, naturally, represent the core contemporary values of the politically dominant middle classes in the prosperous Western societies. With the collapse of Communism and the Cold War, NGOs and 'civil society' – a term encompassing the self-appointed guardians of high moral values of the West – have become the main voice for opposition and criticism. The internet has allowed to bring much more rapidly together geographically distanced people and groups and to organise actions aimed at capturing public opinion, thereby both influencing formal political processes resulting in 'law', but also, for the NGOs engaged in intense competition, to develop profile, i.e. a kind of public-opinion 'brand value' which helps to raise funds, efforts and support. Political parties, suddenly subject to such competition from the outside of the oligopoly of election contesting, are compelled to pay attention and to hang-on and follow NGO campaigns which are proving attention-getters. What does, though, all of this have to do with the external dimension of EU energy law?

The EU institutions, in particular the Commission, with very little political legitimacy, have to be particularly careful to be seen to respond to demands from 'civil society' in order not to alienate the modest support they have. The OECD, for the public a largely faceless discussion club of bureaucrats, has learned through the failure of the MAI that an international organisation now has to develop the capability to engage in meaningful play with 'civil society',[88] something that has been taken up with more much effort by the World Bank and the WTO.[89] NGO pressure therefore works directly on the Commission, but also through the EP as this institution as well, or even more so, badly needs to develop a level of political acceptance that is closer to its formal political legitimacy, itself in heavy deficit. As energy markets internationalise, political attention, now largely activated by NGOs in conjunction with the educated media[90] focuses on what international agencies and multinational companies do. As NGOs in combination with the media do not make a living out of positive news or support, but out of focusing and highlighting 'scandal' accompanied by outrage, their influence is both negative, i.e. to make existing activities more difficult, and positive, i.e. by pushing international agencies in particular into desired direction.

---

[88] David Henderson, *The MAI Affair: A story and its lessons*, Royal Institute of Int'l Affairs, London 1999; Jan Huner, Lessons from the MAI: a view from the negotiating table, in: Brack & Ward, *op. cit.* 2000, 242.

[89] Bergesen/Lunde *op. cit.* 1999.

[90] Not to forget: A significant influence even on EU external energy policy comes the discussion and interpretation of events in the Financial Times, The Economist, Wall Street Journal, Le Monde; New York Times; Frankfurter Allgemeine Zeitung; Neue Zuercher Zeitung. Political capital dissipated from the MAI negotiations not only because of NGO criticism (as a rule misinformed and emotionally agitated), but because of critical reporting in the Financial Times (Guy de Jonquieres). The Secretary General of the Energy Charter Secretariat was ousted in December 1999 largely because of FT criticism.

The confrontation between NGOs/ 'civil society' and international energy companies is typically focused on a particular situation: The (legal and approved) dumping of an offshore platform into the Sea (Shell – Brent Spar case) and the – legal – exploitation of oil in Nigerian Delta areas characterised by conflictual relations between the federal governments and several, competing local populations with likely breaches of rules of criminal procedure regarded in Western countries as fundamental (Ogoniland trial of Saro-Wiwa), exploration for oil in areas with indigenous people (Ecuador), mineral exploitation in an area characterised by tensions between central government and local people (Ok Tedi and Bougainville, Papua New Guinea), oil development under a – legal – concession from the – legal – government involved in a secession civil war (Talisman in Sudan), human rights violations by security forces to protect a BP pipeline in Colombia, use of forced labour by government services to support infrastructure for a oil pipeline in Myan-Mar are just a sample of relevant recent cases.[91] In all of these cases, companies were acting legally, in full conformity with national law and the consent of the national government. The government, though, employed practices reflective the 'underdeveloped' (in the 19th century terms 'uncivilised') practices in its tensions with secessionary movements or local, often indigenous people. NGO campaigns are aimed not only at the companies (where they have an effect), but also at capturing the regulatory power of governments and international organisations such as the EU. The stated aim is to use the financial and political leverage of the EU – as well as that of multinational companies – to improve the 'governance' of the developing countries. Energy, here oil and gas development, are one of the prime targets. The reason is that oil and gas has to move where a not yet discovered geological target is, and that tends to be increasingly in developing countries and remote areas. The EU is hence under increasing pressure to take action, or at least show action, in combating visible violations of human rights and environmental disasters in the oil and gas operations of in particular EU-based companies.

The issue, though, is wider. The failure of statist systems in developing countries to supply enough energy for the exploding needs has led to large-scale privatisation and opening of energy investment opportunities. EU companies – in order not to lose out in competition with the more agile US energy companies – have now followed suit and acquired and established power plants, transmission grids, distribution systems and gas pipelines in particular in resource-rich or energy-hungry large developing countries (Pakistan, India, Indonesia, Argentina, Brazil, Bolivia). These operations may sometimes have the human rights and environmental implications of the typically more remote-area investment of oil and gas; but mainly such

---

[91] G. Akpan, 20 *JENRI*, 55 (2002); Shell, Brent Spar case, Stephen Howarth, *A Century in Oil: The Shell Transport and Trading Company 1897–1997*, London, Weidenfeld 1997 at 334–336, 338.

investment is carried out under governance conditions which do not correspond to the reality, or ideal, of Western countries. This applies in particular to widespread corruption required to do business, or at least in the equivalent practice of having to co-opt cronies of the strong men.[92] As these matters have now become widely known, in particular in relation with energy facility disputes in Pakistan, India and Indonesia,[93] pressure is mounting both on companies and the EU/national governments to introduce national and international regulation to combat such features of bad governance. The EU is certainly responding to these pressures. 'Good Governance' items, reflecting NGO and EP pressure, is now a mandatory part of international agreements.

The rapid recent progress on these matters can be observed by comparing the Energy Charter Treaty, the Bulgaria Europe Agreement and the Cotonou Agreement. The ECT, negotiated 1992–94, includes no specific 'governance' provision. The Bulgaria Europe agreement (signed 1994, amended up to 2001) already has a reference to the observance of human rights (Art. 6, referring to the Helsinki Act) and prevention of money laundering (Art. 87). The Cotonou agreement of 2001 is replete with 'civil society' elements: 'civil society in all its forms' and NGOs are specifically mentioned as actor of cooperation (Art. 6); arms trade, organised crime, ethnic, religious or racial forms of discrimination, but also human rights, democratic principles, the rule of law and good governance (Art. 8). Human rights and sustainable development, the quality of men and women, transparent and accountable governance (Art. 9), greater involvement of civil society and justice (Art. 10), rights of girl children (Art. 26), access of women to economic and other resources (Art. 31), corruption (97). The EC has with these provisions a basis to exercise leverage, be it by the dialogue envisaged under the agreement, formal arbitration (Art. 98) and presumably by withdrawal of financial and technical assistance, but also of the significant trade concessions for the ACP countries under the Treaty ('appropriate measures', Art. 96. In essence, the agreement provides a political, financial and trade stick to the EC to sanction ACP countries (i.e. former colonies) that do not mend their ways. The legal reciprocity of this treaty should not cover the fact that it is in essence an instrument to legitimise the overwhelming leverage of the EU against misconduct by developing countries which, by definition, have weak governance structures. For the energy sector this means that projects with a governance liability – this is virtually any project in any developing country, is now burdened with the risk of NGO campaigning, reverberating in shareholder pressure and sometimes

---

[92] Francois Vincke, April 1997, Dealing with corruption – effectiveness of existing regimes on doing business, 91st *AJIL* Meeting 1997.

[93] 91st Annual Meeting of ASIL 1997; Theodore Moran, Political and regulatory risk in infrastructure, Report for World Bank Infrastructure investment risk conference, Rome 1999 (*www.worldbank.org/riskconference*), Thomas Waelde, International Treaties and Regulatory Risk in Infrastructure Investment, 34 *JWT* 1–61 (2000); Regular reporting in the Financial Times, see: Waelde, *JWT* April 2000 with further references.

public-opinion focused litigation,[94] with economic sanctions by the US government, but also now the prospect of the blacklisting of the country and the withdrawal of financial assistance and trade concessions by the EU. It is not that business can not continue under these conditions, but it is likely to become a 'rogue business' in the shadow, with heavy profit margins for adventurous companies and an entry for international crime.[95]

The implication of this emerging international law of 'good governance', embodied in treaties such as the Cotonou agreement, the OECD anti-bribery convention, international human rights treaties, numerous guidelines, codes of conduct serving as aid conditionalities, but also emerging civil law of corporate liability of multinational companies is:

Companies, international organisations and governments cannot rely on defense of 'compliance with national law'. The strong emphasis on non-intervention into the domestic affairs of another state, enshrined in the UN Charter and the World Bank Convention[96] are de-facto superseded in the eyes of the 'civil society' movement in the Western countries. The pendulum which in the period of the call for a 'New International Economic Order' (NIEO) emphasised to an extreme 'absolute state sovereignty', Calvo-clause, permanent sovereignty over natural resources and economic activity and inadmissibility of any foreign intervention into the affairs and exclusive jurisdiction of host (developing) states has swung back 180% to its opposite.[97]

As yet an inchoate principle of international customary or comparative law of major Western countries may be emerging according to which multinational companies bear some responsibility for serious of breaches of good governance principles when their investment is supporting the activities of such governments. The recent compensation settlements for WW II corporate 'connivance' in human rights violations by the Nazi regime may in fact herald the recognition of such a principle, such as the Nuremberg tribunal provided the precedent for the current human rights tribunals in The Hague and Arusha.

But these developments are not as 'good' or 'godly' as they may appear to the activists at first sight. They place the principal targeted actors in a series of dilemmas: The EU and member states are dependent, and increasingly so, on

---

[94] Harold Hongju Koh, Transnational Public Law Litigation, 100 *Yale LJ* 2335 (1991); Akpan (*op. cit* supra); special issue of *Texas J Intl Law*, 2000.

[95] See report of panel of experts for UN security council on conflict diamonds: (*http://www.niza.nl/uk/campaigns/diamonds/docs/sierra_leone/index.html*; earlier the Bingham report on oil supply against UN sanctions to South Africa:, Report on the supply of petroleum and petroleum products to Rhodesia, T.Bingham/S. Gray, London: HMSO, 1978.

[96] Ibrahim Shihata, The World Bank and the Environment: A Legal Perspective, in: 16 *Maryland J. Int'l Law & Trade* 1 (1992).

[97] Thomas Waelde, A requiem for the 'New International Economic Order', in: *Festschrift Ignaz Seidl-Hohenveldern* (Ed. Gerhard Hafner et.al.), Kluwer International, The Hague. 1998, 771–804.

energy import which overwhelmingly is from states that could easily become sanction targets. Most of the petroleum producers (notably Saudi Arabia) have not acceded to the major human rights conventions; Russian or Chinese practices against secessionist movements are not that different from Sudan. The raison d'etre of oil companies is to go out and get the oil where it is located – if this would be forbidden, they would go out of business, and Western societies would go into crisis. The idea that outside, benevolent intervention will solve deep domestic problems has as a rule not worked; financial, technical and trade are ways to make well-functioning economies more prosperous, and civilised, but can not much contribute to solve deep internal government problems. Five development decades have not eradicated bad-governance or poverty, and there is no indication that changing the tack towards imposing Western cultural concepts borne out of specific Western experiences would suddenly prove more successful. The current solution to both governments and the EU (and its member states) is to emphasise the human rights element as much as possible for public consumption, but try to minimise taking treaty language meant more for public relations too serious. While Sudan and Sierra Leone might be suitable targets for trade sanctions, China, Russia and Saudi Arabia are clearly not, a pattern that replicates the internal EU pattern of political sanctions – e.g. well against Austria, but not against Italy. A system of partly recognised hypocrisy is of doubtful value, as it downgrades the moral acceptance of both the values that are pursued hypocritically, and of the institutions involved in such hypocritical pursuit.

There is more to the issue of good-governance pursuit through treaties. Imposing Western values via treaties, money, aid and trade against the former colonies may seem workable at this time. It did not work in a period when there was a balance of power between East and West; developing countries, fresh out of decolonisation, have then much more breathing space for then exaggerated notions of absolute sovereignty. But the condition for such pressures clothed in treaties to work is there is at this time no power to balance the power of the united West (US plus EU). If a balancing power would emerge (e.g. in Asia), that might well put an end to our current good-governance mode of relations with the Third World. It should be hard to deny that modern 'civil society' use of EU, governmental and market powers to impose values on the weaker countries, much meant to 'their' benefit, has a strong taste of the 19th century. Then as now, missionary societies went out, privately funded, but with government support, to civilise the savage people. Trade, aid and missionaries went hand in glove. The condition for this was a strong imbalance of power and the absence of effective opposing force – the colonising countries may have struggled over carving up the globe, but there was no fundamental dissent in the 'concert of the great powers' over the missionary mandate of the colonial powers. Perhaps such revival of a neo-colonialism which accepts the formal trappings of statehood acquired in the decolonisation process, but not the rule of non-intervention, is an inevitable reflection of highly unequal relationships of economic,

technological, cultural, political and military power in our era. But it is not
guaranteed to last.

As to its future influence on EU external energy policy and law, mainly
through treaties based on EU economic leverage, it may work best with
weaker countries (e.g. excepting Russia, India, China) and in countries with
no large and therefore crucial petroleum potential than in major oil and gas
producers (e.g. Saudi Arabia, Iran and Iraq).[98] In addition, we will see if the
leverage potential in agreements such as the Cotonou-agreement can
realistically be activated. Any imposition from abroad is bound to lead to
resistance, as the colonial and post-colonial history shows.

Economic sanctions are one of the principal instruments of international
coercion. For the energy sector, with its needs to go out into problem countries
because of the location of energy resources, sanctions have been a particular
problem. They bring an additional politicisation to commercial relationships
which are made more difficult in the first place by both host state, home state
and often transit state internal and international politics.[99] Corporate management now faces not only the challenge of managing very complex political risks
in the source-of-oil&gas states, but the new and additional risk of both US (and
EU) sanctions plus the new type of public relation and market-based sanctions
engineered by NGOs. They are still expected to bring the petroleum to market,
but are now also held liable for uncivilised governments over which companies
have little, if any, influence. As part of external EU energy-related law,
sanctions have two sides: As a sender country, the EU issues sanctions (based on
Art. 301 for political sanctions, also Art. 113 for trade-related sanctions);[100] the
EU has not been subject to political sanctions,[101] but its oil companies have been
subject to US economic sanctions for investment in Cuba, Libya and Iran; here,
the EU is not a sender of sanctions, but rather a defender of its own companies
against US sanctions. Both sides need a closer look.

As a sender of sanctions (prohibition of trade; interruption of services) the
EU as a rule participates in sanctions decided by the UN Security Council and
binding on member states according to Art. 25 of the UN Charter. The
sanctions are decided by qualified majority vote by the Council, usually as a
regulation, on a proposal by the Commission following the formulation of a

[98] It is not surprising that the so far major restraint on petroleum sovereignty arrangement has
been applied to Chad and not, say, for one of the large petroleum producers, Friday, Dec, 8,
2000 Washing Post Comment: Tough Choice in Africa.
[99] On Sanctions in respect of oil and gas: T. Waelde, *Texas JIL*, 2001; Bruno Cova, The
European Response to US Extraterritorial legislation, 353 in: 15 *OGTLR* October 1997.
Most recently and comprehensively on economic sanctions: K. Rodman (2001).
[100] McGoldrick, 158–159; Macleod, 352–356.
[101] With the exception, naturally, of GATT-based trade sanctions, mainly by the US (i.e. higher
tariffs; import restrictions and quota, anti-dumping measures). Energy was only affected in the
case of cars with high gasoline consumption; EU companies will have been subject to sanctions
for dealing with Israel (anti-Israel boycott blacklist by Arab League).

common position or joint action under the rules of the Common Foreign & Security Policy (CFSP).[102] Pertinent sanctions have been taken in implementation of UN SecCouncil Resolution 661 (1990) against Iraq after the invasion of Kuwait forbidding all commercial transactions promoting, inter alia, the export of oil/ oil products from Iraq, and by Resolution 748 (1992) against Libya (Lockerbie-bombing) with a more limited scope against trade in goods and services. Ancillary regulations prohibit contractual performance, including on performance bonds given by contractors to the sanctioned countries.[103] A contractor of a sanctioned country suffering commercial losses is not entitled to compensation.[104] The problem of economic sanctions is that they provide a competitive advantage to companies that are either not subject to sanctions – either by law or by non-enforcement by their home state. Economic sanctions typically engender a grey and black market of sanction breakers – such as subsidiaries of respected international oil companies in the 1970s sanctions against Rhodesia. Effective sanctions in most cases require a multilateral regime, normally initiated by a UN Security Council Resolution, followed by serious enforcement by all UN member countries. The more unilateral a sanction, the less is it usually effective, the more multilateral, the more universally and more effectively enforced, and the most embedded in public opinion, NGO attention and corporate management, the better it usually works. Large EU energy companies usually – different from the 1970s – comply with sanctions. They are also unlikely to participate in the grey and black market of sanction breaking where the profit usually corresponds to the risk – the better the enforcement, the higher the profit premium and the greater the sanction breaking incentive for risk-taking commercial and criminal operators.

One of the effect of not perfectly enforced sanctions (which are rare) is that the sanctioned country has to pay implicitly the risk premium by the sanction breakers. There is also usually a quiet race among oil companies to occupy positions within the sanctioned country (e.g. Iraq, Libya and Iran) and thereby foreclose more compliant competitors to be able to start exploration, production and export rapidly once the sanctions are lifted. Both US companies in Iran (sanctioned by the US, not by the EU) and EU, Russian and Asian companies in Iraq are believed to have preliminary agreements for investment in Iraq in case sanctions are lifted. Oil trade, being much less visible and notoriously difficult to control, is likely to involve many more oil trading firms than the much more visible investment. It is hard to make a

---

[102] McGoldrick, 159; Macleod 357.

[103] M. Nolan, US Sanctions Law: A complex web for US and foreign companies, in: 1998 *Oil &Gas Law & Taxation Review*, 112–116; Hans van Houtte, Trade Sanctions and Arbitration, in: 25 *Int'l Business Lawyer*; Ricardo Pavoni, UN Sanctions in EU and National Law: The Centro-Com case, 48 *ICLQ* 582 (1999) 166, 168 (April 1997).

[104] so the ECJ in: Dorsch Consult v. Council and Commission, 93 *AJIL* 685–190 (1999).

judgement on the effectiveness of sanctions. It is believed that they only work, to some extent, when issued by an overwhelming coalition of economic and political power against a relatively weak target (e.g. Haiti, Yugoslavia). In case of success, it is usually more than just the sanctions which have brought about political reversal in the target state, but then sanctions may contribute to such internal developments. The majority of sanctions, though, is considered to have failed its principal diplomatic purpose, that of coercing the will of the government of the target state. They also bring about a climate of criminality which is later difficult to do away with. Sanctions may, however, be more important as a political signal by the sender countries (e.g. the EU) both to the target state, its allies and as a symbol of a proper response (even if ineffectual) to domestic political pressures.

The other side of the EU coin on sanctions is if EU companies are penalised by US sanctions affecting non-US citizens and activities on EU territory ('extraterritorial sanctions'). Energy, again, is a primary area of application for such sanctions. The US is the most active producer of economic sanctions, and largely to satisfy its large number of émigré communities harbouring a particular grudge, and, more recently, the NGO movement.[105] The problem is that sanctions which are not shared by the major economic actors tend to do nothing but confer a competitive advantage on companies from countries outside the US. To issue sanctions and then see economic competitors benefit from it, with little damage to the target, is clearly not very satisfactory in the US political process. Therefore, and also by the tradition of missionary politics[106] and US hegemony[107] the US have several times over the last 50 years designed sanctions which were applicable to subsidiaries of US companies incorporated abroad (Fruehauf case), to European companies involved in the purchase of Russian gas and construction of pipelines in the early 1980s and, more recently, against non-US companies investing in the oil&gas sector in Libya and Iran and in any business in Cuba.[108] The EU considers the extraterritorial reach of these sanction laws a contravention against international law; international law does not, though, condemn extraterritorial regulation per se, there are several recognised exceptions; in addition, a multilateral, UN-covered sanction regime can probably legitimately affect persons and activities outside the territorial jurisdiction of the sanctioning state. The EU itself applies, in particular its competition law, with an

---

[105] Extensive literature: Waelde (2001); most recently: Rodman (2001).

[106] Henry Kissinger, Diplomacy, 1994.

[107] Lea Brilmayer, *American Hegemony, Political Morality in a one-superpower world*, Yale University Press, New Haven 1994.

[108] For a pro/contra commentary: A. Lowenfeld: Congress and Cuba: The Helms-Burton Act, 90 *AJIL* 419 (1996) considering the most recent US legislation; different: B. Clagett, Title III of the Helms-Burton Act is consistent with international law, 90 *AJIL* 434 (1996); Statement of Monroe Leigh before Western Hemisphere Subcommittee of Senate Foreign Relations Committee of July 30, 1996 (on file with the author).

extraterritorial reach based on the 'effects' doctrine.[109] But US sanctions – mainly imposing specific sanctions related to access to the US capital markets on non-US companies – that are only unilateral, not covered by a formalised international consensus and for actions that do not directly affect US rights – are seen as incompatible with the international law principle of territorial sovereignty, quite universally and even to a large extent within the US international law community.[110] The EU, as other states, have reacted with 'blocking statutes'[111] which forbid compliance with US sanctions and contain some counter-sanctions on US persons trying to enforce in particular the Helms-Burton-act rights against non-US persons dealing in Cuba. The EU also initiated proceedings through the WTO dispute settlement system asserting breach of a number of WTO disciplines. These matters have up to 2001 come to a preliminary halt; the US has not (yet) prosecuted actively major EU oil companies involved in Iran (Shell, Total, ENI) and Libya.[112]

It is difficult to make a conclusive judgement on the EU's recent opening up to 'civil society' as this is a matter very much in flux. It is here difficult to distinguish between what is current fashion of political correctness, and what is a longer, lasting trend towards applying Western cultural ideas about good governance to non-Western societies, on the instigation and under pressure from NGOs, mainly self-appointed, but through public opinion often, though not consistently, influential guardians of these values. There are elements of hypocrisy, of missionary proselytising for values against societies who may not want such values, but are too weak to fight back. There may also be elements which help to make international relations more civilised and indirectly prosperous by providing a social dimension to the otherwise purely economic impact of globalisation. It is likely that we will see perhaps on one hand minimum rules of civilised governance, and on the other increasing contradiction between values promoted by quite different interest and quasi-religious value groups. The EU would do well to take a very cautious line. If it embraces the 'civil society' with arms that are too much open, it also risks that its growing legitimacy gets undermined by the inevitable contradictions

---

[109] Daniel Tarullo, Norms and Institutions in Global Competition Policy, in: 94 *AJIL* 478–505 (2000).

[110] It is interesting to observe that the US Foreign Corrupt Practices Act includes a not dissimilar extraterritorial obligation on non-US persons employed abroad by US subsidiaries incorporated abroad to refrain from USFPCA-defined bribery. No opposition is known to the author to this far-reaching scope. The reason must be that, first, it is not very politic to be seen as facilitating bribery and, second, there is at least general coverage for the US action against international corruption by the OECD anti-bribery convention.

[111] EU Council Regulation No. 2271/96 of 22 November 1996 – published with the similar Canadian Foreign Extraterritorial Measures Act and the Mexican Act to Protect Trade and Investment from Foreign Norms that contravene international law are all published with notes in: 36 *ILM* 125 (1997), 36 *ILM* 111 (1997) and 36 *ILM* 133 (1997).

[112] S. Smis/ Kim van der Borght, the EU-US Compromise on the Helms-Burton and D'Amato Acts, 93 *AJIL* 227 (1999).

between solid interests (e.g. in energy supply and prosperous commercial relationships under a commonly agreed legal order) and the much more fuzzy and volatile ideologies of the day. There is an argument for helping societies move to more law, order and security if they are on that way already and if there are vigorous domestic forces in that direction; but there is little practical argument in trying to push European values and system on societies, which are not prepared, not interested and which perhaps are even, surprising as this may seem to neo-missionaries, attached to their own, distinct system of values. A safe and civilised international intercourse may be a more reasonable and realistic goal than taking up again the 'white person's burden' and better the modern day 'sullen people'.

3.   Assessment of EU international energy law and policy

3.1 Conclusion and assessment

Given the challenges of the integration process, and in particular, the delayed, much resisted and technically difficult integration of the energy markets, it is perhaps not surprising that the external dimension of EU energy law has not received that much attention. Perhaps also reflecting the absence of a separate energy chapter in the Treaty, there is very little that is energy-specific about international EU law; the Energy Charter Treaty[113] is the major, and only, specific achievement in this area, and even this treaty has loose ends (the draft Supplementary Treaty). But it is in energy that the EU is more than in other areas most dependent on smooth functioning of international trade. Trade here is as a rule with volatile, high-risk and from a governance perspective problematic countries close to the Eastern and Southern fringes of the Community. Energy is affected in most of the economic cooperation treaties of the EU. In most cases, the move towards customs union, the principles of investment promotion and environmental attention include the energy sector, with some more specificity in the accession ('Europe') agreements. But even these treaties have something intangible about them. There are replete with high-sounding intentions and objectives, but, apart perhaps from trade, short on tangible and specific mechanisms. The EU has not, so far, and apart from the ECT, achieved a tangible, creative mechanism which goes beyond a marginal and moral support to facilitation of trade and investment. There is no innovative institution, no working mechanism to bring Russian and Central Asian gas to Europe, no clear-cut result in making former Soviet

---

[113] T. Wälde, *The Energy Charter Treaty*, Kluwer 1996.

nuclear reactors safe, no deal with OPEC involving prices, taxes, production and climate change (though I think that is now becoming more feasible), but rather lots of words, good intentions and aid funds dissipated by a directorate general without an energy focus among a large number of countries and projects. Why is that so? Perhaps, it reflects that the navel-gazing approach of the EU has not yet grasped fully that much of the energy challenges are in building solid structures with the supplier countries, and that one has to look not only at one's own interests and constraints (of which there are many) but at the interests and constraints of the supplier countries to find workable deals. That requires a dramatic change in the mental outlook – from inside to the outside, perhaps hard for an organisation such as the EU and its services to make. Possibly, there is also a vacuum of leadership, perhaps reflecting the difficulty of foreign policy in general in a federated system where national jealousy, in particular from former imperial countries, keeps the centre from exercising leadership, and with not enough power, space and legal competences for individual member states to act as laboratories and strike out pilot deals any more. National power and leadership potential seems to have vanished, but rather into a black hole than into the Commission and the CSFP structures. That is possibly the price of having a federation, and not a European 'superstate'. Who can speak with authority and strike a deal?[114]

On the other hand, the Commission and EP in parliament are on a slippery slope when giving in without in-depth discussion to 'civil society'. If one takes the many rules and sanctions of the Cotonou agreement in particular serious (and it is not certain that should be done), then there is the risk of alienating the major energy suppliers (who can turn their attention easily to the much more dynamic markets less encumbered by morality in Asia) and at the same time getting into a re-play of 19th century missionary colonialism, without that the political circumstances really require and allow that in the long term. Relations with NGOs (organisations without accountability and not exposed to elections or market-based competition) and 'civil society' need to be thought through and debated much more carefully. The EU system and culture may favour a facile accommodation to capture short-term popularity rather than a serious debate. If energy supplies are imperilled, that is much more serious for the EU than efforts to morally upgrade societies which either can not be upgraded so easily or which in the end resent the missionary sermons from a far away party with little appreciation of local circumstances.

The EU should perhaps focus on exploring the potential for lasting deals to facilitate smoothly functioning energy markets: With Russia on pipelines, with OPEC on prices, production, tax and climate change and within the WTO on a global liberalisation (perhaps through a reference paper modelled on the energy directives). The EU is, surprisingly, not a member of the International

---

[114] A US complaint on negotiating with the Commission, FT (2000): Richard Holbrooke, 17 April 2001.

Energy Agency (IEA),[115] where member states, and not the EU, play the dominant role.[116] The EU has a dominant role in the European Investment Bank (EIB) who is used for financing energy infrastructure investment and could be built up as a major institution for both financing and guaranteeing risky infrastructure facilities and long-term contracts, something that may be necessary in energy relations with Russia and Central Asia. The EU is not a member of the EBRD. Again, this may reflect the still somewhat neutered nature of EU international energy policy.

[115] Richard Scott, IEA, The First Twenty Years, Vol. I OECD/IEA 1994. The IEA administers a legally binding oil sharing mechanism in case of supply crisis. It is also involved in high-quality research on energy issues and participates in energy-related initiatives (e.g. discussions with OPEC).

[116] The IEP Agreement says (Art 72.1) 'This Agreement shall be open for accession by the European Communities'. That did not occur. It would not convey voting rights, which are reserved for participating states. The European Commission 'takes part in the work of the IEA pursuant to a 1974 invitation of the Governing Board, which recites that it refers to Supplementary Protocol No. 1 to the OECD Convention, providing that the Commission shall take part in the work of the OECD. As a practical matter, the Commission participates in the same manner as a Member, except that it cannot vote. The EU states caucus before IEA meetings, and the country that holds the chair may speak on behalf of the EU states.

GERHARD HAFNER[1]

General Principles of Sustainable Development: From Soft Law to Hard Law

I. Introduction

The main task of this short introductory paper is to offer certain ideas regarding the particular issue of the link between codification in the broad meaning and the principles of sustainable development as applied to natural resources. There is certainly no need to emphasise the importance of the topic; quite a lot of ink has already been spilled on it and extensive negotiations have been conducted.[2]

---

[1] Gerhard Hafner, Professor of International Law, Vienna University. This paper was presented at a seminar on Exploitation and Management of Natural Resources in the 21st century: The Challenge of Sustainable Development, organized by the British Institute of International and Comparative Law and the Department of Law, Queen Mary, University of London, 26–27 October 2001.

[2] The issue of sustainable development has a prominent place in the preparatory negotiations concerning the World Summit for Sustainable Development held in Johannesburg in 2002; see e.g. the Chairman's Text for Negotiation of 9 May 2002 (advance unedited text), UN Doc. of the Commission on Sustainable Development Acting as the Preparatory Committee for the World Summit for Sustainable Development, Fourth Session.

M. Fitzmaurice and M. Szuniewicz (eds.), Exploitation of Natural Resources in the 21st Century, 53–66.
© *2003 Kluwer Law International. Printed in Great Britain.*

Nevertheless, certain of its aspects did not gain the necessary attention, although they undoubtedly deserve it. Without taking them into account questions would be left in abeyance and problems would be raised which do not need so. In particular, such aspects should be identified which are necessary in order, at least, to establish the right parameters for these questions and problems. This discussion aims at identifying the requirements for a better efficiency of these principles in practice.

For this purpose, it is first necessary to ponder on the question of the objective of the formulation of rules in international law, followed by the discussion of the scope of sustainable development, its basic meaning and the problems involved therein, before the problems of their formulation in more or less legal terms can be embarked upon. In the latter context, the question of the pros and cons of codification, i.e. of endowing these principles with a written form, should be discussed first before the advantages and disadvantages of, including the obstacles to, such a written formulation either in the form of soft or hard law could be analysed.

1.1 *What is the purpose of the formulation of rules of international law?*

International law, as any law, serves as parameter of international politics, both phenomena are interconnected and they mutually influence each other. To put it in different terms, international law reduces the complexities of international politics since it provides the broad spectrum of possible activities in international relations with a structure guided by international law.

A further effect of legal rules is the stabilisation of the relations governed by them. Any social system needs a regulation of the conduct of its principal actors for the purpose of its stabilisation and maintenance and ensuring the survival of mankind. In particular, such a regulation enables the actors to include the behaviour of others into the shaping of their own conduct and to react reasonably to the former, i.e. with the intention to achieve a given result. Lacking such an order a reasonable conduct would be impossible; the only alternative would be chaos or the settlement of conflicts by unregulated use of force. The increasing interdependence of actors, the growing number of conflict situations and the intensified interconnectedness of different activities within the international social context still increase the need for regulation. This development is typical of matters of environmental concern and, in particular, the use of natural resources.

It is the international normative system or the international legal order which mainly serves the purpose of creating the parameters for such reasonable conduct. As such, it exercises not only a conflict preventing role, as originally manifested in prohibitions and in the delimitation of sovereign powers, but enables also the actors to perform jointly activities which they could not carry out individually.

2. Meaning of sustainable development – its vagueness

Sustainable Development is an expression which has been the object of the most different interpretation. As Brownlie states, for the present, the concept remains problematic and nebulous, appearing more as a statement of issues than as a resolution of the basic problems.[3] It must be emphasised that the Stockholm Declaration on Human Environment of 1972[4] did not yet include such a principle or objective.

Twenty years later, the situation has totally changed: According to the Brundlandt Report this principle could be understood as 'Development that meets the needs of the present without compromising the ability of future generations to meet their own needs'[5].

The Rio Declaration of Environment and Development of 1992[6] refers to sustainable development in various contexts, namely in the context of eight different Principles:

- Principle 1 confirms the anthropocentric concept and all encompassing scope of the principle of sustainable development.[7]
- Principle 4 forms the consequence of the former principle bringing it into the context of development.[8]
- Principle 7 states the objective of Principle 1 as well as the differentiated scope of obligations in the pursuit of this principle.[9]

---

[3] Ian Brownlie, *Principles of Public International Law* (1998), 287.

[4] UN Doc. A/CONF. 48/14.

[5] World Commission on Environment and Development (Brundlandt Commission), *Our Common Future* (1987).

[6] UN Doc. A/CONF. 151/26 (vol. I).

[7] 'Human beings are at the centre of concerns for sustainable development. They are entitled to a healthy and productive life in harmony with nature'.

[8] 'In order to achieve sustainable development, environmental protection shall constitute an integral part of the development process and cannot be considered in isolation from it.'

[9] 'States shall cooperate in a spirit of global partnership to conserve, protect and restore the health and integrity of the Earth's ecosystem. In view of the different contributions to global environmental degradation, States have common but differentiated responsibilities. The developed countries acknowledge the responsibility that they bear in the international pursuit of sustainable development in view of the pressures their societies place on the global environment and of the technologies and financial resources they command.'

- Principle 8 explains the ways and means to achieve the objective of Principle 1.[10]
- Principle 9 refers to the need of capacity-building in order to achieve the objective of sustainable development.[11]
- Principle 22 emphasises the contribution of indigenous people and their communities, and other local communities, to achieving the objective of sustainable development.[12]
- Principle 24 brings this principle in the context of warfare.[13]
- Principle 27 obliges States to cooperate in good faith and in a spirit of partnership in the development of the law regarding this principle.[14]

Despite these frequent references to this principle, even this declaration nowhere contains a precise definition so that the impression of a very vague and broad scope remains. The broad scope is also reflected in the mandate of the Committee of Sustainable Development of the UN since the founding resolution only refers to the results of the Rio Conference without adding any further clarification.[15]

In view of the absence of a more concrete reference, it seems that the broad scope of this term is now intended or at least generally accepted as a basis for further work. This equivocal understanding which addresses not only an intergenerational distributive equity, but also a horizontal equitable distribution has also to apply to resource management. It can therefore be concluded that if one speaks of the application of that objective to the exploitation and management of natural resources, this management must address not only the balance in the intergenerational field, but also a balance in horizontal perspective, namely between the States of different levels of development. In

[10] 'To achieve sustainable development and a higher quality of life for all people, States should reduce and eliminate unsustainable patterns of production and consumption and promote appropriate demographic policies.'
[11] 'States should cooperate to strengthen endogenous capacity-building for sustainable development by improving scientific understanding through exchanges of scientific and technological knowledge, and by enhancing the development, adaptation, diffusion and transfer of technologies, including new and innovative technologies.'
[12] 'Indigenous people and their communities, and other local communities, have a vital role in environmental management and development because of their knowledge and traditional practices. States should recognise and duly support their identity, culture and interests and enable their effective participation in the achievement of sustainable development.'
[13] 'Warfare is inherently destructive of sustainable development. States shall therefore respect international law providing protection for the environment in times of armed conflict and cooperate in its further development, as necessary.'
[14] 'States and people shall cooperate in good faith and in a spirit of partnership in the fulfilment of the principles embodied in this Declaration and in the further development of international law in the field of sustainable development.'
[15] UN Doc. A/RES/47/191.

this regard the natural resources could be conceived as a common good which has to be distributed according to this objective.

This conception of course necessarily comes into conflict with other well established principles such as territorial sovereignty. This latter principle grants a State the right for the unrestricted exploitation of its resources, subject only to certain restrictions stemming from the right of good neighbourliness.

But despite the restrictions envisaged by Principle 21 of the Stockholm Declaration which stimulated the development of international environmental law, the question posed by Birnie and Boyle nevertheless remains: How far can it be assumed that international law now imposes on States a general obligation of conservation and sustainable development of natural resources and the natural environment?[16] It is to be added that, in particular, the precise scope of such an obligation seems rather vague and obscure.

3. Problems of definition

Obviously, there exists a shared expectation among the States concerning such a principle as is proven by the extensive discussions and negotiations in this matter,[17] which presuppose this principle. However, its broad and vague concept inevitably impedes any elaboration of a norm in written form or at least makes it substantially difficult.

Any further investigation into the scope of this principle reveals that it embodies two different elements which have to be distinguished: the duty to comply with conservation measures or the prohibition of unfettered exploitation on the one hand (limitative aspect), and the objective of the conservation or restriction on the other (distributive aspect).

3.1. Which resources are addressed?

If applied to natural resources, the core of this distributive obligation appears to consist in a limitation of the exploitation of resources, this limitation being defined by the objective to be achieved. But irrespective of the more concrete definition of natural resources, it must be asked whether resources are addressed only if their exploitation would have a transboundary impact or whether they are addressed even without such an impact. The origin of international environmental law in the law of good neighbourliness favours the

---

[16] Patricia W. Birnie, Alan E. Boyle, *International Law and the Environment* (1992), 122.
[17] See in particular the vast amount of documents for the preparation of the Johannesburg Summit, *supra* fn. 2.

more restrictive approach insofar as a limitation would be required only if otherwise other States were be affected.

3.2. The objectives of the limitation

However, the expectations of the States regarding this principle already extend beyond this limited understanding insofar as three different objectives of limitation or of distribution can presently be distinguished. The first two are categories of limitations aiming at generating a horizontal equity:

(i)   A limitation in the interest of neighbouring countries[18] insofar as there exists an obligation to take into account the exploitation rights of countries detrimentally affected by the exploitation, sometimes governed by the principle of optimum utilisation;[19]

(ii) a limitation in the interests of the international community as a whole effectuating a global distribution;[20]

(iii) and, finally, intergenerational equity.[21]

But any attempt to identify existing rule of an all encompassing nature must fail: As yet, international law has only developed certain rules to be applied either relating to the first kind of distribution or for specific areas or resources:

---

[18] This limitation is obviously the original obligation resulting from the principle of good neighbourliness.

[19] See e.g. the Convention on the law of the non-navigational uses of international watercourses, Article 5 which reads:
'Equitable and reasonable utilization and participation
1. Watercourse States shall in their respective territories utilize an international watercourse in an equitable and reasonable manner. In particular, an international watercourse shall be used and developed by watercourse States with a view to attaining optimal and sustainable utilization thereof and benefits therefrom, taking into account the interests of the watercourse States concerned, consistent with adequate protection of the watercourse.
2. Watercourse States shall participate in the use, development and protection of an international watercourse in an equitable and reasonable manner. Such participation includes both the right to utilize the watercourse and the duty to cooperate in the protection and development thereof, as provided in the present Convention.'

[20] The term 'international community as a whole' is to be understood in the sense of the Articles on International Responsibility of States for Internationally Wrongful Acts according to UN Doc. A/RES/56/83.

[21] The concept of intergenerational sustainability is based on the conception of the Earth and its resources 'not only as an investment opportunity but as a trust, passed to us by our ancestors, to be enjoyed and passed on to our descendants for their use.' Edith Brown Weiss, Intergenerational equity: a legal framework for global environmental change, in: Edith Brown Weiss, ed., *Environmental change and international law: New challenges and dimensions, http://www.unu.edu/unupress/unupbooks/uu25ee/uu25ee00.htm.*

so for the marine resources, regarding international watercourses, outer space and certain terrestrial living resources.

The most developed rule pertaining to the international legal order applies to the first kind of distribution where a certain field of customary international law, *lex lata*, can be identified. In this regard, the equitable principles as elaborated in different instruments from various resolution such as from the WCED in 1987[22] to the most recent draft articles of the ILC on prevention,[23] as well as the rich practice of the ICJ in the field of maritime delimitation in particular[24], could serve as useful guidance. Although it would go too far to embark on the content of these formulations and elaborations of the equitable principles, whether it is rather a procedural device or contains substantive criteria of distribution, it nevertheless has to be acknowledged that certain common patterns of their interpretation have already surfaced. However, even in this regard, it must be asked whether the individual distribution scenarios are not too different to allow for a general regulation applying to all the different resources, be it territory, fresh water, maritime resources, air, shared oil deposits etc.

In contrast, the criteria of distribution under (ii) and (iii) are not yet so clear and no common or generally accepted pattern has emerged. Even if in this context reference is made to equitable principles, their particular impact on this distribution has not yet been tested so that this is a task de *lege ferenda* if a codification in the broader sense seems advisable.

3.3. Other problems encountered by a formulation of this principle

There are also other reasons which generate certain doubts concerning the possibility to reach a more general regulation of this matter, additional to the first mentioned distribution scenario. The work of the International Law Commission delivers two examples which substantiate these doubts:

-   The first example is taken by the work undertaken by the Commission so far: Although in various instances the ILC has dealt with different issues of what could be considered as falling under sustainable

---

[22] See the Principles Specifically Concerning Transboundary Natural Resources and Environmental Interferences, elaborated by the Expert Group on Environmental Law of the World Commission on Environment and Development UN Doc. WCED/86/23/ADD.1.

[23] See the draft articles on Prevention of transboundary harm from hazardous activities submitted to the General Assembly in 2001; Report of the International Law Commission, Fifty-third session, UN Doc. A/56/10, 370.

[24] A substantial number of cases presently on the docket of the ICJ deal with maritime delimitation; see Report of the International Court of Justice, UN Doc. A/56/4, 2.

development,[25] it was unable to treat this issue under a broad perspective. Instead, it addressed only individual topics. As far as primary rules are concerned, it dealt with environmental issues in particular in connexion with the law of the sea[26] and the law of the non-navigational uses of international watercourses,[27] less so in the context of the law of State responsibility[28] or reservations.[29] A more general approach was taken with regard to prevention[30] and the draft code of crimes.[31] But even in the latter two cases, the topic dealt with environmental matters only in a very restricted manner so that for the purposes of sustainable development very little can be gained from the Commission's work although it must not be ignored that already very early environmental concerns influenced the work of the ILC within the issue of the law of the sea.

–   The second example is a more recent one: The ILC placed on its agenda for the forthcoming quinquennium the question of shared natural resources of States.[32] It did however not define what should be understood under natural resources. Hence, a group of the International Law Seminar which is usually held during the session of the ILC dealt with this issue and identified different areas where separate international law regimes have so far been developed. They include particular regimes for the sea relating to its various kinds of resources

[25]   The Commission has not yet dealt with international environmental law properly, but in various instances it had to include in its work aspects of this field of international law; see in particular, Gerhard Hafner, Holly Pearson, Environmental Issues in the Work of the ILC, 11 *YBIEL* 3 (2000).

[26]   This work resulted in the Geneva Conventions on the Law of the Sea of 1958, the Convention on the Territorial Sea and the Contiguous Zone, the Convention on the High Seas, the Convention on the Continental Shelf and the Convention on Fishing and Conservation of the Living Resources on the High Seas; United Nations, The Work of the International Law Commission, New York 1996, 250.

[27]   Cf. the Convention on the Law of the Non-Navigational Uses of International Watercourses of 1997, UN Doc. A/51/869.

[28]   Hafner, Pearson, *supra* fn. 25, 15.

[29]   Hafner, Pearson, *supra* fn. 25, 30.

[30]   The draft articles on Prevention of transboundary harm from hazardous activities were submitted to the General Assembly in 2001; Report of the International Law Commission, Fifty-third session, UN Doc. A/56/10, 370.

[31]   The draft Code of Crimes was never presented to the General Assembly, because of the elaboration of the Statute of the International Criminal Court of 1998. See Hafner, Pearson, *supra* fn. 25, 30.

[32]   See Report of the International Law Commission, Fifty-second session, UN Doc. A/55/10, 292.

such as living and non-living,[33] for watercourses,[34] for special regions like the Antarctica,[35] for the Outer Space,[36] or regimes established by treaties relating to locally more specific areas and resources.

Hence, even if the principle of sustainable development is restricted to the management of resources alone, i.e. with a more restricted scope, nevertheless the question whether a general formulation encompassing all three categories of distribution is reachable still remains open. Taking this situation into account, one may wonder how far any elaboration of the overall principle would be possible or even beneficial.

4. Establishment of a vertical and horizontal balance: the problem of codification

This vagueness of the objective or principle of sustainable development renders any attempt of codification rather difficult, if possible at all, and raises the question whether in such a situation a forced codification could be of certain use or rather be detrimental to the further development of a legal regime.

In order to obtain a certain clarity, it has first to be asked why a codification is sought or intended at all. Admittedly, already the meaning of codification is not entirely clear; it can extend to a continuum which reaches from the written reflection of existing customary law (exchange of the legal basis, codification *stricto sensu*) and its systematisation to the formulation of new legal rules of general-abstract nature (including 'soft law', codification *lato sensu*).

The written formulation of legal norms, irrespective of whether in treaty or any other form, has certain advantages and disadvantages in comparison with unwritten law – advantages insofar as it systematises the legal regulations, leads to their harmonisation, broadens knowledge of such rules. It also contributes to conflict prevention insofar as it facilitates access to the legal regulations and is able to provide a more formal procedure of enforcement than customary law, which frequently is spelled out in the relevant instrument itself.[37] Beyond that, it

---

[33] Cf. e.g. the United Nations Convention of the Law of the Sea of 10 December 1982 or the Agreement for the Implementation of the Provisions of the United Nations Convention of the Law of the Sea of 10 December 1982 Relating to the Conservation and Management of Straddling Fish Stocks and Highly Migratory Fish Stocks, UN Doc. A/CONF. 164/37.

[34] See *supra* fn. 27.

[35] See the Antarctic Treaty, 402 UNTS 71.

[36] See the Treaty on Principles Governing the Activities of States in the Exploration and Use of Outer Space, Including the Moon and other Celestial Bodies, 610 UNTS 205.

[37] If the regulation is embodied in a treaty, the customary secondary rules of international law, e.g. the law on State responsibility, provide the necessary enforcement mechanism. In other cases, the relevant instrument can produce its own enforcement mechanism.

offers States a greater influence in the formation of the rules than in the case of customary law: Whereas the creation of the latter is influenced by the exercise of power, the codification process is governed by the majority of the participants.

A major disadvantage of codification, particularly *stricto sensu*, is that it petrifies the law at a given moment, providing only limited mechanisms for adjustment, i.e. means of dynamic adjustment are mostly absent or it produces a detrimental effect to the evidence of customary law if the latter differs from the codification.

Nevertheless, even if the advantages of a written elaboration and formulation are given priority over keeping the unwritten situation, the question remains whether it would be worthwhile to strive for a formulation in the form of hard law or of soft law.

Whereas for the classical doctrine international law in written form comprised solely the totality of 'binding legal norms' i.e. 'hard law', amounting to international treaties or binding resolutions of international organisations, the present view extends the meaning of international law to all regulations which are susceptible of steering the conduct of actors in international relations.[38] In the field of posited or written rules, namely, rules formulated by the main actors in international relations, the States, international law *lato sensu* encompasses not only the legally binding treaties, but also instruments agreed upon by the actors and articulated in the form of legal norms, which entail the possibility of obtaining legal force, i.e. 'prenormative instruments' or 'soft law'. Although these latter regulations are of most different kind and mostly not ensured by classical instruments of enforcement or secondary norms of international law, they are nevertheless capable of guiding the conduct of actors, by supplying this conduct with the presumption of legality, by creating the conviction of the need of new regulations in the form of hard law and even by proving the existence of the *opinio iuris* for the purposes of establishing customary law.[39] Since such regulations in the form of, *inter alia*, 'declarations', 'guiding principles' 'codes of conduct', are not legally binding, their adoption is easier to achieve.[40] They have, however, first to stand the test of their 'legal effect' (or, in different terms, the effect of creating normative expectations) because only their observance by the actors or their conversion into formally binding law (binding resolutions of international organisations, treaties) furnish them with legal force.

---

[38] See e.g. Ian Brownlie, *Principles of Public International Law*, 2 (1998).

[39] See e.g. the judgment of the ICJ in the case Nicaragua v. United States (merits), ICJ Reports 1986, 98, 107.

[40] An interesting practice has recently emerged in the General Assembly with regard to some works of the ILC: In the case of the 'Draft articles on nationality of natural persons in relation to succession of States' and 'Draft articles on responsibility of States for internationally wrongful acts' the General Assembly only took note of the drafts which where annexed to the resolution, see UN Doc. A/RES/55/153 and A/RES/56/83.

As to the advantages and disadvantages of these two kinds of formulation, reference could be made to discussion within the ILC on the draft articles on State Responsibility when it was asked whether these articles should obtain the form of a convention or a non-binding instrument.

Some members argued in favour of a convention that a binding form was needed in order to give these rules additional certainty to customary rules, more reliability and a binding force. Any other form of formulation would create an imbalance in the international legal order whereby primary rules received a more stringent legal force than secondary rules. Even, if the convention would remain unratified, it nevertheless continued to play an important role. Since all States participated in the treaty's elaboration on an equal footing more democracy would be involved in the law creating process. In the case of a non-binding instrument doubts could be casted on the value of the text since a 'mere' General Assembly resolution could not have the same normative value as a treaty. And a declaration entailed the same problems as a convention, but without the advantages, since it would be unrealistic to expect the General Assembly to adopt the text as a declaration without first substantially amending the draft articles. There was no guarantee that States would not attach interpretative declarations to the instrument.

In favour of a non-treaty form it was argued that it could be difficult to state the basic elements of international law (which the law on State responsibility undoubtedly is) in a convention; unlike for example the law of State immunity, the law of State responsibility did not require implementation in national legislation. In the case of a convention, double standards would be achieved applying to parties and non-parties. Further dangers would result from the possibility of reservations or of States adopting a non-cooperative stance. A codification conference of plenipotentiaries would result in a lengthy process, unpredictable in outcome, and could call into question the balance of the text, laboriously achieved over 40 years. It would not be desirable to give the General Assembly a stark choice between a convention or nothing. A resolution or declaration adopted unanimously by the General Assembly would be more effective than a convention adopted after many years of preparatory work and ratified by a small number of States, thereby contributing to legal stability and predictability in international relations. Such a declaration would place the burden on opposing States to prove that it was not binding. It was observed that such soft law instruments did have a decisive impact on international relations and the conduct of States, as evidenced by the jurisprudence of the International Court of Justice.

The impact of the elements of progressive development in the draft to the question of the final form could be seen under two different angles. On the one hand, it could be argued that because of the progressive elements, the appropriate form would be a multilateral convention since no binding law existed, but if the draft articles merely codified existing rules, there would be no need for a convention. On the other hand, precisely because of the elements of progressive development, practice showed that States were in general not in favour of such elements being included in internationally binding instruments.[41]

It seems that similar reasons militating against a codification *stricto sensu* might be put forward with regard to the question whether or not an attempt should be made to codify the principle of sustainable development in the form of a treaty.

Additional reasons which result from the particular nature of the principle of sustainable development and did not so much apply to the question of State responsibility could however still be added: This principle has not yet obtained even a rough outline of its content; States are still divided on its content and the various already existing legal regulations apply only to specific issues and do not yet permit general conclusions. The petrifying effect of any codification would cut off and, consequently, bar any further attempts to find generally acceptable solutions. A situation would be frozen which is not yet generally acceptable.

Further, this principle is necessarily applied not only in a bilateral setting, but is frequently seen as possessing a normative structure according to which the obligation is owed to the international community as a whole, or at least to an unspecified addressee. Therefore, the traditional mechanisms of ensuring performance, including the principle of reciprocity, is absent so that new devices have to be sought which are mostly still in discussion. In such a situation it must be ascertained that States or other actors which are not directly injured by a wrongful act are entitled to take measures to ensure compliance. Otherwise, wrongful acts which do not injure another State directly would run the risk of remaining without reaction. In this respect, reference can be made to the different forms of compliance mechanisms[42] which depend on the political and ideological environment in which they are embedded: Such a mechanism within an integrated community of States looks certainly differently from that in a global context. The particular difficulties encountered in such a situation are revealed by the futile attempts of the ILC to formulate a right of other than injured States to take countermeasures: Despite serious efforts to provide such a right, no agreement could be reached so that in the final outcome, the matter could be solved only through a saving clause in Article 54.[43]

---

[41] Report of the International Law Commission (2001), *supra* fn. 30, 38.

[42] See Gerhard Loibl, The proliferation of international institutions dealing with international environmental matters', in: Blokker/Schermers (Hrsg.), *Proliferation of International Organisations* (2001), 151.

[43] This provision is contained in Article 54 of the Articles on the Responsibility of States for internationally wrongful acts, *supra* fn. 40:
'Measures taken by states other than an injured state
This chapter does not prejudice the right of any State, entitled under article 48, paragraph 1 to invoke the responsibility of another state, to take lawful measures against that state to

It would therefore be difficult to elaborate immediately a convention calling for a direct application by the States. However, these considerations do not rule out the possibility of a formulation of this principle in the form of a non-treaty instrument. It is the vagueness of the present conception underlying the principle of sustainable development which makes such a formulation desirable. It would conform to the need of a greater stability and predictability in international relations without closing the door to further developments and adjustments. Any attempt to reach such a formulation or codification *lato sensu* would compel the States to ponder on the definition and, thus, constitute the first steps towards reducing or removing its vagueness and towards providing this principle with sharper contours. Such an instrument would constitute only an intermediary step since it would still have to stand the test of time and to prove whether it is generally acceptable or still needs adjustments in order to acquire a firm legal standing. The non-treaty form would facilitate such necessary adjustments.

5. Conclusions

The following conclusions can be drawn:

- A generally applicable formulation of this principle seems achievable only with great difficulties due to the different structures and the different stages of legal development of its various aspects.
- The structural particularities favour first an attempt to strive for a non-binding instrument; a binding instrument seems possible only in the context of shared resources. The decision of the ILC to include this latter issue in the agenda of the ILC for the next quinquennium reflects the conviction of the Commission that this issue is ripe for a serious codification exercise.
- As to the other aspects of this principle, they are still too vague to be included in a binding instrument; a clear pattern of State conduct necessary for such an attempt has not yet surfaced.
- For this latter part the alternative would consist in an instrument like a resolution which would produce an educative effect. Its benefit would consist in an immediate effect after adoption for all participant actors although without being legally binding. States would become accustomed to it.
- If a treaty is sought there exist different possibilities: A framework

cont.
ensure cessation of the breach and reparation in the interests of the injured state or of the beneficiaries of the obligation breached.'

convention would best suit the particular features of this topic as it would allow for an adaptation to specific cases and situations. However, even such a type of convention requires a particular enforcement and compliance mechanism in order to ensure observance.

— Despite all the difficulties, one must acknowledge the urgent need for the formulation of such a principle in the broad meaning in the interest of a global development and the survival of future generations.

OLUFEMI ELIAS*

Sustainable Development, War Reparations and Environmental Damage

1. Introduction

The aim of this paper is to examine some of the possibilities that may exist for international bodies charged with the resolution of claims for environmental damage to apply the principle of sustainable development. The United Nations Compensation Commission ('the Commission') is a rare example of such bodies, and it will be the focus of this paper. The aim is not to analyse the jurisprudence of the Commission relating to the principle of sustainable development as such, but rather to take a more general view of the place of the principle in the reservoir of legal standards, principles and rules that can be drawn upon by third-party decision-makers such as the Commission, as a contribution to the discussion of the prospects of the principle making, or having made, the transition from soft law to hard law.[1]

---

* Governing Council Secretariat, United Nations Compensation Commission. The views expressed in this paper are those of the author; they are in no way intended to reflect the views of, and are not to be attributed to, the Commission.
[1] This paper was originally presented at the conference in October 2001 under the rubric 'Sustainable Development: From Soft Law to Hard Law'.

M. Fitzmaurice and M. Szuniewicz (eds.), Exploitation of Natural Resources in the 21st Century, 67–90.
© *2003 Kluwer Law International. Printed in Great Britain.*

2. The United Nations Compensation Commission

2.1 *The establishment of the Commission*

The Commission is a subsidiary organ of the United Nations Security Council. It was established in 1991 to process claims and pay compensation for losses resulting from Iraq's invasion and occupation of Kuwait. Security Council resolution 687 (1991), the so-called 'ceasefire resolution', is the most important of the numerous resolutions passed by the Security Council in response to the invasion and occupation of Kuwait.[2] It was adopted five weeks after the suspension of military operations against Iraq by the Allied Coalition Forces. Resolution 687 was adopted under Chapter VII of the Charter of the United Nations. The most important provision in resolution 687 is to be found in paragraph 16, which provides that the Security Council

> Reaffirms that Iraq, without prejudice to the debts and obligations of Iraq arising prior to 2 August 1990, which will be addressed through the normal mechanisms, is liable under international law for any direct loss, damage, including environmental damage and the depletion of natural resources, or injury to foreign Governments, nationals and corporations, as a result of Iraq's unlawful invasion and occupation of Kuwait.[3]

The Security Council accordingly decided to create a fund from which compensation would be paid for losses, damage and injury caused as a direct result of the invasion and occupation of Kuwait, and to establish a commission to administer it,[4] and directed the Secretary-General to develop and present to the

---

[2] S/RES/687 (1991), 3 May 1991. A formal ceasefire was made conditional upon the acceptance by Iraq of all of the provisions of the resolution (see paragraph 33 of the resolution). The texts of these resolutions as well as all decisions of the Governing Council and reports and recommendations made by the panels of commissioners can be found on its website (http://www.uncc.ch). The website also contains a bibliography of the scholarly literature on the Commission.

[3] Paragraph 8 of the earlier Security Council resolution 674 (1990) (29 October 1990) provides that the Security Council '[r]eminds Iraq that under international law it is liable for any loss, damage or injury arising in regard to Kuwait and third states and their nationals and corporations, as a result of the invasion and illegal occupation of Kuwait by Iraq'.

[4] On the Security Council's competence in adopting resolution 687 and in establishing the Commission and the rules according to which it operates, see, e.g., see D. Caron, 'The Legitimacy of the Collective Authority of the Security Council', 87 *American Journal of International Law* (1993), 352 ff; R. C. O'Brien, 'The Challenge of Verifying Corporate and Government Claims at the United Nations Compensation Commission', 31 *Cornell Int'l L.J.* (1998), 1, at nn. 15, 18 and 21; F. Kirgis, 'Claims Settlement and the United Nations Legal Structure', in R. B. Lillich, (ed.) *The United Nations Compensation Commission* (Thirteenth Sokol Colloquium) (1995), 103. For different views, see, e.g., P. Malanczuk,

Security Council recommendations for setting up the fund and the commission.[5] The Secretary-General recommended, inter alia, that the commission take the form of a claims resolution body that would verify and value claims and administer the payment of compensation, and also that the commission function under the authority of the Security Council. The commission would be comprised of a Governing Council, panels of commissioners and a secretariat.[6] In Security Council resolution 692 (1991), the Security Council established the Commission and the United Nations Compensation Fund ('the Fund') in accordance with Part I of the Secretary-General's report.[7]

2.2 *The institutional structure of the Commission*

As recommended by the Secretary-General, the Commission is composed of three bodies, namely the Governing Council, the commissioners and the secretariat.

The Governing Council is the main policy-making organ of the Commission. Its membership is the same as that of the Security Council at any given time. It is responsible for the establishment of the criteria for the compensability of claims, the rules and procedures for processing the claims, the guidelines for the administration and financing of the Fund and the procedures for the payment of compensation. In addition, the Governing Council is charged with taking decisions on the reports and recommendations made by the panels of commissioners concerning claims reviewed by the latter. According to article 40(4) of the Commission's Provisional Rules for Claims Procedure, (hereinafter 'the Rules'),[8] these decisions are 'final and are not subject to appeal or review on procedural, substantive or other grounds'. The commissioners are responsible for the review and processing of claims submitted to the Commission. They are required to determine whether the alleged losses or injury arose as a direct result of Iraq's invasion and occupation of Kuwait. They are also required to assess the value of losses considered to be direct and to make written recommendations as to compensation to the Governing Council. The commissioners sit in panels of three, and they are chosen for their integrity and their expertise in areas relevant to the work of the Commission (such as law, accounting, loss

---

cont.

'International Business and New Rules of State Responsibility? – The Law Applied by the United Nations (Security Council) Compensation Commission for Claims against Iraq', in K.-H. Böckstiegel (ed.), *Perspectives of Air Law, Space Law and International Business Law for the Next Century* (1995), at 117 ff, and M. E. Schneider, 'How Fair and Efficient is the United Nations Compensation Commission System?', 15 *Journal of International Arbitration* (1998), 15 ff.

[5]   At paragraphs 18 and 19.
[6]   S/22559, 2 May 1991.

adjustment, insurance, engineering and assessment of environmental damage).[9] Where appropriate, the commissioners are assisted by expert
consultants.[10] The secretariat provides administrative, technical and legal
assistance to the Governing Council and the commissioners,[11] and is also
responsible for administering the Fund.

Funds to pay the awards of compensation are drawn from the Fund which
currently receives 25 per cent of the revenue generated from the export of Iraqi
petroleum and petroleum products, pursuant to Security Council resolution
1330 (2000). At present, funds are made available to the Fund from the
proceeds of the 'oil-for-food' mechanism established by Security Council
resolution 986 (1995) as extended and modified by subsequent resolutions.[12]

2.3 *Overview of the claims submitted*

2.3.1 *General*

Approximately 2.6 million claims seeking compensation with an asserted value in
excess of US$300 billion were submitted to the Commission. Nearly one hundred

---

[7]   S/RES/692 (1991).

[8]   Governing Council Decision 10 (S/AC.26/1992/10), to which the text of the Rules is annexed.

[9]   See section III, articles 18–27, and section IV, articles 28–43, of the Rules.

[10] See article 36 (b) of the Rules.

[11] For further description of the role played by the secretariat, see O'Brien, *op. cit.* supra n.3, at
      9–13. See also N. Wühler, 'The United Nations Compensation Commission: A New
      Contribution to the Process of International Claims Resolution', *Journal of International
      Economic Law* (1999), 249–272..

[12] The revenue derived from the oil sales authorized by resolution 986 (1995), which came into
      effect in December 1996, is deposited in a specially-created UN escrow account. The funds in
      the escrow account are used to meet the humanitarian needs of the Iraqi population, and to
      provide the twenty-five per cent share for the Compensation Fund. The operating costs of
      the Commission are also paid from the Fund. The exact amount coming into the
      Compensation Fund each month depends on the quantity and price of oil sold by Iraq.
         The arrangements in Security Council resolution 986 (1995) were extended and modified
      by resolution 1111 (1997), resolution 1143 (1997), resolution 1153 (1998), resolution 1210
      (1998), resolution 1242 (1999), resolution 1266 (1999), resolution 1275 (1999), resolution
      1280 (1999), resolution 1281 (1999), resolution 1284 (1999), resolution 1293 (2000),
      resolution 1302 (2000), resolution 1330 (2000), resolution 1352 (2001), resolution 1360
      (2001, resolution 1382 (2001) and resolution 1409 (2002). Resolution 1153 (1998) raised to
      US$5.256 billion the ceiling on total revenues that Iraq was authorized to generate through
      the sale of oil. The same ceiling of US$5.256 billion was applied in resolutions 1210 (1998)
      and 1242 (1999). Since the adoption of resolution 1284 (1999), there has not been any ceiling
      on total revenues that Iraq is authorized to generate through the sale of oil.
         The mechanisms governing the distribution of compensation to successful claimants are
      contained in Governing Council Decisions 17 (S/AC.26/Dec.17 (1994)), 73 (S/AC.26/Dec.73
      (1999)) and 100 ((S/AC.26/Dec.100/Rev.1 (2002)). See also Decisions 18 (S/AC.26/Dec.18
      (1994)) and 48 (S/AC.26/Dec. 48 (1998)).

Governments have submitted claims for their nationals, corporations and/or themselves. Furthermore, thirteen offices of the United Nations Development Programme (UNDP), the United Nations High Commissioner for Refugees (UNHCR) and the United Nations Relief and Works Agency for Palestine Refugees in the Near East (UNRWA) have also submitted claims for individuals who were not in a position to have their claims filed by Governments.[13]

For the purposes of processing and payment of the claims, the Governing Council has established six categories of claims. Category 'A' claims are claims of individuals who had to depart from Kuwait or Iraq between the date of Iraq's invasion of Kuwait (2 August 1990) and the date upon which the Security Council adopted resolution 686 (1991) which acknowledged the suspension of combat operations by Kuwaiti forces and the UN Member States co-operating with Kuwait (2 March 1991). Category 'B' claims are claims of individuals i) who suffered serious personal injury or ii) whose spouse, child or parent died as a result of Iraq's invasion and occupation of Kuwait. For present purposes, it should be noted that certain claims in category 'B' relate to environmental damage. In its report and recommendations concerning the first instalment of category 'B' claims, the category 'B' Panel found that 'claims for serious personal injury caused by the pollution emitted from Kuwaiti oil wells are compensable as the environmental damage from burning oil wells was, according to United Nations reports, caused by Iraqi occupying forces'.[14] The claims in categories 'A' and 'B' are for fixed amounts.[15] Category 'C' claims are claims of individuals for damages up to US$100,000 each. Category 'C' claims include claims arising from departure from Kuwait or Iraq; personal injury; mental pain and anguish; loss of personal property; loss of bank accounts, stocks and other securities; loss of income; loss of real property; and individual business losses. Category 'D' claims, which are claims for losses similar to those under category 'C', are claims for damages above US$100,000 each. Claims in categories 'A' to 'D' constitute the overwhelming majority of the total number of claims submitted to the Commission.

Category 'E' claims are claims submitted by or on behalf of corporations and other private legal entities, as well as public-sector enterprises.

---

[13] Deadlines were established for the filing of the various categories of claims. All of the filing deadlines have now expired with the exception of claims put forward on behalf of missing persons and claims for damage and losses resulting from land mine or ordnance explosions (see Governing Council Decision 12 (S/AC.26/1992/12). In exceptional circumstances, the Governing Council has allowed the filing of claims after these deadlines where the criteria established for the acceptance of late claims are met; see, e.g. the second paragraph of the preamble to Governing Council Decision 101 (S/AC.26/Dec.101 (2000)).

[14] See the *Recommendations Made by the Panel of Commissioners Concerning Individual Claims for Serious Personal Injury or Death* (S/AC.26/1994/1), the first report and recommendations made by a UNCC panel of commissioners, at paragraphs 121–123.

[15] See Governing Council Decision 1 (S/AC.26/1991/1), at paragraphs 10–13.

Approximately 5,900 category 'E' claims, with a total asserted value in excess of US$83 billion, were submitted to the Commission.[16]

Category 'F' claims are claims filed by Governments and international organizations. Approximately 300 category 'F' claims were submitted to the Commission by 43 governments and 6 international organisations, seeking compensation with a total asserted value of approximately US$210 billion. These claims have been divided into four sub-categories. Category 'F2' claims are claims submitted by the Governments of Jordan and Saudi Arabia, category 'F3' claims are claims submitted by the Government of Kuwait and category 'F1' claims are claims submitted by other Governments and international organizations. The claims in these three sub-categories are for losses including expenses incurred in evacuating and providing other relief to citizens and property-related losses, but not claims for environmental damage. Claims for environmental damage and the depletion of natural resources form a sub-category of their own, namely category 'F4'.

2.3.2 *Claims for environmental damage*[17]

The 'F4' category comprises 170 claims, with a total amount claimed of approximately US$63 billion.[18] The more significant proportion of these claims was submitted by claimant States in the Persian Gulf region on whose territory environmental damage and depletion of natural resources are alleged to have occurred (the 'regional Governments', namely Iran, Jordan, Kuwait, Saudi Arabia and Syria). Claims were also submitted by non-regional claimants for expenses incurred in the provision of assistance in responding to the environmental damage caused as a result of the invasion and occupation of Kuwait.[19]

---

[16] The Well Blowout Control Claim was filed by the state-owned Kuwait Oil Company on behalf of the Kuwaiti oil sector, and was reviewed in 1995–1996 by a special panel of commissioners that subsequently became the category 'E1' Panel. This claim was filed as a corporate claim and not as an environmental claim (See S/AC.26/1996/5/Annex generally, especially paragraphs 47–61). The claim concerned the work performed to extinguish the well-head fires that were burning upon the withdrawal of Iraqi forces from Kuwait, the initial sealing of the wells to stop the flow of oil and gas, and the making safe of the wellheads so that work on the reinstatement of production of oil could be started. The 'E1' Panel also reviewed the claims by the Kuwait Petroleum Corporation that could be considered as claims for depletion of natural resources (see S/AC.26/2000/16, paragraphs 89 *ff*).

[17] See, generally, M. Kazazi, 'Environmental Damage in the Practice of the UNCC', in A. Boyle (ed.), *Environmental Damage in International and Comparative Law* (2002).

[18] At the time of writing, the Panel had reviewed and made recommendations in respect of 105 'F4' claims, with 69 claims being awarded a total amount of US$ 243, 234, 967 out of a total claimed amount of approximately US$986 million. See Governing Council Decision 132 (S/AC.26/Dec. 132 (2001)) 21 June 2001. These claims are discussed more fully in section 3.4 below.

[19] See General Assembly resolutions 46/216 (20 December 1991) and 47/151 (18 December 1992) (both entitled, 'General Assembly resolution concerning international cooperation to mitigate the environmental consequences on Kuwait and other countries in the region resulting from the situation between Iraq and Kuwait').

The claims in category 'F4' cover a wide range of issues.[20] These include the following: clean up operations and other costs relating to the oil spill; the depletion of natural resources including oil fish and other water resources; damage to terrestrial resources such as agricultural land, wetlands, the surface of the desert, rangelands, forests, livestock and recreational resources and groundwater aquifiers; damage to public health including post-traumatic shock syndrome and increased public health monitoring and public medical care costs, as well as expected increase in the incidence of illnesses arising from the conflict; and damage to marine resources, including marine flora and fauna. [21]

2.4 The Nature of the Commission and its procedure[22]

As Iraq's liability under international law for environmental damage resulting from its invasion and occupation of Kuwait has been affirmed by resolutions of the Security Council,[23] the role of the Commission, in particular, the panels of commissioners, is essentially administrative in nature. This is reflected in the recommendation made by the Secretary-General in his report to the Security Council, to the effect that

> the Commission is not a court or an arbitral tribunal before which the parties appear; it is a political organ that performs an essentially fact-finding function of examining claims, verifying their validity, evaluating losses, assessing payments and resolving disputed claims. It is only in this last respect that a quasi-judicial function may be involved.[24]

This recommendation is reflected in the functioning of the Commission, and the compensation process established by Security Council Resolution 692 (1991) is distinct from previous mechanisms established for the resolution of international claims.[25] Proceedings before the Commission are inquisitorial rather than adversarial in nature, given the need to avoid excessive delays in the processing of the claims, and the Rules generally allow for more limited

---

[20] See, for example, the Report to the Secretary-General by a United Nations mission led by Mr. Abdulrahim Farah, assessing the scope and nature of damage inflicted on Kuwait's infrastructure during the Iraqi occupation of the country' (S/22535, 29 April 1991).

[21] See, further, sections 3 and 4 below.

[22] For a comprehensive analysis of the Rules, see M. Raboin, 'The Provisional Rules for Claims Procedure of the United Nations Compensation Commission: A Practical Approach to Mass Claims Processing', in Lillich, supra n. 4, 119.

[23] See n. 3 supra and accompanying text.

[24] S/22559, paragraph 20.

[25] See, e.g., B. G. Affaki, 'The United Nations Compensation Commission – A New Era in Claims Settlement?', 10 *Journal of International Arbitration* (1993), 21.

participation in the proceedings by claimants and Iraq than is the case in traditional courts and tribunals.[26] The panels of commissioners operate within strict time-limits, and it is left to the discretion of the panels of commissioners to decide whether additional information and documentation, or oral proceedings, are required.[27]

wo sets of general criteria were established for the processing of the claims submitted to the Commission. One set of criteria was laid down by the Governing Council in its first decision for the review and processing of 'urgent' claims, namely, claims submitted by individuals in categories 'A', 'B' and 'C'.[28] Priority was accorded to these claims out of humanitarian considerations, and a shorter time frame is accorded for the review of these claims and payment of compensation where appropriate.[29] As pointed out earlier, the overwhelming majority of the claims submitted to the Commission are in this category. For claims in categories 'A' and 'B', for example, simple documentation of the fact and date of departure, serious personal injury or death is all that is required to prove the loss, and given that the claims are for fixed amounts, there is no need to prove the actual amount of loss.[30] The review and processing of these claims is virtually complete, and much of the compensation awarded in respect of successful claims has been made available to the Governments or other submitting entities that submitted the claims for distribution to the claimants.[31]

---

[26] Claimants are generally permitted only one submission in which to prove their claims. See the Report and Recommendations made by the Panel of Commissioners Concerning the Fourth Instalment of 'E3' Claims (S/AC.26/1999/14), paragraphs 61–62. More generally, see also articles 16 and 36–39 of the Rules. Similarly, the fact that Iraq's participation, as a matter of right, is limited to providing its written views on significant legal and factual issues under the procedure laid out in article 16 of the Rules has routinely been taken into account by the panels of commissioners, see, e.g., S/AC.26/1999/14, paragraph 40.

[27] See article 36 of the Rules.

[28] See Governing Council Decision 1, (S/AC.26/1991/1), entitled 'Criteria for the Expedited Processing of Urgent Claims'. See also article 37 of the Rules.

[29] 'Given the traditional emphasis in previous claims resolution processes on the losses suffered by governments and corporations, this humanitarian decision to focus first on urgent individual claims marked a significant step in the evolution of international claims practice'; Wühler, *op. cit.* supra n. 11, 13. In addition to priority in the processing of these claims, priority was also accorded regarding the payment of compensation to successful claimants in these categories. See the Governing Council Decisions cited in the third paragraph of n. 12 above.

[30] Claims in category 'C', in contrast, must be 'documented by appropriate evidence of the circumstances and the amount of the claimed loss. The evidence required will be the reasonable minimum that is appropriate under the circumstances involved, and a lesser degree of documentary evidence would ordinarily be required for smaller claims, such as those below $20,000'; Governing Council Decision 1, supra n. 28, paragraph 15. See also article 35 of the Rules.

[31] For further information on the status of claims processing, see the Commission's website, supra, n.1.

Claims in categories 'D', 'E' and 'F' (including claims for environmental damage and the depletion of natural resources), in contrast, being larger and more complex, are governed by a different set of procedural rules.[32] The Rules contain more elaborate procedures, including the provision of a longer time-period for the review of these claims and the discretionary power of the commissioners to ask for additional written submissions and oral proceedings where it is considered appropriate. The Rules provide also that these claims 'must be supported by documentary and other appropriate evidence sufficient to demonstrate the circumstances and amount of the claimed loss'.[33] A higher evidentiary standard therefore has to be met by the claimants in these categories.[34] It is also commonplace for the panels of commissioners to issue interrogatories requesting further clarification from the claimants for claims in these categories. It is mainly in relation to this group of claims that the 'quasi-judicial function' referred to in the Secretary-General's recommendations to the Security Council is performed.

Between 2000 and mid-2001, the Governing Council conducted a review of the claims review process and adopted a number of significant procedural changes,[35] with a view to increasing the level of Iraq's participation in the claims review process, and many of these changes are applicable to category 'F4' claims. In the first place, the Governing Council encouraged the Commissioners, in their discretion, to send a greater number of claims files to Iraq for its written comments and observations.[36] Secondly, the Governing Council called for the convening of oral proceedings in certain circumstances, including 'where the claims under review are substantive 'F4' environmental claims',[37] and this has been reflected in the practice of the 'F4' Panel thus far.

---

[32] See Governing Council Decision 7 (S/AC.26/1991/7/Rev.1) and article 38 of the Rules.
[33] See article 35(3) of the Rules.
[34] See Governing Council Decision 46 (S/AC.26/Dec.46 (1998)).
[35] See generally, C. L. Lim, 'On the Law, Procedures and Politics of United Nations Gulf War Reparations', *Singapore Journal of International and Comparative Law* (2000), 435.
[36] See Governing Council Decision 114 (S/AC.26/Dec.114 (2000)), paragraphs 14 –15:
    '14. It is the Working Group's understanding that the criteria used by the panels to determine whether to transmit a claim file to Iraq normally include: (a) the Government of the Republic of Iraq is a party to a contract forming part of the subject matter of the claim; or (b) if the situs of the alleged loss is in Iraq; or (c) if the Panel determines that the transmission of the claim file will otherwise facilitate the Panel's verification and valuation of the claim; or (d) the amount claimed is more than USD 100 million.
    15. It is the understanding of the Working Group that, when the criteria referred to in paragraph 14 are fulfilled, as a practical matter, full claim files (consisting of the claim form, statement of claim and all of the documents provided by the claimant as attached to the statement of claim) are sent to Iraq unless such claims fall outside the jurisdiction of the Commission.
    19. Iraq's written responses concerning the claims under consideration by the panel will be reflected by the panels in their reports'.
[37] *Ibid.*, paragraph 21.

Thirdly, and perhaps most significantly, the Governing Council established an arrangement for the provision of 'technical assistance' to Iraq,[38] the aim of which is 'to facilitate the promotion of legitimate interests of Iraq with respect to 'F4' claims, which give rise to particular questions due to their complexity and the limited amount of relevant international practice', and is also aimed at 'assisting the 'F4' Panel of Commissioners in the conduct of its tasks, through ensuring the full development of the facts and relevant technical issues, and in obtaining the full range of views including those of Iraq.'[39] The role of the experts is to assist Iraq in preparing responses to article 16 reports,[40] written submissions and oral proceedings before the panel, and any other communication with the Commission on 'F4' claims. The effect of these procedural modifications is to ensure the participation of Iraq in the review of 'F4' claims, and the Panel is guaranteed the benefit of Iraq's oral and written responses to the claims.

3. Sustainable Development and the Law Applicable to Environmental Damage Claims

3.1 Article 31 of the Rules

Article 31 of the Rules provides that the Commissioners 'will apply Security Council resolution 687 (1991) and other relevant Security Council resolutions, the criteria established by the Governing Council for particular categories of claims, and any pertinent decisions of the Governing Council. In addition, where necessary, Commissioners shall apply other relevant rules of international law'.

Accordingly, in the hierarchy of sources enumerated in this provision, relevant resolutions of the Security Council are the primary source of law in the Commission, in particular resolution 687. The reference to Iraq's liability 'under international law' is to be noted, as sustainable development could inform the review of the claims if it is considered a part of international law.

Next in the hierarchy of sources are the decisions of the Governing Council, which lay down more detailed criteria regarding 'direct' losses and for the compensability of claims in general. With respect to claims in categories 'D', 'E' and 'F' (including 'F4' claims), Governing Council Decision 7 provides that direct losses include those suffered as a result of:

---

[38] See Governing Council Decision 124 (S/AC.26/Dec.124 (2001)).
[39] At paragraph 2.
[40] See article 16 of the Rules.

(a) Military operations or threat of military action by either side during the period 2 August 1990 to 2 March 1991;
(b) Departure from or inability to leave Iraq or Kuwait (or a decision not to return) during that period;
(c) Actions by officials, employees or agents of the Government of Iraq or its controlled entities during that period in connection with the invasion or occupation;
(d) The breakdown of civil order in Kuwait or Iraq during that period; or
(e) Hostage-taking or other illegal detention 7[41]

These heads of loss are not exclusive.[42] Furthermore, the Council has elaborated further rules on what counts as 'direct' losses, for example in relation to business losses[43] (an important issue given that losses that are attributable to the trade embargo[44] imposed against Iraq in response to its invasion and occupation of Kuwait are not compensable) and on claims for environmental damage and the depletion of natural resources. Paragraph 35 of decision 7 provides that direct environmental damage and the depletion of natural resources as a result of Iraq's unlawful invasion and occupation of Kuwait will include losses or expenses resulting from:

---

[41] Supra n. 32, at paragraphs 6, 21 and 34. The laying down of lists of compensable losses in claims resolution bodies is not new; see Wühler, *op. cit.* supra n. 11, 250–251.

[42] Supra n. 32, at paragraphs 2, 17 and 31, which provide that these heads of loss described above 'are not intended to resolve every issue that may arise with respect to these claims. Rather, they are intended to provide sufficient guidance to enable [claimants] to prepare consolidated claims submissions.' Paragraph 36, on category 'F' claims, provides that '[t]hese payments will include loss of or damage to property of a Government, as well as losses and costs incurred by a Government in evacuating its nationals from Iraq or Kuwait. These payments are also available to reimburse payments made or relief provided by Governments or international organizations to others – for example to nationals, residents or employees or to others pursuant to contractual obligations – for losses covered by any of the criteria adopted by the Council'; see also paragraphs 7 and 22. It should also be noted that the same five non-exclusive criteria apply to claims in categories 'A', 'B' and 'C'; see paragraph 18 of Governing Council Decision 1 (S/AC.26/1991/1).

[43] Governing Council Decisions 9 ('Propositions and Conclusions on Compensation for Business Losses: Types of Damages and Their Valuation', S/AC.26/1992/9) and 15 ('Compensation for Business Losses Resulting from Iraq's Unlawful Invasion and Occupation of Kuwait Where the Trade Embargo and Related Measures Were Also a Cause', S/AC.26/1992/15).

[44] Pursuant to Security Council Resolution 661 (1990). In addition to decisions 9 and 15 (see the previous footnote), see *Reports and Recommendations made by the Panel of Commissioners Concerning the Egyptian Workers' Claims* (Jurisdictional Phase), (S/AC.26/1995/R.20), paragraphs 223–230; *Report And Recommendations made by the Panel of Commissioners Concerning Part One of the Second Instalment of Individual Claims for Damages Above US$100,000*, (S/AC.26/1998/11), paragraphs 19–20 and *Report and Recommendations made by the Panel of Commissioners Concerning the First Instalment of 'E2' Claims*, (S/AC.26/1998/7), paragraphs 98–100, 164–173, 206–210.

(a) Abatement and prevention of environmental damage, including expenses directly relating to fighting oil fires and stemming the flow of oil in coastal and international waters;
(b) Reasonable measures already taken to clean and restore the environment or future measures which can be documented as reasonably necessary to clean and restore the environment;
(c) Reasonable monitoring and assessment of the environmental damage for the purposes of evaluating and abating the harm and restoring the environment;
(d) Reasonable monitoring of public health and performing medical screenings for the purposes of investigation and combating increased health risks as a result of the environmental damage; and
(e) Depletion of or damage to natural resources.

Where an issue has not been covered conclusively in any resolution of the Security Council or in any decision of the Governing Council, the commissioners are to have recourse to the third source of law, namely 'other relevant rules of international law'. This provision has provided the commissioners with a rich reservoir from which to identify supplementary rules and principles and the commissioners have accordingly drawn from a wide range of sources. For example, it has been decided that 'international law' is the basis of interpretation of the provisions of the Commission's 'rules and directives'.[45] Other examples include reference to 'general principles of law' in the context of article 38 of the Statute of the International Court of Justice,[46] the jurisprudence of the International Court of Justice and the International Criminal Tribunal for the Former Yugoslavia,[47] rules contained in multilateral treaties,[48] 'general principles of private international law',[49] the

---

[45] See the *Report and Recommendations made by the Panel of Commissioners Concerning Part One of the First Instalment of Claims by Governments And International Organizations*, (S/AC.26/1997/6), paragraph 55.

[46] See the *Report And Recommendations made by the Panel of Commissioners Concerning the Second Instalment of 'E2' Claims*, (S/AC.26/1998/7), paragraphs 71–72.

[47] *Ibid.*, paragraphs 55 and 61 respectively (regarding the rules of interpretation of non-treaty documents).

[48] In the context of a claim for pre-paid rent for diplomatic premises in Kuwait where those premises could not be used as a result of the invasion and occupation, it was held that, according to article 45 of the Vienna Convention on Diplomatic Relations, 'the mere permanent or temporary closure of a diplomatic mission, even in time of armed conflict, does not give rise to a claim for compensation. In such situations, under article 45 of the Vienna Convention on Diplomatic Relations of 1961, the only obligation of the receiving State, even in the case of armed conflict, is to 'respect and protect the premises of the mission, together with its property and archives'. Accordingly, the claim was rejected; *Report Recommendations made by the Panel of Commissioners Concerning Part Two of the First Instalment of Claims by Governments and International Organizations* (S/AC.26/1998/4), paragraph 55.

[49] In the context of family claims, the category 'B' Panel of Commissioners stated that 'Decision 1 does not contain any further definition of the terms 'parent' or 'child', and taking into

practice in several national jurisdictions regarding the use of sampling methodologies and statistical methods in mass claims processing,[50] and a number of different rules and principles of the law relating to contracts.[51]

3.2   *The legal status of the principle of sustainable development*

The issue, then, is whether there is any role for the concept of 'sustainable development' in the determination of compensability of category 'F4' claims. The threshold question is whether the principle of sustainable development is applicable under the rubric 'other relevant rules of international law' in article 31 of the Rules.

The status of sustainable development has been the subject of extensive discussion, and it is widely acknowledged that there is no settled definition of 'sustainable development'.[52] The basic idea behind the principle of sustainable development is to ensure 'development that meets the needs of the present without compromising the ability of future generations to meet their own needs'.[53] It is quite well-established that the principle comprises at least four elements, namely (a) the need to integrate environmental protection and economic development; (b) the need to preserve natural resources for the

---

cont.

account the comments and views made by Governments in response to this issue as raised in article 16 reports, the Panel finds it appropriate, in conformity with general principles of private international law, to apply to each claimant his or her own national law in interpreting these terms. Where national laws accord a claimant legal rights similar to those accorded to a biological parent or child, the claimant will be treated as a biological parent or child for the purposes of the processing of the claims in category 'B'"; *Recommendations Made by the Panel of Commissioners Concerning Individual Claims for Serious Personal Injury or Death*, supra n. 14, at paragraph 45.

[50] See *Report And Recommendations Made by the Panel of Commissioners Concerning the Fourth Instalment of Claims for Departure From Iraq or Kuwait*, (S/AC.26/1995/4), paragraphs 9–34.

[51] For further examples of the rules of law applied by the panels, see the Index of Jurisprudence on the website of the Commission, supra n. 2. See also the *Report of the Working Group of Experts on Liability and Compensation for Environmental Damage Arising from Military Activities*, U.N. Doc. UNEP/Env.Law/3/Inf.1, 15 October 1996. This report deals with all aspects of the work of the Commission regarding claims for environmental damage and the depletion of natural resources, and was written prior to the commencement of the review of these claims. The Working Group considered, interestingly, the role of sustainability in the valuation of environmental damage. Needless to say, the conclusions of the Working Group are not binding on the 'F4' Panel of Commissioners, and no reference was made to it in the Panel's first report. The report however contains a number of conclusions regarding the anticipated tasks of the 'F4' Panel.

[52] See. e.g., P. Birnie and A. Boyle, *International Law and the Environment* (2002), 84–97.

[53] See the Bruntland Report, *Our Common Future*, World Commission on Environment and Development (1987).

benefit of future generations; (c) the sustainable utilization of renewable and non-renewable natural resources; and (d) the redressing of economic inequities within the existing system.[54] The answer to the question whether sustainable development can be considered a *legal* principle is, however, generally negative. In spite of the 'near universal' endorsement at the Rio Conference of its 'defining role' in the development of international environmental law and policy, its subsequent adoption in major treaties and its role in the development of the law and policy of various international organizations, it is widely acknowledged that it is difficult to identify the parameters of sustainability or the specific criteria for determining whether the conduct of States or other actors is in compliance with whatever normative consequences the principle might imply.[55]

Nevertheless, it has been argued the principle of sustainable development, or its component elements, are 'not legally irrelevant although factors such as inter- and intra-generational equity, or the integration of environment and development, may lack normative or justiciable content, a court or international institution can ensure that they are taken account of in decision-making, even if it cannot review judgments made in the light of these factors'.[56]

One argument in favour of the legal relevance of the principle is based on the premise that the entirety of international law, at least as far as third-party adjudication is concerned, is not to be sought exclusively within the traditional sources of international law, for example, as listed in article 38(1) of the Statute of the International Court of Justice. Lowe, taking a lead from dicta in

---

[54] See, e.g., Fred L. Morrison and R. Wolfrum (eds.), *International, Regional and National Environmental Law* (2000), 20–23; P. Sands, *Principles of International Environmental Law* (1995), 198–208. Other enumerations of the components of the principle of sustainable development contain more items, but the difference is not material for present purposes; see, e.g. A. Boyle and D. Freestone (eds.)., *International Law and Sustainable Development* (1999), Ch. 1; Birnie and Boyle, supra n. 52, include the 'polluter-pays' principle and procedural obligations as elements of sustainable development.

[55] See Birnie and Boyle, supra n. 52, at 84–5, where it is also mentioned that, while the elements of sustainable development can be identified, it is not clear how these elements relate to each other or to human rights law and international economic law. V. Lowe ('Sustainable Development and Unsustainable Arguments', in Boyle and Freestone, supra n. 54, 19, esp. 22–31), concludes that the concept of sustainable development cannot 'be regarded as having sufficient identifiable normative meaning to be capable of generating a self-contained norm of customary international law, no matter what its utility as a description of policy goals in international treaties might be ... The argument that sustainable development is a norm of customary international law, binding on and directing the conduct of states, and which can be applied by tribunals, is not sustainable' (30).

[56] *Ibid.*, 17. It should be pointed out that the full subtlety and sophistication of Lowe's thesis is not fully captured in this short summary.

the Separate Opinion of Judge Weeramantry in the *Gabcikovo-Nagymaros* case,[57] argues that all legal systems contain (primary) rules and principles that (potentially) overlap or conflict in relation to a specific set of facts (for example, 'the right to development' and 'environmental protection'), and there exist 'modifying norms' that serve to enable a decision-maker to choose which rules or principles are to be given decisive force in a given situation. Sustainable development is of this character, and like other modifying norms (of which canons of interpretation in municipal law and the 'Rule of Reason' and the 'balancing of interests' test in disputes concerning extraterritorial jurisdiction are also examples), it does not depend upon state practice and *opinio juris*; nor does it necessarily carry a prescriptive charge. As Lowe puts it, '[W]hile the concept is insufficiently precise for it to be possible to say that it requires a state to do this or that, as a goal or policy it is perfectly adequate to offer some guidance to judges in their approach to establishing priorities and accommodations between primary norms'. As such, sustainable development 'can properly claim a normative status as an element of the process of judicial reasoning', exemplifying 'another species of normativity which is of great potential value in the handling of concepts of international environmental law'. The point is also made, however, that the concept of sustainable development may need to undergo further evolution before it becomes well suited for application by tribunals in this way.[58] Nevertheless, on this analysis, the lack of precision attending the implications of 'sustainable development' does not prevent it from having a role to play in the review of category 'F4' claims as a part of international law,[59] as a 'modifying norm' that operates in a parasitic fashion on, and informing choices as to the operation of, other primary rules of more traditionally-acknowledged pedigree, be it those that are determined to be applicable in accordance with the traditional methods of international law-making, or those that are otherwise applicable on the basis of article 31 of the Rules.

Another argument in favour of the legal importance of the principle is put forward by Birnie and Boyle, who argue that even if international law as it stands cannot be said to require that development be sustainable, 'it does require development decisions to be the outcome of a process which promotes sustainable development'.[60] This argument finds some ready support in the *Gabcikovo-Nagymaros* case, where the International Court of Justice ruled that the concept of sustainable development, for the purposes of the case before it, required that

---

[57] I.C.J. Reports (1997), 7.

[58] As Lowe points out, modifying norms also have a role to play even when states negotiate, and not only when third-party decision-makers are involved; supra n. 55.

[59] See P. Sands, 'International Law in the Field of Sustainable Development', 65 *B.Y.B.I.L.* (1994), 303.

[60] Birnie and Boyle, supra n. 52, 96.

'the Parties should look afresh at the effects on the environment of the operation
of the Gabcikovo power plant ... It is not for the Court to determine what shall
be the final outcome of these negotiations to be conducted by the Parties. It is for
the Parties themselves to find an agreed solution that takes account of the
objectives of the Treaty, which must be pursued in a joint and integrated way, as
well as the norms of international environmental law and the principles of the
law of international watercourses'.[61]

Rather than having to decide on what is sustainable and what is not,
adjudicators can further the aim of sustainable development by requiring that
environmental impact assessments be carried out, or that environmental
considerations, including the elements of sustainable development however
enumerated, be taken into account in decision-making in a demonstrable
fashion. However, whether this argument indicates an independent normative
status for sustainable development is open to question, as it could be argued
that the procedural obligations to be complied with have their own normative
status (albeit of varying strengths depending on the obligation in question)[62]
whether they are brought under the umbrella term of 'sustainable development' or not.[63]

These two arguments suggest that there is a role for sustainable
development to play in the resolution of environmental disputes, as part of
international law.

3.3 The role of sustainable development in the context of war reparations

Even if sustainable development has a role to play as described in the previous
sub-section, there exists another possible obstacle to the reference to the
principle in the context of institutions such as the Commission. It will be
recalled that paragraph 16 of Security Council resolution 687 (1991) re-
affirmed Iraq's liability for environmental damage and the depletion of
natural resources that arose as a direct result of its invasion and occupation of
Kuwait. The actions in respect of which compensation is sought are acts of war
on the part of Iraq, and Iraq's liability therefor has been determined in
principle. Sustainable development, on the other hand, appears to require that
there be an element of (economic) development in the actions to be reviewed
by any adjudicator. In the context of the Commission, that would seem to

---

[61] Supra n. 54, at paragraph 140–141.
[62] See Morrison and Wolfrum, supra n. 54, for a discussion of the normative force of the various
      elements of sustainable development.
[63] See section 4 below.

require that the actions undertaken by Iraq in invading Kuwait be considered an act of (economic) development. While economic motives may or may not have been a basis for Iraq's invasion of Kuwait, it would seem odd to view the invasion and occupation of Kuwait as an act of development; international law does not prohibit economic development but it prohibits the use of force other than in self-defence. Sustainable development, which may be considered as having at its core the idea that decisions about economic development should take account of environmental considerations in both the planning and the implementation of those decisions, would appear to have little to do with a scheme set up for compensating war damage.

However, it could be argued that the principle of sustainable development does have a role to play in such a context. In the first place, the concept of sustainable development is amorphous and multi-faceted and embraces a number of discrete ideas. Common to all these components is the idea of conservation and sustainability of components of the environment. It could be argued that this 'sustainability' aspect of the concept can be considered independently of the 'economic development' aspect referred to in the previous paragraph. This view finds support in the consideration that some of the elements of sustainable development necessarily imply a sustainability aspect but do not imply a 'development' aspect. The element of the principle that calls for the integration of economic development and environmental protection clearly refers to the 'economic development' aspect, but not so with the other elements. For example, the element of sustainable development that refers to future generations is very easily formulated with no reference to the 'economic development' aspect; neither 'the need to preserve natural resources for the benefit of future generations'[64] nor the requirement that 'each generation use and develop its natural and cultural heritage in such a manner that it can be passed on to future generations in no worse condition than it was received'[65] necessarily require any reference to economic development. If the various elements of the principle can be considered independently of each other in this way, it follows that a) the damage caused as a result of the invasion of Kuwait cannot be regarded as a sustainable use of the components of the environment, and b) it is not necessary to consider the actions of Iraq as 'economic development' for the principle of sustainable development to be relevant. There would then be a role for the principle in the context of category 'F4' claims.[66]

---

[64] Morrison and Wolfrum, supra n. 54, 20; and Sands, supra n. 54, 199, both use this exact formulation.

[65] Birnie and Boyle, supra n. 52, 89.

[66] See the views of Birnie and Boyle, supra n. 55, concerning the relationship between the various elements of the principle. See also section 4 below; measures taken to remedy environmental damage, particularly on a large scale, are akin to the kind of (development) projects that would normally be associated with the principle of sustainable development. There would not seem to be any reason to take the phrase 'economic development' so

In any event, environmental damage of the kind caused as a result of the invasion of Kuwait can have consequences for the economic development of a state, in a more general sense. If the large amounts sought in compensation by the regional claimants are anything to go by, then amounts spent on remedying the effects of the invasion on the environment can be expected to lead, at least to some extent, to reconsideration of economic priorities for the injured state, which may well have adverse consequences for the priority accorded to environment considerations in overall economic planning. In other words, the ability of injured states to meet the requirements of sustainable development can be expected to have been impaired as a result of war; or conversely, the exercise of the so-called 'right to development', which developing country advocates had succeeded in bringing into negotiations at Rio on the principle of sustainable development, could be impaired if resources are taken up in protecting the environment.[67] It will be recalled, in this context, that Principle 24 of the Rio Declaration, for what it is worth, provides that:

> Warfare is inherently destructive of sustainable development. States shall therefore respect international law providing protection for the environment in time of armed conflict and co-operate in its further development, as necessary.

Furthermore, in the case of category 'F4' claims, to be eligible for compensation under any of the heads of loss set out paragraph 35 of Governing Council Decision 7,[68] claimants will have to demonstrate the reasonableness of expenses incurred in respect of measures taken or proposed in response to the environmental damage. Sustainability could well have a role to play in determining whether and to what extent claims for such expenses are compensable, and it is to this that we now turn.

---

cont.
    literally as to exclude remediation projects from the ambit of the principle of sustainable development.
[67] It could also be argued that the environmental damage and depletion of natural resources by Iraq did not take account of the needs of future generations that might be expected to benefit from the components of the environment of the Persian Gulf Region in general and Kuwait in particular.
[68] See section 3.1 above.

3.4. Claims for the monitoring and assessment of environmental damage – the first report and recommendations of the 'F4' panel of Commissioners

Paragraph 35(c) of Governing Council Decision 7 provides that compensation will be provided for the costs of reasonable monitoring and assessment of environmental damage for the purposes of evaluating and abating the harm and restoring the environment. Prior to the expiration of the deadline established by the Governing Council for the submission of 'F4' claims, a number of governments submitted claims for environmental damage and the depletion of natural resources, including claims for compensation for expenses resulting from monitoring and assessment of such damage. In 1998, Saudi Arabia, on behalf of itself, Iran, Jordan, Kuwait, and Syria, presented a proposal requesting the Governing Council to agree to a procedure under which awards for the monitoring and assessment claims would be made in advance of the review of the related substantive claims, and any awards would be made by the Governing Council on the basis of recommendations of the Panel. The Governing Council, in response, requested the Executive Secretary of the Commission to invite the claimants as well as other similarly situated claimant Governments, if any, to identify and file separately, within the period to be specified by the Executive Secretary, those portions of their claims already filed with the Commission that pertained to the monitoring and assessment of environmental damage. The Governing Council also decided that appropriate priority should be given to the processing of such claims, so that the claims could be resolved separately from the resolution of the related claims for environmental damage. Most of the monitoring and assessment claims were related to substantive claims for environmental damage and depletion of natural resources under the other heads of paragraph 35, because the information obtained from the monitoring and assessment activities would also be used by the claimants to support their substantive claims, thereby assisting the Panel in its subsequent review of those claims. The Governing Council's decision to authorize expedited review of monitoring and assessment claims was, in large part, intended to make funds available to claimants to finance activities that might produce information to support the substantive 'F4' claims.

Accordingly the Panel considered, in its first and only report and recommendations available at the time of writing, claims for compensation for expenses resulting from monitoring and assessment activities undertaken or to be undertaken to identify and evaluate damage or loss suffered by claimants as a result of the invasion and occupation of Kuwait.[69] These activities relate to

---

[69] S/AC.26/2001/16, especially paragraphs 15–18 and 28–49 for a discussion of the issues arising from the claims for costs of monitoring and assessment.

measures taken to monitor and assess the damage caused by, inter alia, a) the release and transport, into the claimants' territories, of airborne pollutants caused by oil fires resulting from the ignition of hundreds of oil wells in Kuwait by Iraqi forces during Iraq's invasion and occupation of Kuwait; (b) numerous oil rivers and lakes formed by oil from the destroyed oil wells that did not ignite; (c) the release, by Iraqi forces, of millions of barrels of oil into the sea from oil pipelines, off-shore terminals and oil tankers; (d) disruption of fragile desert and coastal terrain caused by the movement of military vehicles and personnel, coupled with the construction of thousands of kilometres of military trenches and the emplacement of mines, weapons caches and other fortifications; and (e) adverse impacts on the environment resulting from the transit and settlement of the thousands of persons who departed from Iraq and Kuwait as a result of Iraq's invasion and occupation of Kuwait. Some of the claims raised issues of sustainable development.

The claim of Jordan was based mainly on its allegation that large numbers of refugees entered its territory from Iraq and Kuwait as a result of the invasion, and that their presence resulted in considerable damage to water resources, coastal areas and the terrestrial environment.[70] In particular, groundwater extraction rates were increased in order to supply water to the refugees, which resulted in over-extraction, saline intrusion into aquifers and degradation of water resources and water supply infrastructure. Other damage included the pollution of water supply by wastes from refugee camps and settlements and a decrease in the quantity and quality of irrigation water, which resulted in damage to agricultural resources. Jordan sought compensation for the costs of a number of monitoring and assessment projects; for example, to investigate and establish the temporal and spatial distribution of refugees across Jordan, to assess degradation in quality and reduction in quantity of water resources in Jordan that may have arisen as a result of the use of unlined cesspits at the refugee camps, to determine the extent of bacterial contamination of freshwater springs in Jordan's four main water extraction areas that may have resulted from disposal of human wastes, to quantify the damage to its water resources and related infrastructure and to assess and quantify damage to wetlands ecosystems, coastal marine environment and desert ecosystems.[71] The Panel reviewed all of these proposed projects, and, taking into account the oral and written responses of Iraq to the claims, it found that the expenses arising therefrom were all compensable in principle, subject to the substantial adjustments made by the Panel on various grounds such as overstatement of costs, especially labour costs, the likely utility of the results to be produced by the projects, the reasonableness and cost-effectiveness of the proposed measures and the fact that some costs were measures that were incurred as a result of

---

[70] *Ibid.*, paragraphs 297–362.
[71] The technical details of the projects are considered in the report and recommendations, supra n. 69.

non-compensable activities.[72] It is clear that the uses to which the natural resources in question were put, as a result of the invasion and occupation of Kuwait, were not sustainable. However, it is to be noted that, as may be expected, the Panel did not refer to the principle of sustainable development in determining whether the costs of these projects were compensable, which makes it difficult to draw further conclusions as to the actual (as distinct from the potential) role played by the principle.

To take another example from the 'F4' Panel's report and recommendations illustrating the relevance of the principle of sustainable development, Kuwait sought compensation for the monitoring and assessment of the impacts of the war on its terrestrial environment.[73] One claim was for a project to monitor and assess the damage caused by the oil lakes and to assess treatment technologies to abate harm and restore the environment,[74] while another was for a project to monitor and assess areas of its desert surface contaminated by the tarcrete formed as a result of oil releases and fallout from the oil fires. After reviewing these claims, the Panel stated that it

'urges that the risks of remediation be carefully considered, especially when it involves excavation that causes additional disturbance to sensitive desert soils. Although in some areas, the degree of contamination might make excavation unavoidable, in less contaminated areas, excavation could pose a greater threat than natural recovery'.[75]

---

[72] The Panel stated as follows: "[h]owever, expenses to determine the areas affected by operations of Jordanian military personnel and equipment are not eligible for compensation because, pursuant to paragraph 34(a) of Governing Council decision 7, damage caused by military activities is only compensable if it results from 'military operations or threat of military action by either side'. The 'E2' Panel found that, 'to find a threat of military action by Iraq outside Iraq or Kuwait for the purpose of establishing the Commission's jurisdiction over a claim based on that threat ... a specific threat by Iraq must have been directed at that location ... [and] ... the target of that threat, if any, must have been within the range of Iraq's military reach'. The 'F2' Panel noted that 'military operations did not take place within the land territory of Jordan. Nor was that land territory the subject of an Iraqi threat of military action, even though it was within the range of Iraqi military reach' . ... Moreover, Jordan has provided no evidence that its territory was the subject of military action or the threat of military action from Iraq" (ibid., at paragraph 346).

Of a total amount claimed of US$ 12,488,949, the Panel recommended compensation of US$7,060, 625 for the Jordanian projects, which sum has been made available to Jordan; see Governing Council Decision 132 (S/AC.26/Dec.132 (2001)).

[73] See paragraphs 363–562, at paragraphs 451–493.

[74] See paragraphs 451–464 and paragraphs 472–480.

[75] See paragraphs 480, and the slight (and inconsequential for present purposes) difference in the wording of paragraph 464. See also paragraphs 481–488, concerning a claim for the costs of monitoring and assessing environmental damage caused by saturation bombing and the open burning or detonation of unexploded ordnance, in respect of which the Panel urged Kuwait to consider the risks of excavation especially in cases where the ordnance disposal sites had been subjected to low levels of contamination. See also the discussion of the claim of Saudi Arabia at paragraphs 651–655.

This indicates that the programmes and policies undertaken as part of the process of remediation of environmental damage may themselves be subject to the requirement of sustainability. In these examples, the risk posed by excavation for the purposes of monitoring and assessment were not so great as to cause the Panel to decide that the project was not 'reasonable'; a margin of discretion is thus accorded to the claimant in implementing the project. The Panel did however reject certain projects where the risks posed by remediation were considered to be too great. In one claim,[76] Iran sought compensation for a study on the use of genetically modified bacteria to combat residual oil pollution that may have resulted from the war. The aim of the study was isolate a number of bacteria from the Persian Gulf, genetically modify them and release them into its marine environment to assist biodegradation of any remaining hydrocarbons and tarballs. The Panel however considered that a more effective way to encourage bacterial biodegradation of oil would be to add nutrients or oxygen to the contaminated area and thus assist naturally occurring bacteria to grow more rapidly, rather than introducing additional bacteria into the environment. The Panel also pointed out that, according to the evidence, bacterial biodegradation of oil is most effective if undertaken soon after an oil spill, so that the procedure was unlikely to be effective after such a long period of time had elapsed after the occurrence of the act causing the damage. The Panel continued:

> In addition, the Panel has serious reservations about the deliberate release of genetically modified organisms into the environment. It notes that widespread concerns have been expressed that the release of such organisms could pose risks to the environment and to human health. In the absence of reliable scientific knowledge about the threat posed by these organisms, it is not advisable for Iran to undertake such a potentially risky procedure. This is particularly so in view of the low probability that the experiment would have any practical utility.

Accordingly the claim was rejected for not amounting to 'reasonable monitoring and assessment'. Again it appears that sustainable development has a role to play in the process of remediation of environmental damage, even if the Panel did not refer to it in explicit terms. In this example, the principle could be considered to have assisted the Panel in choosing between different options open to Iran for the monitoring and assessment of environmental damage, with that choice being made in favour of the option that was compatible with sustainability and environmental protection.

The following observation can also be made regarding paragraph 35(c) of the Governing Council Decision 7. That paragraph makes it clear that the costs of monitoring and assessment of environmental damage are a distinct head of loss in itself, alongside losses suffered as a result of depletion of natural

---

[76] See paragraphs 169–172.

resources and costs of measures taken to abate and prevent environmental damage or to clean and restore the environment. It was suggested earlier[77] that, even if the content of the principle of sustainable development is not sufficiently precise to allow it to enable adjudicators to decide whether a given activity is sustainable or not, the decision to undertake that activity should itself be the outcome of a process that promotes sustainable development. This understanding of the role of the principle would appear to find a certain degree of real expression in the decision to consider the costs of monitoring and assessment as a distinct head of loss. As illustrated in the Panel's report, the purpose of monitoring and assessment is to enable a claimant to develop evidence to establish whether environmental damage has occurred and to quantify the extent of the resulting loss, provided that there is a sufficient nexus between the activity and environmental damage or risk of damage that may be attributed directly to Iraq's invasion and occupation of Kuwait.[78] Accordingly, the projects undertaken for the purposes of monitoring and assessment are themselves subject to the requirement of environmental impact assessment, a central element of 'sustainable development as procedure', and will not be considered 'reasonable' and therefore compensable if they do not take sufficient account of the demands of sustainability. Reasonableness, compensability and sustainability appear to be easy bedfellows.

4. Conclusions

It could be that the principle of sustainable development is no more than the aim of international environmental law as a whole, and that the component elements of the principle are indistinguishable from the most fundamental components of any conception of contemporary international law. A less general version of this view would be that the principle is no more than an umbrella term for other principles and rules of environmental law, such as those to be found in the fields of conservation and environmental impact assessment, so that 'application' of the principle is actually no more than the application of these other and better established exigencies of international environmental law. Such views would accord with the notorious difficulties that attend the concept, and may find some support in the fact that the 'F4' Panel has not made any explicit reference to the principle even if the aims of the principle are being fulfilled. But even if this view is correct, it would not mean that the principle is not applicable by adjudicators charged with resolving claims for environmental damage. It would mean, rather, that the principle does not exist as such, but that other principles and rules are being

---

[77] See section 3.2, infra.
[78] See paragraphs 29–32 of the report and recommendations, supra n. 69.

applied to serve the aims of sustainable development. But such a view may be questionable in view of the wide recognition accorded to the principle as a separate idea, and it is hoped that this paper has made a few suggestions as to the role that it can play in the work of institutions such as the Commission. This is so even if the principle is no more than a non-normative goal to which activities of States should aspire.[79]

---

[79] See Lowe, supra n. 55. The role the principle can play in the context of valuation of environmental damage is one question that is worthy of further analysis; see n. 51 above.

DAVID FREESTONE*

Incorporating Sustainable Development Concerns into the Development and Investment Process – the World Bank Experience

This paper will explain briefly the main ways that the World Bank[1] addresses sustainable development issues within the context of its development mandate.[2] It looks at the key instruments available for sustainable development, the development of an environment portfolio together with

---

* Chief Counsel, Environmentally and Socially Sustainable Development and International Law Group, Legal Vice-Presidency World Bank. The views expressed in this chapter are the personal views of the author and should not be taken to represent the official views of the World Bank.
[1] Hereinafter used interchangeably with 'the Bank'.
[2] The World Bank is comprised of five associated institutions: the International Bank for Reconstruction and Development (IBRD), the International Development Association (IDA), and the International Finance Corporation (IFC), the Multilateral Investment Guarantee Agency (MIGA) and the International Centre for the Settlement of Investment Disputes (ICSID). The cases before ICSID include environmental issues. The 'World Bank' as used in this paper refers to the IBRD and IDA.

M. Fitzmaurice and M. Szuniewicz (eds.), Exploitation of Natural Resources in the 21st Century, 91–112.
© *2003 Kluwer Law International. Printed in Great Britain.*

necessary internal technical capacity. It considers the development of the ten 'Safeguard Policies' and the role of the Inspection Panel in overseeing these. It then looks at the growth of the modalities to fund and encourage global environmental 'public goods', through the Global Environment Facility (GEF) and other trust funds and partnership arrangements.

1. Financing sustainable development

The financial instruments available to the World Bank to promote sustainable development include the full suite of Bank Group financial and technical assistance. These include the normal loan arrangements of the IBRD, the long term low interest concessional credits available to the poorest countries through IDA,[3] partial risk guarantees through IBRD and the Multilateral Investment Guarantee Agency (MIGA). Private sector debt and equity is provided through the International Finance Corporation (IFC) and over the last decade or more the Bank has committed itself to act as trustee or implementing agency for a number of significant trust funds designed to address global environmental issues. These include the Global Environment Facility (GEF), the Montreal Protocol Multilateral Fund, the Rain Forest Trust Fund, the Prototype Carbon Fund.[4] It has also entered into strategic partnerships with a number of NGOs and other bodies to address environmental issues. The Critical Ecosystem Partnership Fund (CEPF) is such a strategic partnership with Conservation International and other donors, as is the Forest Alliance between the Bank and WWF under which both institutions commit themselves to work with other stakeholders, including governments, to reduce the loss and degradation of all forests types worldwide, by promoting effective conservation, management and sustainable uses of forests.

---

[3] Because IDA is a concessional facility it depends on replenishment every three years. This provides opportunities for the donor countries to introduce policy requirements for the way in which IDA will be committed and is the origin of many of the environmental and disclosure requirements.

[4] This is $US 180 million fund with contributions from both public and private participants which aims to finance projects designed to generate emissions reductions capable of being registered under the requirements of the Kyoto Protocol of the UN Convention on Climate Change. For more details see David Freestone, 'The World Bank's Prototype Carbon Fund: Mobilising new Resources for Sustainable Development' in (Sabine Schemmer-Schulte and Ko-Yung Tung, eds.), *Liber Amicorum for Ibrahim S.I. Shihata*, Kluwer Law International, The Hague, 2001, 265–341.

2. Establishment of an environment department

The basic constitution of the International Bank for Reconstruction and Development (IBRD) is to be found in its Articles of Agreement. The IBRD Articles of Agreement require, inter alia, that investments be 'for a productive purpose' (Article I) and Article IV (10) prohibits political interference in the internal affairs of member states and requires that '... only economic considerations shall be relevant to their decisions, and these considerations shall be weighed impartially in order to achieve the purposes stated in Article I.' By the early 1980s the World Bank was accepting that investments made for environmental objectives were for productive purposes and that environmental considerations could legitimately be taken into account in assessing the suitability of projects for investments. The World Bank issued its first environment policy instruction: the Operational Manual Statement (OMS2.26) on Environmental Aspects of Bank Work in 1984.[5]

In 1987 – before the Report of the World Commission on Environment and Development (the Brundtland Commission)[6] had been published – the Bank was in the process of a major restructuring and its high level Development Committee considered an important paper on the environmental agenda for the Bank.[7] It was in mid-1987 that the Environment Department was established. It was placed in the policy and research complexes of the Bank and small environmental units were established in each of the Bank's Regional Vice Presidencies. In 1988, Dr. Kenneth Piddington was appointed as the first Director of the Environment Department. The Bank had by then started to finance the preparation of a series of 'Environment Issues' papers for borrowers-an initiative which lead quickly to the development of National Environment Action Plans (NEAPs), especially for African countries.[8]

3. Development of an environment portfolio

The recruitment of environmental specialists within an separate department, and the establishment in 1991 of the Pilot Phase of the Global Environment Facility[9] ushered in an increase in the World Bank commitment to the financing of environmental projects, particularly those which combined local

---

[5] OMS 2.36 *Environmental Aspects of Bank Work.* (May 1984).

[6] World Commission on Environment and Development, *Our Common Future*, Oxford, 1987,.

[7] Environment, Growth and Development (World Bank, 1987) cited by Kenneth Piddington, 'The Role of the World Bank' in A. Hurrell and B. Kingsley, eds., *The International Politics of the Environment*, Oxford, 1992, 212–227, 215.

[8] *Ibid.*, Piddington, 216.

[9] Together with other developments noted elsewhere.

and global benefits, categorised by the influential 1992 World Development Report, as 'win-win' opportunities.[10]

By 2002 the World Bank had more than 300 specialist environmental and social staff members, of whom the majority had been recruited since 1992. Since 1988 it has developed an environment portfolio in the order of US $15 billion. For example, in Fiscal Year 2000 it funded some 40 projects in which the primary or major objectives were environmental to the level of US$ 1.4 billion (about 10% of Bank financing as a whole), with around the same level of co-financing (i.e. total project finance of nearly US$ 3 billion.).

The composition of that portfolio is set out in the attached diagram. In addition to project lending the Bank also provides technical assistance to build institutional capacity in introducing environmental policies legislation and enforcement. It also provides training through the World Bank Institute (WBI).

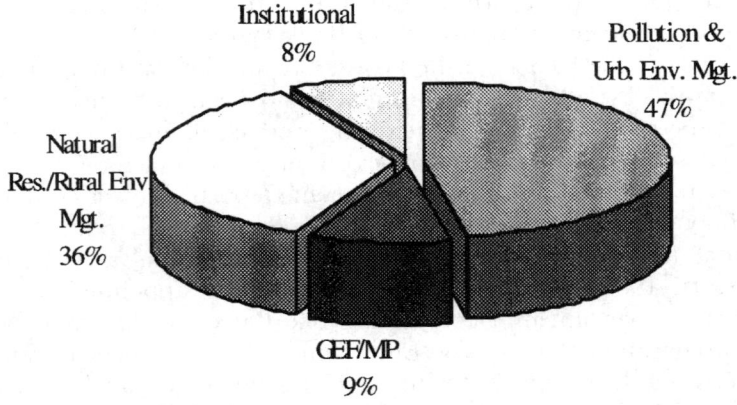

Figure 1: Composition of World Bank Environment Portfolio, 2000

4.   2001 World Bank environmental sector strategy

On July 12, 2001, the Bank's Board of Executive Director endorsed the World Bank's Environment Sector Strategy. Entitled 'Making Sustainable Commitments', it is designed to promote environmental improvements as a fundamental element of development and poverty reduction strategies and actions. The strategy outlines how the Bank will aim to help its client countries address environmental challenges and to ensure that its projects and programmes integrate principles of environmental sustainability. Environmental problems threaten the quality of life of the millions of people who

---

[10]   *Development and the Environment* (World Development Report 1992), The World Bank, Washington, D.C., 1992.

depend directly on environmental and natural resources for their livelihoods and they threaten the health of millions, e.g. through the impacts of water born diseases or indoor air pollution. It is clear also that it is the poor who suffer the worst consequences of environmental disasters such as flooding or storms. The Environmental Strategy acknowledges that attention to environmental problems is not a luxury but a necessity. The main objectives of the strategy are therefore threefold: improving the quality of life, improving the prospects for, and quality of, growth; and protecting the global commons.

- Improving the quality of life through (i) reducing environmental health risks by reducing people's exposure to environmental factors such as indoor and urban air pollution, water-borne and vector borne diseases and toxic substances); (ii) enhancing livelihoods of the poor who depend on land, water, forests and biodiversity by helping them secure access to resources and creating circumstances in which they can manage those resources sustainably; (iii) reducing people's vulnerability to environmental risks such as natural disasters, severe weather fluctuations and the impacts of climate change by providing information to governments, the private sector and poor communities and empowering them to adapt.

- Improving the quality of growth though interventions that will focus on promoting better policy, regulatory, and institutional frameworks, which are essential to sustainable growth and through strengthening of safeguard systems and practices in client countries to ensure that projects and policy changes do not adversely affect the environment, and promote environmentally and socially sustainable private sector development.

- Improving the quality of the global commons. Bank assistance to countries to address local environmental issues also generates regional and global environmental benefits, and the Bank Group has a mandate to channel finance to poorer countries to meet environmental goals under the Global Environment Facility (GEF) and Montreal Protocol. A poverty-focused environmental agenda will require interventions to protect the global environmental commons that are carefully targeted to benefit developing countries and local communities.

In implementing the strategy, the Bank will ensure that country assessments and programmes consider and reflect regional and global situations and priorities with a view to harmonizing local, regional, and global benefits. The strategy aims to ensure that environmental issues that have too often been the concern of a small, specialized group are fully internalized into all Bank operations. The Bank plans to take a leadership role in measuring more precisely the impact of environmental interventions.

5. The development of the World Bank safeguard policies

The basic constitution of the Bank is to be found in its Articles of Agreement.[11] Under the Articles the Board of Executive Directors comprised of the Bank shareholders and chaired by the President is the ultimate decision making body; the Articles even give the Executive Directors the authority to interpret the Articles themselves.[12] While the Executive Directors are the final authority on the determination of issues of Bank policy, there has been a long-standing practice for Bank Management to issue instructions to staff on operational policies and procedures. These are collected in an Operational Manual. Until 1987, the Bank's policies on a wide range of issues were largely found within Operational Manual Statements (OMSs), complemented at times by Operational Policy Notes (OPNs). Although the Operational Manual reflected policies generally agreed by the Board, the individual statements and notes were not generally discussed by the Board, although some of them related to issues that would now be regarded as sensitive, including environment and social issues.[13] The evolution of these policies has been described elsewhere[14] but the first environmental policy statement dates from 1983.[15]

When the Bank was reorganized in 1987, the previous statements and notes were generally redrafted into 'Operational Directives' (ODs). These too served as policy and procedural instructions, binding on Bank staff. Because these were essentially internal management documents the general practice continued of not putting the draft ODs to the Board for discussion although a few, because of their sensitivity or complexity were discussed with the Board prior to being issued. These included the Operational Directive on environmental assessment[16] and the procedures for investment projects under the newly established GEF.[17] Subsequent developments, as the late Ibrahim

---

[11] Articles of Agreement of the International Bank for Reconstruction and Development . Original text at 2 United Nations Treaty Series (UNTS) 134. For current amended text see *www.worldbank.org*. For original text of the Articles of Agreement of the International Development Association see 439 UNTS 249 and current version at same website.

[12] IBRD Articles of Agreement, Article IX, subject to reference to the IBRD Board of Governors.

[13] An exception was OMS 2.32(1985) on *Projects in International Waterways*, the text of which was approved by the Board, Shihata *op. cit.*, 41.

[14] Robert Wade, 'Greening the Bank: The Struggle over the Environment' in *The World Bank: Its First Half Century*, (Davesh Kapur, John P. Lewis, Richard Webb, eds.) Brookings Institution Press, Washington D.C., 1997, pp. 611–734; I.F.I. Shihata, *The World Bank Inspection Panel* (Oxford, 2nd ed. 2000), pp. 41–49.

[15] OMS 2.36 *Environmental Aspects of Bank Work* (May 1984).

[16] OD 4.00 1989, replaced by OD 4.01 in 1991 and in 1999 by OP 4.01.

[17] OD 9.01 (1992) – the draft of which was circulated to the Executive Directors under a no-objections procedure.

Shihata, former General Counsel of the World Bank, put it, 'resulted in the Board's increased interest in discussing ODs before they were issued by Management.'[18] Some of these developments included the issuance of policies on a range of environmental, social and international law issues raised by projects. The distinction between those ODs which have and those that have not been approved by the Board has significance internally if circumstances dictate that an exception be sought to the OD. Exceptions to policies approved by the Board require Board approval, others could be agreed by Senior Management, nominally the President but in practice, by delegation, a Managing Director.[19]

Toward the end of 1992, the Bank's practice was changed again, with the goal of distinguishing policy from procedure and clarifying those aspects of the policies which are obligatory – mandatory upon staff – and those which are hortatory – aiming at the development of good practice. The Bank is now codifying previous policy directives (and designing new ones where necessary) and converting them into a different format: (1) Operational Policies (OPs) which include the substantive policy instructions with which Bank staff are expected to comply and (2) Bank Procedures (BPs), which describe the procedural steps to be followed in the preparation of Bank operations. These OP/BPs are binding on staff. It was originally intended to develop a third limb to these instruments, so called 'Good Practice' (GP) statements, which would offer practical advice to Bank staff and borrowers on the topics addressed by the OPs/BPs. Experience has shown that it is difficult to collect good practice in such a format and for key policies – such as the environmental and social policies – a more systematic treatment of the issues involved has been developed through separate source books which are available, and continually updated, on line so as to be available to field as well as HQ staff.[20] The development of new GPs has been discontinued.

In 1998 a proposal was approved to group the Bank's policies into five areas: Operational Strategies, Safeguards, Fiduciary Requirements, Project Analysis and Review Requirements and Internal Processing Requirements. Under this re-grouping, the ten polices which covered the key environmental, social and international law issues were renamed the 'Safeguard Policies'.[21] These policies cover the following areas: Environmental Assessment;[22] Natural

---

[18] I.F.I. Shihata, *The World Bank Inspection Panel*, (Oxford, 2000, 2nd ed.) p. 42.

[19] E.g. in 2002 an Exception was granted to the application of OD 12.00 on Disbursements so as to allow GEF funds to be disbursed to Conservation Trust Funds.

[20] See e.g. source books on environmental assessment, involuntary resettlement, pest management, etc.

[21] see *World Bank Operational Policy Reform: Progress Report* (CODE98–13 March, 1998.) The texts of these policies are available on the Bank website at *www.worldbank.org*.

[22] Environmental Assessment – OP 4.01, January 1999.

Habitats;[23] Forestry;[24] Pest Management;[25] Involuntary Resettlement;[26] Indigenous Peoples;[27] Cultural Property;[28] Safety of Dams;[29] International Waterways;[30] Projects in Disputed Areas.[31] In addition Disclosure, of Information (updated in early 2002) is increasingly being grouped with the ten safeguard policies.[32]

6. Benchmarking of environmental and social requirements

The Bank's policies do not purport to set objective international standards; nor are they formally instructions to borrowers. They are requirements that must be fulfilled by Bank staff in order for a project to qualify for Bank financing. If a borrowing or grant recipient country refuses to allow a Bank requirement to be met – e.g. the publication in country of an environmental assessment report for an IDA investment project- then Bank staff are required to discontinue the operation.[33] However, for a number of reasons the impact of the policies is in practice much wider. First, the Bank requires that its policies be complied with even in operations where it is not the only, or indeed the major, financier. This means that all the components of a project must comply with Bank policies – not only those components actually co-financed by the Bank but also those project components financed by other agencies – whether from the public or private sector – and those components financed with counterpart financing from the borrowing country's own money. The 'leveraging' effect is therefore substantial.

Second, many borrowing countries have internalised these procedures and incorporated them into national law. A recent study found that twenty-four countries in Sub-Saharan Africa have Environmental Impact Assessment legislation and that the majority of these incorporate the key requirements of the Bank policy on Environmental Assessment – which includes consultation and disclosure requirements.[34] Other borrowers too have reflected many

---

[23] Natural Habitats   – OP 4.04, September 1995.
[24] Forestry   – OP 4.36, September 1993.
[25] Pest Management   – OP 4.09, December 1998.
[26] Involuntary Resettlement   – OP 4.12, December 2001.
[27] Indigenous Peoples   – OD 4.20, September 1991.
[28] Cultural Property   – OPN 11.03, September 1986; Draft 4.11.
[29] Safety of Dams   – OP 4.37, September 1996.
[30] International Waterways   – OP 7.50, October 1994.
[31] Projects in Disputed Areas – BP 7.60, November 1994.
[32] Disclosure of Information   – BP 17.50, Updated Spring 2002.
[33] As required by OP 4.01 para 19 for projects classified as A.
[34] Mohammed A. Bekhechi and Jean Roger Mercier, *The Legal and Regulatory Framework for Environmental Assessments: A Study of Selected Countries in Sub-Saharan Africa*, The World Bank: Law, Justice and Development Series, Washington D.C., 2002.

Bank policies and procedures into their own legal and administrative procedures.

Third, it is clear that the private sector also uses these policies for its own purposes. Although they are not standards they are often termed 'World Bank standards' by the private sector, and the Bank has even received requests to certify that third party, non-Bank-financed projects, are in compliance with Bank 'standards' or policies – something the Bank has consistently refused to do.[35] In addition it is worth noting that many other development agencies – the bilateral agencies as well as the regional development banks also have policies on many of the same issues. Over the last two years or so, the Bank has been involved in a discussion process with other international financial institutions aimed at the development of common principles on, *inter alia*, environmental assessment.

The final point to make is that although these are internal Bank policies the process by which they are developed has become highly politicised. When revising, or simply converting, the safeguard policies, there is always a protracted consultation process both within and outside the Bank once a working draft has been developed. For reasons that sometimes have little to do with the business of the Bank, and much more to do with placing an issue on a wider international agenda, the finalization of the texts can take a great deal of time. For example, the conversion of the OD on involuntary resettlement to an Operational Policy took some five years to complete, and the parallel conversion of OD 4.20 on indigenous peoples has already taken five years.[36]

7. The Inspection Panel

The Inspection Panel was established in 1993 by Resolution of the Board of Executive Directors of the World Bank.[37] A number of factors had contributed

---

[35] Another example is the *Pollution Prevention and Abatement Handbook* published in 1998 by the Bank (in collaboration with UNEP, WHO and UNIDO). This publication sets out emission levels from a range of industrial practices that will normally in Bank financed projects. Although again this Handbok does not set standards, it has been significant in providing benchmarks for other bodies, including other international financial institutions and the private sector.

[36] For a discussion of the evolution of some of the key safeguard policies, notably involuntary resettlement, indigenous peoples and forestry see Freestone, et.al., 'The World Bank' in *Yearbook of International Environmental Law 2001*, Vol. 12, Oxford University Press 2003, pp 763–778.

[37] Resolution No. IBRD 93–10; Resolution No. IDA 93–6; reproduced in I.F.I. Shihata, *The World Bank Inspection Panel: In Practice*. Oxford, 2000, at 271ff. D.D. Bradlow and S. Schlemmer-Schulte, 'The World Bank's New Inspection Panel: A Constructive Step in the Transformation of the International Legal Order,' (1994) 54 *Zeitschrit für Ausländisches Öffentliches Recht und Völkerrecht (Heidelberg Journal of International Law)* 392–415; S.

to the move to establish some form of review or 'appeals' commission.[38] In 1991, Lewis T. Preston became President of the Bank. One of his early concerns was to investigate ways to improve the efficiency of Bank operations largely because of publicly expressed concerns at the impacts of some major projects.[39] One such operation in particular, the two Narmada projects in India, had attracted a great deal of criticism from NGOs for the way in which environmental assessment and resettlement issues were being dealt with. An independent review chaired by Bradford Morse, former Executive Director of the United Nations Development Programme, had been commissioned in 1991 by the previous President to assess the implementation of these projects in relation to 'existing Bank operational directives and guidelines' looking particularly at the environmental and resettlement issues. The Morse Report, submitted to the Bank's Board in June 1992 was critical of the way in which these Bank policies had been implemented[40] and added fuel to a campaign by NGOs and others to pressure the Bank's major donors to with-hold contributions to the Tenth IDA Replenishment (IDA 10) unless some form of accountability mechanism were established.

Shihata points out that similar demands were then being made of other international organizations – including the UN.[41] What form such a mechanism could take was unclear. Proposals ranged from the setting up of an in-house project implementation evaluation unit, to the appointment of an Ombudsman, or to the establishment of an Independent Appeals Commission. In June of 1993 a discussion paper was presented to the Board by Bank Management which examined the various proposals, reviewed the experience of existing inspection functions in some member countries, and itself proposed an independent but in-house Inspection Panel comprised of three inspectors who would be appointed by the Board on the recommenda-

cont.
  Schlemmer-Schulte, 'The World Bank's experience with its Inspection Panel' (1998) 58 *Zeitschrit für Ausländisches Öffentliches Recht und Völkerrecht* 353–388; A. Rigo Sureda, 'Process Integrity and Institutional Independence in International Organizations: The Inspection Panel and the Sanctions Committee of the World Bank,' Laurence Boisson de Chazournes, L., Romano C. and Mackenzie, R. eds., *International Organizations and International Dispute Settlement: Trends and Prospects.*, New York, 2002, pp. 165–218.

[38] These are discussed extensively in Shihata, ibid., at 1–21.
[39] He established a Task Force under Willi Wappenhans – a senior Bank manager – which recommended inter alia the development of better ways of monitoring performance of projects. Bank Management response to this report included consideration of an inspection mechanism, ibid., 2.
[40] Projects were Narmada River Development (Gujarat) Sardar Sarova Dam and Power Project (IDA Credit Agreement No. 1553-IN) and the Narmada River Development (Gujarat) Water Delivery and Drainage Project (IBRD Loan Agreement No 2497-IN). The Morse report was published by its authors as B. Morse and T. R. Berger, *Sadar Sarovar: The Report of the Independent Review*, Resource Futures International, Ottawa, 1992.
[41] *Ibid.*, 4.

tion of the President. After extensive discussion and a number of revisions to the proposal during the summer of 1993, a Resolution establishing the Panel was eventually approved by the Board on September 22, 1993. The Resolution envisaged a review of the operation of the Panel two years after the date of appointment of the first Panel members. The first review was completed in 1996 and resulted in the Board agreeing to certain 'clarifications' of aspects of the Resolution in October 1996.[42] A second review of the Panel's experience in 1999 resulted in further 'clarifications.'[43]

7.1 Composition

In accordance with the Resolution, the Inspection Panel is comprised of three independent members appointed by the Board – on the recommendation of the President after consultation with the Board.[44] The members must be persons of different nationalities drawn from Bank Member countries.[45] They should be selected on the basis of their ability to 'deal thoroughly and fairly with the request brought to them, their integrity and their independence from Bank Management and their exposure to developmental issues and to living conditions in developing countries.'[46] The Resolution also indicates that 'knowledge and experience of the Bank's operations would also be desirable.'[47] The Panel members hold office for five-year non-renewable terms and elect their chair annually. The chair is full time, but the other members are part-time – their duties depending upon the Panel's work load.[48] The Panel has a permanent secretariat, headed by a full time Executive Secretary with a staff of four.

A number of provisions of the Resolution are designed to re-inforce the independence of Panel members. They may serve only one, non renewable,

---

[42] '1996 Review of the Resolution establishing the Inspection Panel: Clarification of Certain Aspects of the Resolution, October 17, 1996' reproduced in Shihata, *op. cit.*, 320–22.

[43] 'Conclusions of the Board's Second Review of the Inspection Panel April 20, 1999' reproduced ibid., 323–328.

[44] Paragraph 2.

[45] In practice the Panel has always had a North American, a European and a developing country member.

[46] *Ibid.*, Paragraph 4.

[47] Ibid.

[48] In the performance of their functions, Panel Members are officials of the Bank who enjoy the privileges and immunities accorded to Bank officials, and subject to the requirements of the Bank's Articles of Agreement concerning exclusive loyalty to the Bank. Res. s. 10. At the time of writing the current members are Professor Edward Ayensu (current Chair) (Ghana, 1998 -), Maartje van Putten (Netherlands, 1999-) and Edith Brown Weiss (US, 2002-). Previous Members have been Jim MacNiell (Canada, 1997–2002), Ernst-Gunther Bröder(Germany, 1994–9); Richard Bissell (US, 1994–97); Alvara Umana (Costa Rica, 1994–1998).

five year term of office,[49] and may be removed from that office only by a decision of the Board, and 'for cause'.[50] In the performance of their functions, Panel Members are officials of the Bank who enjoy the privileges and immunities accorded to Bank officials.[51] Staff members and other employees of the World Bank Group may not serve on the Panel until two years have elapsed since the end of their service.[52] A Panel member is disqualified from participating in the hearing and investigation of any request related to a matter in which he or she has a personal interest or had significant involvement in any capacity.[53] Following the end of their service on the Panel, members are disqualified from any further employment by the Bank Group.[54]

7.2 *The powers of the Panel*

The Panel is authorized to receive requests for inspection from 'an affected party in the territory of a borrower which is not a single individual.' That affected party must present evidence that its rights and interests have been, or are likely to be, directly affected by an act or omission of the Bank as a result of 'failure of the Bank to follow its operational policies and procedures with respect to the design, appraisal and/or implementation of a project' financed by the Bank[55] provided that in all cases such failure has had, or threatens to have, a material adverse effect. In addition, any one Executive Director may 'in special cases of serious alleged violations' of the Bank operational policies and procedures ask the Panel for an investigation and the Executive Directors, acting as the Board, may at any time instruct the Panel to conduct an investigation.[56] The Panel's mandate is to investigate 'failure of the Bank to follow its operational policies and procedures with respect to the design, appraisal and/or implementation of a project.'

Since 1993, the panel has received twenty-seven requests, of which it has registered all but three. (Twenty-four) investigations have been authorized.

---

[49] Paragraph 3.
[50] Paragraph 8.
[51] Paragraph 10.
[52] Paragraph n 5.
[53] Paragraph 6.
[54] Paragraph 10, final sentence. The Board felt very strongly about this issue as an unsuccessful attempt was to made to make an exception for the first Panel members, see Shihata, *op. cit.*, 92.
[55] Including situations where the Bank is alleged to have failed in its follow up on the borrower's obligations under loan agreements with respect to such policies and procedures. Section 12.
[56] Paragraph 12.

8. International environmental 'public goods'

In the run up to the 1992 Rio Earth Summit proposals were put forward by a number of European Members of the Bank for it to play a key role in the mobilization of resources which could be used to finance activities which address 'global public goods' issues. Some of the key funds established are discussed below, starting with the Global Environment Facility, but the Bank has also entered into strategic partnerships with a number of other bodies – including leading conservation NGOs. As well as signing Memoranda of Understanding for co-operation with a number of bodies, including the World Conservation Union (IUCN), the Bank and the World Wide Fund for Nature and Natural Resources (WWF) agreed on a Forest Alliance under which both organizations agreed to work with others for the achievement of global targets for the designation of forest protected areas and for the certification of sustainable forestry.

In 2000 the World Bank and the GEF agreed with Conservation International to finance a Critical Ecosystem Partnership Fund This fund, hosted by CI which now has collaboration and financing from the John D. and Catherine T Macarthur Foundation and the Government of Japan, is designed on the premise that there are a number of critical 'hotspots' in the world which combine high levels of biodiversity with high levels of threat.[57] A strategy designed to preserve global biodiversity should, it argues, focus attention on these areas as a matter of first priority. These areas often cross national boundaries and are identified by ecosystem type. The fund also seeks to ensure that civil society is engaged in conservation efforts in the hotspots.[58]

8.1 The Global Environmental Facility

Peter Sand[59] has pointed out that the origins of the Global Environment Facility (GEF) can be traced back to a suggestion by the Brundtland Commission for the 'development of a special international banking programme or facility linked to the World Bank'.[60] This idea was developed

---

[57] See Russell A. Mittermeier, et. al., *Hotspots: Earth's Biologically Richest and Most Endangered Terrestrial Ecosystems*, Cemex, Mexico City, 1999.

[58] To date ecosystems identified for strategic assistance by the CEPF include- the Vilcabamba-Amboro (Tropical Andes), Madagascar, and Upper West Guinean Forest (West Africa), the Atlantic Forest, the Cape Floristic region, Choco-Manabi Corridor (Choco-Darien, W. Ecuador) the Philippines Southern Mesoamerica and Sumatra (Sunderland).

[59] See Peter Sand, 'Trusts for the Earth' in *Transnational Environmental Law*. Kluwer Law International , The Hague, 2000, 300–303.

[60] *Our Common Future* (Oxford, 1987) 338.

by the Washington DC based World Resources Institute as a proposal for a International Environmental Facility (IEF)[61] The idea was operationalised by a French and German proposal at the 1989 World Bank Annual Meeting, and as a consequence a meeting was held in Paris in November 1990 to finalise a proposal for a Global Environment Facility with a commitment of some US$1 billion over a three year pilot phase. The Global Environment Trust Fund was established within the Bank in 1991. By procedural resolutions of October 1991 the United Nations Development Programme (UNDP), the UN Environment Programme (UNEP) and the World Bank agreed to cooperate in the implementation of the Facility. The World Bank acts as Trustee of the Fund as well as one of the three Implementing Agencies.[62]

At the 1992 UN Conference on Environment and Development in Rio di Janeiro, a great deal of discussion focussed on the governance of the GEF. Agenda 21 recommended that the GEF should be 'restructured' so as to, inter alia, 'ensure a governance that is transparent and democratic in nature, including in terms of decision-making and operations, by guaranteeing a balanced and equitable representation of the interests of developing countries, as well as giving due weight to the funding efforts of donor countries.'[63] A similar provision is expressly included in the text of Article 21 of the UNFCCC.[64] The restructuring process, involving negotiations among 73 states, was completed in Geneva in March of 1994; since then it has been replenished twice with pledges from both donors and host countries.[65] In March 1998 in Paris the negotiations for the second replenishment – GEF-2 – were completed with commitments totalling 2.75 billion for the four year period to 2002.[66] In August of 2002 a third replenishment was agreed of over US$ 2.9billion for the four year period to 2006.

---

[61] *Natural Endowments: Financing Resource Conservation for Development* (F. van Bolhuis ed.) WRI, 1989, p.14.
[62] A proposal for the establishment of a Global Environment Trust Fund was approved by the Bank's Board of Executive Directors by Resolution No. 91–5 on March 14 1991. 30 I.L.M. 1735. See also I.F.I. Shihata, 'The World Bank and the Environment: a Legal Perspective' (1992) 16 *Maryland Journal of International Law and Trade* 1–42.
[63] Chapter 33.16 (a)(iii).
[64] The final sentence of UNFCCC, Article 21(3) reads: '... The Global Environment Facility should be appropriately restructured and its membership made universal to enable it to fulfil the requirements of Article 11.'
[65] For text of the Instrument for the Establishment of the Restructured Global Environment Facility (The Instrument), Report of the GEF Participants Meeting, Geneva 14–16 March 1994 see 33 ILM 1273 (1994). See further I.F.I. Shihata, 'The World Bank's Contribution to the Development of International Environmental Law' *Liber Amicorum Professor Seidl-Hohenveldern – in honour of his 80th birthday* G. Haffner, G. Loibl, A. Rest, L. Sucharipa-Bermann and K. Zemanek, (eds.), Kluwer, 1998, 631–657.
[66] See Freestone, *et. al.* "The World Bank Group' (1998) 9 *Yearbook of International Environmental Law* 669, 671.

In the words of the Instrument establishing it, the GEF operates as a 'mechanism for international co-operation for the purposes of providing new and additional grant and concessional financing to meet the agreed incremental costs of measures to achieve global environmental benefits in the following focal areas:

(a) Climate Change;
(b) Biological Diversity;
(c) International Waters; and
(d) Ozone Layer depletion.'[67]

The first two areas reflected the concerns of the two Rio Conventions and when the GEF, as envisaged, became a financial mechanism for these conventions the work programmes as required by the Instrument reflected the guidance provided by the Conferences of the Parties (COPs) of the those conventions.

The new institutional structure established by the 1994 Instrument[68] has the following elements:

- Three Implementing Agencies (World Bank, UNDP and UNEP)
- A Secretariat under CEO
- A Council with 32 members (14 from developed countries, 14 from developing countries and 4 from countries with economies in transition (EITs), which meets twice a year.
- An Assembly, with representatives of all members, meets tri-annually.[69]

GEF Programmes provide funding for

- Enabling activities (for countries to fulfil their international environmental law treaty obligations
- Project Grants (which include project preparation grants up to $1m.)
- Small grants for NGOs (administered by the UNDP)
- Medium Size projects – up to $1m aimed at NGO executors.

The procedures for the approval of GEF-funded operations treat these operations in the same manner as other Bank operations. Approval by the Bank's Board of GEF projects proposed by the Bank helps ensure that the

---

[67] GEF Instrument, para. 2. Note that para. 3 reads: 'The agreed incremental costs of activities concerning land degradation, primarily desertification and deforestation as they relate to the four focal areas shall be eligible for funding.'

[68] GEF Instrument, Part III, paras 11–24.

[69] The first Assembly was in New Delhi in 1998, The next meeting of the Assembly will be in Beijing in October 2002.

quality of the Bank's work as Implementing Agency meets the usual standards of quality, including cost-effectiveness, of Bank operations. In the course of the project preparation, Bank-GEF projects are circulated to members of the GEF Council before they are considered by the Bank's Board. The GEF Council approves the work program. It receives project documents before their final approval by the implementing agency and may discuss their conformity with GEF policies and procedures (at the request of four of the Council members).

In 1999 the GEF Council decided to expand opportunities for other entities – such as the regional development banks – to access GEF resources, either through the existing three Implementing Agencies (IBRD, UNDP and UNEP) or direct to the GEF Secretariat. Under this initiative such projects would be approved by the appropriate boards or other governing bodies of such entities and would not go to the Bank's board.

Over the last ten years nearly US$ 4 billion has been committed to support activities in the four focal areas: Ozone Depletion, International Waters, Conservation of Biodiversity and Climate Change. Climate Change alone has attracted commitments of over US$ 1 billion.[70] What is even more striking is that this project financing has 'leveraged' nearly four times as much again – largely through associated loans for which the recipient countries have borrowed money from the IBRD or other sources for environmental projects.

Now that the negotiations for the third GEF Replenishment for the four-year period 2002-2006 are complete, two new focal areas have been added to the GEF mandate by an amendment of the Instrument – approved at the second GEF Assembly in Beijing in October, 2002 – Persistent Organic Pollutants (POPs) and Land Degradation.[71]

The International Conference finalizing the Stockholm Convention on Persistent Organic Pollutants in 2001 requested the Global Environment Facility to be its financial mechanism. The GEF Council at its meeting in May 2002 considered this request and the Council approved proposed amendments to the Instrument to allow it to accept this invitation. The GEF Council has also designated FAO and UNIDO as executing agencies that will be able assist with the implementation of projects in this new focal area.[72]

In Marrakech in November 2001, at the seventh Session of the Conference of the Parties of the UN Convention on Climate Change, the COP invited the GEF as financial mechanism to establish and administer three new 'Climate

---

[70] *The Difference GEF makes*, GEF 2000 Annual Report, Washington D.C., 2001, 6–7.
[71] See GEF Instrument, para. 14.d: 'The Assembly shall ... (d) Consider for approval by consensus, amendments to the present Instrument on the basis of recommendations by the Council.'
[72] Under the 'Expanded Opportunities for Executing Agencies' Program – which also includes the four Regional Development Banks and IFAD.

Change Funds' – of which one will be concerned with financing 'adaptation' projects for those states most vulnerable to the effects of Climate Change.[73]

8.2 Ozone Projects Trust Fund

The 1987 Montreal Protocol on Substances that Deplete the Ozone Layer to the Vienna Convention on the Ozone Layer[74] is one of the most comprehensive and successful international environmental agreements to date. After ratification by 29 countries and the EC, representing approximately 82 percent of world consumption of Ozone Depleting substances, the Montreal Protocol came into force on January 1st, 1989.

In 1990, the Parties to the Montreal Protocol established the Multilateral Fund to Implement the Montreal Protocol (MFMP) to provide financial and technical assistance, including the transfer of technology, to developing countries. Article 10 of the London Amendments to the Montreal Protocol details the institutional arrangements in relation to the Fund. It is administered by a Secretariat and an Executive Committee which develops and monitors the implementation of specific operational policies, guidelines and administrative arrangements, including the disbursement of resources, for achieving the objectives of the Fund and the Protocol.

In 1991 – as the GEF was being established – the World Bank agreed with UNDP and UNEP to assist in implementing what was then the interim Multilateral Fund and in June 1991 entered into a bilateral Ozone Project Agreement with the Protocol's Executive Committee to manage investment projects with resources which would be transferred from the Multilateral Fund to a newly established Ozone Projects Trust Fund (OTF) established by the same Resolution of the Board as that which established the GEF.[75]

After the decision to convert the interim fund to a permanent facility, UNIDO join the implementing agencies. The World Bank continues to act as implementing agency for investment operations and as of July 20 2001, the contributions made to the Multilateral Fund by some 32 industrialized countries amounted to US$ 1.3 billion. The World Bank's Montreal Protocol

---

[73] Such a Fund is envisaged by Article 12 of the Kyoto Protocol to the UNFCCC. See further GEF/C 19/6, Arrangements for *The Establishment of The New Climate Change Funds.* Available on www.gefweb.org.

[74] For a discussion of the innovative legal methods the Convention and the Protocol has used to keep pace with developments of scientific understanding in this field see David Freestone, 'The Road from Rio: International Environmental Law after the Earth Summit' (1994) 6 *Journal of Environmental Law* 193–218.

[75] Resolution 91–5, above. See further Peter Sand, 'Trusts for the Earth', *op. cit.,* 301–302. The Bank has a specific Operational Policy (OP/BP 10.21) on *Investment Operations Financed by the Multilateral Fund for the implementation of the Montreal Protocol* (November 1993).

program has developed a portfolio of over 450 investment projects under the MFMP. To date, the Bank as implementing agency has provided financing for the phase out by its country partners of more than 80 percent of the Ozone Depleting Substances (ODS) targeted for support from the Multilateral Fund, with grant financing of over US$420 million, which is about 45 per cent of the total funding made available for investment projects.

In 2001, the Executive Committee approved US$35.8 million to phase out completely the consumption of chlorofluorocarbons (CFCs) through Bank implemented projects in the Bahamas, Malaysia, Thailand, and Turkey. Whereas for the first decade of the Fund's operations the Bank implemented relatively large investment projects to convert single industrial plants to ozone friendly technology, the next step is to move to more comprehensive national programmes phase-out which cover the whole sector of CFC consumption and production. The National CFC Phase-out Plans for Malaysia and Thailand are the first of such comprehensive phase-out strategies that include a long-term plan that will assist the two countries to meet their Montreal Protocol obligations. These plans were developed through active participation by all stakeholders in the respective countries, including private, government and non-governmental organizations. The plans consist of a combination of tailored investment, policy and regulatory support measures, which seek to phase-out CFCs in all sectors. Their significance is that they will allow these two countries to channel much needed technical and financial assistance to a large number of small and medium-scale enterprises in order to eliminate their dependency on CFCs.

The Bank, in partnership with UNEP, is also financing a Terminal CFC Phase-out Management Plan for the Bahamas. This will enable the Bahamas to completely phase out its consumption of all CFCs by 2008-two years in advance of the Montreal Protocol deadline. The Bank's legal department has prepared the grant agreements for these projects which include the development of an innovative way of disbursement of funds through a voucher scheme. The Bank can thus cost-effectively make grants available for medium size and small conversions of equipment while safeguarding the quality of the project and the success of the conversions.[76]

8.3 The Rain Forest Trust Fund

The Rain Forest Trust Fund was established by Resolution of the Board of Executive Directors of the World Bank in March 1992,[77] to provide financing for

---

[76] I am grateful to Charlotte Streck of the ESSD and International Law Practice Group in the Legal Vice-Presidency of the Bank for this current information.

[77] Resolution No. 92–2 establishing the Rain Forest Trust Fund of March 24 1992. See further Peter Sand, 'Trusts for the Earth', *op. cit.*, 304–306.

a pilot programme to conserve the Brazilian Amazon and Atlantic rain forest. As the first preamble to that Resolution recounts 'The Government of Brazil, with the assistance of the International Bank for Reconstruction and Development and the Commission of the European Communities, has prepared a pilot program with the overall objective of maximizing the environmental benefits of Brazil's rain forests in a manner consistent with its developmental goals through the implementation of a sustainable development approach that will contribute to a continuing reduction of the rate of deforestation.'

The Fund and the programme it supports were the outcomes of a proposal of the Brazilian Government to the G7 Summit in Houston in July 1990. Following a series of technical and high level meetings, a more detailed programme was put to the London G7 Meeting in July 1991 supported by a paper prepared by the World Bank and the European Commission. A donors meeting was held in Geneva in December of that year at which representatives of the G7 and other donors pledged support for the pilot programme and the establishment of the Trust Fund.[78] It is for this reason the Programme is known as the PPG7 (the G7 Pilot Programme). The World Bank assists Brazil in coordinating the Programme and administers the multi-donor Rain Forest Trust Fund.

The Programme is currently pursuing five lines of action, including testing, institutional strengthening, gathering scientific knowledge, and dissemination of lessons learned. At the Participants Meeting in June 2001 the donors agreed however that the Pilot Programme will undergo a gradual shift from its earlier focus on piloting, learning and catalyzing effect to progressive mainstreaming. After a transition period, the Programme should enter a second phase in 2003 that is planned to run for about four years. Donors also agreed that the World Bank would continue to exercise its fiduciary role as trustee of the fund.

In June 2001 agreement was reached to fund a second phase of the Fire Prevention and Mobilization Project (PROTEGER II), aimed at supporting a campaign to mobilize and train the rural population of the Amazon in controlled burning and fire prevention techniques. An agreement on a second phase of the Extractive Research Project was already reached earlier. During the first phase of that Project, four extractive reserves have been established and consolidated in the Amazon. In these conservation areas, families of rubber tappers and Brazil-nut gatherers are both protecting this environment and using it to make a living – without recourse to clearing the forest.

The Program was also instrumental in introducing and gaining wide acceptance for the concept of rain forest corridors, networks that link protected areas and the buffer zones around them, thus creating wider spaces for dispersal of species and genetic flux. Under this new model, conservation

---

[78] For further details see the Background note dated March 13, 1992 which supported the application to the Bank's Board – reproduced with the Resolution on the website (www.worldbank.org).

of biodiversity will be coordinated on a regional scale rather than through individual 'conservation islands'. In the autumn of 2001 agreement was reached to fund a five-year project that will focus initially on two large rain forest corridors. One, in the central Amazon, encompasses 245,500 sq. km, an area the size of the United Kingdom. The other, in the northern Atlantic Forest, measures 77,500 sq. km – an area larger than Ireland. For this purpose Brazil's Ministry of Environment (MMA); the Brazilian Institute of the Environment and Renewable Natural Resources (IBAMA); concerned state environmental agencies; corridor project units will collaborate with public and private stakeholders; and civil society organizations and community groups.[79]

9. The Prototype Carbon Fund

On July 20, 1999 the Executive Directors of the Bank approved IBRD Resolution 99-1- on the establishment of a Prototype Carbon Fund.[80] This Fund, which it recommended should not be launched until after the Fifth meeting of the Conference of the Parties (CoP-5) to the UN Framework Convention on Climate Change,[81] represents a first attempt to demonstrate systematically the way that the innovative market mechanisms introduced in the 1997 Kyoto Protocol to the UNFCCC might operate to the advantage of the Bank's borrowing countries. It was recognised by the Bank's Board that although the Parties to the UNFCCC still had to reach decisions on a number of issues which could be crucial to the ultimate success of such a Fund, nevertheless there were important ways in which a demonstration Fund such as the PCF could actually assist the Parties in the process of identifying key practical issues for their deliberation. As a prototype the Fund has three principal objectives. First, to demonstrate how projects which are designed to reduce emissions of greenhouse gases can promote and contribute to the sustainable development of the Bank's borrowing member countries, and the ways in which these projects can channel additional public and private capital for development as well as providing both

---

[79] I am grateful to Hanneke van Tilburg for this information about the current status of the RFTF.

[80] For more details see David Freestone, 'The World Bank's Prototype Carbon Fund: Mobilising new Resources for Sustainable Development' in (Sabine Schemmer-Schulte and Ko-Yung Tung, eds.), *Liber Amicorum for Ibrahim S.I. Shihata*, Kluwer Law International, The Hague, 2001, 265–341.

[81] The United Nations Framework Convention on Climate Change was concluded in New York on 9th May 1992 (UN Doc. Distr. General A/AC.237/18 (Part II)/Add.1.15 May 1992). It was opened for signature at the United Nations Conference on Environment and Development in Rio di Janeiro on 4 June 1992. It came into force on March 21 1994 and on 17 May 2000 had 184 Parties. The Fifth Conference of the Parties took place in Bonn from October 25–November 5, 1999.

financiers and project host countries with an equitable share of the resulting benefits.[82] Second, to provide the Parties to the UNFCCC an opportunity to 'learn by doing' as they themselves deliberate on the rules, regulations and procedures which will govern such GHG emission reduction projects under the framework of the UNFCCC/Kyoto Protocol, and third, provide an important example of how the Bank can work in partnership with both the public and private sectors to mobilise new resources for its borrowing member countries while addressing global environmental concerns.

The Instrument of the fund approved by the Resolution envisaged two closings. The first closing was in April 2000, when it began operations. Participation in the fund required public sector entities to subscribe $US10 million and private sector entities US5 million. At the first closing the Fund stood at US$ 135 million including six governments[83] and 16 companies.[84] A second closing was held in late 2000 at which point two further companies joined and the fund reached US $145 million and was closed for subscription.[85] The first organisational meeting of the Participants was held in Washington in April of 2000 and the annual meetings have taken place in June 2000, 20001 and 2 in 2002. The Instrument also establishes a host country committee comprised of representatives of states which have endorsed a project for the PCF or which have signed an Memorandum of Understanding with the Bank to collaborate with the PCF. In August of 2002 the number countries participating in the host country Committee stands at over 30 and a number countries are still considering joining.

The first project of the Fund was a solid waste, methane capture project in Liana Latvia for which a newly developed legal instrument – an Emission Reduction Purchase Agreement (ERPA) was signed in 2000. In fiscal year 2002 the terms of a further 13 projects were agreed. At an extraordinary meeting in Paris in February 2002 the Participants agreed to allow the Trustee to seek 'supplementary voluntary contributions' from existing Participants up to the overall cap of US$ 180 million imposed by the PCF Instrument. This increased capitalization was completed in December 2002.

---

[82] As well as promoting the transfer of environmentally sound and socially acceptable technology, and reducing local pollution.

[83] Governments of Canada, Finland, Netherlands, Norway, Sweden, and Japan (through JBIC).

[84] Private sector entities at first closing were Chubu Electric Power (EP), Chugoku EP, Kyushu EP, Shikoku EP, Tokyo EP and Tohoku EP, Mitsubishi and Mitsui from Japan; BP Amoco (UK); Deutsche Bank (Germany); RWE (Germany); Electrabel (Belgium); Gaz de France; Norsk Hydro (Norway); Statoil (Norway).

[85] The two are Rabobank (through Gilde Strategic Situations BV., Netherlands)and Fortum (Finland).

10. Conclusion

Writing in 1996 Robert Wade, historian of the role of environment in the World Bank, remarked that 'No other field of Bank operations has grown as fast as its environmental activities.'[86] Starting with the appointment of one environmental adviser in 1971, which grew to five specialists in the mid-1980s, it now has a Vice Presidency of Environmentally and Socially Sustainable Development. and what is probably the largest number of environmental and social experts in any international organization.

Environmental activities have now gone beyond the 'do no harm' agenda of the 1980s. The Bank is currently assessing ways in which it might assess the environmental impacts of operations other than investment projects, e.g. structural adjustment lending. Its environmental and social policies, as well as its Pollution Prevention and Abatement handbook do provide benchmarking of project finance environmental requirements emulated and adopted by many others. It has also played a major role in the development of international environmental financing and, in collaboration with the GEF, is currently the biggest financier of global environment projects. It is still experimenting with ways of mobilizing new and additional resources, including those of the private sector, with new forms of alliances.

[86] *Op. cit.*, 611.

DAVID M. ONG*

The Progressive Integration of Environmental Protection within Offshore Joint Development Agreements

1. Introduction: the integration principle in the International Law of Sustainable Development

One of the main aims of the sustainable development agenda is the progressive integration of environmental considerations within socio-economic development policies and their related laws. Addressed in Principle 4 of the 1992 Rio Declaration on Environment and Development,[1] the

---

* Department of Law, University of Essex, UK. Also Research Associate, Joint Development Regimes project, British Institute of International & Comparative Law, London.
[1] Adopted on 13 June, 1992 at the UN Conference on Environment and Development (UNCED) in Rio de Janeiro, Brazil, also known as the 'Earth Summit'. Principle 4 states: 'In order to achieve sustainable development, environmental protection shall constitute an integral part of the development process and cannot be considered in isolation from it.'

M. Fitzmaurice and M. Szuniewicz (eds.), Exploitation of Natural Resources in the 21st Century, 113–141.
© *2003 Kluwer Law International. Printed in Great Britain.*

integration principle arguably finds its most legally significant expression in the latest, amended version of the 1957 EC Treaty, where it is provided for in Article 6.[2] A persistent concern however relates to the decision-making *level* at which such integration of environmental considerations takes place. While ostensibly directed at engendering the progressive integration of environmental concerns within domestic government socio-economic development policies, the inclusion of this principle within a multilateral convention like the EC Treaty also has important legal implications for the conduct of states in their relations with one another. For example, the lack of such integration of environmental protection within domestic socio-economic activities raises issues of due diligence between states in the event of transboundary environmental damage resulting from such activities.

An ideal scenario would ensure that *all* public, and arguably even private, decision-making processes that could conceivably have environmental implications would implement the integration principle and thereby incorporate environmental considerations. In this sense the most recent and progressive incarnation of the integration principle within the EC Treaty in turn requires the permanent and continuous 'greening' of all Community policies,[3] and arguably serves to highlight its immense potential for 'horizontal' application, even as between private legal and natural individuals. Arguably this implies the integration of environmental concerns within the corporate, as well as government and EC, decision-making processes. The integration principle thus has a transcendental ambit, extending beyond inclusion within purely environmental policies to insinuation within all government, and possibly even corporate, planning and decision-making structures and policies.

---

[2]   In fact, this principle has been amended successively by the 1992 Maastricht and 1998 Amsterdam Treaties, respectively, and more significantly, has been re-positioned within the overall EC Treaty. The initial, 1987 version of this principle formulated in Art. 130R(2) (now Art. 174(2)) of the EC Treaty by the Single European Act (SEA) provided as follows: 'Environmental protection requirements shall be a component of the Community's other policies.' It was then amended in the 1992 Maastricht Treaty to provide that: 'Environmental protection requirements must be integrated into the definition and implementation of other Community policies.' Finally, and perhaps most importantly, this principle was moved to Article 6 of the EC Treaty under Title I: Principles, thereby transcending its 'mere' environmental status and taking its place as one of the guiding principles of the whole European Union project. Here, it was re-phrased as follows: 'Environmental protection requirements must be integrated into the definition and implementation of the Community policies and activities referred to in Article 3, in particular with a view to promoting sustainable development.'

[3]   Krämer notes that this re-positioning in Article 6 has 'certainly further strengthened the importance of the integration requirement in environmental matters which is, because of its horizontal nature, probably the most important of all the different principles,' pointing out that the integration clauses for culture (Art. 128, now Art. 151) and health (Art. 129, now Art. 152) were not similarly re-evaluated in the Amsterdam Treaty. See: L. Krämer, *E.C. Treaty and Environmental Law*, 3rd Ed., London: Sweet & Maxwell (1998) at 71.

Taken to its logical conclusion, the integration principle would require the explicit consideration of the environmental impact of business activities at the corporate boardroom level. Thus, the integration principle has the potential to be a fundamental justification for the inclusion of environmental considerations within corporate governance. The as yet unanswered question is the extent to which future EC and domestic legislation will provide for the incorporation of this principle within corporate decision-making structures. In other words, is it merely to be applied at the operational or business end of corporate activities, or introduced at a higher, corporate management level, or indeed at the highest possible corporate level, to be included as part of the directorial duties of the chairperson and the board of directors.[4] As Bär and Kraemer have noted, '(a)lthough in legal terms the integration principle will not give priority to the environment, the changes are evidence of a strong political will to strengthen the integration of environmental aspects into other policy areas.'[5] The integration principle therefore has the potential to become a cornerstone of the whole European Union legal system and intrinsic to the fulfillment of the overall aims and objectives of the EU project itself. Bär and Kraemer conclude however that '(t)he degree to which ... the integration principle will lead to environmental protection being taken into account in practice, remains to be seen.'[6]

Indeed, it is possible to argue that the true test of the successful implementation of the integration principle will only be passed when environmental concerns form part of the *a priori* considerations of *any* policy decision-making process, irrespective of whether in fact environmental concerns are significant to the matter at hand. Only the transcending of environmental concerns beyond their otherwise limited confines of the environmental law and policy sub-discipline will bring about truly integrated decision-making processes. The implications of such an inclusive project would be far-reaching. Clearly, present environmental law and policy is a long way from arriving at this transcendental point. Nonetheless, it is a useful exercise to subject successive legal instruments in the same subject area to the test of how far they have included and hopefully integrated environmental considerations within their text and implementation. The present analysis targets a series of bilateral offshore joint development agreements (hereinafter JDAs) for this purpose. The chronological period within which this exercise takes place

---

[4] For a comparative study of how far this principle is now incorporated within several domestic jurisdictions, see: David M. Ong, 'The Impact of Environmental Law on Corporate Governance: International and Comparative Perspectives', *European Journal of International Law,* Vol. 12, No. 4 (September, 2001) 685–726.

[5] S. Bär and R. A. Kraemer, 'European Environmental Policy after Amsterdam', *Journal of Environmental Law,* Vol. 10 (2) (1998) 315–330, at 319.

[6] Bar and Kramer (1998) *op. cit.*

ranges from the late 1950s to the most recent agreements adopted in 2001,[7] thereby encompassing a similar time-frame with the recognition, acceptance and implementation of the legal imperative for environmental protection.

## 2.	The joint development concept under international law

'Joint Development' is a generic term given to international agreements between states whose main function is to provide for the co-operative exploitation of hydrocarbon resources that come under the jurisdiction of two states. While the 'joint development' concept itself has not been understood or used in a uniform way,[8] JDAs have nevertheless proven to be an effective

---

[7]	See further below for the 2001 Nigeria-Sao Tome agreement and the 2001 Cambodia-Thailand MOU providing the legal basis for negotiation of a future maritime boundary delimitation/joint development agreement.

[8]	Section IV, paragraph 1 of the Conclusions and Recommendations of the lawyers' group at the Second Workshop on Geology and Hydrocarbon Potential in the South China Sea and Possibilities of Joint Development, held in Honolulu during August, 1983 defined 'joint development' as extending from unitization of shared resources to unilateral development of a shared resource beyond a stipulated boundary, and various gradations in between. See: M. Miyoshi, 'The Basic Concept of Joint Development of Hydrocarbon Resources on the Continental Shelf', *International Journal of Estuarine (now Coastal) Law*, Vol.3, No. 1 (1988) 1–18, at 5 & Appendix II, at 17.

	Gault defines 'joint development' as 'a decision by one or more countries to pool any rights they may have over a given area and, to a greater or lesser degree, undertake some form of joint management for the purposes of exploring and exploiting offshore minerals.' See: I. Townsend-Gault, 'Joint Development of Offshore Mineral Resources – Progress and Prospects for the Future', *Natural Resources Forum*, Vol.12 No. 3 (1988) at 275.

	Lagoni restricted the scope of 'joint development' to co-operation between States based on agreement with regard to the exploration for and exploitation of certain deposits, fields or accumulations of non-living resources which either extend across a boundary or lie in an area of overlapping claims. See: The International Committee on the EEZ, Report on Joint Development of Non-Living Resources in the Exclusive Economic Zone for the International Law Association (ILA), 1988. (Hereinafter, 1988 ILA Report) Rapporteur: R. Lagoni at 2.

	Miyoshi too favours a restrictive version of 'joint development', limited to an inter-governmental agreement, to the exclusion of joint ventures between a government and an oil company, or a consortia of private companies for capital participation. He therefore defines 'joint development' as an inter-governmental arrangement of a provisional nature, designed for functional purposes of joint exploration for and/or exploitation of the hydrocarbon resources of the sea-bed beyond the territorial sea. See: M. Miyoshi, 'Basic Legal Issues of Joint Development of Offshore Oil and Gas in relation to Maritime Boundary Delimitation', *Maritime Briefing*, Vol.2, No. 5 Durham: International Boundaries Research Unit (IBRU) (1999) at 4.

	Finally, the British Institute of International and Comparative Law (BIICL) Research Team's definition of 'joint development' is an agreement between two States to develop so as

option for co-operation in the exploration and exploitation of shared offshore mineral resources.

There are now numerous bilateral JDAs. Significantly, these agreements can now be found in many different regions of the world.[9] Both their increasing numbers and geographical diversity preclude any attempt at dismissing their repeated occurrence as merely coincidental state practice. This leads to the preliminary observation that the lack of a binding obligation to co-operate in the joint development of an international common deposit has less to do with the lack of state practice than with the absence of that other imperative in the formation of customary international law, namely the psychological or subjective element of acceptance of the specific obligation as binding in law, *opinio juris*.[10] Indeed, the burgeoning state practice in joint development of late, with three new agreements adopted in 2001 alone,[11] suggests that states are increasingly viewing these arrangements as viable legal alternatives to otherwise intractable maritime boundary delimitation negotiations. As Orrego Vicuña has remarked:

'Joint development and management zones have thus far accomplished a useful role in relation to the exploration and exploitation of deposits connected with boundaries between States, with the process of agreeing on a delimitation, and with situations where delimitation is pending. There is a trend here which is likely to continue in view of the fact that such arrangements provide a management tool in situations which otherwise lead to disputes and confrontations.'[12]

Supportive judicial opinion can also be found in favour of the joint development solution when overlapping claims or a transboundary deposit is the subject of an international dispute. The joint development principle has received authoritative judicial support at the highest international level, namely the International Court of Justice in the *North Sea Continental Shelf*

---

cont.

to share jointly in agreed proportions by inter-State co-operation and national measures the offshore oil and gas in a designated zone of the seabed and subsoil of the continental shelf to which both or either of the participating States are entitled in international law. See: H. Fox *et al*, *Joint Development of Offshore Oil and Gas*, Vol. I, London: British Institute of International and Comparative Law (1988) at 45.

9   Specifically, the North Sea, Middle East and East and Southeast Asian regions, although two of the more recent agreements are situated in the South-West (UK-Argentina, 1995) and East (Nigeria-Sao Tome, 2001) Atlantic Ocean, respectively.

10   For a fuller discussion of this issue, see: David M. Ong, 'Joint Development of Common Offshore Oil and Gas Deposits: 'Mere' State Practice or Customary International Law?', *American Journal of International Law*, Vol.93, No. 4 (October, 1999) 771–804.

11   These are respectively, the Nigeria-Sao Tome, Timor Sea and Cambodia-Thailand agreements. See below for further details.

12   Francisco Orrego Vicuña, 'Regional cooperation in non-living resources: Joint management zones', in Peter Bautista Payoyo (ed.) *Ocean Governance: Sustainable Development of the Seas*, Tokyo: United Nations University Press (1994) 171–82, at 179.

cases, where it was held to be particularly appropriate when it is a question of preserving the unity of a deposit.[13] Most recently, the Arbitral Tribunal in the *Eritrea-Yemen Arbitration (Phase II-Maritime Delimitation)* case[14] observed that 'in the last thirty years there has grown up a significant body of cooperative state practice in the exploitation of resources that straddle maritime boundaries'.[15] According to the Tribunal, such cooperative state practice in the exploitation of resources that straddle maritime boundaries had particular relevance in the instant case between Yemen and Eritrea as they face each other across a relatively narrow body of water,[16] very much like the present situation between Australia and East Timor. The Tribunal held that the two Parties are bound to inform and consult one another on any oil and gas deposit that may be discovered to straddle the recommended single maritime boundary between them or lie in its immediate vicinity.[17] The Tribunal concluded that state practice dictates that 'Eritrea and Yemen should give *every consideration* to the shared or joint or unitised exploitation of any such (straddling) resources.'[18] (emphasis added) Commenting on this decision, Reisman notes that 'the Tribunal seemed to assume that some of these (state) practices were rapidly acquiring, but have not yet attained, customary international law status.'[19]

Thus, it is arguable that joint development is now mandated under international law for the specific resolution of common hydrocarbon deposits that are legitimately subject to the sovereign rights of two or more interested states.[20] This is especially true in regions such as the North Sea, Persian Gulf, Southeast Asian waters and most recently in the sub-regions of the Atlantic Ocean, where the great majority of these agreements were adopted. A legal presumption in favour of joint development is clearly pertinent in regions where previous state practice is prevalent.[21]

The bilateral JDAs featured in this study will first be grouped into three different joint development models (JDA Models I, II & III) for analytical

---

[13] See: North Sea Continental Shelf cases, *ICJ Reports* (1969) at 52, para.99.
[14] Arbitral Tribunal Award, 17 December, 1999. Accessed from: < http:// www.pca-cpa.org > .
[15] At para. 84, *ibid.*
[16] *Ibid.*, at para. 85.
[17] *Ibid.*, at para. 86.
[18] *Ibid.*, at para. 86.
[19] W. Michael Reisman, 'Eritrea-Yemen Arbitration Award Phase II-Maritime Delimitation', International Decisions, *American Journal of International Law*, Vol. 94, No. 4 (October, 2000) 721–36, at 735.
[20] See: David M. Ong, 'The New Timor Sea Arrangement, 2001: Is Joint Development Mandated under International Law?' *International Journal of Marine & Coastal Law*, Vol.18, No. 1 (January, 2002) 79–122, at 105.
[21] See: David M. Ong, 'The 1979 and 1990 Malaysia-Thailand Joint Development Agreements: A Model for International Legal Co-operation in Common Offshore Petroleum Deposits?', *International Journal of Marine & Coastal Law*, Vol. 14, No. 2 (May, 1999) 207–246, at 244–5.

purposes. They are as follows: The first JDA Model (I) comprises of an agreement between the interested States whereby one State manages the development of a designated joint zone on behalf of the other State(s) concerned, with the other State(s) sharing the revenues arising from the exploitation of the resources, once the costs incurred by the first State have been subtracted.

The second JDA Model (II) consists of an agreement establishing a system of compulsory joint ventures between their national or other nominated oil companies, either in designated joint development zones, or in order to exploit deposits lying across already delimited boundary lines. This latter sub-species of Model II JDAs has also been described as the international or transboundary unitization of deposits. A common feature of both variations of Model II JDAs is the compulsory nomination of a single operator to exploit the shared deposit(s) found in the designated joint development zone, or lying across the delimited boundary. The third JDA Model (III) is the most complex and institutionalized type of JDA, requiring a much higher level of bilateral co-operation between the interested states, and consequently, greater reduction of individual national sovereignty and autonomy than the previous two options.

Model III JDAs consist of agreements between the interested states establishing inter-governmental joint authorities or joint commissions, normally with their own legal personalities, and provided with both licensing and regulatory powers as well as comprehensive mandates to manage the development of the designated joint zone on behalf of the states concerned.

Regardless of the joint development model utilized in state practice, similar types of provisions can be found in most of these agreements. These common features include provisions on the following issues: non-prejudice exceptions to the sovereign rights of each party over the disputed overlapping claims area or shared, transboundary deposits; criminal and civil jurisdictional allocations; joint institutional arrangements and harmonized or uniform hydrocarbon licensing regimes; dispute settlement mechanisms and procedures; third party rights within the designated joint development zones; and last but certainly not least, provisions for environmental protection from such joint development activities. The present study focuses upon the progressive inclusion of environmental provisions within these bilateral JDAs in line with the integration principle as part of the general requirement to strive for sustainable development that is now arguably part of the international legal obligations of all states.

3. The inclusion of environmental provisions within bilateral joint development agreements

A previous study of JDAs from an environmental perspective focused on the body of general international environmental law that would be applicable to these agreements.[22] The present discussion eschews this approach in favour of an examination of the contribution by the agreements themselves to the trend for progressive incorporation and integration of environmental provisions within organized human socio-economic activities. Thus, it examines how far environmental considerations either included or otherwise alluded to within these JDAs lay bare the integration of such concerns within co-operative but otherwise exploitatively oriented agreements. As Birnie notes, marine environmental protection was not foremost in the collective mindsets of the states that negotiated and adopted these JDAs.[23] It will be seen that later JDAs more readily include environmental protection requirements, thereby at the very least denoting the raised level of environmental consciousness within the parties that negotiated, adopted and now charged with implementing these joint development agreements.

On the other hand, it should be noted that JDAs, regulating as they do sovereign rights over shared oil and gas resources, are particularly apt instruments for this type of study. This is because the primary focus of these type of agreements is usually upon the level of bilateral co-operation required for the successful joint exploration and exploitation of international common hydrocarbon deposits. Marine environmental protection then becomes a useful side issue that the interested parties can reach agreement fairly easily on and therefore contribute to the forward momentum of any bilateral negotiations on the joint development regime itself. It has been observed that some of the most recent JDAs have included co-operative clauses on the exploitation of living resources, environmental protection, scientific research activities, search and rescue operations, etc.[24]

The present trend towards better provision of environmental protection within more recently adopted JDAs also needs to be viewed against a backdrop of ever increasing international and domestic environmental regulation of the oil and gas industry generally.[25] There is clear evidence that the industry has taken on board the environmental agenda within its production cycle, if not its overall managerial decision-making processes. Wojtanowicz, for example, notes the development of environmental control technology (ECT) through various evolutionary stages from an initial PCD (produce-consume-dispose) approach, through to a WMT (waste manage-

---

[22] See: Patricia Birnie, 'Protection of the Marine Environment in Joint Development', in Hazel Fox (ed.), *Joint Development of Offshore Oil and Gas*, London: British Institute of International and Comparative Law, Vol. II (1990) 202–222.

[23] *Ibid.*, at 218.

[24] Orrego Vicuna (1994) *op. cit.*, at 179.

[25] For a comprehensive analysis of these developments, see: David M. Ong, 'International Legal Developments in Environmental Protection: Implications for the Oil Industry', Chapter 2 in S.T. Orszulik (ed.), *Environmental Technology in the Oil Industry*, London: Blackie Academic & Professional, an imprint of Chapman & Hall, 1997, 16–72. Reprinted in *Australasian Journal of Natural Resources Law and Policy*, Vol.4, No. 1 (1997) 55–106.

ment technology) approach before finally arriving at the present ECT approach embodying the preventive principle.[26] The offshore petroleum industry's embrace of the preventive approach is mainly due to increasing pollution and waste disposal costs,[27] that in turn reflect the progressive internalization of what were previously considered external costs to the industry.[28] Thus, in contrast to both the previous PCD and WMT approaches, the ECT approach is conceived as an integral part of the entire petroleum development process.[29] Read confirms that prevention is now an 'essential element' in any offshore oil and gas exploration programme, although his conception of this approach is limited to the prevention of operational leaks, spills and blowouts,[30] as opposed to the clearly integrationist approach to environmental considerations advocated by Wojtanowicz.

Within this context, we can now proceed to examine JDAs from each of the three different Joint Development Models described above in respect of their provision for environmental protection from such joint exploration and exploitation activities.

4. Environmental provisions in Model I type joint development agreements

The 1958 *Saudi Arabia-Bahrain*,[31] 1969 *Qatar-Abu Dhabi*[32] and 1971 *Iran-*

---

[26]   A. K. Wojtanowicz, 'Environmental control technology in petroleum drilling and production', Chapter 3 in Orszulik (1997) *ibid.*, 73–180 at 74.

[27]   *Ibid.*, at 76.

[28]   See generally: C. S. Pearson, *International Marine Environment Policy: The Economic Dimension*, Baltimore MD: John Hopkins University Press (1965).

[29]   Wojtanowicz (1997) *op. cit.*, at 77.

[30]   A. D. Read, 'Protection of the Marine Environment: A View from Industry', in Fox (ed.) Vol. II (1990) *op. cit.*, 223–232, at 223–4.

[31]   Full title: Agreement concerning the Delimitation of the Continental Shelf in the Persian Gulf between the Shaykhdom of Bahrain and the Kingdom of Arabia. The agreement was made on 22 February, 1958 but signed and entered into force on 26 February, 1958. Source: Charney & Alexander (eds.), *International Maritime Boundaries*, Dordrecht: Martinus Nijhoff. Report No. 7–3, Vol. II (1993) 1495–7. Also see: Churchill *et al* (eds.) *New Directions in the Law of the Sea*, Vol. V, 207; UN Doc. No. ST/LEG/SER.B/16, 409 (1974). Clause 6 provides that the agreement shall come into effect from the date on which it is signed by the two parties. Hence although the agreement was initially made on 22 February, 1958 it was only signed on 26 February, 1958 and entered into force on this date. See: R. F. Pietrowski, Jr., 'Bahrain-Saudi Arabia', Report No. 7–3, in Charney & Alexander, *International Maritime Boundaries*, Vol. II, *op. cit.*, 1489–93, at 1489. Also see: A. A. El-Hakim, 'Bahrain-Saudi Arabia boundary agreement', *The Middle Eastern States and the Law of the Sea*, Manchester: Manchester University Press (1979) 86–91, at 86, fn. 7.

[32]   Full title: Agreement on the Settlement of Maritime Boundary Lines and Sovereign Rights over Islands between Qatar and Abu Dhabi. Signed: 20.3.1969; in force: 20.3.1969. Source: UN Doc. No. ST/LEG/SER.B/16, 403 (1974). Also see: Charney & Alexander (eds.) Vol. II, Rep. No. 7–9 (1993) 1547–8.

Sharjah[33] agreements are early examples of Model I-type bilateral offshore JDAs. Neither of these provided for the rights of third parties, environmental protection, or dispute settlement measures for resolving problems between the respective parties. The 1969 Qatar-Abu Dhabi agreement does however provide for consultation on all matters concerning exploitation of the designated field, which presumably includes any disputes between Parties over environmental concerns.

5. Environmental provisions in Model II type JDAs

The 1965 *Kuwait-Saudi Arabia* agreement[34] is a good example of the first variation of a Model II-type JDA described above. The rights of both Parties to the shared natural resources in the partitioned Neutral Zone are maintained notwithstanding the division of land territory of the Neutral Zone and territorial waters up to 6-nm offshore between the two Parties.[35] Beyond 6 nautical miles, Article VIII also provides that the equal rights of the two parties shall be exercised by means of shared exploitation. This agreement provides for voluntary (as opposed to compulsory) joint ventures between concessionaires in the divided Neutral Zone. It allows the respective concessionaires of each Party, both onshore and offshore, to enter into joint operating agreements providing for the unitization of fields lying across their concession area boundaries. In keeping with early state practice on joint development no specific provision for environmental protection is made in the agreement but a private arrangement on pollution control establishing a joint monitoring system was devised amongst the companies granted concessions by Bahrain, Kuwait, Saudi Arabia and Iraq.

In the *France-Spain* JDA,[36] each Party is required to encourage joint venture agreements between companies of each nationality to participate in the natural resource development of the zone on the basis of equal partnership and financing of operations in accordance to their respective shares in the joint venture.[37] This agreement is therefore a good example of the first variation of

---

[33] Full Title: Memorandum of Understanding (MOU) between Iran and Sharjah. Adopted by exchange of letters between the Parties and the concession-holder: Buttes Co. in November, 1971. Source: Supp. to *Middle East Economic Survey*, Vol. XV, No. 28 (May,1972).
[34] Full title: Agreement between the State of Kuwait and the Kingdom of Saudi Arabia Relating to the Partition of the Neutral Zone. Adopted: 7.7.1965. Source: (1965) 4 *ILM* 1134.
[35] Arts. IV and VII, *ibid.*
[36] Full Title: Convention between the Government of the French Republic and the Government of the Spanish State on the Delimitation of the Two States in the Bay of Biscay. Signed: 29.1.1974; in force: 5.4.1975. Source: Churchill *et al* (eds.), *New Directions in the Law of the Sea*, Vol.V (1976) 251–60.
[37] Annex II, para.2, *ibid.*

the Model II-type JDA noted above. Unlike earlier joint development agreements where the provision for environmental protection was conspicuous in its brevity or even total absence, Article 7 provides that the Parties shall by mutual consultation make every effort to prevent interference with the ecological equilibrium and other legitimate uses of the marine environment from natural resource development activities in the Bay of Biscay continental shelf. The recognition of threats to natural ecosystems beyond the usually anthropocentric focus of such environmental provisions highlights the progressive approach adopted by this agreement. However, the more comprehensive nature of environmental protection embodied within this agreement as compared to the simpler arrangements established in the Persian Gulf above has not been tested todate as no petroleum exploitation has taken place in the joint zone.

Another prime example of the first type of Model II JDA is the 1974 *Japan-Republic of (South) Korea* Agreement.[38] This Agreement provides for petroleum exploration and exploitation in a defined Joint Development Zone (JDZ).[39] This is to be carried out within further divided subzones.[40] The Agreement also provides that each of the subzones delineated within the overall JDZ will be subject to the jurisdiction of one of the Parties. The designation of the appropriate national jurisdiction applicable to each subzone is in turn dependent on the nationality of the operator chosen by the nominated concessionaires to that subzone.[41] The Parties require their nominated concessionaires to enter into a Joint Operating Agreement (JOA)[42] within each of the subzones designated.[43] The resolution of navigational and fisheries issues involving both Parties and third states is specifically provided under Article XXVII. Provision for the co-ordination of bilateral fisheries interests within each subzone is also included within the joint operating agreements between the nominated concessionaires.[44] Article XX provides for the Parties to agree on measures to prevent and remove marine pollution from activities in the joint development zone, and prevent collisions at sea.

[38] Full title: Agreement between Japan and the Republic of Korea concerning the Joint Development of the Southern Part of the Continental Shelf Adjacent to the Two Countries. Signed: 5.2.1974; in force: 22.6.1978. Source: Churchill *et al* (eds.), *New Directions in the Law of the Sea*, Vol. IV, 117.

[39] Delineated by Art. II(1) of the 1974 Agreement *ibid.*, and encompassing some 24,101 sq. nautical miles.

[40] Art. III(1), *ibid.*

[41] Art. XIX, *ibid.*

[42] Art. V(1), *ibid.*

[43] Initially nine, later reduced to six as a result of an Exchange of Diplomatic Notes on 31 August, 1987.

[44] Art. V(1), *ibid.*

The 1976 *United Kingdom-Norway* Frigg Field agreement[45] and similar ones agreed subsequently between the same two Parties, namely the 1979 Statfjord[46] and Murchison Field Agreements, as well as the 1982 Markham Field Agreement between the UK and Netherlands are international transboundary field unitization agreements made pursuant to relevant provisions in previously agreed continental shelf delimitation treaties in the North Sea. As Taylor *et al* have noted, 'Where part of an oil or gas field falls within the UK sector of the continental shelf and the remainder falls within an area over which another state has sovereign rights, any unitization will need to be agreed at two levels. First, the two states will need to reach agreement and secondly, the respective licensees will need to enter into a unit operating agreement.'[47] The 1976 Frigg Field agreement, for example, was made pursuant to Article 4 of the Anglo-Norwegian Continental Shelf Agreement, 1965. All these agreements are therefore excellent examples of the second variation of the Model II-type JDAs described above.

In terms of environmental protection, Article 23 of the 1976 agreement provides that the Parties undertake, jointly and severally, to ensure that the exploitation of the Frigg field, including any installation or pipeline involved, shall not cause pollution of the marine environment or damage by pollution to the coastline, shore facilities or amenities, or vessels or fishing gear of any country. Thus, each state retains jurisdiction over the offshore installations situated in its own sector of the continental shelf but consultation is required on the implementation of uniform safety and presumably also environmental standards.

However, as Birnie notes, it has not proved easy to harmonise the respective discharge standards already in place within each Party's domestic sector.[48] Furthermore, international discharge standards were not yet in place when these JDAs were adopted and in any case may be less stringent than certain national standards. An additional progressive measure allows state inspectors from either Party access to all installations in the field, regardless of which side of the boundary line they are situated.[49] Moreover, according to Birnie, a 'foreign' inspector can, in the absence of a national one, inform the person in charge of the national installation and the corresponding government

---

[45] Full title: Agreement between the Government of the United Kingdom of Great Britain and Northern Ireland and the Government of the Kingdom of Norway relating to the Exploitation of the Frigg Field Reservoir and the Transmission of Gas therefrom to the UK. Signed: 10.5.1976; in force: 22.7.1977. Source: 1977 *UK Treaty Series (UKTS)* 113.

[46] Both signed: 16.10.1979, in force: 30.1.1979; sources: (1981) *UKTS* 44 (Statfjord) and (1981) *UKTS* 39 (Murchison).

[47] Michael P G Taylor, T P Winsor and Sally M Tyne, *The Joint Operating Agreement (in) Oil and Gas Law*, London: Longman at 71.

[48] Birnie (1990) *op. cit.*, at 217.

[49] Art. 8(3) of the 1976 Frigg Field Agreement, *op. cit.*

authorities of any accident involving serious pollution.[50] Ultimately, inspectors can order the complete cessation of all operations if they judge this necessary to avert or minimise an accident involving danger to life.[51]

Recently, another pressing environmental issue that was not adequately catered for by the initial transboundary unitisation agreement has reared its ugly head. This relates to the environmental implications of the Frigg field decommissioning process as it completes its final production phase. A variety of jurisdictional and substantive environmental questions too numerous to treat adequately on this occasion have arisen during the decommissioning phase due to the transboundary nature of the field and the sheer size of the installations put in place to extract the natural gas from it.[52]

The 1981 *Iceland-Norway* Jan Mayen agreement[53] applies a hybrid of Joint Development Models I and II. Article 2 established a rectangular joint development zone of some 45,470 sq. km. A previously agreed (1980) single continental shelf-EEZ boundary cuts across the zone, leaving approx. 32,750 sq. km. within Norwegian jurisdiction and the rest (12,720 sq.km.) within Icelandic jurisdiction. Norwegian law applies in relation to petroleum activities, safety measures and environmental protection within the Norwegian sector and likewise in the Icelandic sector. The initial exploration phase of the joint zone is funded by Norway, with any net profit from the sale of seismic data shared between the Parties.[54] Specific exploration and production licenses are awarded on the basis of joint venture contracts.[55]

There are no specific provisions regarding environmental protection in the joint zone but jurisdiction over environmental protection follows the sectoral allocation of the joint zone between the Parties by the earlier, 1980 agreement.[56] Unlike the previous transboundary unitisation agreements considered above, the present JDA provides for a specific dispute settlement procedure in the event of disagreement over the marine environmental protection regime within the designated joint zone.[57] If one of the Parties

---

[50] Birnie (1990) *op. cit.* at 217.

[51] Art. 8(4) of the 1976 Frigg Field Agreement, *op. cit.* .

[52] For a preliminary discussion of the legal, technical and other issues raised by the Frigg field decommissioning process, see: Det Norske Veritas, *Frigg Field Cessation Environmental Impact Assessment*, Draft Technical Report for Elf Petroleum, Report No. 99–4030 (15 August, 2000) This Report has now been incorporated into Part 2 of the overall Frigg Field Cessation Plan that can be downloaded from the following website: *http://www.totalfinaelf.no/cessation*. See also: Department of Trade and Industry (UK), *Decommissioning of Offshore Installations and Pipelines under the Petroleum Act 1998 – Guidance Notes for Industry* (May, 2000).

[53] Full title: Agreement on the Continental Shelf between Iceland and Jan Mayen Signed: 22.10.1981; in force: 2.6.1982. Source: 21 ILM (1982) 1222; Charney & Alexander (eds.) Vol.II (1993) Report 9–4, 1762–65.

[54] Art. 3, *ibid.*

[55] Art. 4, *ibid.*

[56] Arts. 5 and 6, *ibid.*

[57] Art. 9, *ibid.*

considers that the safety or environmental regulations fail to provide adequate protection during exploration or production in the joint zone, then the Parties are required to consult each other. If the Parties disagree during such consultations, the question shall be referred to a Conciliation Commission. The Conciliation Commission shall consist of three members, one appointed by each Party and the Chairman jointly appointed by the Parties. The Commission's recommendations are not binding on the Parties but they are required to pay reasonable regard to them.

The 1992 *Malaysia-Vietnam* Memorandum of Understanding (MOU)[58] provides for the two Parties' nominated state oil companies to enter into an agreement between them for the exploration and exploitation of petroleum (art. 3) in a Defined Area (art. 1) of overlapping continental shelf claims between the two countries. Unlike the two previous Southeast Asian examples of joint development (considered below), namely the 1979/90 Malaysia-Thailand and 1989 Australia-Indonesia agreements, this MOU does not provide for the establishment of a complex institutional framework in order to implement the joint development concept. It merely requires the two explicitly nominated state oil companies to enter into a joint operating agreement for their petroleum development and extraction activities in the Defined Area. Rather unusually for a modern JDA, there are no explicit provisions or even references to environmental protection within this agreement. However, both Parties have agreed to ensure that petroleum development in the Defined Area in this arrangement shall be conducted with due regard to marine environmental protection.[59]

6. Environmental provisions in Model III type JDAs

The 1974 *Sudan-Saudi Arabia* Agreement[60] was probably the first of this new breed of JDA providing for an altogether more sophisticated legal and institutional framework for the joint development of non-living resources. This is the first JDA that provides for a supranational institution to oversee the exploration and exploitation of the natural resources of a designated joint

---

[58] Full title: Memorandum of Understanding between Malaysia and the Socialist Republic of Vietnam for the Exploration and Exploitation of Petroleum in a Defined Area of the Continental Shelf Involving the Two Countries. Signed: 5.6.1992; in force: 4.6.1993. Source: Ted L. McDorman, 'Malaysia-Vietnam', Report No. 5–19, in J. I. Charney & L. M. Alexander (eds.) *International Maritime Boundaries*, Dordrecht: Martinus Nijhoff, Vol.3 at (1998) 2335–44, at 2341.

[59] Pers. Comm. from the Malaysian Ministry of Foreign Affairs, Wisma Putra, Kuala Lumpur.

[60] Full title: Agreement between Sudan and Saudi Arabia relating to the Joint Exploitation of the Natural Resources of the Sea-bed and Sub-soil of the Red Sea in the Common Zone, 1974. Adopted: 16 May 1974. Source: ST/LEG/SER.B/18 452–5.

development zone. It is therefore the first example of the third Joint Development Model in the typology described above. Both Parties expressly recognise that they each retain exclusive sovereign rights over the sea-bed area adjacent to their respective coastlines in the Red Sea up to the 1000m isobath. (arts. III & IV) The two Parties also expressly recognise that they have no rights over the sea-bed adjacent to the other Party's coastline within the 1000m isobath. (arts. III & IV)

The sea-bed area lying between the two areas defined above, *i.e.*, beyond the 1000m isobath, is designated as the Common Zone. Here, the Parties agree that they have equal sovereign rights over the natural resources therein to the exclusion of other, third parties. (art. V) The Parties undertake to protect their sovereign rights and defend them *(sic)* against third parties. (art. VI) Natural resources are defined here as only the non-living substances, including hydrocarbon and mineral resources.(art. I(2)). But the application of this agreement shall not affect the high seas legal status of the superjacent waters over the Common Zone, nor obstruct navigation. (art. XV)

The Joint Commission is endowed with legal personality and extensive powers to exercise its functions. It is established as a body corporate in both Parties (art. VIII), to ensure the prompt and efficient exploitation of the natural resources therein. (art. VII) The Joint Commission is charged with: (a) surveying and delimiting the Common Zone; (b) undertaking studies on the exploration and exploitation of the Zone; (c) encouraging specialized bodies *(sic)* to explore in the Zone; and most importantly, (d) considering and deciding on license/ concession applications. It also expedites and supervises the production stage; and has regulatory powers necessary for its functions. Any dispute between the Parties shall be settled by amicable means initially. Should this fail, it will be submitted to the ICJ, both Parties accepting the compulsory jurisdiction in this respect. Either Party can also request interim measures from the ICJ. (art. XVI)

However, the generally more sophisticated nature of this Model III type JDA is conspicuously lacking when it comes to provisions for environmental protection as there are none to speak of. The lack of such provisions only serves to highlight the relatively recent evolution of the sustainable development concept and its corollary principles such as the integration principle. On the other hand, Birnie notes that given the Joint Commission's general regulatory functions and powers, it could presumably provide for safety and pollution regulations governing exploitation activities taking place within the designated Common Zone in the Red Sea seabed.[61]

---

[61] Birnie (1990) *op. cit.*, at 218.

The 1979 *Malaysia-Thailand* Memorandum of Understanding (hereinafter, MOU)[62] established a Joint Development Area (art. I) and a Joint Authority (art. III(1) of MOU & art. 2 of the 1990 Agreement) to assume all rights to explore and exploit the non-living natural resources of the sea-bed in the area of overlapping continental shelf claims for a period of 50 years, commencing from the date the 1979 MOU came into force (24 October, 1979). Following more than a decade of further bilateral negotiations over the specific legal and institutional regime for joint development in the designated Area, the parties adopted the 1990 Agreement establishing the Constitution of the Malaysia-Thailand Authority,[63] (arts. 1–7) including a petroleum development regime based on the production-sharing model. (art. 8) This Agreement also provides for financial (arts. 9–12), customs and excise and taxation (arts. 16-17) arrangements in the JD Area. If the Parties reach agreement on the delimitation of the continental shelf boundary before the expiry of the 50 years, the Joint Authority shall be wound up. (art. VI(1) of MOU) However, if no satisfactory solution is found within 50 years, the existing arrangement will continue. (art. VI(2))

The 1979 MOU divided the criminal jurisdiction of both Parties within the JD Area by means of a straight line through the Area, roughly corresponding to the equidistance line from the two parties' adjacent coastlines.(art. V) In addition, the rights (including powers of enforcement) exercised by the parties over fishing, navigation, marine scientific research, and marine pollution shall extend to the JD Area. (art. IV) Article V of the 1979 MOU also provides that the designated areas of criminal jurisdiction shall not in any way be construed as indicating the boundary line of the continental shelf between the two Parties in the JD Area. In line with the jurisdictional dividing line through the designated JD Area, the Joint Authority does not have jurisdiction over environmental protection in the JDA. Art.IV of MOU provides that the enforcement powers exercised by the national authorities of either Parties in relation to, *inter alia,* the prevention and control of marine pollution shall extend to the JDA and shall be recognised and respected by the Authority.

The 1989 *Australia-Indonesia* Timor Gap treaty,[64] along with its 4

---

[62] Full title: The 1979 Memorandum of Understanding between Thailand and Malaysia establishing a Joint Authority for the exploitation of the resources of the sea-bed in a defined area of the continental shelf of the two countries in the Gulf of Thailand, 1979. The texts of both this 1979 MOU and the 1990 Agreement noted below are included in Appendices to David Ong, "Thailand/ Malaysia: The Joint Development Agreement 1990', Current Legal Developments, *International Journal of Estuarine (now Marine) and Coastal Law,* Vol. 6, No. 1 (February 1991) 57–72.

[63] Full title: Agreement between Malaysia and Thailand on the Constitution and other matters relating to the establishment of the Malaysia-Thailand Joint Authority, 1990.

[64] Full title: Treaty between Australia and the Republic of Indonesia on the Zone of Cooperation in an Area between the Indonesian Province of East Timor and Northern Australia. Adopted: 11 December, 1989; entered into force: 9 February, 1991.

annexes,[65] is probably the most sophisticated joint development regime agreed to date.[66] Both the geographical division and institutional design are complex. Area A, which lies in between the other two Areas (B and C), is subject to a true joint development arrangement, incorporating joint control and equal revenue sharing.[67] Petroleum resource exploration and exploitation in this area is administered by a Ministerial Council[68] and Joint Development Authority[69] on the basis of production-sharing contracts.[70]

The sophisticated nature of the treaty is evident from the complex institutional framework laid down for the joint development of petroleum resources in Area A. It creates a hierarchical, two-level arrangement composed of a Ministerial Council and a Joint Authority.[71] The Ministerial Council (MC) has overall responsibility for all matters relating to the development of the petroleum resources in Area A of the Zone of Co-operation. (art. 6(1)) In exercising its functions, the MC shall ensure the optimum commercial utilization of the petroleum resources consistent with good oilfield practice and *sound environmental practice*. (art. 6(2)) (emphasis added)

Part IV of the 1989 treaty established a Joint Authority (JA) (art. 7(1)), that has juridical personality and such legal capacities under the two Parties' laws as necessary to exercise its powers and perform its functions, in particular capacity to contract, acquire and dispose property, to institute and be party to

---

[65] Under Art. 1(o), Annexes A, B, C, and D are included within the meaning of the 'Treaty'. Annex A contains the designation and description including maps and coordinates of the areas A, B and C comprising the Zone of Cooperation and is incorporated into the Treaty by Article 1. Annex B contains the Petroleum Mining Code for Area A of the Zone of Cooperation. This Code governs operational activities relating to exploration and exploitation of the petroleum resources in Area A subject to the power of the Ministerial Council under Article 6.1(b) of the Treaty to amend it (Article 1.1(i)) Annex C to the treaty contains the Model Production Sharing Contract between the Joint Authority and contractors on the basis of which production sharing contracts for Area A are to be concluded subject to modification by the Ministerial Council under Article 6.1(c) of the treaty (Articles 1.1(g)).

[66] For an early analysis of its provisions see: Anthony Bergin, 'The Australian-Indonesian Timor Gap Maritime Boundary Agreement', *International Journal of Estuarine (now Marine) and Coastal Law*, Vol.5, No. 4 (November, 1990) 383–93. It should be noted however that unique as the Timor Gap treaty is, it is but one of three such joint development arrangements in Southeast Asian waters alone. The other two are the 1979 Malaysia-Thailand MOU followed by the 1990 Agreement *op. cit.*, and the 1992 Malaysia-Vietnam MOU *op. cit.*

[67] Art. 2(2)(a) and 3, *ibid.*

[68] Part III, arts. 5 and 6, *ibid.*

[69] Part IV, arts. 7–11, *ibid.*

[70] Based on a model production-sharing contract in Annex C, *ibid.*

[71] Unlike the Malaysia-Thailand Joint Authority, for example, which ostensibly at least retains control over all aspects of policy and decision-making for the exploration and exploitation of the non-living natural resources in the Joint Development Area. See: Article 3(2) of the 1979 Memorandum of Understanding and article 7(1) of the 1990 Agreement on the Constitution of the Joint Authority. For analysis of this issue, see: David M. Ong, *IJMCL* (1999) *op. cit.*, at 233.

legal proceedings. (art. 7(2)) The most important contractual function the Joint Authority has performed relates to entering production-sharing contracts (PSCs) with corporations for the extraction of petroleum. The JA is subordinate to the MC, and is responsible to the Council for the day-to-day management of the petroleum activities in Area A. (arts. 7(3) and 8) In this context, it is empowered to issue regulations on all matters related to petroleum development activities, including work safety and *environmental protection* matters. (art. 8(j)) (emphasis added)

The 1989 treaty also provides that the Parties shall co-operate in Area A to prevent and minimise pollution of the marine environment arising from the exploration and exploitation of petroleum (art. 18(1)), in particular by providing assistance to the JA as may be requested pursuant to art. 8(m) and where pollution in Area A spreads beyond it. (art. 18(1)(a) & (b)) Apart from issuing regulations for marine environmental protection in Area A as noted above, the JA shall also establish an oil spill contingency plan. (art. 18(2)) Contractors shall be liable for damage or expenses incurred as a result of marine environmental pollution arising out of petroleum operations in Area A in accordance with contractual arrangements with the Joint Authority and the law of the State in which a claim in respect of such damage or expenses is brought. (art. 19) Thus, we can see that that environmental concerns are incorporated within the remits of both the MC and JA, as well as being the object of co-operation between both the Parties to the 1989 treaty themselves.[72] Such environmental considerations are also written into the Petroleum Mining Code (Annex B) and the Model Production Sharing Contract (Annex C) that form two of four Annexes to the treaty.[73]

More recently, on 5 July, 2001 the UN Transitional Administration of East Timor (UNTAET)[74] and Australia culminated sixteen months of negotiations[75] with the adoption of a Memorandum of Understanding (MOU)

---

[72] See: D. Zahar, 'The Timor Gap Treaty's Provisions on the Protection and Preservation of the Marine Environment', Appendix 2, attached to Mochtar Kusuma-Atmadja, 'Joint Development of Oil and Gas by Neighbouring Countries', in M. Kusuma-Atmadja, Thomas A. Mensah and Bernard H. Oxman (eds.), *Sustainable Development and the Preservation of the Oceans: The Challenges of UNCLOS and Agenda 21*, Proceedings of the Law of the Sea Institute's 29th Annual Conference, Denpasar, Bali, Indonesia, 19–22 June 1995; Honolulu: William S. Richardson School of Law, University of Hawaii (1997) 592–609, at 604–9.

[73] *Ibid.*, at 606–8..

[74] The UNTAET was established by UN Security Council Resolution 1272 (1999) adopted on 25 October, 1999. S/RES/1272 (1999) see: 38 ILM (2000) at 240. UNTAET is endowed with overall responsibility for the administration of East Timor and is empowered to exercise all legislative and executive authority, including the administration of justice. (para.1).

[75] Negotiations between Australia and the UNTAET, along with representation from the East Timor Transitional Administration (ETTA), began in March, 2000.

providing for a new Timor Sea Arrangement.[76] This Arrangement is to be adopted by Australia and East Timor upon East Timor's full independence.[77] This new joint development arrangement will therefore in due course replace the currently applicable 2000 MOU also agreed between the UNTAET and Australia,[78] which in turn continues the terms of the 1989 Timor Gap Zone of Co-operation Treaty[79] agreed between Indonesia and Australia. This is indeed a significant achievement in the prospects for future joint development of the petroleum resources in the Timor Gap. The adoption of the 2001 MOU, incorporating the new Timor Sea Arrangement, represents the application of a modified version of the joint development principle enshrined by the earlier Timor Gap treaty in a manner which should prove much more favourable to the imminent East Timor state. In particular, government revenues from the initial upstream activity in the designated Joint Petroleum Development Area

[76] Memorandum of Understanding between Australia and the UNTAET, 2001 incorporating the Timor Sea Arrangement as Attachment 'A'. Adopted on 5 July, 2001. Source: Department of Foreign Affairs and Trade (DFAT) Australia. See: DFAT website: *http://www.dfat.gov.au*. The MOU also includes Annexes A to F. Under Article 19(a), the 'Arrangement' also means these Annexes and any others subsequently agreed between East Timor and Australia. The Arrangement will enter into force 30 days after East Timor and Australia have notified each other in writing that their respective requirements for its entry into force have been fulfilled. (Article 25).

[77] This was achieved on 20 May, 2002. See: Luke Harding, 'East Timor celebrates becoming a nation', *The Guardian* newspaper, Monday, 20 May, 2002 at 13.

[78] Full Title: Memorandum of Understanding between the Government of Australia and the UNTAET, acting on behalf of East Timor, on Arrangements Relating to the Timor Gap Treaty, 10 February 2000. Adopted in an Exchange of Notes constituting an Agreement between the Government of Australia and UNTAET concerning the continued operation of the treaty between Australia and the Republic of Indonesia on the Zone of Co-operation between the Indonesian Province of East Timor and Northern Australia of 11 December 1989. Performed at Dili, 10 February 2000. Entry into force: 10 February, 2000 but with effect from 25 October 1999. This arrangement was brought into force by an exchange of Diplomatic Notes on 10 February, 2000 that retrospectively applied the provisional agreement as from 25 October 1999, *i.e.,* the date when UNTAET took over government functions on behalf of East Timor. See: Australian Treaty Series 2000, No. 9, accessed at the following website: < http:www.auslii.edu.au/au/other/dfat/treaties/2000/9.html > In April, 2000 Australia approved legislation giving effect to the above treaty with UNTAET. See: Timor Gap Treaty (Transitional Arrangements) Act 2000.

[79] Full title: Treaty between the Australia and the Republic of Indonesia on the Zone of Co-operation in an Area between the Indonesian Province of East Timor and Northern Australia, signed (in the airspace) over the Timor Gap on 11 December, 1989; entered into force on 9 February, 1991. (hereinafter: the Timor Gap treaty) Sources: 29 *ILM* 469 (1990) and V. Prescott, 'Australia-Indonesia (Timor Gap)', Report No. 6–2(5), in Jonathan I. Charney & Lewis M. Alexander (eds.), *International Maritime Boundaries*, Vol. II, The Hague: Martinus Nijhoff (1993) at 1245–1328. Also in H. Fox (ed.): *Joint Development of Offshore Oil and Gas*, Vol. II, London: The British Institute of International and Comparative Law (1990), Part III, 235–51. For an early analysis of the background and main features of the Treaty, see: V. L. Forbes and F. M. Auburn, 'The Timor Gap Zone of Co-operation', *Boundary Briefing*, No. 9, Durham: IBRU (1991).

(JPDA) will be shared on a 90:10 basis in favour of the new East Timor state, rather than the present 50:50 split initially provided by the 1989 Timor Gap treaty and continued under the present 2000 MOU.

The 2001 Timor Sea Arrangement is a good example of how environmental considerations have become prioritised in later JDAs. The high level of co-operation engendered by the joint development regime established under the 2001 Arrangement is also manifest with regard to marine environmental protection in the JPDA. Article 10(a) provides that East Timor and Australia shall co-operate to prevent and minimise pollution and *other environmental harm.* (emphasis added) This provision is significant because it appears to acknowledge that environmental damage can occur despite the lack of pollution from petroleum activities in the JPDA.[80] For example, damage to ecosystems such as coral reef during hydrocarbon extraction activities is considered to be environmental damage. However, such damage does not necessarily fall within the meaning of 'pollution of the marine environment' under article 1(1)(4) of the 1982 LOSC. This is defined as 'the introduction by man, directly or indirectly, of substances and energy into the marine environment, including estuaries, which results or is likely to result in such deleterious effects as harm to living resources and marine life, hazards to human health, hindrance to marine activities, including fishing and other legitimate uses of the sea, impairment of quality for use of sea water and reduction of amenities.' Thus, environmental damage caused by petroleum exploration activities on the sea bed would not qualify as marine pollution under this definition as such activities do not necessarily introduce substances or energy into the marine environment.

Article 10(a) also requires the parties to consult as to the best means to protect the JPDA marine environment from the harmful consequences (*i.e.,* not merely pollution) of petroleum activities. Article 10(a) specifies that special efforts are to be made to protect marine wildlife including marine mammals, seabirds, fish and coral. In respect of all these endeavours, the designated Authority shall issue regulations to protect the JPDA marine environment. (art. 10(c)) Should pollution nevertheless occur, the parties shall co-operate in mitigating and eliminating such pollution. (art. 10(b)) Moreover, companies shall be liable for damage as a result of pollution within the JPDA marine environment, with claims allowed to brought in either party's jurisdiction (art. 10(d)(ii)).

---

[80] For more details of the legal relationship between pollution and environmental damage, see: David Ong, 'The Relationship between Environmental Damage and Pollution: Marine Oil Pollution Laws in Malaysia and Singapore', Chapter 10 in M W Bowman & A E Boyle (eds.), *Environmental Damage in International and Comparative Law,* Oxford: OUP (2002) 191–212.

The 1993 *Guinea-Bissau-Senegal* Agreement[81] and its 1995 Protocol[82] provide for a cone-shaped joint exploitation zone extending to either side of the 1960 maritime boundary between the two Parties. They also provide for a joint Agency of Management and Co-operation (AMC) to exploit both the fishery and continental shelf resources of the zone. The resources of the continental shelf shall be shared between the Parties in the following proportions: (Senegal) 85:15 (Guinea-Bissau), subject to the provision that in the event of discovery of additional resources, these proportions shall be reviewed, having regard to the magnitude of such discoveries. (art. 2 of 1993 Agreement). By the 1993 Agreement, the Parties shall pool the exercise of their respective rights, without prejudice to legal titles previously acquired by each of them and confirmed by judicial decisions, and without prejudice to claims previously formulated by them in respect of non-delimited areas. (art. 6)

The Agreement and its Protocol thus establish a joint development arrangement that corresponds with the Model III-type JDA described above. The Agreement entered into force at the same time as the Protocol concerning the establishment and functions of the joint Agency was concluded and the exchange of ratification instruments for both instruments occurred (21 December, 1995). (art. 6) It shall remain in force for a period of twenty years and shall be automatically renewable. (art. 8) The Parties established a joint International Agency (art. 4 of the 1993 Agreement), later renamed the Agency of Management and Co-operation (AMC) by the 1995 Protocol. (art. 2 of 1995 Protocol) The organisation and operation of the Agency was to be the subject of a joint agreement within one year of the signing of the 1993 Agreement. (art. 4) However, the 1995 Protocol was signed more than a year later on 12 June, 1995.

The Agency for Management and Co-operation (AMC) succeeds the Parties with respect to the rights and obligations arising out of agreements concluded by each of them relating to exploitation of the resources of the joint zone. (art. 5 of the 1993 Agreement) The Agency comprises two organs: 1) the Authority made up of the Heads of State, or Government, or persons delegated by them, and the Secretariat of the Agency; (art. 9 of the 1995 Protocol) and 2) the Enterprise, which is the organ through which the Agency shall execute the mission assigned to it under the 1993 Agreement. (arts. 6 & 12 of the Protocol)

---

[81] Full title: 1993 Management and Co-operation Agreement between the Government of the Republic of Senegal and the Government of the Republic of Guinea-Bissau. Adopted: 14.10.1993; in force: 21.12.1995. Source: 31 Law of the Sea (LOS) Bulletin 40 (1996); Charney & Alexander (eds.) Vol.III (1998) 2257–2278.

[82] Full title: 1995 Protocol of the Agreement Relating to the Organization and Operation of the Agency of Management and Co-operation between the Republic of Senegal and the Republic of Guinea-Bissau. Adopted: 12.6.1995; in force: 21.12.1995.

The Authority defines the general policy of the Agency.(art. 10.1) It meets at least once a year to examine and approve the administration and co-operation policies proposed by the Secretary-General. (arts. 9 & 10.2) It has the following functions: (a) providing the Enterprise with guidance as to its performance; (b) upon the recommendation of the Board of Directors, in a manner not incompatible with the aims of the Protocol and Agreement, amending the regulations governing prospecting, exploration, and exploitation of the resources of the area, as well as those governing monitoring and scientific research; (c) supervising the application of the Agreement & Protocol, regulations applicable to the Enterprise and recommending to the Board of Directors (BoD) any necessary modifications; and finally (d)determining and exercising the scope of police powers in the zone. The Authority shall ensure that resource development in the zone is carried out in an optimal manner, in conformity with good mining or oil industry practices and with regard to the marine environment and conservation of fishery resources. (art. 10.5)

The Agency is an international organization with responsibility for managing the resources of the zone, either directly by means of the Enterprise or its subsidiaries, or indirectly through other companies. It is also responsible for promoting co-operation between the Parties. (art. 4) The Agency has general and specific functions in the fields of mineral and petroleum resource development (art. 5(a)) and fisheries (art. 5(b)). Its general functions include the rational exploitation of the zone's resources, co-operation with parties and competent international organizations, safety, and protection of the marine environment. (art. 5(c)) The Agency holds the exclusive title to mineral and oil and fishing rights in the joint zone. It shall act in this connection through the Enterprise. (art. 6)

The Parties shall co-operate with the Agency to prevent or minimise pollution and all other forms of marine environmental degradation from activities in the zone. (art. 23.1) In particular, the Parties shall assist the Agency as may be requested of them under art. 11(4)(m) & (n) of the 1995 Protocol; and when marine pollution in the zone extends, or presents the risk of doing so, the Parties shall co-operate to prevent, reduce and eliminate this pollution. (art. 23.1) Under art. 11, the Agency shall enact regulations to protect the marine environment in the zone. It shall also establish an emergency or management plan for combating pollution or any form of degradation from activities in the zone. (art. 23.2) Companies shall be liable for the damage and expense caused by pollution or any form of degradation resulting from activities in the zone of the marine environment. (art. 23.3) (The term 'companies' is defined in art. 1.15 to mean juridical person(s) with a fishing or hydrocarbon resource development contract, and any other juridical person to which an interest is assigned and may be described as a company under art. 24 on the applicable law.)

The 1993 *Colombia-Jamaica* Maritime Boundary Delimitation Treaty[83] is a hybrid between JDA Models II and III. This Agreement partly delimits an apparently multi-purpose single maritime boundary, presumably incorporating both EEZ and Continental Shelf boundaries between the two Parties.(art. 1) It also establishes a Joint Regime Area (JRA), where pending the determination of the jurisdictional limits of each Party, the designated JRA will be a zone of joint management, control, exploration and exploitation of the living and non-living resources. (art. 3(1)) In the JRA, the parties may carry out the following activities: exploration and exploitation of the natural resources, whether living or non-living, of the waters superjacent to the seabed and the seabed and its subsoil, and other activities for the economic exploration and exploitation of the JRA (art. 3(2)(a)); the establishment and use of artificial islands, installations and structures (art. 3(2)(b)); marine scientific research (art. 3(2)(c)); the protection and preservation of the marine environment (art. 3(2)(d)); the conservation of living resources (art. 3(2)(e)); and such measures as are authorized by this Treaty, or as the Parties may otherwise agree for ensuring compliance with and enforcement of the regime established by this Treaty.(art. 3(2)(f)) In the JRA, each party has jurisdiction over its nationals and vessels flying its flag over which it exercises management and control in accordance with international law. (art. 2(5))

Activities relating to exploration and exploitation of non-living resources, as well as marine scientific research and the protection and preservation of the marine environment will be carried out on a joint basis agreed by both Parties. (art. 3(3)) Towards these ends, the Parties have agreed to establish a Joint Commission (JC) which shall elaborate the modalities for the implementation and carrying out of the activities set out in art. 3(2), the measures adopted pursuant to art. 3(6), and any other functions which may be assigned to it by the Parties for the purpose of implementing the Treaty provisions. The modalities for the implementation of the task of protection and preservation of the JRA marine environment are to be elaborated by the Joint Commission (art. 4(1)), and carried out by the Parties.(art. 3(2)(d))

By the 1995 *Argentina–UK* Joint Declaration,[84] the two Governments agreed to co-operate in order to encourage offshore activities in the South West Atlantic. Exploration and exploitation of hydrocarbons by the offshore oil and gas industry will be carried out in accordance with sound commercial principles and good oilfield practice, drawing upon the Governments'

---

[83] Full title: Maritime Delimitation Treaty between Jamaica and the Republic of Colombia, 1993. Signed: 12.11.1993; entered into force: 14.3.1994. Source: 26 LOS Bulletin 50 (1994); Also see: Charney & Alexander (eds.), *op. cit.*, Vol. III (1998) 2179–2204.

[84] Full title: UK-Argentina Joint Declaration on Co-operation over Offshore Activities in the South West Atlantic. Adopted: 27.9.1995. Source: 35 ILM 301 (1996) See also: *International Journal of Marine & Coastal Law*, Vol.11, No. 1 (1996) 113–8. It is unlikely that this Declaration is to be considered as a legally binding treaty instrument between the two states concerned.

experience in both the South West Atlantic and in the North Sea.[85] (para.2) In this sense, the present Declaration paves the way for the possible further agreement and implementation of a unitization arrangement based on the second Joint Development model.

Co-operation has been furthered by the establishment of a Joint Commission (para. 2(a)) and by means of co-ordinated activities in up to 6 tranches, each about 3,500 sq. km. (para. 2(b)) The number of tranches have been reduced to 4 as a result of the latest technical advice on the basis of the geological data obtained so far. The Joint Commission is essentially facilitative in function, akin to that established by the 1974 Japan-South Korean agreement.[86] It does not have supranational authority nor juridical personality like the Joint Authorities established by a couple of other bilateral Model III type JDAs, such as those between Malaysia-Thailand (1979/1990)[87] and Indonesia-Australia (1989).[88] The Joint Commission (JC) has the following functions, *inter alia,* co-ordinate activities in the 6 (now 4) tranches which are designated as a Special Co-operation Area (SCA) (para.4(b)), and promote the development of hydrocarbon resources in the South West Atlantic maritime areas. (para.4(c))

Provisional agreement has been reached that petroleum companies licensed in the Special Co-operation Area (SCA) will operate on a joint venture basis, with one half of the joint venture licensed by the Falkland Islands Government (FIG) and the other half by Argentina. It is envisaged that companies will operate in the Special Co-operation Area (SCA) on the basis of an unincorporated joint venture with 50% licensed by the Falkland Islands Government (FIG) to companies incorporated under UK company law and 50% by Argentina to Argentinean-based companies.[89] These licences will be issued on a parallel basis with common bid assessment procedures and similar conditions on such issues as, *inter alia,* health and safety, *environmental protection* (emphasis added) and taxation.

Apart from its functions in relation to petroleum development activities in the designated Area of Special Co-operation, the JC also submits to both Governments recommendations and proposed standards for the protection of the marine environment of the South West Atlantic, taking into account relevant international conventions and recommendations of competent international organisations (para. 4(a)) The two Governments also agreed to co-operate throughout the different stages of offshore activities undertaken by commercial operators, including the regime for the eventual abandonment of installations.

---

[85] See: the Norway-UK Frigg and Murchison Fields and Netherlands-UK Markham Field Agreements, respectively, *op. cit.*
[86] See: 1974 Japan-Korea Agreement, *op. cit.*
[87] See: 1979 Malaysia-Thailand MOU and 1990 Agreement, *op. cit.*
[88] See: 1989 Australia-Indonesia Timor Gap treaty, *op. cit.*
[89] This information was obtained from UK FCO sources on Chatham House rules basis.

(para. 7) This Joint Declaration is therefore possibly the only JDA so far that explicitly provides for regulation of the decommissioning process, presumably covering the environmental implications of abandonment or disposal of offshore installations or platforms. It is therefore yet another indication of the application of the integration principle through the inclusion of environmental considerations for the full life-cycle of offshore platforms installed within the SCA.

The 2001 *Nigeria-Sao Tome* Treaty,[90] is another one of the new breed of Model-III type JDA. It has the following important provisions for marine environmental protection from any activities undertaken within the Joint Development Zone designated under this agreement. First, art. 30(1) requires the Authority, acting either itself or through a national body or third party, to inspect petroleum activities, related installations and pipelines situated in the designated Zone. Under Article 30(5), unless otherwise directed, the inspectors referred to in paragraph 1 may order the immediate cessation of any or all petroleum operations in the Zone if such a course appears necessary or expedient:

(a) for the purpose of avoiding an accident involving loss of life or danger to life:
(b) for the purpose of avoiding actual or threatened damage;
(c) to protect the coastline or other maritime interests of either State Party, including fishing interests, against actual or potential pollution;
(d) due to *force major* distress or an emergency which may give rise to reasonable fears of major harmful consequences; or
(e) to minimise the consequences of such a casualty or accident

Secondly, Article 38 provides for the prevention of pollution and marine environmental protection. Here, the Authority shall take all reasonable steps to ensure that development activities in the Zone do not cause or create any appreciable risk of causing pollution or other harm to the marine environment. (Art. 38.1) In accordance with paragraph 1, the States Parties on the recommendation of the Authority shall agree necessary measures and procedures to prevent and remedy pollution of the marine environment resulting from development activities in the Zone. (Art. 38.2) In order to facilitate the effective monitoring of the environmental impact of petroleum activities in the Zone both States Parties shall regularly provide the Authority with such relevant information as they obtain from contractors or inspectors concerning levels of petroleum discharge and contamination. (Art. 38.3) In particular the States Parties shall immediately inform the Authority of the occurrence of the following events:

---

[90] Full title: Treaty between the Federal Republic of Nigeria and The Democratic Republic of São Tome e Principe on the Joint Development of Petroleum and other Resources, in respect of Areas of the Exclusive Economic Zone of the two States. Adopted at at Abuja the 21st day of February 2001. Unpublished. Copy of text on file with the author.

    (a) any petroleum spillage or event likely to cause pollution and requiring remedial measures beyond the capacity of the operator;
    (b) discharge into the sea of large quantities of petroleum from an installation or pipeline:
    (c) collisions at sea involving damage to an installation or pipeline;
    (d) evacuation of personnel from an installation due to *force majeure*, distress or other emergency.

Such notification shall include any measures taken or proposed with respect to such events.

Finally, it is provided that nothing in this Treaty shall prejudice the taking or enforcement by each State Party or by the States Parties jointly of measures in the Zone proportionate to the actual or threatened damage to protect their coastline or exclusive maritime areas from pollution or threat of pollution which may reasonably be expected to result in major harmful consequences. (Art. 38.4)

On 4 June 2001, a *Cambodia-Thailand* Memorandum of Understanding (MOU) was adopted regarding 'the Area of their Overlapping Maritime Claims to the Continental Shelf'[91] in the Gulf of Thailand. The 2001 MOU purports to resolve a three-decade long dispute involving overlapping continental shelf claims between these two countries in the Gulf of Thailand. The proposed resolution includes the negotiation of a traditional maritime boundary delimitation of the territorial sea, continental shelf and exclusive economic zone in the northern part of the overlapping claims area, called the Area to be Delimited (Art.2(b)) and a more co-operative solution in the form of a Joint Development Treaty in the southern part of this area, called the Joint Development Area. (Art.2(a)) To this end, the MOU has established an institutional framework consisting of a Joint Technical Committee to draw up the agreed terms for both the joint development and maritime boundary delimitation treaties. (Art.3(a) & (b)) The proposed Joint Development Treaty will include a mutually acceptable basis for sharing the costs and benefits of any hydrocarbon resource exploitation in the Area. (Art.3(a))

The 2001 MOU itself does not provide for environmental protection within the Area, presumably leaving this issue to be negotiated by the two Parties in the forthcoming Joint Development Treaty. Moreover, the regular meetings of the Joint Technical Committee should provide a suitable bilateral forum to address any environmental concerns arising from activities taking place in the Area. (Art.4)

Finally, we should note the proposed inclusion of environmental protection provisions within the British Institute's proposed Model Joint Development Agreement as further evidence of recognition of the progressive integration of

---

[91] Unpublished. Copy on file with author.

environmental considerations within the international legal regime for joint development.[92] Article 21(1) of the Model Agreement provides for States Parties to use all reasonable efforts to ensure that the petroleum activities in the Joint Development Zone,[93] including installations and pipelines, shall not cause nor be likely to cause marine environmental pollution. However, as the British Institute's research team notes, there is no generally accepted 'pollution' definition,[94] so it is important to note that this definition is a progressively modified version of that which was proposed by the Group of Experts on Scientific Aspects of Marine Pollution (GESAMP) in 1969.[95] 'Pollution' is defined in Article 1(15) of the revised Model Agreement as the introduction by petroleum activities of substances or energy into the marine environment which results or is likely to result in such deleterious effects as harm to living resources and marine life, hazards to human health, impairment of sea water quality and reduction of amenities. It is important to note that this definition effectively mirrors that which was adopted by State parties at UNCLOS III (1973-1982) and is now included in Article 1(1)(4) of the 1982 UNCLOS. By including petroleum activities that 'may' or are 'likely' to cause pollution this definition also goes further than the *UK-Norway* 1976 Frigg Field Agreement, for example, which includes only those activities that necessarily result in marine environmental pollution.

Institutionally, under the Model Agreement the Joint Commission is to be given a mandate to recommend that State Parties agree necessary measures to 'prevent and remove' any marine environmental pollution. This obligation appears to be more stringent than the 'prevent, reduce and control' norm in Part XII of the 1982 UNCLOS. Such measures must also be based on good oilfield practice and international standards embodied in UNEP and IMO instruments.[96] These *a priori* measures are supplemented by *ex-post facto* requirements. For example, in the unfortunate event of a pollution incident

---

[92] See: Article 21 of the Model (Joint Development) Agreement in Fox *et al* (1989) *op. cit.*, 409–10, with commentary in Chapter 15, 355–75. For the revised version of this Model Agreement resulting from an extensive consultation process, see: Article 21 in Fox (ed.) (1990) *op. cit.*, at 18–19, and Birnie in Fox (ed.) (1990) *op. cit.*

[93] As defined in Article 2 of the revised Model (Joint Development) Agreement in Fox (ed.) (1990) *ibid.*, at 5.

[94] See: Fox *et al* (1989) *op. cit.*, at 363.

[95] In fact, as Yturriaga notes, the definition of 'marine pollution' adopted in the 1982 UNCLOS differs in three material aspects from the GESAMP definition: (a) pollution can be caused not only by the introduction of substances or energy into the marine environment in a way that results in deleterious effects but also when it is 'likely to result' in such effects; (b) hindrance to marine activities includes, in addition to fishing, 'other legitimate uses of the sea'; and finally, (c) the harm envisaged refers both to 'living resources' and 'marine life' generally. See de Yturriaga, 'Regional Conventions on the Protection of the Environment' (1979) *Recueil des Cours* I, 323 at 332.

[96] See: Art. 21(2)(b) of the Model Agreement.

occurring, contingency plans must be established[97] and recourse to both Parties' legal systems for prompt and adequate compensation in respect of pollution damage must be ensured.[98] This reflects and extends the provision in the *Japan-Korea* agreement enabling nationals from the two State Parties, as well as third party nationals, to sue in the courts of either Party.[99] Effective monitoring of petroleum activities is facilitated by provision of reporting requirements of both Parties to the Joint Commission.[100]

7. Conclusions

As noted in the Introduction, there is a clear trend that runs in parallel to the increasing level of institutional provision within the later JDAs, especially those that are Model III JDAs. This trend is for environmental provisions to be increasingly manifest in these more recent JDAs as well. An obvious explanation for this trend is that it reflects growing public consciousness of environmental protection issues generally and marine oil pollution issues in particular. Hence the need to include environmental considerations within the negotiation, adoption, and implementation of more recent JDAs.

Aside from this general trend towards the inclusion of environmental considerations within JDAs, several other more specific characteristics of these provisions can also be observed. First, conceptual advances in what constitutes 'environmental protection' are now reflected in such provisions within JDAs. These include: protecting ecosystem integrity as opposed to merely preventing pollution from joint development activities[101] and recognising that environmental damage does not necessarily only occur as a result of pollution.[102]

Second, environmental protection provisions within JDAs now also extend to apply to the entire life-cycle of the joint petroleum development activities. The 1989 Timor Gap treaty, for example, contains requirements to consider or include environmental concerns in many of its operative decisions. This emphasis on the inclusion of environmental considerations within every aspect of offshore petroleum activities now specifically includes the final, abandonment or decommissioning phase of any such activity.[103]

Third, more recent JDAs increasingly establish sophisticated legal and

---

[97] Art. 21(2)(cc), *ibid.*
[98] Art. 21(2)(d), *ibid.*
[99] Art. XXI(1) of the 1974 Japan-Korea Agreement, *op. cit.*
[100] Art. 21(3) of the Model Agreement.
[101] See art. 7 of the 1974 France-Spain Bay of Biscay JDA, *op. cit.*
[102] See art.10(a) of the proposed 2001 Timor Sea Arrangement, *op. cit.*
[103] See, for example, the 1995 *Argentina-UK* Declaration which provides for environmental protection even in the abandonment/decommissioning phase, as opposed to the 1976 *Norway-UK* Frigg Field Agreement that does not.

institutional frameworks for joint exploitation of resources and many other wide-ranging functions including, *inter alia,* environmental protection within the designated joint development zone or transboundary unitization field. This is particularly true of many of the Model III type JDAs that are characterised by the establishment of Joint Commissions/Authorities with powers to provide for environmental protection. This allows for increased flexibility and adaptability of these measures to take into account the different types of environmental threats and conditions under which joint development is undertaken. In the long run, such qualities may prove to be more effective at ensuring overall environmental protection from joint development activities.

Finally, we should note the apparently trite but nonetheless important observation that simply by agreeing to negotiate, adopt and implement bilateral joint development agreements, States are taking steps to avoid ultimately wasteful and potentially environmentally hazardous unilateral action over common hydrocarbon deposits. Thus, the practice of joint development itself can be seen as environmentally responsible behaviour by the interested States concerned, notwithstanding the provision, or otherwise, of adequate environmental protection measures within such joint development agreements.

JOSEPH W. DELLAPENNA

The Customary International Law of Transboundary Fresh Waters

1. Introduction

Water is one of the most important of the resources necessary for human survival and thriving, yet the resource is under increasing stress because of the growth of human populations and changing patterns of use by those populations.[1] All 264 of the world's largest water river basins – home to about 40 percent of the world's population – are shared by more than one nation.[2] This reality requires mechanisms for the cooperative waters if water is

---

[1] See generally Hillel, D. (1994) *Rivers of Eden: The Struggle for Water and the Quest for Peace in the Middle East* 20–23, 28–37; McDonald, A. and Kay, D. (1988) *Water Resources: Issue and Strategies*; Petts, G. (1984) *Impounded Rivers: Perspectives for Ecological Management*; Powledge, F. (1982) Water 12–39; Dellapenna, J. (1997) 'Population and water in the Middle East: The challenge and opportunity for law', *Int. J. Envt. and Pollution*, Vol. 7, 72–110.

[2] Aaron Wolf, 'Conflict and cooperation along international waterways', *Water Policy* Vol. 1, 251–65, 251–52 (1998).

M. Fitzmaurice and M. Szuniewicz (eds.), Exploitation of Natural Resources in the 21st Century, 143–190.
© *2003 Kluwer Law International. Printed in Great Britain.*

not to become a major problem for each nation's security.[3] This in turn requires the creation of legal structures to govern interstate cooperation.[4] Without such a structure, competition over water could eventually lead to serious conflict.

This chapter surveys the evolving body of customary international law as a vehicle for addressing the need for cooperative management of internationally shared fresh water resources, beginning with a discussion of the sources (and nature) of customary international law generally. There follows an analysis of the customary international law of internationally shared fresh water resources and of the recent efforts of the United Nations to codify that body of customary law. The chapter closes with a discussion of the proposal to redraft the'Helsinki Rules' of the International Law Association[5] in light of all the changes in the customary law in the 31 years since the Helsinki Rules were first approved.

2. Sources of customary international law

The international legal system viewed as a whole lacks the superstructure of specialized institutions – executive, legislative, judicial, and administrative – found in modern national legal systems. But to conclude from these omissions that international law is not really law is to confuse particular institutional arrangements with what law really is and how it really operates. Similar institutions, useful and necessary as they have proven to be in large communities, might yet develop in the international system. The absence of those institutions no more indicates an absence of law in the international system than the absence of those institutions indicated the lack of law in pre-industrial societies the world over.[6] The international system's less formal processes similarly are law and must be examined carefully to learn both its capabilities and its limitations.

The *Statute of the International Court of Justice* lists four sources of international law for the Court to apply: conventions; custom; general principles of law; and the writings of the 'most highly qualified publicists' for evidence of what the

---

[3] Westing, A.H. (editor) *Global Resources and International Conflict*; Kukk, C. and Deese, D. (1996) 'At the water's edge: regional conflict and cooperation over fresh water', *UCLA J. Int. L. and For. Aff.*, Vol. 1 21–64.

[4] Dellapenna, ref. 1, 89–91.

[5] International L. Assoc., *The Helsinki Rules on the uses of the waters of international rivers* (Rep. of the 52d Conf., Helsinki 1966) ('Helsinki Rules').

[6] Barkun, M. (1968) *Law without Sanctions*; Bohannan, P. (1957) *Justice and Judgement among the Tiv*; Hooker, M.B. (1978) *Adat Law in Modern Indonesia*; Li, V. (1978) *Law without Lawyers*; Nader, L. (1990) *Harmony Ideology: Justice and Control in a Zapotec Mountain Village*; Starr, J. (1978) *Dispute and Settlement in Rural Turkey: An Ethnography of Law*.

law is, as opposed to what they think the law should be.[7] Of these, only conventions (treaties) have the high degree of formality and the sort of definite content – at least in the verbal sense – that one finds in legislation or even in caselaw in highly developed legal system. And even conventions do not bind a participating state without its specific consent, in sharp contrast with what individual members of a national polity can expect when the state authorities have spoken.

There are today literally hundreds of bilateral or regional treaties regarding the cooperative management of shared waters.[8] None of these treaties has achieved such wide adherence that it could be said to lay down the law of internationally shared fresh waters generally. There is a movement today towards the codification of the customary international law regarding non-navigational uses of international watercourses in a general convention.[9] As we shall see, this convention has a long ways to go to gain the sort of general acceptance that could lead to its elevation as the governing law between states generally. Instead, one must turn to customary international law for the general rules applicable to such problems.[10]

Customary international law is more complex and uncertain than formal agreements such as treaties or conventions. Customary international law consists of the practices of states undertaken out of a sense of legal obligation, that is out of a sense that the practice is required by law (*opinio juris sive necessitatus*, often referred to as simply *opinio juris*).[11] If these two elements

[7] Statute of the Int'l Ct. of Justice, art. 38.

[8] The treaties are collected in UN Doc. A/CN.4/283, (1974) *Y.B. Int. L. Comm'n*, Vol. 2, 33–264. See also Burchi, S. (editor) (1993) 'Treaties concerning the non-navigational uses of international watercourses – Europe', FAO Legislative Study no. 50; Christy, L. (editor) (1993) 'Treaties concerning the non-navigational uses of international watercourses – Africa', FAO Legislative Study no. 61; United Nations (1964) Legislative Texts and Treaty Provisions Concerning the Utilization of International Rivers for Other Purposes than Navigation, ST/LEG/SER.B/12 ('Legislative Texts'); Dellapenna, J. (1994) 'Treaties as instruments for managing internationally-shared water resources: restricted sovereignty vs. community of property', *Case-W. Res. J. Int. and Comp. L.*, Vol. 26, 27–56; McCaffrey, S. (1986) 'Second report on the law of non-navigational uses of international watercourses', UN Doc. A/CN.4/399, [1986] *Y.B. Int. L. Comm'n.*, Vol. II, pt. 2, 87–144, at 134–38; Schwebel, S. (1982) 'Third report on the law of non-navigational uses of international watercourses', UN Doc. A/CN.4/348, [1982] *Y.B. Int. L. Comm'n*, Vol. 2, pt. 2, 65–197, at 76–82, 88–90.

[9] UN Convention on the law of non-navigational uses of international watercourses, approved May 21, UN Doc. No. A/51/869, reprinted in *Int. Legal Materials* vol. 36, 700–20 ('UN Convention').

[10] International Court of Justice (1998), The Gabcíkovo-Nagymoros Case (Hungary v. Slovakia), 1997 ICJ No. 92 reprinted in *Int Legal Materials* vol. 37, 162-242.

[11] The North Sea Continental Shelf (Federal Rep. of Germany v. Denmark and Netherlands), [1969] *ICJ* 3, 44; The SS Lotus (France v. Turkey), [1927] *PCIJ*, Ser. A, no. 10, at 18, 28. See generally Brierly, J.L. (Waldock, H. editor) (1963) *The Law of Nations*, 52, 59–60; Brownlie, I. (1990) *Principles of Public International Law*, 4th ed. 4–11; D'Amato,

combine, law results regardless of how long – or how briefly – the practice has continued.[12] As with treaties, the operative theory on which the binding effect of the customary rule depends is that a state has consented to the rule.[13]

Customary international law (special or general) develops through a process of claim and counterclaim between states.[14] When one state undertakes an action that affects other states, those other states will either acquiesce in the action or take steps to oppose it, usually first by employing rhetorical strategies. If the matter is important enough to the objecting state, it eventually will escalate its opposition by imposing a variety of sanctions up to the possibility of military operations. Regardless of which state prevails, over a period of time a pattern of practice will emerge that describes how states behave and allows one to predict how states will behave. If nothing more were involved, one might well question whether we were talking about anything that could properly be termed law. Beginning with the simplest rhetorical strategies, however, and continuing right through to outright war, states on both sides of a controversy will refer to international law as a primary justification of their claims and their practices.[15]

Diplomats know very well the difference between appeals to law, appeals to morality, and appeals to expedience. They often express these differences at

cont.

A. (1971) *The Concept of Custom in International Law*, 1–10; Danilenko, G.M. (1993) *Law-Making in the International Community*, 75–77, 81–82; Henkin, L. (1995) *International Law: Politics and Values*, student ed., 29–37; Lauterpacht, H. (1958) *The Development of International Law by the International Court*, 368–93; Restatement (Third) of Foreign Relations Law of the United States § 102(2) (Henkin, L., Lowenfeld, A. and Vagts, D. reporters. 1987) ('Restatement Third'); Shaw, M. (1991) *International Law*, 3rd ed., 60–76; Tunkin, G.I. (Butler, W. translator) (1974) *Theory of International Law*, 89–203; Verzijl, J.H.W. (1968) *International Law in Historical Perspective*, 31–47; Wolfke, K. (1993) *Custom in Present International Law*, 2nd rev. ed., 1–51, 58–64, 66–67, 96–98; Condorelli, L. (1991) 'Custom', in Bedjaoui, M. (editor) *International Law: Achievements and Prospects*, 179–211 ('Achievements and Prospects').

[12] The North Sea Continental Shelf (Federal Rep. of Germany v. Denmark and Netherlands), [1969] *ICJ* 3, 43; Asylum (Colombia v. Peru), [1950] *ICJ* 266, 276–77; D'Amato, ref. 11, 56–58; Danilenko, ref. 11, 77–81; Wolfke, ref. 11, 59–60.

[13] The SS Lotus (France v. Turkey), [1927] *PCIJ* Ser. A, no. 10, at p.18 ('The rules of law binding upon States ... emanates from their own free will.'). See also Wolfke, ref. 11, 50, 160–67.

[14] De Visscher, C. (1961) *Theory and Reality in International Law*, 3rd ed.; Wolfke, ref. 11, 56–58; Chinkin, C. and Sadurska, R. (1991) 'The anatomy of international dispute resolution', *Ohio St. J. Dispute Resol.*, Vol. 7, 39–81, at 70–74; McDougal, M. and Schlei, N. (1955) 'The Hydrogen bomb test in perspective: lawful measures for security', *Yale L.J.*, Vol. 64, 648–710.

[15] Higgins, R. (1963) *The Development of International Law through the Political Organs of the United Nations* ('Higgins, Political Organs'); Higgins, R. (1970) 'The place of international law in the settlement of disputes by the Security Council', *Am. J. Int. L.*, Vol. 64, 1–18. See also Hart, H.L.A. (1961) *The Concept of Law*, 222–25; Levi, W. (1991) *Contemporary International Law: A Concise Introduction*, 2nd ed., 21.

appropriate points in their statements and assertions, whether speaking generally or in the course of a dispute with another nation. References to law connect a customary practice to a sense of legitimacy, and thus constitutes the practice as law in the highly decentralized and institutionally undeveloped system of international law. The same is just as true for customary law among subsistence farmers or nomadic tribesmen.

The changing structure of the international community that creates and effectuates international law complicates the picture of customary international law. Until recently, international law governed a relatively small and largely structureless society of states, a society in which other sorts of actors did not have a recognized status. The United Nations, an organization that has grown from 51 at its founding in 1945 to nearly 200 now, as well as other international organizations, certainly count as full players ('legal persons') in the international legal system today.[16] Rapidly proliferating non-governmental and other official and semiofficial participants are also now playing a distinct, albeit thus far a subordinate, role.[17] Even natural and artificial persons (people and corporations) are now recognized to a growing extent as participants in the international legal community.[18] As a result, the

---

[16] Advisory Opinion on Reparations for Injuries Suffered in the Service of the United Nations, [1949] ICJ 174. See generally Bekker, P. (1994) *The Legal Position of Intergovernmental Organizations: A Functional Necessity Analysis of Their Legal Status and Immunities*; Brownlie, ref. 11, 63–64, 679–89, 694–98; Restatement (Third), ref. 11, § 219); Bedjaoui, M. (1991) 'Introduction to Subjects of International Law', in Bedjaoui, M. (editor) *International Law: Achievements and Prospects*, 1–18, 23 ('Achievements and Prospects'); Schermers, H. (1991) 'International Organizations', *Achievements and Prospects*, 67–100.

[17] Yoder, A. (1992) *The Evolution of the United Nations System*, 2nd ed., 35–36; Cohen, C.P. (1990) 'The role of non-governmental organizations in the drafting of the covenant of the rights of the child', *Hum. Rts. Q.*, Vol. 12, 137–55; Manno, J. (1993) 'Advocacy and diplomacy in the Great Lakes: a case history of non-governmental-organization participation in negotiating the Great Lakes Water Quality Agreement', *Buff. Envtl. L.J.*, Vol. 1, 1–61; Sands, P. and Bedecarré, A. (1990) 'The convention on international trade in endangered species: the role of public interest non-governmental organizations in ensuring the effective enforcement of the ivory trade ban', *B.C. Envtl. Aff. L. Rev.*, Vol. 17, 799–882; Shelton, D. (1994) 'The participation of non-governmental organizations in international judicial proceedings', *Am. J. Int. L.*, Vol. 88, 611–42; Tolbert, D. (1991) 'Global climate change and the role of international non-governmental organisations', in Churchill, R. and Freestone, D. (editors) *International Law and Global Climate Change*, 95–108; Trubek, D. et al. (1994) 'Global restructuring and the law: studies of the internationalization of legal fields and the creation of transnational arenas', *Case-W. Res. L. Rev.*, Vol. 44, 407–98, 474, 489–93. The awkward phrase 'non-governmental organizations' (NGO's) persists because it is the term used in the United Nations Charter. UN Charter, art. 71.

[18] Danzig Railway Officials (Poland v. Danzig), [1928] *PCIJ*, Series B, no. 15, digested in *Int. L. Rep.* Vol. 4, 287–92. See generally Brownlie, ref. 11, 67–69, 553–602; Restatement (Third), ref. 11, §§ 701–03; Seidl-Hohenveldern, I. (1991) *Corporations in and under International Law* (1987); Shaw, ref. 11, 178–81; Cassese, A. (1991) 'Individuals', in *Achievements and Prospects*, ref. 11, 113–20; Rigaux, F. (1991) 'Transnational corporations', *Achievements and Prospects*, supra at 121–32; Sohn, L. (1982) 'The new international law: protection of the rights of individuals rather than states', *Am. U. L. Rev.*, Vol. 32, 1–64.

international legal system in the last 50 years evolved from the relatively simple structure of the past to an increasingly diverse and complex community of actors who too often no longer know much about each other. This growing community furthermore reflects more sharply differentiated cultural traditions than the smaller community from before World War II.

Such a transformation is precisely the situation in which one would predict that the participants would welcome the emergence of more specialized and more formal legal structures.[19] And, on a regional level this appears to be happening (consider, for example, the Association of Southeast Asian States, the European Union, or the North American Free Trade Association).[20] This is even true on a global scale for specialized forms of activity (consider, for example, the International Atomic Energy Agency, the International Civil Aviation Organization, and the newly created World Trade Organization).[21] Still, in large measure, the international legal system remains institutionally underdeveloped and decentralized.[22] Thus even for non-state actors, customary international law remains central.

Despite its diffuse nature with a consequent vagueness and instability, customary international law has worked satisfactorily when there are only a few participants in a particular international process (a regional or special custom) or when a general customary international rule operates without major controversy.[23] A special custom, binding only a few states (usually in a particular region), binds only those states that can be shown to have actually consented to the custom. A general custom, which is deemed to bind all states, is presumed to bind a state unless the state can show that it has consistently resisted (or objected to) the custom.[24]

---

[19] De Visscher, C., ref. 14, 161–62.

[20] Bowett, D. (1982) *The Law of International Institutions*, 4th ed., 199–248; Merrills, J.G. (1991) *International Dispute Settlement*, 2nd ed., 207–29; Shaw, ref. 11, 127–28, 762–71.

[21] Bowett, ref. 20; Shaw, ref. 11, 742–61, 771–82.

[22] See, e.g., Handl, G. (1997) 'Compliance control mechanisms and international environmental obligations', *Tulane J. Int. and Comp. L.*, Vol. 5, 29–49.

[23] Henkin, L. (1979) *How Nations Behave: Law and Foreign Policy*, 2nd ed., 25–26, 47, 89–98, 320–21; Brownlie, I. (1981) 'The reality and efficacy of international law', *Brit. Y.B. Int. L.*, Vol.52, 1–8.

[24] The Right of Passage over Indian Territory (Portugal v. India), [1960] *ICJ* 6, 39–43; U.S. Nationals in Morocco (France v. United States), [1952] *ICJ* 21, 199–200; The Fisheries Case (United Kingdom v. Norway), [1951] *ICJ* 116, 131; The Right of Asylum Case (Colombia v. Peru), [1950] *ICJ* 266, 268–269, 276–278; Brownlie, ref. 11, 5–6, 9–11; D'Amato, ref. 11, p.223; Danilenko, ref. 11, 109–13; Restatement (Third), ref. 11, § 102 comments c, d; Shaw, ref. 11, 76–79; Wolfke, ref. 11, 58–61, 66–67, 86–90, 160–68; Charney, J. (1986) 'The persistent objector rule and the development of customary international law', *Brit. Y.B. Int. L.*, Vol. 56, 1–24; Colson, D. (1986) 'How persistent must the persistent objector be?', *Wash. L. Rev.*, Vol. 81, 957–70; Condorelli, ref. 11, 202–07; Loschin, L. (1986) 'The persistent objector and customary human rights law: a proposed analytical framework', *U.C. Davis J. Int. L. and Pol'y*, Vol. 2, 147–72; Stein, T. (1985) 'The approach of a different drummer: the

The process of determining customary international law is not elegant.[25] In determining what customary international law actually is, diplomats, international tribunals, lawyers, and scholars must examine a wide variety of sources of state practice; finding evidence regarding the reasons for the practice is more challenging.[26] Decisions by international courts or international arbitrators are useful for determining whether a practice has become a rule of customary law.[27] A widespread pattern of treaties or other international agreements has been used to demonstrate that a practice is so widely followed that it has become a rule of customary law binding even on states that are not parties to such treaties.[28] Under some circumstances, even an unratified treaty might be indicative of customary law.[29] General Assembly resolutions, as well as similar resolutions of other international organizations, have been taken as strong evidence that states consider a particular rule to be a legal obligation, leaving one only to determine whether state practice actually is consistent with

cont.

principle of the persistent objector in international law', *Harv. Int. L.J.*, Vol. 26, 457–82; Weil, P. (1983) 'Toward a relative normativity in international law?', *Am. J. Int. L.*, Vol. 77, 413–42, at 433–38.

[25] Janis, M. (1993) An Introduction to International Law, 2nd ed., 52–54. See also Condorelli, ref. 11, 181–83.

[26] Brierly, ref. 11, 60–62; Brownlie, ref. 11, 5, 11, 24; Danilenko, ref. 11, 82–128; Levi, ref. 15, 36–38; Wolfke, ref. 11, 8–29, 67–85, 116–159; Condorelli, ref. 11, 187–92.

[27] Brownlie, ref. 11, 19–24; Lauterpacht, ref. 11, 1–25; Rosenne, S. (1985) The Law and Practice of the International Court, 2nd ed., 611–14, 616–19; Shaw, ref. 11, 678–80.

[28] The North Sea Continental Shelf (Federal Rep. of Germany v. Denmark and Netherlands), [1969] *ICJ* 3, 31, 42–43; The Wimbledon (United Kingdom, France, Italy and Japan v. Germany), [1923] *PCIJ*, ser. A, no. 1, at p.25, digested in *Int. L. Rep.* Vol. 2, 99–102; The Panevezys-Saldutiskis Ry. (Estonia v. Lithuania), [1939] *PCIJ*, ser. A/B, no. 76, at 51–52; The Pacquett Habana, 175 U.S. 677, 687–88 (1900). See Brownlie, ref. 11, 3–4, 11–14, 180–181, 201, 214–17, 604; D'Amato, ref. 11, 103–66; Danilenko, ref. 11, 156–72; McNair, A.D. (1961) *The Law of Treaties*, 2nd ed., 216–18; Restatement (Third), ref. 11, § 102 comment f; Shaw, ref. 8, 81–82; Wolf, ref. 11, 68–72; Charney, J. (1986) 'International agreements and the development of customary international law', *Wash. L. Rev.*, Vol. 81, 971–96; Kishoiyian, B. (1994) 'The utility of bilateral investment treaties in the formulation of customary international law', *Nw. J. Int. L. and Bus.*, Vol. 14, 327–75; McCaffrey, S. (1991) 'The restatement's treatment of sources and evidence of international law', *Int. Lawyer*, Vol. 25, 311–30, at 319–21; Tunkin, G. (1993) 'Is general international law customary law only?', *Eur. J. Int. L.*, Vol. 4, 534–41; Weil, ref. 24, 434–35, 438–40; Weisburg, A. (1988) 'Customary international law: the problem of treaties', *Vand. J. Transnat'l L.*, Vol. 21, 1–46.

[29] Delimitation of the Continental Shelf Boundary (Libya v. Malta), [1985] *ICJ* 13, 29–34; The Gulf of Maine (Canada v. United States), [1984] *ICJ* 246, 294–95 (merits); Fisheries Jurisdiction (United Kingdom v. Iceland), [1973] *ICJ* 3, 18; Advisory Opinion on the Status of Namibia, [1971] *ICJ* 16, 47. See generally Brownlie, ref. 11, 181, 201-02, 217, 232; Lee, L. (1983) 'The law of the sea convention and third states', *Am. J. Int. L.*, Vol. 77, 541–68; Sinclair, I. (1986) 'The Impact of the Unratified Convention', in Bos, A. and Siblesz, H. (editors) *Realism in Law-Making* 211–29; Sohn, L. 'Unratified treaties as a source of customary international law', in Bos and Siblesz, supra at 231–46; Weil, ref. 24, 435–38.

this *opinio juris*.[30] Even unilateral acts of states can demonstrate that the particular state embraces a particular customary rule of law.[31]

Identifying when a practice has crystallized as customary law, turning as it does on a question of motive, any examination of the primary evidence for a customary rule is often inconclusive. The international legal system therefore sometimes will turn to the leading scholars of international law (the 'most highly qualified publicists') for evidence regarding the presence or absence of the necessary *opinio juris*.[32] This approach does not authorize such scholars to create law according to their notions of what the law ought to be, although this can be a fine distinction to say the least.

As the foregoing suggests, often the inquiry into customary international law leaves gaps and ambiguities. Treaties and other international agreements only sometimes fill the gaps or clarify the ambiguities in customary international law. International decision-makers sometimes fill in gaps or clarify ambiguities through recourse to 'general principles of law' – principles of law found in most or all national legal systems in their internal operation.[33]

---

[30] Military and Paramilitary Activities in Nicaragua (Nicaragua v. United States), [1986] *ICJ* 14, 99–100; Advisory Opinion on the Western Sahara, [1975] *ICJ* 12, 31–37; UN GA Res. 3232, 32d Sess., Preamble (Nov. 12, 1974). See generally Brownlie, ref. 11, 14–15, 30–31, 698–700; Bokor-Szegö, H. (1978) *The Role of the United Nations in International Legislation*; Bowett, ref. 20, 41–51; Castaneda, J. (1969) *Legal Effects of United Nations Resolutions*; Elias, T.O. (1972) *Africa and the Development of International Law*, 71–75; di Qual, L. (1967) *Les effect des résolutions des nations unies;* Higgins, *Political Organs*, ref. 15, 1–10; Restatement (Third), ref. 11, §§ 102(3), 103(2)(c); Schachter, O. (1995) *International Law in Theory and Practice* (student ed.) 84–101; Sloan, F.B. (1991) United Nations General Assembly Resolutions in *Our Changing World*; Wolfke, ref. 14, 79–84, 100-04; Bleicher, S. (1969) 'The legal significance of re-citation of general assembly resolutions', *Am. J. Int. L.*, Vol. 63, 444–78; Chodosh, H. (1991) 'Neither treaty nor custom: the emergence of declarative international law', *Tex. Int. L.J.*, Vol. 26, 87–124; McCaffrey, ref. 24, 323–24, 326–30; Schwebel, S. 'United Nations Resolutions, recent arbitral awards and customary international law', in Bos and Siblesz, ref. 25, 203–10; Weil, ref. 17, 416–18.

[31] The Nuclear Tests Case (Australia and New Zealand v. France), 1974 *ICJ* 255, 267–70. See generally Janis, ref. 25, 14, 38–43; Wolfke, ref. 11, 77–78; Skubiszewski, K. (1991) 'Unilateral acts of states', in *Achievements and Prospects*, ref. 11, 221–40; Rubin, A. (1977) 'The international legal effects of unilateral declarations', *Am. J. Int. L.*, Vol. 71, 1–30.

[32] The North Sea Continental Shelf Case (Federal Rep. of Germany v. Denmark and Netherlands), [1969] *ICJ* Vol. 3, 33–35. See generally Brierly, ref. 11, 65–66; Brownlie, ref. 11, 24–25; Lauterpacht, ref. 11, 23–25; Restatement (Third), ref. 11, § 103(2)(d); Rosenne, ref. 27, 614–16; Schachter, ref. 30, 38–39; Shaw, ref. 11, 91–93; Wolfke, ref. 11, 76–77; Sourang, M. (1991) 'Jurisprudence and Teachings', in *Achievements and Prospects*, ref. 11, 283–88.

[33] Brierly, ref. 11, 62–63, 67–68, 366–73; Brownlie, ref. 11, 15–19, 153–62; Danilenko, ref. 11, 173–89; de Visscher, ref. 14, 356–58; Janis, ref. 25, 54–61; Levi, ref. 15, 39–44; Restatement (Third), ref. 11, § 102(4); Rosenne, ref. 27, 608–11; Rossi, C. (1993) *Equity and International Law: A Legal Realist Approach to International Decisionmaking*, 87–154; Schachter, ref. 30, 49–61; Shaw, ref. 11, 84–89; Tunkin, ref. 11, 190–203; Wolfke, ref. 11, 105–08; Bokor-Szegö, H. (1991) 'General principles of law', in *Achievements and Prospects*, ref. 11, 213–20; Chemillier-Gendreau, M. (1991) 'Equity', in *Achievements*

General principles, however, seldom amount to more than the most general abstractions about justice and judicial economy, and thus are even less likely to fill the lacunae in customary international law with definitive content given the increasingly heterogeneous nature of an international legal community.[34]

Successful areas of customary law tend to be codified under United Nations auspices. The principal organ through which the United Nations initiates the codification of cusomary international law is the International Law Commission, a body created by the General Assembly in 1947 to help codify and 'progressively develop' customary international law.[35] The rules developed by the Commission often are accorded 'quasi-legal effect' as rules of international law even before they take the form of a binding legal document.[36] Yet even when a body of customary law has been codified, parts (or even a great deal) of the relevant law often survive as customary law.[37]

cont.

    and Prospects, supra at 271–82; Ford, C. (1994) 'Judicial Discretion in International Jurisprudence: Article 38(1)(c) and "General Principles of Law" ', *Duke J. Comp. and Int. L.* vol. 5, 35–86.

[34] Chen Tiqiang (1984) 'The People's Republic of China and public international law', *Dalhousie L.J.*, Vol. 8, 3–31; Danilenko, G. (1991) 'The changing structure of the international community: constitutional implications', *Harv. Int. L.J.*, Vol. 32, 353–61; Flory, M. (1982) 'Adapting international law to the development of the third world', *J. African L.*, Vol. 26, 12–20; Gunther, K. (1982) 'Re-defining international law from the point of view of decolonisation and development and African regionalism', *J. African L.* Vol. 26, 49–67; Hazard, J. (1985) 'Socialism and international public law', *Colum. J. Transnat'l L.*, Vol. 23, 251–63; Hoya, T (1985) 'Marxism and international private law', *Colum. J. Transnat'l L.*, Vol. 23, 265–79; Murphy, jr., E. (1981) 'The diminishing world of western law', *Tex. Int. L.J.*, Vol. 16, 1–10; Ntambirweki, J. (1991) 'The developing countries in the evolution of international law', *Hastings Int. and Comp. L, Rev.*, Vol. 14, 905–28; Park, No-Hyoung (1987) 'The Third world as an international legal system', *B.C. 3rd World L.J.*, Vol.7, 37–60; Sathirathai, S. (1984) 'An understanding of the relationship between international legal discourse and third world countries', *Harv. Int. L.J.*, Vol. 25, 395–419; Thomas, J. (1990) 'International law in Asia: an initial review', *Dalhousie L.J.*, Vol. 13, 683–724; Wang Tieya (1983) 'The Third world and international law', in *Selected Articles from the Chinese Yearbook of International Law*, 6–40 (Chinese Soc'y Int. L.).

[35] UN Charter, art. 13(1); GA Res. 174(II), Nov. 21, 1947. See generally Brierly, ref. 11, 78–86; Briggs, H. (1965) *The International Law Commission*; Sinclair, I. (1987) *The International Law Commission*; UN Secretariat, (1988) *The Work of the International Law Commission*, 4th ed.; Condorelli, ref. 11, 194–97; Graefrath, B. (1991) 'The International Law Commission tomorrow: improving its organization and methods of work', *Am. J. Int. L.*, Vol. 85, 595–612.

[36] Kirgis, F. (1977) *International Organizations in Their Legal Setting: Documents, Comments, and Questions*, 250–51.

[37] Consider the example of the law of the sea: Delimitation of the continental shelf boundary case (Libya v. Malta), [1985] *ICJ* 13, 29–34; The Gulf of Maine Case (Canada v. United States), [1984] *ICJ* 246, 295 (merits); The North Sea Continental Shelf Case (Federal Rep. of Germany v. Denmark and Netherlands), [1969] *ICJ* 3, 31. See generally Churchill, R.R. and Lowe, A.V. (1988) *The Law of the Sea*, 2nd ed., 5–19; O'Connell, D. (1982) (Shearer, I.A. editor) *The International Law of the Sea*, Vol. 1, 22–28, 37–53; Restatement (Third), ref. 11, §§ 513 comment j, 514 comment a, 515 reporters' note 1, 523 comment b; Shaw, ref. 11, 337–92; Condorelli, ref. 11, 184–85, 197–200.

Despite the obvious difficulties in determining the precise content of customary international law, even as supplemented by general principles, the system has been rather remarkably successful. Many forms of international life could not exist without a shared set of norms that are largely self-effectuating in the conduct of that life.[38] Customary international law empowers international actors by legitimating the claims they make, but it also limits the claims international actors can make.[39] Customary international law is, in some respects, ill fitted to perform these functions given its often poorly defined and highly uncertain nature.[40]

Even when a norm of customary international law has been determined with some certainty, however, customary forms of enforcement – claim and counterclaim among states – proceed without a neutral enforcement mechanism, always leaving a suspicion that national interest overrides any real commitment to law. Without a neutral enforcement mechanism, international law ultimately has nothing better to offer for punishing violations than the vendetta.[41] Coupling a recognized mode of expert analysis with woefully inadequate institutional development produces a serious imbalance in international law. The 'most highly qualified publicists' often devise doctrinal schemes of considerable sophistication without being able to translate those schemes into effective institutional arrangements. That task has fallen to diplomats and politicians with predictably mixed results.

Today, institution building rarely succeeds through customary processes. The lack of institutional machinery for impartial dispute resolution and reasonably efficient enforcement for even strongly supported international norms can seriously undermine the effectiveness of international law. The institutional limitations of international law have always been most clear

[38] Merrills, ref. 20, 86–90. See generally Rittgerger, V. and Mayer, P. (editors) (1993) *Regime Theory and International Relations*.

[39] Haas, P. (1989) 'Do regimes matter? Epistemic communities and Mediterranean pollution control', *Int. Org.*, Vol. 43, 377–403, at 401–02. See generally Rittgerger and Mayer, ref. 34.

[40] These are characteristics of all customary law, and not just customary international law. See Bloch, M. (Manyon, L.A. translator) (1961) Feudal Society, p.114; Havelock, E. (1963) Preface to Plato, 121–22; Kern, F. (Chrimes, S.B. translator) (1939) *Kingship and Law in the Middle Ages*, p.179; Collins, R. and Skover, D., (1992) 'Paratexts', *Stan. L. Rev.*, vol. 44, 509–52, at 516–21.

[41] Naff, T. and Matson, R. (editors) (1984) *Water in the Middle East: Conflict or Cooperation?* p.161. See also Henkin, ref. 11, 60–62; Bilder, R. (1982) 'Some limitations of adjudication as an international dispute settlement technique', *Va. J. Int. L.*, Vol. 23, 1–12; Chinkin and Sadurska, ref. 14, 57–60; Doxey, M. (1983) 'International sanctions in theory and practice', *Case-W. Res. J. Int. L.*, Vol. 15, 273–88; Radinsky, M. (1994) 'Retaliation: the genesis of law and the evolution toward international cooperation: an application of game theory to modern international conflicts', *Geo. Mason U. L. Rev.*, Vol. 2, 52–75.

during periods of major crisis.[42] A fully developed institutional framework is essential for resolving any serious, long-term crisis, including competition over critical water shortages.[43] To get beyond the limitations of custom, states must combine the sophisticated insights of international lawyers with the practical structures of political actors through institutions for managing water cooperatively and resolving conflicts over water before its escalates to injurious levels.

3. The customary international law of water management

A rich body of custom regarding internationally shared fresh water has emerged, largely in the last century or so. International disputes regarding non-navigational uses of fresh water were rare and rather easily resolved before the modern industrial era.[44] Historically, the process of claim and counter-claim relating to internationally shared fresh waters focused on surface waters, with the application of the resulting norms to aquifers being a relatively recent development. This section opens with analysis of the evolution of the customary norms applicable to surface waters through state practice and the elaboration of those norms through the work of the leading scholars on the topic, including in particular the Helsinki Rules of the International Law Association.[45] After a brief look at the application of the resulting norms to groundwater, this section closes by evaluating the effectiveness of the customary law of internationally shared fresh waters.

3.1 State practice and opinio juris

Industrialization brought intensive use and extensive diversion of water from its source of origin. The resulting international claims and counterclaims

---

[42] Morganthau, H. (1967) *Politics among Nations*, 4th ed., 282–83; Schachter, ref. 30, 227–46.

[43] Teclaff, L. (1967) *The River Basin in History and Law* 13–203; Dellapenna, J. (1994) 'Designing the legal structures of water management needed to accomplish the Israeli-Palestinian Declaration of Principles', *Palestine Y.B. Int. L.*, Vol. 7, 63–103, at 98–103 ('Dellapenna,"Designing"'); Dellapenna, J. (1990) 'The waters of the Jordan Valley: the potential and limits of law', *Palestine Y.B. Int. L.*, Vol. 5, 15–47, at 40–45; Dellapenna, ref. 8, 51–56.

[44] See generally Teclaff, ref. 43, 75–112; Teclaff, L. (1985) *Water law in historical perspective*, 78–128 ('Teclaff, Historical Perspective').

[45] Helsinki Rules, ref. 5.

quickly settled into a predictable pattern, depending on the riparian status of the state making the claim. There is one point on which all states agree: Only riparian states – states across which, or along which, a river flows – have any legal right, absent agreement, to use the water of a river, lake, or other surface source.[46] Beyond that point, however, the patterns of international claim and counterclaim initially diverged sharply according to the riparian status of the state making the claim. The uppermost riparian state always initially claims 'absolute territorial sovereignty'.[47] By this claim, the upper riparian state asserts a right to do whatever it chooses with the water regardless of its effect on other riparian states. Downstream states, on the other hand, generally open by claiming a right to the 'absolute integrity of the watercourse'.[48] These lower riparian states claim that upper riparian states can do nothing that affects the quantity or quality of water that flows down the watercourse. Friedrich Berber noted that these claims 'are grounded in an individualistic and anarchical conception of international law in which personal and egotistical interests are raised to the level of guiding principles and no solution is offered for the conflicting interests of the upper and lower riparians'.[49]

The utter incompatibility of such claims guarantees that neither claim will prevail in the end, although the process of negotiating or otherwise resolving the dispute embodied in these claims might require decades. The usual solution is a concept of 'restricted sovereignty' that goes by the name

[46] Int. L. Comm'n, Draft articles on the law of non-navigational uses of international watercourses ('Draft Articles II'), art. 4, in Report of the 46th Meeting of the International Law Commission, 2 May–22 July, 1994, A/49/10 ('ILC Report'), 195–236; *Water in the Middle East*, ref. 41, 166–67; Benvenisti, E. (1996) 'Collective action in the utilization of shared freshwater: The challenges of international water resources law', *Am. J. Int. L.*, Vol. 90, 384–415, at 384, 388; Fahmi, A. (1967) 'International river law for non-navigable rivers with special reference to the Nile', *Revue égyptienne de droit international*, Vol. 23, 39–62, at 51.

[47] Berber, F.J. (Batstone, R.K. translator) (1959) *Rivers in International Law*, 14–19, 77–78, 108; Bruhàcs, J. (1993) *The Law of Non-Navigational Uses of International Watercourses*, 41–47; Caponera, D. (1992) *Principles of Water Law and Administration*, 212–13; Elmusa, S. (1996) *Negotiating Waters: Israel and the Palestinians*, 37–38; Godana, B.A. (1985) *Africa's Shared Water Resources: Legal and Institutional Aspects of the Nile, Niger, and Senegal River Systems*, 32–35; Smith, H.A. (1931) *The Economic Uses of International Rivers*, 7–8; Lipper, J. (1967) 'Equitable utilization', in Garretson, A., Hayton, R. and Olmstead, C. *The Law of International Drainage Basins*, 15–88, at 18, 20–23; Maluwa, T. (1992) 'Towards an internationalisation of the Zambezi River regime: the role of international law in the common management of an international watercourse', *Comp. and Int. L.J. S. Afr.*, Vol. 25, 20–43, at 25–26; McCaffrey, ref. 8, at 88, 105–110; Sheng Yu (1991) 'International rivers and lakes', in *Achievements and Prospects*, ref. 23, 989–98, at 990.

[48] Berber, ref. 47, 9–22; Bruhàcs, ref. 47, 43–47; Caponera, ref. 47, 213; Godana, ref. 47, 38–40; Lipper, ref. 47, 18–20; Maluwa, ref. 47, 24–25; Sheng Yu, ref. 47, 990.

[49] Berber, ref. 47, 14.

'equitable utilization'.[50] States that are both upper and lower riparians on the same stream (usually relative to different states) often are the first to assert the theory of equitable utilization under which each state recognizes the right of all riparian states to use water from a common source so long as their uses do not interfere unreasonably with uses in other riparian states.

Documenting the process of claim and counterclaim that converts a convenient practice into a customary rule of law is easy for internationally shared waters. Perhaps the most famous claim of absolute territorial sovereignty was made by the United States in 1895. A dispute arose in the 1890's when the Mexican government complained that Americans were wastefully diverting water from the Rio Bravo del Norte (the river the Americans call the Rio Grande) to the injury of Mexicans down river. The Mexican Minister to the United States complained that the American practices violated both treaties and customary international law.[51] The US Attorney-General, Judson Harmon, gave the US Secretary of State a legal opinion that international law did not impose any obligation on the United States regarding how it used waters within its sovereign borders.[52] Eventually, after nearly 12 years of dispute, the two states negotiated an agreement whereby the United States promised to 'deliver' (by way of the river) 60,000 ac-ft. (74 million cubic meters ['MCM']) of water annually to the lower reaches of the Rio Grande for Mexican use.[53] Later, the two nations revised the allocation of the lower Rio Grande and agreed that the United States would 'deliver' 1,850 MCM (1,500,000 ac.-ft.) of water to

[50] Berber, ref. 47, 11–14, 78–79; Bruhàcs, ref. 47, 45–48; Caponera, ref. 47, 213–14; Godana, ref. 47, 40; Bush, W. (1981) 'Compensation and the utilization of international rivers and lakes: the role of compensation in the event of permanent injury to existing uses of water', in Zacklin, R. and Caflisch, L. (Editors) *The Legal Regime of International Rivers and Lakes*, 309–29; Lipper, ref. 47, 23–38; Maluwa, ref. 47, 26–30; McCaffrey, ref. 8, 110–33; Sheng Yu, ref. 47, 991.

[51] Letter of Minister Matías Romero to Secretary of State Richard Olney, Oct. 21, 1894, in (1894) *Foreign Rel.* of the U.S. 395.

[52] Op. Att'y Gen. (1895) Vol. 21, 274, at 281–82, reprinted in Moore, J. (1906) *Digest of International Law*, Vol. 1, 654. See generally Hyde, C. (1945) *International Law Chiefly as Interpreted and Applied by the United States*, 2nd ed., 565; Kriskau, K. (1966) *Die Harmon Doktrin – cine These der Vereinigton Staaten zum inernationalen Flussrecht*; Mackay, R.A. (1928) 'The international joint commission between the United States and Canada', *Am. J. Int. L.*, Vol. 22, 292–318; McCaffrey, S. (1996) 'The Harmon Doctrine one hundred years later: buried, not praised', *Nat. Resources J.*, Vol. 36, 549–90, at 556–68; Simsarian, J. (1938) 'The diversion of waters affecting the United States and Mexico', *Tex. L. Rev.*, Vol. 17, 27–61, at 59.

[53] Convention providing for the equitable distribution of the waters of the Rio Grande for irrigation purposes, signed May 21, 1906, *Mexico-United States*, Stat., Vol. 34, 2953 ('Rio Grande Convention'). See generally Berber, ref. 47, 110–11; Teclaff, Historical Perspective, ref. 44, 429–33; McCaffrey, ref. 8, 105–07; McCaffrey, ref. 52, 745–57; Utton, A. (1998) 'Mexican International Waters', in Robert Beck (editor) *Waters and Water Rights* (replacement volume) Vol. 5, § 51.02.

Mexico by way of the Colorado River.[54] Years later, the US State Department concluded that the United States had never considered the Harmon Doctrine to be anything more than special pleading and decisively repudiated the so-called Doctrine.[55]

Note the interplay in the Mexican-US disputes between treaty and custom. The original Mexican claim relied on both forms of law, and Attorney-General Harmon rejected both in similar terms. The dispute was resolved through a series of treaties. The treaties created legal obligations between the two nations and they demonstrate state practice which, if sufficiently widespread, could amount to an international custom. The question arises whether the ensuing treaties in addition demonstrate the *opinio juris* necessary to make that custom law. At one time that question was hotly disputed, with several leading experts on international law in general and on the law of internationally shared rivers in particular concluding that these treaties could not rise to the level of customary law.[56] Their conclusion was disputed at the time, and the consensus has decisively swung in favor of the conclusion that indeed a consistent pattern of treaties can demonstrate both state practice and the necessary *opinio juris* sufficiently to prove the existence of a rule of customary international law.[57] A customary rule of restricted sovereignty ('equitable utilization') can be said to rest on the now nearly innumerable treaties regarding internationally shared waters.[58]

[54] Treaty respecting utilization of waters of the Colorado and Tijuana Rivers and of the Rio Grande, signed Feb. 3, 1944, *Mexico-United States*, UNTS, Vol. 3, 313 ('Colorado Treaty'). See generally McCaffrey, ref. 8, 107–08; Utton, ref. 53, § 51.03.
[55] Memorandum to the legal advisor, Nov. 23, 1942, reprinted in Whiteman, M. (1964) *Digest of International Law*, Vol. 3, 950. See also State Dep't (1958) 'Legal aspects of the use of systems of international waters', *Sen. Doc.* No. 118, 85th Cong., 2d Sess., 89–91, reprinted in Whiteman, supra, Vol. 3, 939–42. See generally Deener, D.R. (1957) *The United States Attorney Generals and International Law*, 253–57, 308–09; McCaffrey, ref. 52, 757–67.
[56] Berber, ref. 47, 149; Hyde, ref. 52, vol. 1, 12.
[57] See, e.g., Bruhàcs, ref. 47, 15, 59–65, 71–73, 156; Kaeckenbeeck, G. (1919) *International Rivers*, 24–29; Saliba, S. (1968) *The Jordan River Dispute*, 48–62; Teclaff, *Historical Perspective*, ref. 44, 428–43; Lipper, ref. 47, 33–35; Sheng Yu, ref. 47, 993–96. See generally The North Sea Continental Shelf case (Federal Rep. of Germany v. Denmark and Netherlands), [1969] *ICJ* 3, 31; The Wimbledon case (France, Italy, Japan, and United Kingdom v. Germany), [1923] *PCIJ*, ser. A, no. 1, at 25, digested in *Int. L. Rep.* Vol. 2, 99–102; The Panevezys-Saldutiskis Ry. Case (Estonia v. Lithuania), 1939, ser. A/B, no. 76, 51–52; The Pacquett Habana, (1900) 175 U.S. 677, 687–88; Brierly, ref. 11, 59; Brownlie, ref. 11, 3–4, 11–14, 180–81, 201, 214–17, 604; D'Amato, ref. 11, 51, 104, 134; Danilenko, ref. 11, 156–72; McNair, ref. 28, 216–18; McDougal, M., Lasswell, H. and Vlasic, I. (1963) *Law and Public Order in Space*, 82–83, 115–19; Restatement (Third), ref. 11, § 102 comment f; Shaw, ref. 11, 81–82; Wolfke, ref. 11, 68–72; Jennings, R. (1991) 'Treaties', in *Achievements and Prospects*, ref. 11, 135–77, at 146–48; Tunkin, ref. 28.
[58] The treaties are collected in UN Doc. A/CN.4/283, ref. 8, 33–264. See also Berber, ref. 47, 52–127; Smith, ref. 47; Burchi, ref. 8; Christy, ref. 8; Legislative Texts, ref. 8; Dellapenna, ref. 8, 42–47; McCaffrey, ref. 8, 134–38; Schwebel, ref. 8, 76–82, 88–90.

Establishing that state practice conforms to the general principle that each state's sovereignty over its water resources is restricted by the obligation not to inflict unreasonable injury on another state is easy in light of the numerous treaties. The treaties generally are so tailored to the particulars of a specific drainage basin, however, that it is impossible to derive a more specific mandate applicable to the waters of a basin not yet allocated by treaty.[59] As in the agreements between Mexico and the United States, the nations involved often share the water according to historic patterns of use, although occasionally some other more or less objective measure of need is substituted (population, area, arable land, etc.).[60] Yet other treaties simply assured each state of 'equal shares.' Several treaties speak in more general terms. A watercourse treaty between Norway and Sweden declares the obligation of each state to prevent 'any considerable inconvenience' to persons in the other country.[61] The Treaty of 'peace, friendship, and arbitration' between the Dominican Republic and Haiti assures each of the right to make 'just and equitable use' of their shared waters.[62] The General Convention relating to the development of hydraulic power affecting more than one state ('Hydraulic Power Convention'),[63] ratified by 17 states, speaks in similarly broad terms of an obligation not to 'cause serious prejudice' to another state.

These treaties certainly establish state practice relative to internationally shared waters. Demonstrating that these treaties taken as a whole, along with other indicia of the motives behind such arrangements, amount to the requisite *opinio juris* is not so easy. After all, the treaties were convenient even if no rule of law supported the result – in fact, that must certainly have been the reasoning underlying the earliest of these treaties.[64] Few of the treaties say anything about the customary law that informs their negotiation, interpretation, and

---

[59] Berber, ref. 47, 148–59; Brownlie, ref. 11, 272; Bruhàcs, ref. 47, 16–17, 60–61; Godana, ref. 47, 66; Hyde, ref. 52, Vol. 1, 563; Smith, ref. 47, 56; Fahmi, ref. 46, 46–48; Goldenman, G. (1990) 'Adapting to climate change: a study of international rivers and their legal arrangements', *Ecol. L.Q.*, Vol. 17, 741–802, at 771; Lipper, ref. 47, 42; Maluwa, ref. 47, 28–29.

[60] See generally Saliba, ref. 57, 51–54, 57–59; Teclaff, ref. 43, 157–65; Teclaff, *Historical Perspective*, ref. 44, 429–43.

[61] Convention on certain questions relating to the law of watercourses, signed May 11, 1929, Norway-Sweden, art. 12(1), *LNTS* Vol. 120, 277.

[62] Signed Feb. 20, 1929, art. 10, LNTS Vol. 105, 225. See also Agreement concerning the waterpower of the Pasvik River, signed Dec. 18, 1957, Norway-USSR, *UNTS* Vol. 312, p. 274.

[63] Opened for signature, Dec. 9, 1923, *LNTS* Vol. 36, 76. See also General convention regulating navigable waterways of international concern, opened for signature, Apr. 20, 1921, art. 4, *LNTS* Vol. 7, p.35. See Berber, ref. 47, 122–124; Bruhàcs, ref. 47, 11; Caponera, ref. 47, 209–210.

[64] Teclaff, L. (1991) 'Fiat or custom: the checkered development of international water law', *Nat. Resources J.*, Vol. 31, 45–73; Young, O. (1989) 'The politics of international regime formation: managing natural resources and the environment', *Int. Org.*, Vol. 43, 349–403.

application. Some treaties even expressly deny any effect as creating or implementing general customary international law. In article 4 of the Rio Grande Convention, Mexico and the United States agreed that '[t]he delivery of water as herein provided is not to be construed as a recognition of any claim on the part of Mexico to said waters'.[65] The same convention stated the premise even more strongly at a later point: '[N]or does the United States in any way concede the establishment of any general principle or precedent by the concluding of this treaty'.[66] Before placing too much emphasis on such disclaimers, one should recall that even the United States, after so carefully insisting on placing the disclaimer in the Rio Grande Convention not once, but twice, has itself since concluded that there is just such a general customary rule of law, relying in part on this very convention as authority for the proposition.[67] This conclusion, however, did not prevent the United States and Canada from including a similar disclaimer in their agreement over the Columbia River Basin just three years later.[68]

On the other hand, a few treaties expressly acknowledge the existence of an underlying customary rule, albeit generally in vague terms. An example is found in the Hydraulic Power Convention: 'The present Convention in no way affects the right belonging to each State, within the limits of international law, to carry out on its own territory any operation for the development of hydraulic power which it may consider desirable'.[69] The recently negotiated Mekong Basin Agreement also committed the signatories to 'utilize the waters of the Mekong River system in a reasonable and equitable manner', and similar expressions are found in bilateral treaties.[70] While there is good reason for considering the appearance of the rule of equitable utilization in a multilateral treaty intended to codify customary international law as more decisive evidence of the customary law than a larger number of bilateral

---

[65] Rio Grande Convention, ref. 53, art. 4.

[66] Rio Grande Convention, ref. 53, art. 6. See also *Indus Waters Treaty*, signed Sept. 19, 1960, India-Pakistan, art. 11, *UNTS* Vol. 419, 126.

[67] State Dep't, ref. 55, 62–63, 89–91. See generally Berber, ref. 47, 110–18; Bloomfield, L.M. and Fitzgerald, G.F. (1958) *Boundary Waters Problems of Canada and the United States: The International Joint Commission, 1912–1958*, 46–47; Saliba, ref. 57, 51–55; Lipper, ref. 47, 25–28; McCaffrey, ref. 8, 106–09.

[68] Treaty for the co-operative development of the Columbia River Basin, Jan. 17, 1961, United States-Canada, art. 17(1), UST, Vol. 15, 1555.

[69] Hydraulic Power Convention, ref. 63, art. 1 (emphasis added).

[70] Agreement on the cooperation for the sustainable development of the Mekong river basin, signed April 5, 1995, Cambodia-Laos-Thailand-Vietnam, art. 5, reprinted in *Int. Legal Materials*, Vol. 34, 864–80 ('Mekong river basin agreement'). See also Agreement on regulation of boundary waters, signed November 20, 1866, Spain-Portugal, Annex 1 (the whole agreement in turn is an annex to the Convention on boundaries, signed on September 29, 1864, Spain-Portugal, in *Legislative Texts*, ref. 58, no. 241); Treaty concerning the regulation of water management of frontier waters, signed Dec. 7, 1967, Austria-Czechoslovakia, art. 19(4), *UNTS* Vol. 728, 313.

treaties, those bilateral treaties count for something. Perhaps most persuasive in this setting is the growing practice of states in a politically, hydrologically, or otherwise dominant position on a river accepting from the start of negotiations that a river or other watercourse is a shared resource over which they cannot claim absolute dominion either in terms of territorial sovereignty or in terms of riparian integrity.[71] Yet, while we can see in these treaties a concept of restricted sovereignty, just what the restrictions are is nowhere indicated.

Many nations have expressed themselves more clearly in international conferences when the topic of internationally shared waters has arisen. The Western Hemisphere states recognized that no state has an absolute right either to do as it pleases with waters it shares with other states or to demand that other states do nothing with those waters.[72] Even nations that objected to the resulting Declaration of Montevideo did so because it was not comprehensive enough, not because they opposed the principle being expressed. Even better evidence of the customary law of internationally shared waters is found in arbitral and judicial decisions applying that law to particular disputes. These decisions are unanimously in favor of the rule of equitable utilization.[73] The best example remains the statement of the Permanent Court of International Justice (the predecessor institution to the International Court of Justice) in discussing the authority of the Permanent Commission of the River Oder:

> When consideration is given to the manner in which states have regarded the concrete situations arising out of the fact that a single waterway traverses or separates the territory of more than one state, and the possibility of fulfilling the requirements of justice and the considerations of utility which this fact places in relief, it is at once seen that a solution of the problem has been sought not in the idea of a right of passage in favour of upstream states, but in that of a community of interest of riparian states. This community of interest in a navigable river becomes the basis a common legal right, the essential features of which are the perfect equality of all riparian states in the use of the whole course of the river

---

[71] See, e.g., The Lake Lanoux arbitration (France v. Spain) (1957), *Int. L. Rep.*, Vol. 24, 101, at 111–112 (France did not assert absolute sovereignty); Papers regarding a treaty of alliance with Egypt – Egypt No. 1, at 31 (UK Cmd. 3050, 1928) (the United Kingdom did not assert absolute sovereignty on behalf of the Sudan). See also Lammers, J.G. (1984) *Pollution of International Watercourses*, 289–90; [Sudanese] Ministry of Irr. and Hydro-Elec. Power (1955), Nile Waters Question 13; Smith, ref. 47, 147; Lipper, ref. 47, 27–28; McCaffrey, ref. 8, 110–13.

[72] Declaration on industrial and agricultural use of international rivers, Montevideo, Dec. 24, 1933 (7th Int. Conf. of Am. States), reprinted in *Am. J. Int. L.*, Vol., 28, 59 (1934 supp.). See generally Berber, ref. 47, 125–127.

[73] See UN Doc. A/CN.4/283, ref. 58, 187–99; Bruhàcs, ref. 47, pp.12–13; Caponera, ref. 47, pp.192–94; Saliba, ref. 57, 62–64; Lipper, ref. 47, 28–31; McCaffrey, ref. 8, 113–22.

and the exclusion of any preferential privileges of any riparian state in relation to others.[74]

3.2. *The teachings of the 'most highly qualified publicists'*

Turning to the 'most highly qualified publicists', one finds general agreement among them on the rule of equitable utilization as the applicable rule of customary international law regarding internationally shared waters. Restricted sovereignty rests ultimately on the concept of an international drainage basin as a coherent juridical and managerial unit, a concept widely supported by naturalists, engineers, lawyers, and economists.[75] We have already seen that the decisions of international arbitral and judicial tribunals strongly embraced this conclusion. The decisions of national courts litigating the rights of states of a federal union have reached similar conclusions. International tribunals cite such national decisions as evidence of customary international law.[76] The Supreme Court of the United States routinely applies

[74] Permanent Commission of the River Oder Case, [1929] PCIJ, ser. A, no. 23, at 27. See also Jurisdiction of the European Commission for the Danube Case, [1927] *PCIJ*, ser. B, no. 14, 61–64; Lammers, ref. 71, 507; Teclaff, *Historical Perspective*, ref. 44, 378–99; McCaffrey, ref. 8, 113–14.

[75] UNCED Report, Agenda 21, 2 UN Doc. A/CONF.151/26, 167–68; Bruhàcs, ref. 47, 17–19, 24–35; Caponera, ref. 47, 185–86; Lammers, ref. 71, 18; McDonald, A. and Kay, D. (1988) *Water Resources: Issues and Strategies*, 190–223, 239–45; Teclaff, ref. 43; Wunderlich, W. and Prins, J. (editors) (1987) *Water for the Future: Water Resources Developments in Perspective*, 245–50; Dworsky, L. and Utton, A. (1993) 'Assessing North America's management of its transboundary waters', *Nat. Resources J.*, Vol. 33, 413–459; Francis, G. (1993) 'Ecosystem management', *Nat. Resources J.*, Vol. 33, 315–45; Linnerooth, J. (1990) 'The Danube Basin: negotiating settlements to transboundary environmental issues', *Nat. Resources J.*, Vol. 30, 629–60; Maluwa, ref. 47, 22–23; Maluwa, T. (1988) 'The legal aspects of the Niger River under the Niamey Treaties', *Nat. Resources J.*, Vol. 28, 671–97; McCaffrey, S. (1991) 'International organizations and the holistic approach to water problems', *Nat. Resources J.*, Vol. 31, 139–65, at 143; Okidi, C.O. (1988) 'The state and the management of international drainage basins in Africa', *Nat. Resources J.*, Vol. 28, 645–69; Xue Hanqin (1992) 'Relativity in international water law', *Colo. J. Int. Envtl. L. and Pol'y*, Vol. 3, 45–57, at 46–48.

[76] The Trail Smelter arbitration, (1941), digested in *Int. L. Rep.*, Vol. 9, 315–33; Bruhàcs, ref. 47, 155; Caponera, ref. 47, 194; Saliba, ref. 57, 64–66; Hayton, R.D. (1967) 'The formation of the customary rules of international law', in Garretson, Hayton and Olmstead, ref. 47, 834–95, at 845–47; Kunz, J. (1951) 'International law by analogy', *Am. J. Int. L.*, Vol. 45, 329–35; Lauterpacht, H. (1929) 'Decisions of municipal courts as a source of international law', *Brit. Y.B. Int. L.*, Vol. 10, 65–95; Lipper, ref. 47, 31–33; Maluwa, ref. 47, 25; McCaffrey, ref. 8, 129–30; Schwebel, ref. 58, 75–76. But see Berber, ref. 47, 168–84 (contra).

international law to disputes between states of the United States.[77] The Court rejected any claim of absolute territorial sovereignty and any claim to the absolute integrity of the river. Courts and commissions in Germany, India, and Switzerland reached similar conclusions.[78] An Italian court reached a similar conclusion in a dispute between a French company and an Italian company regarding a stretch of the Rio Roya, a river that straddled the French-Italian border.[79] The German *Reichsgerichtshof* expressed the point in these straightforward words:

> The exercise of sovereign rights by every State in regard to international rivers traversing its territory is limited by the duty not to injure the interest of other members of the international community. Due consideration must be given to one another by the States through whose territories there flows an international river. No State may substantially impair the natural use of the flow of such a river by its neighbours.[80]

Writing on an individual basis, the most highly qualified publicists are nearly unanimous in support of the theory of restricted sovereignty as a customary rule of international law.[81] A study by the United Nations

---

[77] Texas v. New Mexico, 482 U.S. 124 (1987); Kansas v. Colorado, 475 U.S. 1079 (1986); Colorado v. New Mexico, 467 U.S. 310 (1984); Wisconsin v. Illinois, 388 U.S. 426 (1967); Arizona v. California, 373 U.S. 546 (1963); Texas v. New Mexico, 352 U.S. 991 (1957); New Jersey v. New York, 345 U.S. 369 (1953); Nebraska v. Wyoming, 325 U.S. 589 (1945); Colorado v. Kansas, 320 U.S. 383 (1943); Wyoming v. Colorado, 309 U.S. 572 (1940); Washington v. Oregon, 297 U.S. 517 (1936); Nebraska v. Wyoming, 295 U.S. 40 (1935); Arizona v. California, 283 U.S. 423 (1931); New Jersey v. New York, 283 U.S. 336 (1931); Connecticut v. Massachusetts, 282 U.S. 660 (1931); Wisconsin v. Illinois, 281 U.S. 179 (1930); Wyoming v. Colorado, 259 U.S. 419 (1922); Kansas v. Colorado, 206 U.S. 46 (1907); Missouri v. Illinois, 200 U.S. 496 (1906). See generally Grant, D. (1996) 'Interstate Water Allocation', in Beck, ref. 53, Vol. 4, chs. 43–48; Tarlock, A.D. (1985) 'The Law of Equitable Apportionment Revisited, Updated, and Restated', *U. Colo. L. Rev.*, Vol. 56, 381–411.

[78] The Donauversinkung Case (Württemberg and Prussia vs. Baden) (1927), Entsheidungen des Reichsgerichts in Zivilsachen ('RGZ') Vol. 116, 1 (Staatsgerichtshof ['SGH']), reprinted in Lauterpacht, H. (editor) (1931) *Ann. Digest of Pub. Int. L. Cases* 128; Report of the Rao Commission (1942) 10, 11, quoted in Whiteman, ref. 72, Vol. 3, 943; Zurich v. Aargau (1898), Entcherdungern des Schweizischen Bundesgerichts, Vol. 4, 34, 37. See also Guliati, N.D. (1972) *Development of Interstate Rivers: Law and Practice in India*; Jain, S.N., Jacob, A. and Jain, S. (1971) *Interstate Water Disputes in India*; Schindler, D. (Zeydel, E.H. translator) (1921) 'The administration of justice in the Swiss federal courts in international disputes', *Am. J. Int. L.* Vol. 15, 149–88.

[79] Decision of Feb. 13, 1939 (Societé énergie électrique du littoral méditerranéen v. Compagnia imprese elettriche liguri) (Corte de Cassazione), translated in Lauterpacht, H. (Editor) (1938–40) *Ann. Digest Pub. Int. L.* Cases No. 47.

[80] *Ann. Digest of Public Int. law Cases*, 128.

[81] See Arsanjani, M. (1981) *International Regulation of Internal Resources*; Berber, ref. 47, 185–255; Brierly, ref. 11, 231–32; Brownlie, ref. 11, 271–76; Bruhàcs, ref. 47, 73–79, 155–73; Caponera, ref. 47, 189–90, 212–14; Chauhan, B. (1981) *Settlement of Water Law Disputes*

Economic Committee for Europe surveyed 75 publicists and found only four who favored either of the absolute theories.[82] A study by Stephen Schwebel, then Special Rapporteur for the International Law Commission for the drafting of articles on the non-navigational use of international watercourses, found a similarly one-sided pattern.[83] Schwebel concluded that 'the right of each State to share equitably in the uses of the waters of an international watercourse system is indisputable and undisputed'.[84] Furthermore, every private international organization to consider the customary legal regime governing internationally shared water resources has embraced the rule of equitable utilization in one form or another.[85]

cont.

in International Drainage Basins; Feinberg, N. (1979) *Studies in International Law with Special Reference to the Arab-Israeli Conflict*, 491–97; Godana, ref. 47, 8, 50–57, 338–44; Hackworth, G.H. (1940) *Digest of International Law*, Vol. 1, 621; Kaeckenbeeck, ref. 57, 1–3, 17–23; O'Connell, D. (1970) *International Law*, 2nd ed., 556–58; Oppenheim, L. (Lauterpacht, H. editor) (1955) *International Law*, 8th ed., Vol. 1, 313, 345–47, 474–76; Schwarzenberger, G. (1941) *International Law*, 2nd ed., 13; Smith, ref. 47, 148–51; Teclaff, ref. 43, 152; Teclaff, *Historical Perspective*, ref. 44, 424–56; Verzijl, ref. 11, Vol. 3, 103–220; Alhéritière, D. (1987) 'Settlement of public international disputes on shared resources: elements of a comparative study of international instruments', in Utton, A. and Teclaff, L. (editors) (1987) *Transboundary Resources Law*, 139–49; Ahmed, S. (1990) 'Principles and Precedents in International Law Governing the Sharing of Nile Waters', in Howell, P.P. and Ailan, J.A. (editors) *The Nile: Resource Evaluation, Resource Management, Hydropolitics and Legal Issues*, 225–38; Austin, ref. 52; Benvenisti, E. and Gvirtzman, H. (1993) 'Harnessing international law to determine Israeli-Palestinian water rights: the mountain aquifer', *Nat. Resources J.*, Vol. 33, 543–67, at 547–48; Bilder, R. (1980) 'International law and natural resources policies', *Nat. Resources J.*, Vol. 20, 451–86; Chalabi, H. and Majzoub, T. (1995) 'Turkey, the waters of the Euphrates and public international law', in Allan, J.A. and Mallat, C. (editors) *Water in the Middle East: Legal, Political and Commercial Implications*, 189–236, at 227–29; Dellapenna, ref. 1, 35–38; Fahmi, ref. 46; Goldenman, ref. 59, 775–79; Griffin, W. (1959) 'The use of waters of international drainage basins under customary international law', *Am. J. Int. L.*, Vol. 53, 50–80; Goldie, F.L.E. 'Equity and the international management of transboundary resources', in *Transboundary Resources Law*, supra, 103–37; Lester, A.P. (1963) 'River pollution in international law', *Am. J. Int. L.*, Vol. 57, 828–53, at p.832; Lipper, ref. 47, 62–66; Maluwa, ref. 47, 26–28; Nanda, V. (1977) 'Emerging trends in the use of international law and institutions for the management of international water resources', in Nanda, V. (editor) *Water Needs for the Future*, 15–37; Sewell, W.R. (1964) 'The Columbia River Treaty and protocol agreement', *Nat. Resources J.*, Vol. 4, 309–31; Van Alstyne, W. (1960) 'International law and interstate river disputes', *Cal. L. Rev.* Vol. 48, 596–622; Sheng Yu, ref. 47, 93–96.

[82] Report of the UN Commission for Europe, Legal Aspects of Hydro-Electric Development of Rivers and Lakes of Common Interest, 57–68 UN Doc. E/ECE/136 (1952).

[83] Schwebel, ref. 8, 82–85, 87–88, 91–103. See also Berber, ref. 47, 11–44 (noting that many earlier commentators supported one or the other of the absolute theories, but that the later commentators were coalescing around restricted sovereignty); McCaffrey, ref. 8, 127–29.

[84] Schwebel, ref. 8, 85.

[85] See generally Bruhàcs, ref. 47, 77–79; Caponera, ref. 47, 194–96.

3.3 The Helsinki rules

One particularly influential form of expert opinion is a report or 'codification' by one or another international association of legal experts that have flourished since the nineteenth century. A number of these groups have undertaken to synthesize the experience of nations in coping with the shared management of international surface water sources. These have included the Asian-African Legal Consultative Committee, l'Institut de droit international, and the Inter-American Bar Association.[86] The groups are not lawgivers, yet the importance of the opinions of the 'most highly qualified publicists' in customary international law give them an importance that would be remarkable for a similar group in a national legal system. Their opinions carry special weight because of the stature of the members who worked on these projects, and because the approval of the end result carries the imprimatur of a large and diverse body of expert opinion.

The International Law Association, a highly-regarded non-governmental organization of legal experts founded in 1873, completed the best known study of the customary international law of transboundary water resources in 1966. The result is known as the *Helsinki Rules on the Uses of the Waters of International Rivers*.[87] The *Helsinki Rules* were the first attempt by any international association to codify the entire law of international watercourses. The resulting rules have heavily influenced state practice and other international associations in examining the law of internationally shared fresh waters.[88]

The *Helsinki Rules* treat international drainage basins (watersheds extending over two or more states) as indivisible hydrologic units to be managed as a single unit to assure the 'maximum utilization and development of any portion of its waters'.[89] This rule explicitly includes all tributaries (including tributary groundwater) within the concept of 'drainage basin' and thus extends beyond the primary international watercourse itself. The *Rules* formulated the phrase 'equitable utilization' to express the restricted sovereignty that applies to fresh

---

[86] Asian-African Legal Consultative Comm. (1974) Report of the Fourteenth Session 100; Inter-American Bar Ass'n. (1957) 'Resolution on Principles of Law Governing the Uses of International Rivers and Lakes'; Institut de droit international. (1961) 'Utilization of Non-Maritime International Waters (Except for Navigation)' ('Salzburg Resolution'), Annuaire de l'institut de droit international, Vol. 40, 381. See also Whiteman, ref. 55, vol. 3, 922–24, 929–30; McCaffrey, ref. 8, 124–27; Schwebel, ref. 48, 84, 87.

[87] Helsinki Rules, ref. 5. The project was begun in 1954 and produced an interim report to the Association's Conference in New York in 1958. Int. L. Ass'n, Research Project on the Law and Uses of International Rivers, 197–98 (1959) ('NYU Conference').

[88] See Bourne, C. (1996) 'The International Law Association's contribution to international water resources law', *Nat. Resources J.*, Vol. 36, 155–216, at 155–77, 213–216; Schwebel, ref. 48, 83–84, 87–88.

[89] Helsinki Rules, ref. 5, art. II and comment (a).

waters: 'Each basin State is entitled, within its territory, to a reasonable and equitable share in the beneficial uses of the waters of an international drainage basin'.[90] The International Law Association has continued to draft rules relating to water-centred activities not addressed directly or adequately in by the *Helsinki Rules,* including flood control (1972), pollution (1972 and 1982), navigability (1974), the protection of water installations during armed conflicts (1976), joint administration (1976 and 1986), flowage regulation (1980), general environmental management concerns (1980), groundwater (1986), cross-media pollution (1996), and remedies (1996).[91]

The International Law Association also developed what some see as a second primary principle governing the management of internationally shared water resources, that each nation shall not cause 'substantial damage' to the environment or the natural condition of the waters beyond the limits of the nation's jurisdiction.[92] The American Law Institute, an unofficial association of jurists, lawyers, and scholars that has been highly influential in the development of US law,[93] has also declared that states must 'take such measures as may be necessary, to the extent practicable under the circumstances' to avoid injury to neighboring states.[94] Neither organization attempted to work out the relation between the 'no harm' rule and the 'equitable utilization' rule, a failure that would produce considerable confusion and difficulty in later years.

3.4 Groundwater

Groundwater makes up about 25% of the world's fresh water apart from the polar ice caps and glaciers.[95] Yet in contrast to the considerable state practice

---

[90] Helsinki Rules, ref. 5, art. IV.

[91] The sets of rules (except those approved in 1996) are collected, with ample commentary, in Manner, E.J. and Metsälampi, V. (editors) (1988) *The Work of the International Law Association on the Law of International Water Resources.* For a summary of the provisions of these several documents, see Bourne, ref. 88, 177–208; McCaffrey, ref. 75, 144–50; Schwebel, ref. 58, 85.

[92] International L. Ass'n (1980) Rules on the relationship between water, other natural resources and the environment, art. I (Rep. of the 59th Conf., Belgrade) ('Belgrade Rules'). See also Shaw, ref. 8, 532–39. See also NYU Conference, ref. 87, 197.

[93] See generally Hazard, G. (1994) *The American law Institute: What It Is and What It Does*; Massey, D. (1997) 'Note, how the American Law Institute influences customary law: the reasonableness requirement of the Restatement of Foreign Relations Law', *Yale J. Int. L.,* Vol. 22, 419–45; White, G.E. (1997) 'The American Law Institute and the triumph of modernist jurisprudence', *Law and Hist. Rev.,* Vol. 15, 1–47; Wechsler, H. (1969) 'The course of the Restatements', *ABA J.,* Vol. 55, 147–51.

[94] Restatement (Third), ref. 11, § 601.

[95] Powledge , ref. 1, 23.

regarding the sharing of surface water sources, there has been remarkably little state practice regarding shared underground sources of water.[96] Contributing to the dearth of relevant state practice is the fact that prior to the spread of vertical turbine pumps after World War II, groundwater was a strictly local resource that could not be pumped in large enough volumes to affect users at any considerable distance away.[97] With the newer technologies, and with the exponential growth in the demand for water of the last several decades, groundwater has emerged as a critical transnational resource that has increasingly become the focus of disputes between nations yet for which no consistent body of state practice has yet emerged. An all too typical example is found in the several treaties dealing with waters shared between the United States and Mexico; despite the growing importance of groundwater to the border regions of the two nations, the treaties are silent on groundwater with potentially disastrous results.[98] Among the very few early agreements specifically allocating groundwater are two from the colonial period in Africa whereby the European powers involved agreed to allow the certain wells at or near a boundary to be used 'in common' by residents on either side of the border as they were accustomed to do before colonization.[99]

The most qualified publicists have concluded that sovereignty over groundwater must be restricted in the same way it is over surface water, subjecting groundwater to the same rule of equitable utilization as applies to surface sources.[100] They reason that as the hydrologic, economic, and engineering variables involved are essentially the same for surface and subsurface water sources, the law must also be the same for both sources. They

---

[96] Caponera, ref. 47, 252–53; Hillel, ref. 1, 275–76.

[97] Hillel, ref. 1, 192.

[98] See Colorado Treaty, ref. 54; Rio Grande Convention, ref. 53. See generally Day, J.C. (1978) 'International aquifer management of the Hueco Bolson on the Rio Grande', *Nat. Resources J.*, Vol. 18, 163–80; Hansen, N. (1982) 'Economic growth patterns in the Texas borderlands', *Nat. Resources J.*, Vol. 22, 805–21; Keleher, M. (1988) 'Note, Mexican-United States shared groundwater: can it be managed?', *Geo. Int. Envtl. L. Rev.*, Vol. 1, 113–31; Rodgers, A. and Albert Utton, A. (1985) 'The Ixtapa Draft Agreement relating to the use of transboundary groundwaters', *Nat. Resources J.*, Vol. 25, 715–72.

[99] Agreement Fixing the Frontier between Cyrenaica and Egypt, signed Dec. 6, 1925, Egypt-Italy, art. 6, *Brit. and For. State Papers*, Vol. 133, 976 (1935); Exchange of Notes with Regard to the Somali Coast, Feb. 9, 1888, France-United Kingdom, *Brit. and For. State Papers*, Vol. 83, 672 (1897).

[100] Caponera, ref. 47, 254–55; Teclaff, L and Utton, A. (editors) (1981) *International Groundwater Law*; Barberis, J. (1991) 'The development of the international law of transboundary groundwater', *Nat. Resources J.*, Vol. 31, 167–86; Benvenisti, ref. 46, 398–99; Caponera, D. and Alhéritière, D. (1978) 'Principles of international groundwater law', *Nat. Resources J.*, Vol. 18, 589–619; Hayton, R. (1982) 'The law of international aquifers', *Nat. Resources J.*, Vol. 22, 71–93; Rodgers and Utton, ref. 98; Schwebel, ref. 58, 95; Teclaff, L. (1996) 'Evolution of the river basin concept in national and international water law', *Nat. Resources J.*, Vol. 36, 359–91, at 372–74; Utton, A. (1982) 'The development of international groundwater law', *Nat. Resources J.*, Vol. 22, 95–118.

do not refer to any clearly established pattern of state practice, nor to the discovery of a pertinent *opinio juris*. About the only real state authority these scholars can point to regarding transboundary groundwater is a dispute between two German states in which a German court held that the same international legal principles applied to waters above the ground must also be applied to waters below the ground in a dispute between two German states.[101] Indeed, properly speaking, groundwater and surface water are not merely similar, they are the same thing; groundwater and surface water are simply water in differing stages of the hydrologic cycle, and what is today one will tomorrow be the other.

The International Law Association initially took a more cautious approach to the question of whether equitable utilization applied to groundwater because of the dearth of relevant state practice. The *Helsinki Rules* included only those groundwaters that form part of an international drainage basin, that is, that either contribute 'subflow' to the streams or lakes, or otherwise drain into common terminus of the relevant watershed.[102] Twenty years later, the Association was ready to apply the rule of equitable utilization even to 'non-tributary' groundwater, although state practice still had not developed very much. The Association then adopted the *Seoul Rules on the Law of International Groundwater Resources* that address 'international aquifers' rather than drainage basins, that is any body of groundwater that is intersected by an international boundary.[103] The *Seoul Rules* declare that an international aquifer counts as an 'international drainage basin' subject to the *Helsinki Rules* even if the groundwater in no way connects to an internationally shared surface water source.[104] A gathering of experts on the law of international water recently confirmed this conclusion in a meeting at Bellagio, Italy, where they drafted a model treaty to assure the equitable utilization and management of internationally shared groundwaters.[105]

The United Nations as a whole has never taken a position on international groundwaters generally. At the Mar del Plata Conference, the delegates did adopt a resolution that endorsed equitable utilization as the governing principle for sharing water resources, but without any express mention of groundwater as such.[106] The International Law Commission, in its *Draft Articles on the Non-Navigational Use of International Watercourses,* adopted an

---

[101] The Donauversinkung Case (Württemberg and Prussia vs. Baden), 116 RGZ 1 (SGH 1927), in Lauterpacht, H. (editor). (1931) *Ann. Digest Pub. Int. L. Cases* 128.

[102] Helsinki Rules, ref. 5, art. II.

[103] International Law Ass'n, The Seoul Rules on the law of international groundwater resources (Report of the Sixty-Second Conference, Seoul, 1986) ('Seoul Rules').

[104] Seoul Rules, ref. 103, art. II (2).

[105] Hayton, R. and Utton, A. (1989) 'Transboundary Groundwaters: The Bellagio Draft Treaty', *Nat. Resources J.*, Vol. 29, 663–722.

[106] Report of the United Nations Water Conference, Mar del Plata, 14–25 March, 1977, UN Doc. No. E.77.II.A.12 (recommendations 90, 91).

approach that was even more restrictive regarding groundwater than the original approach of the *Helsinki Rules,* including groundwaters that drain to a 'common terminus' with surface waters within its definition of a 'watercourse'.[107] Such a restrictive definition of included groundwater ignores the fact that groundwater might be interdependent with surface water sources and yet follow other paths to the sea (or other terminus) than the surface watercourses do. Failure to address all groundwater is one of the most serious failings of the *Draft Articles.* Arguably the *Draft Articles* would not apply even to groundwater intimately connected to watercourses covered by the *Articles,* thus effectively precluding effective, system-wide management.[108] Furthermore, as the *Seoul Rules* recognize, even groundwater that has no significant connection to surface watercourses can be international in its effects, and thus should be international in its management. Only at the very end of its deliberations on the law of international watercourses did the International Law Commission finally address the problem, but only through a resolution that reads, in relevant part, as follows:

> [T]he principles contained in its draft articles ... may be applied to transboundary confined (*sic*) groundwater and ... the Commission:
> 1. *Commends* States to be guided by the principles contained in the draft articles on the law of non-navigational uses of international watercourses, where appropriate, in regulating transboundary groundwater;
> 2. *Recommends* States to consider entering into agreements with the other State or States in which the confined transboundary groundwater is located;
> 3. *Recommends also* that, in the event of any dispute involving transboundary confined groundwater, the States concerned should consider resolving such dispute in accordance with the provisions contained in article 33 of the draft articles, or in such other manner as may be agreed upon.[109]

As Stephen McCaffrey commented, 'It appears to be exactly what it is: a hasty effort tacked onto the draft articles at the conclusion of the Commission's work'.[110]

The possibility that equitable utilization is required as a rule of general customary international law is supplemented by the growing recognition of a

---

[107] Draft Articles II, ref. 46, art. 1.

[108] The Donauversinkung case involved a dispute that arose because part of the groundwater underlying the upper Danube discharge into the Aach River which feeds into the Rhine and not into the Danube. The Donauversinkung Case (Württemberg and Prussia vs. Baden), 116 RGZ 1 (SGH 1927), in Lauterpacht, H. (editor) (1931) *Ann. Digest Pub. Int. L. Cases* 128. See also Teclaff, ref. 43, 9.

[109] ILC Report, ref 46, 326. See McCaffrey, S. (1996) 'An assessment of the work of the International Law Commission', *Nat. Resources J.*, Vol. 36, 297–318, at 316–18; Rosenstock, R. (1995) 'The forty-ninth session of the International Law Commission', *Am. J. Int. L.*, Vol. 89, 390–95, at 392.

[110] McCaffrey, ref. 109, 318.

right to development and even of a possible human right to water.[111] Now is
not the time or place to analyze and evaluate these claims. The arguments are
complex and controversial. Here we need only note that neither social and
economic development, nor even the satisfaction of basic survival needs, are
possible if only one community sharing an aquifer monopolizes its waters. Such
supposed human rights, even if they do not provide satisfactory means for
resolving disputes over aquifers, at the least lend weight to the supposition that
the waters of those aquifers must be shared equitably.

Foremost among the problems in applying equitable utilization to an
aquifer is the relative lack of firm knowledge of the hydrologic characteristics
of the resource.[112] We know quite a lot about surface water sources, having
made accurate and ongoing measurements of these sources for a century or
more. We can observe where surface water flows and what variables affect its
behavior. Groundwater is very different. Groundwater, like surface waters,
responds to gravity, seeking its lowest level, yet it does not flow as freely as
surface waters. The structure, porosity, and slope of the rocks or soil through
which it seeps or percolates determine the path of movement for groundwater.
Because of the variability of subsurface conditions, there is a great deal we
simply do not know about the characteristics of particular aquifers. To acquire
more knowledge is expensive. We are then only able to make tentative
allocations that informal processes such as are found in customary regimes are
ill adapted to revise or supplement.

3.5 The failure of customary regimes

Reliance on customary international law to allocate surface or subsurface
waters among states simply has not worked very well.[113] The system is too
informal, lacks precise rules, and also lacks the means for effectuating and
enforcing such rules as it has. The remarkable thing is that this informal system
has worked as well as it has in many parts of the world. To begin to examine

---

[111] See Kanaaneh, H., McKay, F. and Sims, E. (1995) 'A human right approach for access to
clean drinking water: a case study', *Health and Hum. Rts.*, Vol. 1, 191–204; McCaffrey, S.
(1992) 'A human right to water: domestic and international implications', *Geo. Int. Envtl. L.
Rev.* Vol. 3, 1–24. See also Smith, ref. 47, 96; Benvenisti, ref. 46, 405–08; Bourne, C. (1965)
'The right to utilize the waters of international rivers', *Can. Y.B. Int. L.*, Vol. 3, 184–264, at
192–95; Dellapenna, J. (1996) 'Rivers as legal structures: the examples of the Jordan and the
Nile', *Nat. Resources J.*, Vol. 36, 217–50, at 246–47.

[112] Hillel, ref. 1, 194. See generally Murphy, E.F. (1991) 'Geology and hydrology', in Beck, ref.
53, Vol. 3, § 18.03; Tsur, Y. (1995) 'Uncertainty and irreversibility in groundwater resource
management', *J. Envtl. Econ. and Mgt.* Vol. 29, 149–61.

[113] Paisley, R. and McDaniels, T. (1995) 'International water law, acceptable pollution risk
and the Tatshenshini River', *Nat. Resources J.*, Vol. 35, 111–132, at 124–26.

why the customary international regime fails first consider the experience of the United States, a nation in which there has been so much litigation over 'equitable apportionment' between states that the cases of the US Supreme Court are often described as the origin of the international rule of 'equitable utilization'. Even with each state in the United States agreeing on the rule of 'equitable apportionment', and with a highly effective federal judiciary exercising compulsory jurisdiction over competing states, equitable sharing simply has proven too cumbersome and too uncertain to satisfy states involved disputes over interstate sources of water.[114] There have been frequent and recurring disputes over what should be the common standard and the proper application of any agreed standard.[115]

In disputes over international water sharing, the lack of the elaborate federal institutional arrangements found in the United States would ultimately lead back to the law of the vendetta.[116] International law is simply too primitive to solve the continuing management problems in a timely fashion. While uncertainty of legal right can induce cooperation among those sharing a resource, it can also promote severe conflict.[117] Relying upon an informal legal system alone to legitimate and limit claims to use shared water resources is inherently unstable. It becomes unsettled either when one or more states consider that it is so militarily dominant that it can disregard the interests of its neighbours, or when one or more states consider that their interests are so compromised by the existing situation that even the risk of military defeat is more tolerable than continuing the present situation without challenge.[118]

Yet, no solution is possible without the creation of the necessary law. If a cooperative management system is to be put in place for internationally shared fresh waters, that system must entail the creation of some sort of legal

---

[114] See Anderson, S. (1984) 'Note, equitable apportionment and the Supreme Court: what's so equitable about apportionment?', *Hamline L. Rev.*, Vol. 7, 405–29; Dellapenna, J. 'The Delaware and Susquehanna River Basins', in Beck, ref. 53, Vol. 6, 137–50; Grant, ref. 77; Tarlock, ref. 77.

[115] See the authorities collected at ref. 77.

[116] Shapland, G. (1995) 'Policy options for downstream states in the Middle East', in Allan and Mallat, ref. 81, 301–23, at 309; Van Alstyne, W. (1964) 'The justiciability of international river disputes: a study in the case method', *Duke L.J.*, Vol. 1964, 307–40. See generally Falk, R. (1959) 'International jurisdiction: horizontal and vertical conceptions of legal order', *Temple L.Q.*, Vol. 32, 295–320.

[117] See Benvenisti, ref. 46; Radinsky, M. (1994) 'Retaliation: the genesis of a law and the evolution toward international cooperation: an application of game theory to modern international conflicts', *Geo. Mason U. L. Rev.*, Vol. 2, 52–75. See generally Axelrod, R. (1984) *The Evolution of Cooperation*; Ellickson, R. (1991) *Order without Law: How Neighbors Settle Disputes*; Fisher, R. and Brown, S. (1988) *Getting Together*, 197–202; Bendor, J. (1993) 'Uncertainty and the Evolution of Cooperation', *J. Conflict Resolution*, Vol. 37, 709–34; Kornhauser, L. (1992) 'Are there cracks in the foundation of spontaneous order? Order without law: how neighbors settle disputes (book rev.)', *NYU L. Rev.*, Vol., 67, 647–73; Young, ref. 64.

[118] Naff and Matson, ref. 58, 161. Cf. Habeeb, W.M. (1988) *Power and Tactics in International Negotiations: How Weak Nations Bargain with Strong Nations*.

mechanism for resolving disputes. The inevitably of recurring bitter disputes, even overt military conflict, would remain under a concept of restrictive sovereignty even where water consumption is tied to some more or less objective record of need (historic use or the like) so long as there is no effective alternative mechanism for resolving the inevitable disputes. The situation would be even worse if the actors were to measure the right to use water by a vaguely defined equitable utilization. The closest analogue to this system is the riparian rights system (and its interstate analogue of 'equitable apportion-ment') as applied in the eastern Unitd States. We have already noted the difficulties in making the 'equitable apportionment' system work between states of the United States. The 'reasonable use' version of riparian rights applied in the eastern United States is perhaps an even more instructive example of why such vague rules cannot survive as water allocation systems in regions where demand consistently approaches or exceeds supply. The 'reasonable use' theory of riparian rights has barely functioned in areas of the United States that are without chronic water shortages and that have a strong judicial structure to resolve disputes between users.[119] Whenever water use in the eastern United States outstrips the available sources of water, riparian rights have been abandoned in favor of a new system of water rights that are heavily administered by state agencies that allocate water to particular uses by time-limited permits and leave authority in the agencies to determine the most socially beneficial ('reasonable') use of the water.[120]

While stress on water resources creates pressures for cooperative solutions to the problems confronting the communities sharing the resources, the creation of a formal legal system is a necessary prerequisite to preventing conflict over water in any community where water resources are under stress. Cooperative management has taken many forms around the world, ranging from continuing and unceasing consultations, to a system of active cooperative management that remains in the hands of the participating states, to the creation of a variety of regional institutions capable of making and enforcing their decisions directly.[121] Experience as well as theory thus suggests that serious conflict in one form or another cannot be avoided under the rule of equitable utilization without a legal mechanism for the orderly investigation and resolution of the disputes characteristic of that theory.

---

[119] See generally Dellapenna, J. (2001) 'The right to consume water under 'pure' riparian rights', in Beck, ref. 53, Vol. 1, ch. 7 (replacement vol.).
[120] See generally Dellapenna, J. (2001) 'Regulated riparianism', in Beck, ref. 53, ch. 9 (replacement vol.).
[121] See Dellapenna, 'Designing', ref. 43.

4. The United Nations codifies the customary law

When first confronted with the *Helsinki Rules*, the United Nations General Assembly refrained from explicitly endorsing those Rules.[122] Instead, the General Assembly called upon the International Law Commission to prepare a set of 'draft articles' on the 'non-navigational uses of international watercourses'.[123] The Commission worked on the project for 23 years, producing a first draft of the *Draft Articles on Non-Navigational Use of International Watercourses* in 1991,[124] and a final draft in 1994.[125] At that point, the General Assembly instructed the Sixth Committee to prepare a draft convention for the Assembly to consider. This produced a revised text that was approved by the General Assembly on May 21, 1997, by a vote of 104-3.[126] An examination of the evolution of these texts serves to identify the key points and central difficulties with the existing customary international law of transboundary waters.

4.1 The first draft articles of the International Law Commission

The International Law Commission is an organ of the United Nations designed to promote the 'progressive codification of customary international law'.[127] Although the law of international rivers has been on the agenda of the Commission since 1949, nothing much was done until a resolution of the General Assembly asked the Commission to give priority to the issue. Thereafter, the work was plagued by frequent changes of 'Special Rapporteur'

---

[122] Bruhàcs, ref. 47, 19.

[123] Progressive development and codification of the rules of international law relating to international watercourses, GA Res. 2669 (XXV), Dec. 8, 1970, UN Doc. A/8028; Sinclair, ref. 34; UN Secretariat, ref. 34, 27, 40. For summary histories of the Commission's work on international rivers, see McCaffrey, ref. 109; Rahman, R. (1995) 'The law of international uses of international watercourses: dilemma for lower riparians', *Fordham Int. L.J.*, Vol. 14, 9–24, at 10–17; Westcoat, jr., J. (1992) 'Beyond the river basin: the changing geography of international water problems and international watercourse law', *Colo. J. Int. Envtl. L. and Pol'y.*, Vol. 3, 301–30.

[124] Int. L. Comm'n, Draft Articles on the law of non-navigational use of international watercourses, UN Doc. A/CN.4/L.463/Add.4 (1991), reprinted in *Colo. J. Int. Envtl. L.*, Vol. 3, 1–11 (1992) ('Draft Articles I').

[125] Draft Articles II, ref. 46.

[126] UN Convention, ref. 9. The three negative votes were by Burundi, the People's Republic of China, and Turkey.

[127] See generally UN Charter, art. 13(1); Statute of the International Law Commission, UN Doc. A/CN.4 rev. 2 (1982); Sinclair, ref. 35; UN Secretariat, ref. 29; Condorelli, ref. 11, 179, 194–97; Graefrath, ref. 35.

for the project, with five Special Rapporteurs serving in a little more than 20 years. We need not invest time in these early deliberations as the Commission completed a 'first reading' of its *Draft Articles on Non-Navigational Use of International Watercourses* and submitted the resulting *Articles* to the General Assembly in 1991.[128] At this point, the Commission embraced both the rule of equitable utilization and the obligation not to cause appreciable harm to other states, without clearly indicating the relationship between the two rules:

Article 5
Equitable and reasonable utilization and participation
1. Watercourse States shall in their respective territories utilize an international watercourse in an equitable and reasonable manner. In particular, an international watercourse shall be used and developed by watercourse States with a view to attaining optimal utilization thereof and benefits therefrom consistent with adequate protection in the watercourse.
2. Watercourse States shall participate in the use, development and protection of an international watercourse in an equitable and reasonable manner. Such participation includes both the right to utilize the watercourse and the duty to cooperate in the protection and development thereof, as provided in the present articles.

Article 7
Obligation not to cause appreciable harm
Watercourse States shall utilize an international watercourse in such a way as not to cause appreciable harm to other watercourse States.

Some see in article 5's formulation of the rule of equitable utilization a diminution of the right of each state to share in a common watercourse.[129] These critics see article 5 (and the *Draft Articles* generally) as focusing too much on procedural questions and not enough on substantive issues. They object to the omission of the word 'right' and to the focus on 'equitable utilization' rather than an 'equitable share' of the water source, and to the criterion of 'optimal utilization' when, one critic has argued, the criterion should be 'sustainable utilization'. The concepts of 'equitable and reasonable utilization' and 'optimal utilization' are sufficiently open that any of the goals of the critics are compatible with the *Draft Articles*.[130] The *Draft Articles* do not guarantee such goals, however. Flexibility is a real strength of the rule of equitable utilization. The 'no harm' rule is more troubling.

State practice provides some support for a 'no harm' rule. A number of treaties have included promises by each state not to undertake or to permit to be undertaken any works on a river or other water body if the works would cause 'any injury' (or words to like effect) to interests centred in the other

---

[128] Draft Articles I, ref. 124.
[129] Rahman, ref. 123, 16–17, 22–23.
[130] See ILC Report, ref. 46, 218–19.

state.[131] This proposition is simply an application of the Latin legal maxim '*sic utere tuo ut alienam non laedas*': 'Do not use your property so as to injure the property of another'.[132] The arbitral panel in the Trail Smelter case, an international dispute involving air pollution, applied the proposition:

> [U]nder the principles of international law, ... no State has the right to use or permit the use of its territory in such a manner as to cause injury by fumes in or to the territory of another ... when the injury is of serious consequence and the injury is established by clear and convincing evidence.[133]

Finally, the principle was endorsed by the United Nations General Assembly in 1972, and by the Declaration of Asunción on the Use of International Rivers adopted by Argentina, Brazil, and Paraguay the year before.[134]

The problem is not whether some form of the 'no harm' rule is valid, but how is one to reconcile the apparently absolute command expressed in article 7 of the first reading of the *Draft Articles* with the flexibility inherent in the rule of equitable utilization as expressed in article 5 of the same *Articles*. Strict application of a 'no harm' rule prohibits any meaningful use by an upper-riparian state, turning the rule into merely a variant form of the absolute integrity claim. But would not the barring of all development in the upstream state be a harm to it, just as a reduction in the quantity or quality of flow reaching the downstream state is an injury to it? Either the 'no harm' rule

---

[131] Act Regarding Navigation and Economic Co-Operation between the States of the Niger Basin, signed Oct. 26, 1963, Cameroon-Chad-Dahomey-Guinea-Ivory Coast-Mali-Niger-Nigeria-Upper Volta, art. 2, 587 UNTS 9; Convention Concerning the Lakes or Courses of Common Waters, Oct. 26, 1905, Norway-Sweden, art. 11, 34 G.F. de Martens, Nouveau Recueil Général des Traités (2e ser.) 711; Treaty Relating to Boundary Waters between the United States and Canada, Jan. 11, 1909, United Kingdom-United States, art. 2, Legislative Texts, ref. 75, no. 79. See also Colorado Treaty, ref. 54, art. 17.

[132] The Corfu Channel (United Kingdom v. Albania), [1949] *ICJ* 4, at p.22; Godana, ref. 64, 50; Ahmed, ref. 81, 225–26; Goldenman, ref. 59 779–81; McCaffrey, ref. 8, 115–16, 133–34; Report of the United Nations on the Human Environment, Stockholm, 5–16, 1972, UN Sales No. E.73.II.A.14 (principle 21) ('Stockholm Declaration'); Schwebel, ref. 8, 92–95. See also [1911] Annuaire de l'institut de droit international, Vol. 24, 365–366 ('Madrid Declaration'); Berber, ref. 47, 211–215; Bruhàcs, ref. 47, 121–148; Lammers, ref. 71, 525–527; Oppenheim, ref. 81, 345–346, 474–476; Lester, ref. 81, 847; Wouters, ref. 81, 45–46. See also Merrill, T. (1997) 'Golden rules for transboundary pollution', *Duke L.J.*, Vol. 46, 931–1019.

[133] The Trail Smelter arbitration, (1941) *Int. L. Rep.* Vol. 9, 315, 317. See generally Shaw, ref. 11, 532–39; Kirgis, F. (1974) 'The technological challenge of the shared environment: U.S. practice', *Am. J. Int. L.*, Vol. 66, 291–320; McCaffrey, ref. 47, 119–21; Read, J. (1963) 'The Trail Smelter arbitration', *Can. Y.B. Int. L.*, Vol. 1, 213–29.

[134] GA Res. 2995 (XXVII), Dec. 15, 1972; Act of Asuncion, signed June 3, 1971, Argentina-Bolivia-Brazil-Paraguay, art. 4, reproduced in Organization of Am. States (1971) Rios y Lagos internacionales, 4th rev. ed. OEA/Ser. I/Vi, CIJ–75 rev. 2. See also Stockholm Declaration, ref. 133, principle 21 and recommendation 21; McCaffrey, ref. 47, 111, 122.

incorporates some measure of flexibility into its application or the rule is strictly binding with the 'equitable utilization' rule being somehow aberrational, relevant only in certain (unspecified) peculiar circumstances.

Experts on international water law have been nearly unanimous on the primacy of the equitable utilization rule in international water law,[135] including the Special Rapporteurs who collectively drafted articles 5 and 7.[136] Stephen McCaffrey, the fourth Special Rapporteur for the project, later concluded, however, that the International Law Commission intended the 'no harm' rule to be primary, with the rule of equitable utilization to be subordinated to the 'no harm' rule.[137] McCaffrey himself did not seem entirely convinced. He has publicly stated that the 'no harm' rule does not comport with state practice[138] and he has argued that there is a 'human right to water',[139] a right than can hardly exist if the overriding obligation of communities is to defer to pre-existing or downstream uses under the 'no harm' rule.

At least three reasons have been advanced for the primacy of the 'no harm' rule. First, the rule is said to protect a weaker state against harm inflicted by a stronger co-riparian. Second, the 'no harm' rule provides a clear line to determine which state is in the wrong. Finally, the 'no harm' rule is said to be preferable because the most important current issues in managing shared water resources pertain to pollution rather than to allocation as such and in

[135] See the authorities collected in refs. 81–85.

[136] International Law Comm'n, 1785th Meeting, (1983) *Y.B. Int. L. Comm'n*, Vol. 1, 171, 177–78 (statement of Special Rapporteur Jens Evensen); McCaffrey, S. (1985) 'An update on the contributions of the International Law Commission to international environmental law', *Envtl. L.*, Vol. 15, 667–78, at 672–74; McCaffrey, ref. 75, 150–61; McCaffrey, ref. 47, 94–95, 130–34; Schwebel, ref. 58, 82–85, 103. See also Bourne, C. (1992) 'The International Law Commission's draft articles on the law of international watercourses: principles and planned measures', *Colo. J. Int. Envtl. L. and Pol'y*, Vol. 3, 65–92, at 73–77.

[137] McCaffrey, ref. 109, 307–09; McCaffrey, S. (1995) 'The International Law Commission adopts draft articles on international watercourses', *Am. J. Int. L.*, Vol. 89, 395–404, at p.399 ('McCaffrey, "Commission adopts draft articles"'); McCaffrey, S. (1991) 'The International Law Commission and its efforts to codify the international law of waterways', *Annuaire suisse de droit international* vol. 47, 32–55, at 48–52; McCaffrey, S. (1990) 'The law of international watercourses: ecocide or ecomanagement?', *Revista Jurídica U.P.R.*, Vol. 59, 1003–12, at 1005-08 ('McCaffrey, "Ecocide"'); McCaffrey, S. (1989) 'The law of international watercourses: some recent developments and unanswered questions', *Den. J. Int. L. and Pol'y*, Vol. 17, 505–26, at 509–10 ('McCaffrey, "Recent Developments"'). See also Bourne, ref. 136, 77–82; Handl, G. (1992) 'The International Law Commission's draft articles on the law of international watercourses (general principles and planned measures): progressive or retrogressive development of international law?', *Colo. J. Int. Envtl. L. and Pol'y*, Vol. 3, 123–34, at 129–33.

[138] McCaffrey, ref. 109, 309–10, 312; McCaffrey, S. (1990) 'The non-navigational uses of international watercourses', *Proc. Am. Soc'y Int. L.*, Vol. 84, 228–32, at 231 ('McCaffrey, "Non-Navigational Uses"'); McCaffrey, 'Recent Developments', ref. 137, 523 n.71.

[139] McCaffrey, ref. 111.

principle, so it is argued, no pollution should be tolerated.[140] There are, however, a number of reasons why McCaffrey's conclusion that the 'no harm' rule is primary will not withstand careful analysis. The language of the *Draft Articles* themselves does not support the primacy of the no harm rule. One perhaps could conclude that the 'no harm' rule of article 7 is primary by comparing the categorical command in article 7 with the more precatory language of article 5. Such an analysis, however, requires us to ignore the express command of the *Draft Articles* themselves as proposed in the 1991 version of the articles (as well as the current version):

Article 10
Relationship between different kinds of uses
1. In the absence of agreement or custom to the contrary, no use of an international watercourse enjoys priority over other uses.
2. In the event of a conflict between uses of an international watercourse, it shall be resolved with reference to the principles and factors set out in articles 5 to 7, with special regard being given to the requirements of vital human needs.

More important than the language of the Draft Articles is the reality that what harm is 'appreciable' or rises to some other such standard is not an objective truth, but a matter which each state will appreciate for itself – leading not to clear bright lines but to serious disputes that will in the end be negotiated or arbitrated on some equitable basis.[141] While the appearance of harm (or the threat of harm) tends to trigger the process of claim and counterclaim from which customary international law arises, the resolution of any such dispute does not centre on the prevention of harm, but on the equitable allocation of benefits and costs.[142] No resolution of an interstate water dispute has ever been based upon the proposition, logically derived from the 'no harm' rule, that upper-riparian states can make no significant use of a watercourse for fear of inflicting harm downstream.[143] Nor is it always clear which state is the 'weaker state'.

---

[140] See, e.g., ILC Report, ref. 46, 242; Belgrade Rules, ref. 92, art. 1; Bruhàcs, ref. 47, 194–204; Caponera, ref. 47, 219–21, 223–25; Nollkaemper, A. (1993) *The Legal Regime for Transboundary Water Pollution: Between Discretion and Constraint*, 61–69; Teclaff, *Historical Perspective*, ref. 44, 457–77; Ando, N. 'The law of pollution prevention in international rivers and lakes', in Zacklin and Caflisch, ref. 50, 331; Prieur, M. (1991) 'Protection of the environment', in *Achievements and Prospects*, ref. 6, 1017–38, at 1020–22; McCaffrey, 'Ecocide', ref. 137; McCaffrey, ref. 109, 308; McCaffrey, 'Recent Developments', ref. 137, 513–25.

[141] Bruhàcs, ref. 47, 142–43; Bourne, ref. 136, 83–88; Handl, ref. 81, 61–62.

[142] Krishna, R. (1990) 'The non-navigational uses of international watercourses', *Proc. Am. Soc'y Int. L.*, Vol. 84, 232–35, at 234–35; Solanes, ref. 75, 120–21; Young, ref. 64, 368–69.

[143] ILC Report, ref. 46, 212–13. For a contrary view, see Bourne, ref. 111, 230–45, 261–64. Bourne's view was criticized, and Bourne has not repeated his argument in his later writings. See also Bruhàcs, ref. 47, 135–39.

A state seeking to initiate a new use would generally be cast in the posture of the one creating the 'injury'. Therefore the 'no harm' or absolute integrity claim favors the more highly developed states at the expense of their less developed neighbours, particularly as the lower basin states tend to develop earlier and faster than upper basin states.[144] One would expect the downstream state to be in the weaker position relative to upstream state. After all, the upstream state has power to affect the river before it ever reaches the downstream state. If the upstream state dams or diverts the flow, it literally could cut off some or all water from a downstream state. One finds, however, that the 'weaker' state is actually the stronger state.[145] The exceptions generally occur in situations were a region is colonized by a technologically more developed culture from outside the region. Perhaps the most notable example is the USA relative to Mexico.[146]

In practical application, the 'no harm' rule resembles the 'natural flow' theory of riparian rights in US law and also the rule of prior appropriation as found in the western states of the United States.[147] Priority of use, while undoubtedly relevant to an equitable allocation of water among national communities, has never been treated as dispositive in international law.[148] This is implicit in all texts of the ILC Draft Articles, and explicit in the commentary to those articles as adopted on the second reading.[149]

---

[144] Bruhàcs, ref. 47, 132–43; Bourne, ref. 88, 92; Dellapenna, ref. 111, 245–46; Ely, N. and Wolman, A. (1967) 'Administration', in Garretson, Hayton, and Olmstead, ref. 47, 124–59, at 124–25; Garretson, A. (1967) 'The Nile basin', in Garretson, Hayton, and Olmstead, supra at 256–97, at 264–65. See also Ahmed, ref. 81, 225–29. See generally Westcoat, ref. 123.

[145] Dellapenna, ref. 111, 245; Wouters, ref. 81, 82. See also Lammers, ref. 81, 364; Gaines, S. (1991) 'Taking responsibility for transboundary environmental effects', *Hastings Int. and Comp. L. Rev.*, Vol. 14, 781–809, at 798.

[146] See Székely, A. (1992) ' "General principles" and "planned measures" provisions in the International Law Commission's Draft Articles on the non-navigational uses of international watercourses: a Mexican point of view', *Colo. J. Int. Envtl. L. and Pol'y*, Vol. 3, 93–101.

[147] Benvenisti, ref. 46, 403. See generally Beck, R. (2001) 'Prevalence and definition', in *Waters and Water Rights*, ref. 53, Vol. 1, ch. 12 (replacement vol.); Dellapenna, ref. 136, § 7.02(c).

[148] Helsinki Rules, ref. 5, art. V(d); Baxter, R.R. (1977) Legal Questions Arising Out of the Construction of a Dam at Maqarin on the Yarmuk River, 65–68; Bruhàcs, ref. 47, 132–40; Elmusa, ref. 47, 36; Saliba, ref. 57, 70; Smith, ref. 47, 40, 146; Benvenisti, ref. 46, 408–09, 411; Bourne, ref. 111, 233, 257; Dellapenna, ref. 111, 247–49; Garretson, ref. 146, 287–89; Lipper, ref. 47, 57–58; Maluwa, ref. 47, 30–33; Shuval, H. (1992) 'Approaches to resolving water conflicts between Israel and her neighbors – a regional water-for-peace plan', *Water Int.*, Vol. 17, 133–43, at 136–38, 141–42; Wouters, ref. 81, 82. For a contrary view, see Fahmi, ref. 46, 51–54. On the importance of prior uses under international law without making them the determining factor in the allocation of water, see Godana, ref. 47, 62; Batstone, R.K. (1959) 'The utilization of Nile waters', *Int. and Comp. L.Q.*, Vol. 8, 523–58, at 529; Benvenisti, supra at 408–09; Benvenisti and Gvirtzman, ref. 81, 548–49.

[149] Draft Articles II, ref. 46, art. 6(1)(e) (requiring consideration of 'existing and potential uses of the watercourse'); Draft Articles I, ref. 124, art. 6(1)(e) (same); ILC Report, ref. 46, 233 (explaining the text as having been adopted 'in order to emphasize that neither is given priority ....').

To treat priority in time as controlling, or even dominant, would replace the balancing of need and interest characteristic of equitable utilization with an absolute rule derived from history rather than from geography. Nowhere is it made clear why protection should be given to recently developed uses as opposed to long-established historic uses (over centuries or even millennia) simply because, for any number of reasons, the historic uses were in abeyance when the recently established uses began.[150] As Eyal Benvenisti, an Israeli expert on international water law, has noted, to give absolute priority to uses existing at the start of the negotiations destroys any incentive for the 'harmed state' – the state with the 'existing' uses – to negotiate with a state that seeks to initiate new uses.[151] The no harm rule thus would hardly be conducive to the developmental equity proclaimed by the United Nations, let alone sustainable development.[152] Indeed, Stephen McCaffrey, despite his assertion of the primacy of the 'no-harm' rule, has himself argued that there is not only a personal right to water but also a social right for states to receive the water from co-riparian states insofar as necessary for the receiving state to develop and flourish.[153]

We can reconcile the two rules by stressing that the no harm rule actually prohibits, in its various incarnations, only 'appreciable harm', 'sensible harm', 'significant harm', 'substantial harm', or the like.[154] These standards could be interpreted to require a determination whether a use represents a reasonable or equitable utilization.[155] As the German federal supreme court stated in The Donauversinkung case, '[o]ne must consider not only the absolute injury caused to the neighboring State, but also the relation of the advantage gained by one to the injury caused to the other'.[156] By this view, the rule of no appreciable harm is just a variant statement of restricted sovereignty in the water source, that is, of the rule of equitable utilization. This does not deny

---

[150] Beaumont, P. (1994) 'The growing pressures on water resources in the Middle East and the need for new approaches to provide solutions', in Bagis, A.İ. (editor) *Water as an Element of Cooperation and Development in the Middle East*, 201–12, at 209–10. See also ILC Report, ref. 46, 221.

[151] Benvenisti, ref. 46, 403.

[152] Benvenisti, ref. 46, 403–04.

[153] McCaffrey, ref. 111, 17–24. See also Smith, ref. 47, 96; Benvenisti, ref. 46, 405–08; Bourne, ref. 111, 192–95; Dellapenna, ref. 111, 246–47.

[154] Schwebel, ref. 58, 98–100. See also Bruhàcs, ref. 47, 129–30; Magraw, D.B. (1986) 'Transboundary harm: the International Law Commission's study of "international liability"', *Am. J. Int. L.*, Vol. 80, 305–30, at 322; Sachariew, K. (1990) 'The definition of thresholds of tolerance for transboundary environmental injury under international law: development and present status', *Neth. Int. L. Rev.*, Vol. 37, 193–206..

[155] Belgrade Rules, ref. 92, art. 1; Helsinki Rules, ref. 5, art. X commentary; Bruhàcs, ref. 47, 137–40; McCaffrey, ref. 75, 144–50; Schwebel, ref. 58, 99–107.

[156] The Donauversinkung Case (Württemberg and Prussia vs. Baden), 116 RGZ 1, 4 (SGH 1927), Lauterpacht, H. (editor) (1931) *Ann. Digest Pub. Int. L. Cases*, 128, 131. See also Bourne, ref. 111, 82–92; Schwebel, ref. 58, 102. See generally Coase, R. (1960) 'The problem of social cost', *J.L. and Econ.*, Vol. 3, 1–44.

appropriate protection to ecosystems or prevent appropriate regulation of pollution. After all, the leading authorities on the protection of international water resources from pollution or other degradation have all found the rule of equitable utilization to be an appropriate vehicle for accomplishing the necessary protection.[157]

4.2 The final Draft Articles of the International Law Commission

The first *Draft Articles* provoked considerable controversy, both among foreign ministries and among the most highly qualified publicists who have worked on the topic. As a result, the International Law Commission considerably revised *Draft Articles* at their 'second reading' in Geneva in July 1994.[158] Under the leadership of yet another Rapporteur, Robert Rosenstock of the United States, the International Law Commission did not revise either article 5 or article 10, but completely rewrote article 7 on the 'no harm rule':

Article 7
Obligation not to cause significant harm
1. Watercourse States shall exercise due diligence to utilize an international watercourse in such a way as not to cause significant harm to other watercourse States.

---

[157] UN Convention on the protection and uses of transboundary watercourses and international lakes, signed at Helsinki, Mar. 17, 1992, art. 2(2) (qualifying the obligation to reduce transboundary pollution with an obligation to 'ensure that transboundary waters are used in a reasonable and equitable way'). UN Doc. E/ECE/1267, reproduced in *Int. Leg. Mat'ls*, Vol. 31, pp.1312–1329 (1992) ('Helsinki Convention'). See also Lammers, ref. 71, 496–501, 540–43, 580–84, 600; Shaw, ref. 11, 532–37; Brownlie, I. (1991) 'State Responsibility and International Pollution: A Practical Perspective', in Magraw, D. (editor) *International Law and Pollution*, 120–25; Dupuy, P-M. (1991) 'Overview of the existing customary legal regime regarding international pollution', *International Law and Pollution*, supra at 61–89; Goldenman, ref. 59, 786–92; Gaines, ref. 146, 798; Handl, G. (1975) 'Balancing of interests and international liability for the pollution of international watercourses: customary principles revisited', *Can. Y.B. Int. L.*, Vol. 13, 156–94; Kiss, A. (1987) 'The protection of the Rhine against pollution', in *Transboundary Resources Law*, ref. 98, 51–75; McCaffrey, S. (1991) 'International liability and international watercourses: the work of the International Law Commission relating to international pollution', in *International Law and Pollution*, supra at 90–119; Magraw, ref. 155; Nanda, V. (1992) 'The law of the non-navigational uses of international watercourses: draft articles on protection and preservation of ecosystems, harmful conditions and emergency situations and protection of water installations', *Colo. J. Int. Envtl. L. and Pol'y*, Vol. 3, 175–207; Prieur, ref. 137, at 1026–27; Teclaff, L. (1991) 'International control of cross media pollution – an ecosystem approach', in Transboundary Resources Law, supra at 289–321. But see Nollkaemper, ref. 141, 66–69; Boyle, A. (1990) 'State responsibility and international liability for injurious consequences of acts not prohibited by international law: a necessary distinction', *Int. and Comp. L.Q.*, Vol. 39, 1–26, at 19–20.

2. Where, despite the exercise of due diligence, significant harm is caused to another watercourse State, the State whose use causes the harm shall, in the absence of agreement to such use, consult with the State suffering such harm over:

    (a) the extent to which such use has proved equitable and reasonable taking into account the factors listed in article 6;

    (b) the question of ad hoc adjustments to its utilization, designed to eliminate or mitigate any such harm caused and, where appropriate, the question of compensation.

In rewriting Article 7, the Commission went considerably beyond even what Special Rapporteur Rosenstock had recommended.[159] The substitution of the phrase 'significant harm' for the earlier term 'appreciable harm' perhaps itself signals a greater recognition of the need for balancing the interests of the competing states in order to determine whether the infliction of harm violates the norms of customary international law.[160] Others would see the change as merely cosmetic, designed to make the *Draft Articles* consistent with the language usually employed by others summarizing this body of customary international law. One need not resolve this question, however, as the other changes in the text of article 7 appear clearly to subordinate the 'no harm' rule to the rule of equitable utilization.

Former Special Rapporteur Stephen McCaffrey, who wrote the original article 7, reads the revised article 7 as substituting a process for resolving issues relating to harm for the flat prohibition of harm found in the original article 7, without changing the ultimate dominance of the 'no harm' rule over the 'equitable utilization' rule.[161] McCaffrey saw the revision as recognizing that the complex issues that invariably arise during disputes over an internationally shared watercourse must be negotiated within a legal framework, but without a predetermined outcome. Apparently McCaffrey reads the first subsection of the revised article 7 without regard the real import of the changes introduced into article 7 in the second reading. Even McCaffrey concedes that the new subsection 2 of article 7 implies that a use that causes significant harm is not '*per se* a breach of the state's international obligations'[162] and that 'if a state's use is equitable it should be allowed to continue, even if it causes significant harm to another state' while also noting that the two paragraphs are meant to

---

[158] Draft Articles II, ref. 46; Rosenstock, ref. 109, 392.

[159] Robert Rosenstock, Second Report on the Law of the Non-Navigational Uses of International Watercourses, UN Doc. A/CN.4/452, at 11 (Apr. 21, 1994). See generally Bruhàcs, ref. 47, 217–220; McCaffrey, 'Commission Adopts Draft Articles', ref. 137, 399 n.29. All but one of the five rapporteurs were Americans.

[160] See Rahman, ref. 123, 23; Schwebel, ref. 58, 93–107. The permutations of this phrase are summarized in Schwebel, supra at 93.

[161] McCaffrey, ref. 109, 308–11; McCaffrey, 'Commission Adopts Draft Articles', ref. 137, 399–401.

[162] McCaffrey, 'Commission Adopts Draft Articles', ref. 137, 400.

interrelate, with any negotiations about the equitableness of a use being combined with negotiations about adjustments and compensation.[163] McCaffrey never attempted to reconcile these several observations with his overall conclusion that the 'no harm' rule remains intact and dominant.

The new article 7, in subsection 1, reduces the apparently absolute command of the original article 7 to an obligation to use 'due diligence' to avoid significant harm. McCaffrey has argued that this is a cosmetic change, and that the limitation that only due diligence was required to avoid harm was always implicit in the original text of article 7.[164] That may have been McCaffrey's intent when he wrote the original article 7, but unfortunately there is not one word in that text to support such an implication, and even McCaffrey concedes that the new subsection 2 does significantly alter the thrust of the article. In subsection 2, the new article 7 provides an obligation for the state causing harm to consult with the injured state, but qualifies that limited obligation by requiring consultation only over the question of whether the harmful use is 'equitable and reasonable' and the question of whether harm might be reduced or prevented by 'adjustments' to the way the water is used. The reference to 'the question of compensation' at the end of the subsection (2)(b) thus is highly ambiguous.[165] To conclude, as McCaffrey does, that under the revised Article 7 compensation will always be due when significant harm occurs ignores the inclusion of the reference to compensation only in subsection (2)(b). Such a conclusion also ignores the introduction of the obligation to make compensation by the limitation 'where appropriate'. Clearly, even when there is significant harm, compensation will not always be appropriate.

The International Law Commission's commentary to revised article 7 is nearly as confusing as the text. It opens by indicating that the goal is to avoid 'significant harm as far as possible while reaching an equitable result in concrete cases' and that ' "equitable and reasonable utilization" of an international watercourse may still involve significant harm to another watercourse state'.[166] The Commission's commentary then goes on to state that 'the principle of equitable utilization remains the guiding criterion in balancing the interests at stake'.[167] Shortly thereafter, however, the commentary states that the requirement of due diligence 'sets the threshold for lawful State activity' which might be seen as reaffirming the primacy of the no harm rule.[168]

The Commission's endorsements of the primacy of the principle of equitable utilization in the commentary are repeated and explicit. The notion that the

[163] McCaffrey, ref. 109, 310–12.
[164] McCaffrey, ref. 109, 309–10.
[165] McCaffrey, ref. 126, 310–11; McCaffrey, 'Commission Adopts Draft Articles', ref. 154, 400–01.
[166] ILC Report, ref. 46, 236.
[167] ILC Report, ref. 46, 236.
[168] ILC Report, ref. 46, 237.

'no harm' rule sets a legal threshold simply begs the question of what is the obligation to avoid or prevent harm. Indeed, the Commission indicated that the obligation of due diligence 'is an obligation of conduct, not an obligation of result'.[169] The Commission's only attempt to define the obligation of due diligence is to indicate – only in the commentary – that a State violates its obligation of due diligence 'only if it knew or ought to have known that the particular use of an international watercourse would cause significant harm to other watercourse states'.[170] While this tells us that a State cannot be held responsible for an unforeseeable effect of activities for which it is responsible, it does not tell us what diligence is due under circumstances when a State can or should foresee the likelihood of significant harm to another State.[171] For that question, whether a use is equitable is surely relevant both in light of the text of revised section 7, and in light of the commentary's analysis. As the International Law Commission's official commentary on the revised article indicates, even the fact that a use caused significant harm 'would not of itself necessarily constitute a basis for banning it'.[172]

The same ambiguity is found in the *UN Convention on the Protection and Use of International Watercourses and International Lakes*. This convention requires States to take 'all appropriate measures to prevent, control, and reduce any transboundary impact'.[173] The notion that States are only required to take 'appropriate' steps appears again and again throughout the convention. Much the same problem arises in the recently signed *Mekong River Basin Agreement*. That agreement commits the states to 'make every effort to avoid, minimize, and mitigate harmful effects' and obligations the states to cease any harmful activity upon notification by another state.[174] It then goes on to require compensation for 'substantial damage ... in conformity with the principles of international law relating to state responsibility'[175] without mentioning whether those principles include and are controlled by the principle of equitable utilization also adopted in the agreement.[176]

---

[169] ILC Report, ref. 46, 237.

[170] ILC Report, ref. 46, 237.

[171] See generally Dupuy, P.-M. (1977) 'Due diligence in the international law of liability', in OECD, *Legal Aspects of Transfrontier Pollution*, 369; Pisillo-Mazzeschi, R. (1992) 'The due diligence rule and the nature of the international responsibility of states', *Germ. Y.B. Int. L.*, Vol. 35, 9.

[172] ILC Report, ref. 46, 236.

[173] Helsinki Convention, ref. 158, art. 1.

[174] Mekong river basin agreement, ref. 70, art. 7.

[175] Mekong river basin agreement, ref. 70, art. 8.

[176] Mekong river basin agreement, ref. 70, art. 5. See also Treaty concerning the integrated development of the Mahakali River, signed Feb. 12, 1996, India-Nepal, art. 9(1) (declaring that the relations of the parties regarding common waters are to be governed by 'the principles of equity, mutual benefit, and no harm to either Party'), reprinted in (1997) *Int. Legal Materials*, vol. 36, 531–46; Treaty on the sharing of the Ganges Waters at Farakka, signed Dec. 12, 1996, Bangladesh-India, art. IX (declaring that the relations of the parties

The Commission's commentary does indicate clearly that there is one narrow situation where the notion of 'no significant harm' would prevail as a near absolute: 'A use which causes significant harm to human health or safety is understood to be inherently inequitable and unreasonable'.[177] McCaffrey points to this language – not to the text of revised article 7 itself – as indicating the ultimate primacy of the rule of no reasonable harm.[178] Assuming that the commentary accurately reflects the meaning of revised article 7, it hardly affects the question of which rule is primary. The *Draft Articles* themselves devote two entire articles to 'harmful conditions' and emergencies.[179] These include floods, erosion, siltation, and water-borne diseases. States are obligated to take all necessary measures to prevent or mitigate conditions of extreme augmentation, depletion, pollution, or contamination whether caused by natural conditions or by human conduct. That a use undertaken by or in a particular state that induces such an extreme condition is inherently inequitable and unreasonable tells us virtually nothing about the far more common situation where one state's use impairs uses in another state without inducing any such harmful condition or emergency situation – as the *Draft Articles* themselves make clear regarding pollution in general:

> Article 21
> *Prevention, Reduction and Control of Pollution*
> ... (2) Watercourse States shall, individually or jointly, prevent, reduce, and control pollution of an international watercourse that may cause significant harm to other watercourse States or to their environment, including harm to human health or safety, to the use of the waters for any beneficial purpose or to the living resources of the watercourse. ...

Remarkably, one commentator has read article 21 as flatly prohibiting the pollution of international watercourses.[180] The Institut de droit international proposed just such a prohibition when it concluded that pollution is inherently unreasonable even when it does not provoke a crisis in human health or

---

cont.
    regarding common waters are to be governed by 'the principles of equity, fairness, and no harm to either Party'), reprinted in (1997) *Int. Legal Materials*, Vol. 36, 521–28.
[177] ILC Report, ref. 46, 242. See also Utton, A. (1996) 'Which rule should prevail in international water disputes: that of reasonableness or that of no harm?', *Nat. Resources J.*, Vol. 36, 635–41.
[178] McCaffrey, ref. 109, 311.
[179] Draft Articles II, ref. 46, arts. 27, 28. See McCaffrey, ref. 109, 314.
[180] Wouters, P. (1996) 'An assessment of recent developments in international watercourse law through the prism of the substantive rules governing use allocation', *Nat. Resources J.*, Vol. 36, 417–39, at 424.

safety.[181] Article 21 is not a complete prohibition of pollution. The obligation is to prevent, reduce, or control; the latter two requirements clearly include the possibility that pollution to some extent will be lawful. The only criterion proffered by the *Draft Articles* for determining when that might be is the principle of equitable utilization.

In light of the foregoing and given the limited role assigned to compensation in the revised article 7, it is at least arguable that no compensation is due if a harmful use is 'equitable and reasonable'. If so, compensation would be 'appropriate' if adjustments to prevent an 'inequitable or unreasonable' harm are not possible, but one would hardly think the International Law Commission intended that there is no obligation to consult over steps to avoid or minimize harm for uses that were 'equitable and reasonable'. The interpretive problem can be resolved if one reads the second obligation – the obligation to consult over mitigating harm – as explanatory rather than as indicating some independent duty: If harm can be prevented or reduced by reasonable adjustments in the manner, place, or timing of use, the harmful use is neither equitable nor reasonable. Subsection (b)(2)'s function is to make explicit the obligation to compensate for 'inequitable and unreasonable' uses; in other words, the rewritten article 7 is explicitly subordinated to the now clearly primary rule of equitable utilization in article 5.[182]

4.3 The UN Convention

At its first meeting after the International Law Commission completed its work on the *Draft Articles,* the General Assembly directed the Sixth Committee (the legal committee of the Assembly) to rework the 'second reading' of the *Draft Articles* into a draft convention for the Assembly's consideration.[183] The Sixth Committee considered the matter for several weeks in October 1996, and in March 1997.[184] Producing an acceptable text generated considerable controversy, with the final product being approved in the committee by a

---

[181] Institut de droit international, 'Athens Resolution', art. 2, *Annuaire de l'institut de droit international*, Vol. 58, 196 (1979). See Lipper, ref. 47, 36–38; McCaffrey, ref. 47, 125–26; Schwebel, ref. 58, 97–98.

[182] Cf. ILC Report, ref. 46, 243–44. See also Benvenisti, ref. 46, 404; Paisley and McDaniels, ref. 113, 121; Rahman, ref. 123, 23–24.

[183] GA Res. 49/52, UN GAOR, 49th Sess., Supp. No. 49, at 293, UN Doc. A/49/49. On the Sixth Committee generally, see Morris, V. and Bourloyannis, M.C. (1993) 'The work of the sixth committee at the forty-seventh session of the UN General Assembly', *Am. J. Int. L.*, Vol. 87, 306–323, at 306 nn. 1,2.

[184] Morris, V. and Bourloyannis, M.C. (1997) 'The work of the sixth committee at the fifty-first session of the UN General Assembly', *Am. J. Int. L.*, Vol. 91, 542–554, at 546–47.

vote of 42-3, with 18 abstentions.[185] Again, the controversy centred on the relationship of articles 5 and 7, the rule of equitable utilization and the 'no harm' rule.[186]

Article 5 emerged with only minor changes that arguably only clarify the text; article 7 was completely rewritten once again:[187]

Article 5
Equitable and reasonable utilization and participation
1. Watercourse States shall in their respective territories utilize an international watercourse in an equitable and reasonable manner. In particular, an international watercourse shall be used and developed by watercourse States with a view to attaining optimal and sustainable utilization thereof and benefits therefrom, taking into account the interests of the watercourse States concerned, consistent with adequate protection in the watercourse.
2. Watercourse States shall participate in the use, development and protection of an international watercourse in an equitable and reasonable manner. Such participation includes both the right to utilize the watercourse and the duty to cooperate in the protection and development thereof, as provided in the present articles.

Article 7
Obligation not to cause significant harm
1. Watercourse States shall, in utilizing an international watercourse in their territories, take all appropriate measures to prevent the causing of significant harm to other watercourse States.
2. Where significant harm nevertheless is caused to another watercourse State, the States whose use causes such harm shall, in the absence of agreement to such use, take all appropriate measures, having due regard for the provisions of articles 5 and 6, in consultation with the affected State, to eliminate or mitigate such harm and, where appropriate, to discuss the question of compensation.

The only potentially significant change in article 5 was the substitution of the phrase 'optimal and sustainable utilization' for the phrase 'optimal utilization' in the first paragraph of the article.[188] While the failure to include 'sustainability' in the International Law Commission drafts had been criticized as biasing the *Draft Articles* towards development of, and away from protection of, the resource,[189] in fact this is a very small change. Not only did the concept of 'optimal utilization' allow consideration of sustainability, but also the concept of 'sustainability' itself thus far is so open-ended as to enable

---

[185] Morris and Bourloyannis, ref. 184, 547 n. 24.
[186] Morris and Bourloyannis, ref. 184, 547.
[187] UN Convention, ref. 9, arts. 5, 7.
[188] Compare the text quoted at ref. 128.
[189] Rahman, ref. 123, 6–17, 22–23.

one to reach almost any decision one might prefer.[190] We are left then with 'equitable' as the only real criterion under article 5, unless the concept of sustainability can be developed more meaningfully than it has been to date.

The revision of article 7 is far more significant. Paragraph 1 of article 7 has moved from an apparently absolute command to prevent 'appreciable harm' to a duty to use 'due diligence' to prevent 'significant harm', to a duty merely to take 'appropriate measures' to prevent 'significant harm'.[191] Even more clearly than the phrase 'due diligence', a requirement of 'appropriate measures' mandates a consideration of what is appropriate under all the circumstances, including the cost of preventing harm and the feasibility of minimizing harm by redesigning a particular use.[192] As if this were not enough to justify a conclusion that the UN Convention makes the obligation to prevent harm subordinate to the rule of equitable utilization, this relationship is made explicit in paragraph 2 of the article where the obligation to take 'appropriate measures', as well as the obligation to 'discuss compensation', are to be made with 'due regard to the provisions of article 5 and 6' – the principle, in other words, of equitable utilization. Given the reality that each state's actions, if undertaken without regard for the interests of the other state, would inflict harm on the other,[193] one could hardly reach any other conclusion.

The *UN Convention* was approved by a vote of 104-3 (with 27 declared abstentions) in the General Assembly, on May 21, 1997.[194] The UN Convention contains 37 articles dealing with the obligations of riparian states to share the common resource, to consult with each other, to protect the environment, and to resolve disputes. It became open for signature on the day it was approved, but did not obtain sufficient signatures when the period that it was open for signature closed on May 20, 2000. With about 12 ratifacations (of the 35 necessary to enter into effect), the utlimate status of the *UN Convention* remains uncertain. It all depends on whether enough states are willing to accede to the convention without having signed it during the period allowed for signature.

In attempting to apply the *UN Convention*, one must always recall that 'equitable' does not mean 'equal' – a confusion that can arise in some non-

---

[190] Biswas, Jellali, and Stout, ref. 75; Carley, M. and Christie, I. (1993) *Managing Sustainable Development*; Holmberg, J. (editor) (1992) *Making Development Sustainable: Redefining Institutions, Policy, and Economics*; Pearce, D. and Turner, R. K. (1990) *Economics of Natural Resources and the Environment*; Sanwal, M. (1994) 'Sustainable development, the Rio Declaration and multilateral cooperation', *Colo. J. Int. Envtl. L.and Pol'y*, Vol. 4, 45–68; Symposium (1995) 'The promise and challenge of ecologically sustainable development', *Willamette L. Rev.*, Vol. 31, 235–493.

[191] Compare the texts quoted at refs. 128, 159, and 187.

[192] See the text at refs. 162–74.

[193] See the text at refs. 135–58.

[194] GA Res. 51/229.

common law countries where the notion of 'equity' in its common law sense is lacking. 'Equity' means a fair share considering the water needs and the ability to use the water efficiently of the several riparian states.[195] The UN Convention provides some certainty to the broadly stated rule by listing the factors to be considered in evaluating claims relating to equitable utilization:[196]

Article 6
Factors relevant to equitable and reasonable utilization
1. Utilization of an international watercourse in an equitable and reasonable manner within the meaning of article 5 requires taking into account all relevant factors and circumstances, including:
   (a) Geographic, hydrographic, hydrological, climatic, ecological, and other factors of a natural character;
   (b) The social and economic needs of the watercourse States concerned;
   (c) The population dependent on the watercourse in each watercourse State;
   (d) The effects of the use or uses of the watercourse in one watercourse State on other watercourse States;
   (e) Existing and potential uses of the watercourse;
   (f) Conservation, protection, development and economy of use of the water resources of the watercourse and the costs of measures taken to that effect;
   (g) the availability of alternatives, or corresponding value, to a particular planned or existing use.
2. In the application of article 5 or paragraph 1 of this article, watercourse States shall, when the need arises, enter into consultations in a spirit of cooperation.
3. The weight to be given to each factor is to be determined by its importance in comparison with that of other relevant factors. In determining what is a reasonable and equitable use, all relevant factors are to be considered together and a conclusion reached on the basis of the whole.

The *Helsinki Rules* provide a somewhat longer but comparable list of relevant factors.[197]

Non-lawyers, particularly engineers and hydrologists, sometimes see these lists of factors as a poorly stated equation. By this view, if one simply fills in numerical values for each factor, one could somehow calculate each watercourse state's share of the water without reference to political or other non-quantitative variables.[198] They simply ignore that the *UN Convention*, the

---

[195] ILC Report, ref. 46, 221–22; Moustafa, S. (1994) 'Egypt's experience of cooperation and development of the Nile Basin', in Bagis, ref. 151, 101–05, at 104.
[196] UN Convention, ref. 9, art. 6.
[197] Helsinki Rules, ref. 5, art. v.
[198] Probably the most extreme version of attempting to reduce the rule of equitable utilization to an algorithm is found in Moore, J.W. (1994) 'An Israeli-Palestinian Water-Sharing Regime', in Isaac, J. and Shuval, H (editors) *Water and Peace in The Middle East*, 181–92. See

Draft Articles, and the *Helsinki Rules* are legal documents that ultimately are addressed to judges. Judges make judgements, and in the English language, at least, the word judgement carries a strong connotation that the result is not dictated in any immediate sense by the factual and other inputs that the judge relies upon in exercising judgement.[199] Any attempt to treat the list of relevant factors as an algorithm simply misses the point.

That legal judgements necessarily involve a measure of discretion has been the focus of much attention in the United States in recent years.[200] This is not a recent thought, nor has it been ignored in the context of the customary law of transboundary waters. Writing more than 60 years ago, professor Herbert Smith expressed skepticism about the utility of the abstract rules of international law as applied to transboundary waters: 'The practical value of legal discussion is in direct proportion to its concern with actual facts, and experience has shown that all attempts to solve river problems by dogmatic insistence upon abstract legal principles have been either futile or mischievous'.[201]

The Jordan Valley provides a prime example of why an algorithmic approach would result in inequitable utilization. The primary contributors to water in the Jordan basin according to the pre-1967 boundaries are the Lebanese and the Syrians, precisely the two communities that have the greatest alternative sources of water.[202] This situation is normal in a dry region

cont.

also Kliot, N. (1994) *Water Resources and Conflict in the Middle East,* 95–99, 167–72, 259–76; Lonergan, S. and Brooks, D. (1994) *Watershed: The Role of Fresh Water in the Israeli-Palestinian Conflict,* 71–73; Hager, R. (1990) 'Note, the Euphrates basin: in search of a legal regime', *Georgetown Int. Envtl. L. Rev.,* Vol. 3, 207–28, at 219–20; Telerant, N. (1995) 'Riparian rights under international law: a study of the Israeli-Jordanian peace treaty', *Loy. L.A. Int. and Comp. L.J.,* Vol. 18, 175–205, at 194–95; Zarour, H. and Isaac, J. (1993) 'Nature's apportionment and the open market: a promising solution to the Arab-Israeli water conflict', *Water Int.,* Vol. 18, 40–52, at 50–51.

[199] See Benvenisti and Gvirtzman, ref. 81, 548; Bourne, ref. 88, 199; Griffin, ref. 81, 78–79; Picard, E. (1994) 'Aspects of international law of the water conflict in the Middle East', in Bagis, ref. 151, 213. The classic statement of this reality in more general contexts is Hutcheson, jr., J. (1929) 'The judgement intuitive: the function of the "hunch" in judicial decision', *Cornell L.Q.,* Vol. 14, 274–88.

[200] See, e.g., Allott, A. (1980) *The Limits of Law;* Cornell, D., Rosenfeld, M. and Carlson, D.G. (editors) (1992) *Deconstruction and the Possibility of Justice;* Dworkin, R. (1986) *Law's Empire;* Greenawalt, K. (1992) *Law and Objectivity;* Raz, J. (1979) *The Authority of Law;* West, R. (1993) Narrative, Authority, and Law; White, J. (1990) *Justice as Translation.*

[201] Smith, ref. 47, vi. See also Elmusa, S. (1994) 'Towards an equitable distribution of the common Palestinian-Israeli waters: an international water law framework', in Isaac and Shuval, ref. 200, 451–67, at 456–60.

[202] See Dellapenna, J. (forthcoming 2003) *Water in the Middle East: The Limits and Potential of Law* §§ 2.04(c), 2.04(e). Natural contribution might carry more weight in more humid regions where pressing needs in lower riparian states are less compelling. Godana, ref. 46, 58; Benvenisti and Gvirtzman, ref. 81, 549–50.

like the Middle East. For example, Turkey contributes 98% of the precipitation for the Euphrates, yet Turkey has immensely more water available from other sources (whether measured in absolute figures or *per capita*) than Iraq, far and away the major consumer from the Euphrates.[203] Close examination of the controversies over water among the five national communities sharing the Jordan Valley illustrates the shortcomings of the customary international law of transboundary waters generally and why that body of law without more will not solve the water management problems in the Valley.[204] It will be necessary in such a case for the interested states to negotiate an agreement, or for them to have recourse to a third party to resolve any disputes.

5. Time for a revised Helsinki Rules?

At a meeting in Edinburgh of the Committee on Water Resources of the International Law Association in January, 1996, the Committee voted to undertake a compilation and review of the entire body of its work beginning with the Helsinki Rules of 1966 and including the various supplementary rules prepared by the Committee and approved by the Association in the ensuing 30 years. This decision was confirmed by the Committee and by the Association in the biennial meeting of the Association in August 1996, appropriately in Helsinki. Professors Alan Boyle and Joseph Dellapenna undertook the initial step, a consolidated compilation of the various rules approved by the Association over the intervening 30 years. Based upon this consolidated draft, the Committee decided in a meeting in Rome in June, 1997, to undertake to revise the compiled rules, with a view of incorporating the experience of the three decades since the initial Helsinki Rules were adopted, taking into account the development since 1967 of an important and impressive body of international environmental law and the approval of a framework treaty on fresh water resources by General Assembly of the United Nations.

The most significant developments not directly reflected in the current body of rules formulated by the International Law Association are the emergence of environmental concerns, integrated management, and sustainable development as central principles of international resource and environmental law. These concepts, either completely unknown or of peripheral importance in 1967, have become the organizing principles of a large and increasingly effective body of law of which the law of transboundary waters properly is a special instance rather than an independent and competing set of rules. These

---

[203] See Dellapenna, J. (1996) 'The two rivers and the land between: Mesopotamia and the international law of transboundary waters', *BYU J. Pub. L.* Vol. 10, 213–261.

[204] See Dellapenna, 'Designing', ref. 43.

newer concepts are found today in the practice of states (including conventional and customary international law), in the writings of the leading publicists of the international law of environmental and resource management, and in the documentary record of the United Nations and other relevant international organizations.[205]

The rule of equitable utilization, the heart of the original *Helsinki Rules*, still provides the primary rule of customary international law regarding the allocation of waters among states. The new body of international environmental law is not incompatible with the rule of equitable utilization. Yet equitable utilization is sufficiently uncertain in application that some critics have argued the principle focuses too strongly on the procedures for resolving disputes over water and presupposes that water is to be consumed even if consumption is not sustainable.[206] The correct relationship of equitable utilization to standards regarding harm to the environment generally as well as harm to the interests of other states bedeviled the drafting of the *UN Convention* both in the workings of the International Law Commission and in the Sixth Committee of the General Assembly. The resulting convention is hardly the definitive word on the problem that one might hope to see available to those who must cope with the looming global water crisis.[207]

The political processes within the International Law Commission and the Sixth Committee virtually assured that the result of their efforts would be a compromise that elides serious problems where the various competing legal principles conflict most directly. If the law governing the allocation of internationally shared waters is to be a positive contribution to the solution of the looming global water crisis rather than being seen as expressing obsolete formulas reflecting a vanished time of plentiful water, organizations like the International Law Association must undertake to provide the leadership that has been their traditional primary role. The Association is in a unique position to bring to the project the collective expertise of the 'most highly qualified publicists' knowledgeable about the law of internationally shared fresh water resources. To fulfill this goal, the *Helsinki Rules* must be restated to express

---

[205] Rio Declaration on environment and development, UN Doc. A/CONF.151/5/Rev. 1 (1992), reprinted in *Int. Legal Materials*, Vol. 31, 874–80; Carley and Christie, ref. 190; Hohmann, H. (1994) *Precautionary Legal Duties and Principles of Modern International Law*; Lammers, ref. 71; Holmberg, ref. 190; Nollkaemper, ref. 140; Pearce and Turner, ref. 190; Sand, P. (editor) (1992) *The Effectiveness of International Environmental Agreements: A Survey of Existing Legal Instruments*; Sands, P. (editor) (1994) *Greening International Law*; Weiss, E.B. (1988) *In Fairness to Future Generations*; World Comm'n on Environment and Development. (1987) *Our Common Future* ('The Bruntland Report'); Hickey, jr., J. and Walker, V. (1995) 'Refining the precautionary principle in international environmental law', *Va. Envtl. L.J.*, Vol. 14, 423–54; Marini, G. and Sacramozzino, P. (1995) 'Overlapping generations and environmental control', *J. Envtl. Econ. and Mgt.*, Vol. 29, 64–77; Sanwal, ref. 190; Symposium, ref. 190.

[206] Rahman, ref. 123, 16–17, 22–23.

[207] See generally UN Comm'n on Sustainable Dev. (1997) Comprehensive Assessment of the Fresh Water Resources of the World, UN Doc. No. E/CN.17/1997/9.

clearly and properly the relation between the principle of equitable utilization and the relevant principles of international environmental law, particularly the principle of integrated management, the precautionary principle, and the principle of sustainable development. Flexibility is the real strength of the rule of equitable utilization. But it must be a flexibility constrained by the principles necessary to assure a sustainable and ecologically sound environment.

At this time the Water Resources Committee is working on the seventh draft of its *Revised International Law Association Rules on Equitable and Sustainable Use in the Management of Waters*. The project is scheduled to be completed in 2004, and submitted for approval by the International Law Association at its Berlin Meeting of that year. If this project is completed successfully, the resulting revised rules can be expected to carry weight in the deliberations of nations both as a coherent and compelling restatement of the relevant customary international law and as an aid to interpretation of the *UN Convention* when it applies to a particular dispute.

PAULO CANELAS DE CASTRO

New Era in Luso-Spanish Relations in the Management of Shared Basins? The Challenge of Sustainability

Introduction

During the first years of a new century we not only reflect on the past, but we also search for indications that the future will be better.

The case of the Luso[1]-Spanish relations in the management of their shared water basins is an example of this. Indeed, several promising signs appear to be present at the turn of the 21st century which encourage an optimistic perspective of the future in this domain. At least this is the impression projected by the proclamations made by both Parties with regard to the recent

---

[1] The term 'Luso' is frequently used in the Portuguese language and even in official documents such as the 1998 Convention. It stands for Portuguese. The expression is based on the Lusitans who were the valiant ancestors of the Portuguese. They inhabited the occidental part of the Iberian Peninsula even before the Romans. Only after several failed attempts rooted in the bravery and autonomous nature of the Lusitanian tribes did the latter empire eventually defeat the Lusitans and conquer the whole Iberian Peninsula.

M. Fitzmaurice and M. Szuniewicz (eds.), Exploitation of Natural Resources in the 21st Century, 191–234.
© *2003 Kluwer Law International. Printed in Great Britain.*

Convention on Cooperation for the Protection and Sustainable Use of the
Waters of the Luso-Spanish Basins which was adopted at the end of 1998[2]
and entered into force at the beginning of 2000.[3, 4] As we shall subsequently
attempt to demonstrate, these declarations seem to indicate a strong resolve on
the part of both Portugal and Spain to face current and future challenges.
Nonetheless, there should not be any illusions as to the dimension and the
complexity of these challenges or any confusion between the pursued idealism
and the more distant and less utopian reality. Rather, the efforts by these two
nations to reconcile the 'reality' with the 'ideal' must be based on realistic
notions of the difficulties inherent in the shared endeavour.

The present case of the Luso-Spanish river management would appear to
constitute a concrete example of the qualitative progress in attitudes in this
problem-area. This article purports to examine this positive appraisal initially
by presenting a brief summary of the facts (I.A.) and the normative treatment
it has thus far received (I.B.). Subsequently, consideration will be given to the
signs of the future contained in the normative message of the Convention
(II.A.) and the significance that can be gleaned from it (II.B.). Finally, several
questions and difficulties will be identified which are likely to occur in the
process of implementation of the proclaimed programme (III). This article
concludes with a brief discussion of potential avenues which should be followed
(Conclusion).

I

1. The Luso-Spanish experience in water management

1.1. The reality

The physical and socio-political reality of the Iberian Peninsula (which has
been occupied by the Portuguese and the Spanish States for centuries) is
characterised by several factors which naturally impose certain limitations, on
any possible model of management of the shared basins that merits credibility.
Among these, the following elements may be highlighted:

---

[2]   Hereafter, the 1998 Convention or simply the Convention.
[3]   More precisely on January 17, 2000, with the notification of the Spanish ratification.
[4]   The English translation of the text may be consulted on the Portuguese National Water
      Institute website, *in www.inag.pt.*

1. the two States share five principal river basins – namely, those of Minho, Lima, Douro, Tagus and Guadiana.[5] The size of three of those basins[6] may be considered substantial even in the broadest European context;[7, 8]

2. the importance of these basins in terms of the Portuguese territory is appreciable. Indeed, roughly 64% of the Portuguese territory is located within the five shared basins. Even with respect to the whole Iberian Peninsula, they are still significant, totalling 264,700 km2 and representing 45% of the surface area of the Peninsula;

3. in absolute terms, the availability of water per inhabitant per year is considerable[9] and is apparently even deemed to be one of the most 'comfortable' in Europe;[10]

4. extreme inter-seasonal rainfall – both in terms of distribution over the year and from one year to another – as well as variations in flows occur.[11] The rains are usually concentrated in a short period of time (October to March) to which dry periods follow with scarce natural flows;

---

[5] See the map and table on the amount of flows presented basin by basin *in* Francisco Nunes Correia, 'Introduction to the Problems of Shared Water Courses and Transboundary Issues', *in* Luso-American Foundation, *Shared Water Systems and Transboundary Issues with Special Emphasis on the Iberian Peninsula*, Lisbon, 2000, 33.

[6] The basins of the Douro, Tagus and Guadiana rivers. Each of them occupies more than 50.000 km2, with the first two approaching 100.000 km2 respectively. See European Environment Agency, *Europe's Environment – The Dobris Assessment*, Kopenhagen, 1995.

[7] As for their relevance within the context of the entire Iberian Peninsula, see the table by José Maria Santafé Martínez, 'The Hispano-Portuguese Agreement on Cooperation for the Protection and Sustainable Use of Water – A Spanish View', *in* Luso-American Foundation, *Shared Water Systems and Transboundary Issues with special emphasis on the Iberian Peninsula*, Lisbon, 2000, 275.

[8] Thus, the surface areas of the basins (in km2) are shared between Spain (S) and Portugal (P): Minho: (S): 16,212 (P): 869; Lima: (S): 1,303 (P): 4,891; Douro: (S): 78,892 (P): 18,610; Tagus: (S): 55,769 (P): 24,309 and Guadiana: (S): 55,261 (P): 11,525. In terms of natural mean flows (hm3/year), the relationship is as follows: Minho: (S): 11,200 (P): 800; Lima: (S) 1,200 (P): 5,000; Douro: (S): 15,000 (P): 8,200; Tagus: (S): 12,200 (P): 6,400; Guadiana: (S): 5,000 (P): 1,700.

[9] Probably more than 5,000 hm3 *'per capita'* at present, according to the estimates of Pedro Serra, 'O regime de caudais nas Convenções Luso-Espanholas de Rios Transfronteiriços', *Revista do CEDOUA*, forthcoming, 23.

[10] See Francisco Nunes Correia, 'Introduction to the Problems of Shared Water Courses and Transboundary Issues', *in* Luso-American Foundation, *Shared Water Systems and Transboundary Issues with special emphasis on the Iberian Peninsula*, Lisbon, 2000, 30, referring these conditions to studies by M. Falkenmark. See, as well, the table comparing the situation in Portugal to other European countries *in* Pedro Serra, 'The Defense of Portuguese Interests in the Agreement on Cooperation for the Protection and Sustainable Exploitation of the Waters of Luso-Spanish Catchment Areas', *in* Luso-American Foundation, *Shared Water Systems and Transboundary Issues with special emphasis on the Iberian Peninsula*, Lisbon, 2000, 232.

[11] See Francisco Nunes Correia, 'Introduction to the Problems of Shared Water Courses and Transboundary Issues', *in* Luso-American Foundation, *Shared Water Systems and Transboundary Issues with special emphasis on the Iberian Peninsula*, Lisbon, 2000, 31.

5. equally important geographical or spatial imbalances exist whereby the North and the Centre are characterised by relative wealth in water whereas the South – given its climatic features related to semi-arid regions – is distinguished by predominant scarcities;[12]
6. Portugal – structurally a downstream country[13] – is highly dependent on the flows originating in Spain[14] which creates an objective vulnerability;[15]
7. to aggravate the problem socio-political perceptions of vulnerability or potential subjugation exist in Portugal which do not necessarily have a positive impact on any process of the reconciliation of interests;[16]
8. approximately 80% or more of the water consumption is, traditionally, for agriculture.[17] Especially in Portugal, old fashioned methods of irrigation are still being used;
9. furthermore, the needs of the agricultural sector as well as many others are highly seasonal. Moreover, the peaks of water needs are usually concentrated in times of scarce availability;
10. the consumption of water, especially in agriculture, is highly subsidized which deepens imbalances and vulnerabilities;[18]
11. to augment Portugal's natural disadvantage, incongruent development and installed water storage or regulatory capacities exist between Spain and Portugal which have become particularly notorious in the Guadiana Basin since the 1960's;[19]

---

[12] *Idem.*
[13] Spain represents the upstream country for every main river in Portugal with the exception of the final stretch of the Guadiana. Additionally, the final stretches of both the Minho and the Guadiana Rivers are contiguous waters.
[14] Close to 50% on average.
[15] Thus its matching classification *in* L. Roberts (ed.), *World Resources 1998–1999. A Guide to the Global Environment.* New York, 1998.
[16] Pedro Serra rightly speaks of a myth, on this regard: see his 'The Defense of Portuguese Interests in the Agreement on Cooperation for the Protection and Sustainable Exploitation of the Waters of Luso-Spanish Catchment Areas', *in* Luso-American Foundation, *Shared Water Systems and Transboundary Issues with special emphasis on the Iberian Peninsula*, Lisbon, 2000, 237.
[17] Establishing a (causal) link between the importance of irrigation and the quantitative problem in the Peninsula as well as the flows regime of the Convention, see Pedro Serra, 'O regime de caudais nas Convenções Luso-Espanholas de Rios Transfronteiriços', *Revista do CEDOUA*, forthcoming.
[18] The point is made by Ramón Llamas, 'New and Old Paradigms on Water Management and Planning in Spain', *in* Luso-American Foundation, *Shared Water Systems and Transboundary Issues with special emphasis on the Iberian Peninsula*, Lisbon, 2000, 219 and 222.
[19] See José Maria Santafé Martínez, 'The Hispano-Portuguese Agreement on Cooperation for the Protection and Sustainable Use of Water – A Spanish View', *in* Luso-American Foundation, *Shared Water Systems and Transboundary Issues with special emphasis on the Iberian Peninsula*, Lisbon, 2000, 277.

12. several large-scale structures or developments have been undertaken (particularly since the 1960's) which have been predominantly of an industrial-hydroelectric nature in the North and the Douro (to a lesser extent, this kind of development is also of some importance in the case of the Tagus) and of an agricultural nature in the South. In this latter case, the development has been carried out almost exclusively by Spain (Guadiana);

13. social aspirations – adopted at a political level – have emerged, to intensify the general development of the two nations, in considerable part based on the exploitation of the water resources of these river developments which have been occurring particularly since the mid-1970's, especially after the democratization of these two countries;

14. the emergence and development of an environmental (ethical) awareness occurred, especially during the 1990's, in the wake of the accession to the European Community, although one may doubt how widely spread and effective it is;[20] and

15. insistence by both States on friendly and co-operative bilateral policies following the profound political changes in the mid-1970's,[21] with their 'velvet revolutions', which assured the transition from dictatorial to democratic forms of government. The desirability and effectiveness of these policies were reinforced by the simultaneous accession to the European Communities in 1986.

1.2 The normative-institutional response

In light of these factors, the Portuguese and Spanish authorities converged on the definition of a normative and practical response which, at the end of the 20th century and the dawn of a new era, may be retrospectively analysed in terms of three fundamental cycles (§§1, 2 and 3). The first two periods incorporate a reasonably constant, unitary or homogeneous model of management (§2.2) which may have more recently entered into crisis (§3.2).

---

[20] See Viriato Soromenho-Marques, 'A longa marcha da causa ambiental', 46–47; Sérgio Ribeiro, 'Os efeitos político-ambientais da integração europeia', 50–55; Elisabete Figueiredo and Filomena Martins, 'O ambiente no discurso político em Portugal (1976–1995)', all *in* Vértice, 1996, no. 74.

[21] To codify this, see the 1977 Treaty of Friendship and Cooperation between Portugal and Spain.

1.2.1 *From the mid 19th century to the second decade of the 20th century: the ('political') cycle of the delimitation of a development process*

In the mid 19th century, the then still two Kingdoms of Portugal and Spain began considering the problem of managing the Luso-Spanish river basins. This willingness culminated in the adoption of a series of treaties which essentially served to delimit the land borders of the respective States. This process of delimitation also defined the limits of the respective sovereignties with regards to the neighbouring waters which otherwise might be contentious and established some general rules regarding their use.

The expressions of this first normative trend were the Treaties of 1864,[22] 1866,[23] 1906[24] and 1926.[25] In terms of the content, and besides the treatment of the described 'political' problem of entitlement (i.e., to which country waters are to be ascribed and where the border passes[26]), reference should be made to the emergence of a principle of common benefit to the waters of the border sections of the rivers.[27] This is to say that a right existed to use these waters in terms of equality.[28] However, its development was minimal, given the fragility of both economies as well as their dependency on State powers which continued to exercise their authority in these areas. In any case, the foundations for future development were laid.

---

[22] Treaty of Lisbon, of September 29, 1864.
[23] Two Annexes to the Treaty of Limits of 1864, adopted on November 4, 1866.
[24] General Act of Lisbon, December 1st 1906, actual delimitation from the Minho to the confluence of the Caia with the Guadiana.
[25] Agreement of Lisbon, July 29, 1926, delimitation of the Luso-Spanish border from the confluence of the Cuncos with the Guadiana to the mouth of the Guadiana.
[26] The first treaties elected the median line criterium whereas that of 1927, certainly due to development in navigation, was based on the thalweg's.
[27] It is already expressed in article 1 of Annex 1 to the Treaty of Limits adopted in 1864, according to which '*The rivers that form the international border between Portugal and Spain along the line covered by the 1864 Treaty of Limits, shall, without prejudice to the fact that half of their respective flows belong to each country, be used by the people of both countries...*'..
[28] This general rule is expressed in even clearer terms in article 1 of the Agreement of 1912 which was reached by an exchange of notes between the Portuguese and Spanish Governments and come into force respectively on the 29th of August and the 2nd of September 1912. This Agreement – designated by its general aim of governing the *industrial use* of the waters in the border sections – established the following: '*The two nations shall enjoy the same rights in relation to the border sections, and consequently may each dispose of half the water flow during each of the various seasons of the year*'.The rest of the Agreement clarifies that the industrial uses referred to were hydroelectric in nature. However, they were simply envisaged and it would be a long time before they actually came true.

1.2.2 *From the second decade to the final decade of the 20th century*

1.2.2.1 The establishment of a dominant model of management

The 1920's onwards and especially the 1960's, were characterised by normative changes that clearly reflected a new way of thinking about waters and also resulted from the new capacity to mobilise them.

This was initially the case with the Agreement of 1927 that foresaw and expressly governed the hydroelectric development of the boundary waters of the Douro River (the stretch of the river between Miranda and Barca de Alva), until it was superseded by the Agreement of 1964. For that purpose, it authorized the construction by Portugal of three dams[29] and the erection by Spain of two structures.[30, 31]

Like the previous one, the Agreement of 1964 foresaw and governed the hydroelectric development of the boundary sections of the Douro River, but it also included the corresponding waters of its tributaries.[32]

Finally the Agreement of 1968 foresaw and governed developments – primarily (but not exclusively[33]) hydroelectric in nature – of other shared rivers, namely, the Minho, Lima, Tagus and Guadiana Rivers, as well as their tributaries, and especially the Chança River. Although the latter river is not a main river (being instead a tributary of the Guadiana), it was included in the title of the Convention in order to conform with the requirements of and to achieve an equitable result.[34, 35]

---

[29] The reference is to the dams of Miranda, Picote (the first to have actually been built), and Bemposta. They were erected between 1954 and 1964.

[30] The dams which Spain built under the terms of this Agreement on the border section of the Douro were the Aldeadávilla and Saucelle Dams.

[31] The hydroelectric potential of the international section which was materialized by these dams respected the principle of parity of benefits between the two States.

[32] The method for determining the equity of the sharing was based on the attribution to each country of some natural falls inscribed in certain stretches of the river Douro and its tributaries which enabled the economic exploitation of the hydroelectric potential linked thereto. The sum of the hydroelectric potential of the falls reserved for each country had to total a quantity equivalent to the one attributed to the other country following this same procedure.

[33] Indeed, it was foreseen that the waters of the Guadiana's section allocated to Portugal would be used, through the Alqueva, for irrigation and public water supply whereas those of the Chança's section reserved for Spain would be consecrated to irrigation as well as urban and industrial usage in the Huelva region.

[34] In terms of method followed in the process of benefits sharing, Parties concentrated on identifying stretches of rivers deemed to be particularly valuable due to their natural characteristics and economic exploitability. Each of the countries subsequently chose a river or stretch of river of particular interest which was reserved for itself to the exclusion of the other country, if need be even by devolution of rights of exploitation of national tributaries.

With a few exceptions, each of these conventions shares a common outlook or perspective whose characteristics are, namely:

1. the economic nature of the exploitation of the waters (the key word, reproduced in every agreement and in several dispositions, is 'development');
2. the restriction of the geographical scope of the discipline to the boundary waters of the main rivers, and, in the case of the conventions of the 1960's, of their tributaries as well. Exceptional considerations or concerns existed which were related to nearby territories or waters under national jurisdiction but still within the context of this scope;[36]
3. the (almost complete) restriction of the objective-functional scope of the Conventions to hydroelectric developments as is clearly reflected in the titles of the Treaties of 1927 and 1964. The Treaty of 1968 has a different title,[37] although the primary objective and practical function of this Convention continues to be to authorise hydroelectric developments;
4. a minimal normative content, towards authorization of single developments[38] or prescription of solutions which are well represented in a small number of articles in each convention;[39]

---

cont.

Hence, Portugal saw its interest satisfied in the intermediate Guadiana and in the Lima, whereas Spain was attributed the Chança and the Tejo. Since the Parties continued to follow the principle of equal rights of exploitation of the border sections, any residual need to establish a balance resulting from this sharing would be met by a proportionate solution in the common exploitation of the hydroelectric potential of Minho. Thus, the sharing is not river by river, or stretch by stretch, but a global one, in function of the rivers taken into consideration. It is not one of waters sharing but one of sharing the hydroelectric potential of the waters deemed to be exploitable. This ingenious method is different from the one followed in 1964 because of the lack of natural flows in these rivers.

[35] The Chança is a tributary to the Guadiana on its left riverbank and constitutes the border between the two countries in a significant part of its course. Its consideration in the 'water benefits sharing-equation' indicated in the previous note was of particular relevance because it facilitated the determination of a solution respecting the general principle of equivalent profits or rights of the exploitation of waters traditionally followed by the two States in their relations in the sector.

[36] This orientation is particularly relevant in the 1968 Agreement since the Parties even envisage the renunciation to rights of use of adjacent national tributaries so that the balance of the global water sharing equation is assured, as is the respect of the principle of equality of rights traditionally presiding Luso-Spanish relations in this field.

[37] See the preamble and article 6, §2 as well. In the same vein, it is telling that there is no reference to other international sections –such as the ones of the Minho's estuary or the final stretch of the Guadiana, for instance. This is due to the lack of hydroelectric exploitability of these particular sections in those times. See also the fact denoted in the previous footnote.

[38] The linked matters dealt with are the ones of expropriations, emplacement of the dams or other structures, concessions and procedural rules governing the implementation of these projects.

[39] 25 articles in the 1964 Agreement and only one in the Additional Protocol, 26 in the 1968 one and few articles in the Additional Protocol adopted at the same time.

5. this normative content, from a material perspective, may be summarised in a few points:

   5.1. the bilateral structure purports to authorise or mandate the exploitation of certain development projects along the border sections. In this way, the conditions are created for subsequent transfer of rights to concessionaires for long periods of time and as a result their position is almost assimilated to that of States. This solution indicates a State-based, economic management approach which is also supply-oriented and reflects the belief in the virtues of the 'Homo faber';

   5.2. for this purpose (i.e. for the viable economic development of the waters), the focus of these Conventions on water-sharing – 'rectius' on the distribution of the benefits that those waters may generate- constitutes another important dimension which is also economic in nature. The distribution of the development rights is not based on the division of the actual boundary waters. Rather, it rests on the quantifiable potential (especially hydroelectric potential) attributed thereto;[40]

   5.3. the 'key' to the distribution of the border flows is the equity in the balance of the predominantly hydroelectric potential or economic interest attributed to a part of the Douro river in the 1964 Agreement or to a set of rivers under consideration (Minho, Lima, Tagus, Guadiana and Chança Rivers) in the 1968 Agreement;

   5.4. the environmental issues or those of water quality are completely (Treaties of 1927 and 1964) or almost entirely (Treaty of 1968) ignored. Even when exceptionally considered,[41] their treatment is vague and inoperational;

   5.5. the actions or concrete measures of co-operation mentioned are minimal and sporadic (limited in time) and assume the sovereignty of each State. This limitation is in accordance with the restrictive geographical scope of these conventions and their main sense of entitlements to developing certain structures. Further, this solution is also in harmony with and becomes reinforced by the isolationist policies of the two neighbour States which were highly evident after World War II (Salazar, the Portuguese ruler, even proclaimed that the country felt 'proudly alone!');

   5.6. a Joint Commission was created or envisaged (in 1927[42] although

---

[40] In turn, this potential – in the case of hydroelectric developments under the terms of the 1964 Agreement – is based on certain natural *falls* particularly suited to the generation of electricity and in which the structures would be inscribed. This method of 'water allocation' is clearly represented, for instance, in the formula of article 2 of the 1964 Agreement which reads: '*The use of the whole of the fall in elevation along the international section of the Douro in the zone (...) is reserved for Portugal.*' .

[41] This happens nonetheless in article 6, §3 of the 1968 Agreement.

[42] Article 14 of the 1927 Agreement.

only implemented after 1964) to be composed of diplomats, engineers and legal experts and was vested with an apparently vast array of powers.[43] However, after careful consideration, it was extremely limited by the very content of the Conventions. Moreover, it quickly fell in a state of accentuated lethargy after the completion of the established projects. This development weakened its potential as an instance of dialogue and a medium for the exchange of information and views surrounding the problems that were arising.

1.2.2.2 Significance: a clearly economically-oriented model

The importance of this programme is clearly of an economic nature, basically directed towards the facilitation of construction of infra-structures in the border sections of the rivers. Further, it is a part of a development effort of the countries and derives from a purely anthropocentric vision – which is conceived as a mere provider of resources to be harnessed and put to the service of Humankind (itself exalting the 'Homo faber' or the 'Homo economicus' dimensions). Hence, the management problem was fundamentally reduced to a question of assuring the availability[44] of these water resources.[45]

Moreover, it was in fact in this manner that Portugal and Spain implemented the programme, although in somewhat different forms.

In Spain, it was applied in a very consistent and determined manner. Ironically, often even resorting to the prestigious Portuguese engineering school. In addition, the policy generally received social support. Thus, not surprisingly, the projected work has been completed, as can be evidenced by such structures as the Tagus-Segura diversion, the irrigated agricultural fields of the South and the installation throughout Spain of a capacity of water storage equivalent to approximately 1/3 of the current total of the other Member States of the European Union.

In contrast, the image is not as homogeneous in Portugal. Despite the prestige associated with its engineering skills, the truth is that there have been several inconsistencies in the application of this model. This incoherence is clearly exemplified by the delayed 'mega-development' of the Alqueva which was envisaged as a fundamental strategic water reserve. Although the project was taken into account in the Convention of 1968, it remains until today to be

---

[43] Articles 14 to 20 of the 1927 Agreement, 14 as well as 16 to 20 of the 1964 Agreement and articles 4, 12, 17 to 21 and 25 of the 1968 Agreement.

[44] Hence, a typical water-supply strategy.

[45] In our opinion, the term 'resources' adroitely conveys this *anthropocentric* and *utilitarian* approach. A more ecologically-oriented stance would prefer, it would seem, the expression of '(environmental) good'.

completed. This overview is aggravated by a certain loss of references and lack of continuity of actions or influence by the former powerful Hydraulic Administration. These facts were a consequence of the social instability and the ensuing institutional turmoil surrounding the 1974 Revolution. Therefore, they should not be attributed to a diminishing belief in the still dominant model of management, but rather to the socio-political, institutional or even material difficulties associated with the erratic political and economic life. In fact, these destabilizing forces initially emerged as a consequence of the liberation wars which Portugal began facing in its non-self-governing territories in Africa during the 1960's. And subsequently they were the result of the shake-up and the redefinition of policies and processes due to the 1974 Revolution of the Carnations.

Nonetheless, the trend has always been in both cases to delegate the management of the river waters to national authorities. Unfortunately, the Portuguese and Spanish water administrations were, in the vast majority of situations, not cooperating with each other. In other words, they autonomously planned and even executed their plans with only minimal and sporadic contact with each other in order to resolve issues concerning the border sections of the rivers.

1.3 The cycle of controversy

1.3.1 The crisis and ensuing developments

Suddenly, this model began to crumble.

The catalyst was the announcement in 1993 of the megalomaniac Spanish National Water Plan.[46] Still under the aegis of the dominant model previously described, the Plan proposed to meet the mounting but certainly unsustainable agricultural needs of the arid South by extensive irrigation. To this end, enormous volume of water would have to be drawn off from the basins which were considered to be in excess and diverted to those identified as having insufficient resources. More specifically, the Plan suggested an annual drawing off of 1,000 hm of water from the Douro Basin to be diverted to various basins in the South, most likely with considerable losses in the process.[47]

Understandably, this project caused great alarm: First, in Spain whose civil

---

[46] See text *in* Antonio Embid Irujo (ed.), *El Plan Hidrologico Nacional*, Madrid, 1993, 293–366, and the discussion of its properties in the previous pages of this book.

[47] For other projects of likely serious impacts, see Paulo Canelas de Castro, 'Para que os rios unam: um projecto de Convenção sobre a cooperação para a protecção e a utilização equilibrada e duradoura dos cursos de água luso-espanhóis', *in* UAL, *Conferência Portugal-Espanha*, Lisboa, 1997, 67–69.

society protested against it and subsequently, in Portugal, whose authorities, still in 1993, decided to voice their apprehension and displeasure with their Spanish counterparts. In common, both the Spanish civil society and the Portuguese authorities began to demonstrate a concern with the environmental implications of such projects and a progressively more-structured environmentally-friendly thinking. Thus, the 'improvement' in comparison with the previously dominant model of management (and which the PHNE so well represented) stressed, paradoxically, the need to start dealing with the principal cost of the policy followed up to that date: the (unbearable) environmental impacts.

It was precisely on the basis of an increasingly conscious environmental perception and environmental legal-technical perspective that Portugal began to prepare a draft convention. This legal document was meant to be environmentally friendly and holistic, if not partially eco-systemic (as noted in the National Water Council in which the position of the authorities acquired the consensual 'approval' of the representatives of both the public administration and the civil society). Portugal entered into negotiations with Spain with the aim of adopting a new Convention which represented the qualitative leap that, in Portugal's view, was required by the new facts and the emerging new consciousness.

As one may imagine, this action translated into a genuine crisis.

On the one hand, Spain continued to insist on a model rooted essentially in quantitative issues which meant huge diversions of waters which supposedly reflected water balance between the (naturally) water-rich North and the (naturally) water-poor South. However, Portugal was henceforth more concerned with the quality of the waters and the environmental impacts resulting from the upstream reductions in the quantity of available water (Douro) or simply the doubtfully sustainable use of already scarce waters (Guadiana). Clearly, Portugal had begun to realise the merits of the environmental protection.

The ensuing (always courteous) diplomatic, technical and juridical struggle constituted a dispute over the drafting of the Law and solutions which were more favourable to the aspirations, interests and visions of each Party. However, this struggle was not simply confined to the negotiation table (1.), but rather extended to other venues(2, 3 and 4):

1. At the bilateral level, through 5 years of intense negotiations. In the Portuguese case, these talks were largely conducted by a 'Negotiation team' which was chaired by a diplomat. This official was accompanied by strong technical and juridical advisors who were called upon to justify the proposals that were presented to the Spanish counterparts. This group always benefited from a strong political support and, if necessary, ministerial intervention. Further, it also received assistance from a 'Coordinating team'. This group was composed of high officials from different interested Departments which, internally, also contributed to the drafting of further proposals or to the discussion and assessment of the progress of the negotiations.

2. In the sub-regional context of the European Community, as well. During the process leading to the adoption of the Water Framework Directive, Spain not only expressed the view that the text should be directed towards questions of quantity (versus quality) as well as unanimously adopted. It also instituted proceedings at the European Court of Justice, based on this argument, contesting the legal basis found by the Council of the Communities to adopt the 1994 Danube Convention.[48] This forced Portugal, along with other States, to intervene in the aforementioned Case,[49] defending the 'mainstream', more-environmental-friendly orientation. This latter perspective eventually prevailed in the ruling of the Court and also in the final text of the Water Framework Directive which was symbolically adopted on the last day of the Portuguese Presidency of the European Community.

3. At the regional level, because of the Spanish resistance or delay to legally bind itself by the 1992 Helsinki Convention on the Protection and Use of Transboundary Watercourses and International Lakes. Spanish ratification of this regional legal document only happened after the adoption of the 1998 bilateral Convention and contrasts with Portugal. Indeed, this UNECE Convention had always been invoked by Portugal as a valid parameter of the negotiating process, along with the 1991 Espoo Convention on Environmental Impact Assessment in a Transboundary Context which was ratified earlier by Spain.

4. At the global level, through Portugal's active participation in the works of the 6th Committee of the World Organisation which eventually led to the adoption,[50] in May 1997, of the United Nations Convention on the Law of the Non-Navigational Uses of International Watercourses.[51] Portugal made a resolute effort to contribute to the greening of the contents of this international document.[52] In contrast, Spain proved less enthusiastic about the course of the works and abstained in the final vote.

---

[48] See *JOCE*, 1997, L 342, 18.

[49] Case C–36/98, Kingdom of Spain v. Council of the European Communities. The ruling of the Court, dismissing the Spanish case, is of January 30 2001.

[50] On the history of the ILC project eventually leading to the works of the Working Group of the Whole in the 6th Committee, see Stephen McCaffrey, 'The Evolution of the Law of the International Watercourses', 45 *Austrian Journal of Public International Law* 87 (1993); Stephen McCaffrey, 'The International Law Commission Adopts Draft Articles on International Watercourses', 89 *AJIL* 395 (1995); Attila Tanzi, 'Codifying the Minimum Standards of the Law of International Watercourses: Remarks on Part One and a Half', 21 *Natural Resources Forum* 109 (1997); Stephen McCaffrey and Mpazi Sinjela, 'The 1997 United Nations Convention on International Watercourses', 92 *AJIL* 97 (1998).

[51] UN Doc. A/51/869, April 11, 1997. Reprinted in 36, *ILM*, 700 (1997).

[52] See the comments made on the ILC draft in 1996 at the request of the Secretary-General of the United Nations. Copy of the original document on file with the Author.

In any case, it must be admitted that all of these exercises were equally an excellent opportunity to better comprehend the views of the other Party. They also served to integrate, more or less actively, the progress that was being recorded in the Law undergoing profound changes. Moreover, these interactions also contributed to the moderation of initial positions and, almost imperceptibly, the reconciliation of perspectives and interests, in what resulted to be a mutual learning process.

1.3.2. The sense of the new times: towards a paradigm-shift?

The final phase of this period seems to have been one of transition. On the one hand, it entailed the progressive questioning of several aspects of the old model of management which had not yet been completely rejected. On the other hand, it simultaneously involved progressive debate of new ideas and concepts. While it is true that these 'fresh' or innovative notions had been present since the 1970's[53] and particularly following the summit in Rio de Janeiro[54] in the 'symbolic market' of International Environmental Law (under the general mantle of 'environmental protection'), the International Water Law proved particularly resilient to them.[55] Although it is doubtful that the old model has been superseded in its entirety, evidence would seem to suggest that a paradigm-shift[56] or a scientific revolution[57] has, in fact, occurred. Congruent with the epistemological thinking of Thomas Kuhn, it is not surprising that a certain lack of coherence – conceptual and practical inconsistencies – still remains. Indeed, the 'social forces of the past' continue to resist what seems to be the (normative) 'spirit of the time' ('Zeitgeist')[58]

---

[53] Notably with the Stockholm Declaration on the Human Environment, reprinted *in* 11, *ILM*, 1416 (1972).

[54] See Rio Declaration on Environment and Development, reprinted *in* 31, *ILM*, 876 (1992).

[55] This is an apprehension that is discernible in many doctrinal works. For instance, Jutta Brunnée, 'The Challenge to International Law: Water Defying Sovereignty or Sovereignty Defying Reality?', *Nação e Defesa*, nº 86, 1998, 53.Her recognition of the necessity to approximate these two bodies of Law which followed two estranged courses underlies the resolution of the celebrated Water Reources Committee of the International Law Association to revise the array of rules which it had previously elaborated and namely the well-known Helsinki Rules of 1966. See www. Ila-hq.org/pdf/Water Resources/2002 Pre Conference Report. The 7th preliminary draft rules of Equitable and Sustainable Use in the Management of the Waters can also already be consulted on the same website.

[56] Ellen Hey, 'Sustainable Use of Shared Water Resources: The Need for a Paradigmatic Shift in International Watercourses Law', *in* G.H. Blake *et al.* (eds.), *The Peaceful Management of Transboundary Resources*, London, 1995, 127–152.

[57] Thomas Kuhn, *The Structure of Scientific Revolutions*, Chicago, 1962.

[58] This conception is very similar to Ferdinand Lassalle's analysis corresponding to the binomy 'Law in action' (this is to say the realistic and actual relations among the social forces) and 'Law in the books' (the idealistic paper Law). See F. Lassalle, *Was Nun? Zweiter Vortrag über Verfassungswesen*, 3rd. Ed., Leipzig, 1873, 12–13.

but whose rejection would appear to be essential in order for the model to be truly consolidated.

II

2. Prospective: a path to success?

2.1 Signs of (an improved?) future. Analysis of the 1998 Convention

The efforts initially undertaken by Portugal, and subsequently with Spanish collaboration, resulted in the Convention on Cooperation for the Protection and Sustainable Use of the Waters of the Luso-Spanish Basins.

Corresponding to visions of the two State Parties, one of the structural elements of this Convention is that it does not reject the past conventional regime of Portugal and Spain but rather recognizes its value. It even presents the new 1998 treaty as a continuation of the past normative tradition (article 27). This normative conceptualization is particularly evident in the preservation of the patrimony of sharing water benefits at the borders or the rights based on the hydroelectric power of those waters and the corresponding exploitation structures. With respect to this latter case, these rights would apply to the hydroelectric installations which already exist as well as those which are still to be completed (with Alqueva being the most obvious example as its construction was only started at the end of the 1990's, despite being granted recognition in the 1968 Convention[59]).

The same inspiration underlies the new search for other solutions of the balancing of interests, since the theme of equitable sharing continues to be one of the principal dimensions of the most recent regime initiated in 1998. This endeavour is shown, in particular, in its new regime of waterflows, foreseen in article 16 and which constitutes the Additional Protocol to the main body of the Convention.[60] In contrast with the past system of mean flows – which could only be assessed 'ex post facto' and consequently could only have confrontational implications in the case of non-compliance – the quantitative question now appears to be dealt with on more solid, technical bases. More precisely, the 'water sharing' which is presently represented in an obligation of 'facere' and even of 'dare' (i.e. Spain as the upstream country guarantees

---

[59] The elaboration of this project in Portugal is even prior to this.
[60] As for the underlying motivations, see Annex to the Additional Protocol, most appropriately called Bases of the Waterflows Regime.

certain minimal water flows[61]) becomes related to both the infrastructures that exist in the basin[62] and the monitoring system that is envisioned.[63] Moreover, true verification of compliance with this obligation is also possible today.[64]

However, the principal innovations of the Convention lie in the new approach to the entire problem of management – a new understanding which flows back to the most traditional solutions. This innovative strategy is exemplified in the very list of topics and binding solutions which are now dealt with by the Convention. In addition, it is visible in the objectives of the regime which are stipulated as the cooperation for the protection and sustainable use (article 2, §1): a normative idea that is even represented in the very portico of the 1998 Convention which is its own designation.

Among these innovative subject-matters and solutions, the following seem to deserve special reference:

1. The physical and geographical elements (article 2, §1 and article 3, §1) constitue the entire hydrographical basins.[65, 66]

   Departing radically from the modest concentration of the former bilateral regime on the boundary waters, the present one starts by conceptually consisting of surface and underground freshwaters.[67] The land through which the feshwaters flow or percolate is also included,[68] as are the associated ecosystems.[69] It subsequently also integrates the interaction of these freshwaters with marine waters.[70] Moreover, these undeniably broad geographical and physical elements correspond with each other within the scope of the Convention. Indeed, they are included in both the list of responsibilities or actions as defined by articles 4, §2 and 10[71] and the sectors of activities which, according to article 3, §2, are to be regulated by the Convention.

---

[61] See, for instance in the case of the Douro, article 3, §§ 2 and 3 of the Additional Protocol.
[62] See article 16, §3 and article 1, §1 d) of the Additional Protocol.
[63] See article 1, §2 of the Additional Protocol and §1 of articles 2 to 5 of the same document.
[64] This may be a key to the understanding of article 7, §2, on the report to be made by Parties.
[65] Moving from north to south, the hydrographical basins of the five main shared rivers are as follows: Minho, Lima, Douro, Tagus, Guadiana (article 3, §1).
[66] The definition of hydrographical basin, in article 1, §1 b) is equally relevant.
[67] Articles 1, §1 b) and 2, §1.
[68] Article 1, §1 b).
[69] Article 2, §1.
[70] Article 14, §2.
[71] The list is certainly impressive: exchange of information, consultations and other activities in the cooperative organs, water quality measures, pollution fighting, assessment and prevention of impacts, promotion of the rationality, efficiency and economy of uses, droughts and floods mitigation, prevention and control of incidents of accidental pollution, promotion of the security of infra-structures, establishment of monitoring system, research and development, compliance control and promotion of the efficiency of the Convention.

2. The pursued objectives are also more ambitious and complex. The new 1998 Convention points to a close and intense cooperation. As previously noted, this collaboration occurs in such a wide scope of areas of management of waters that it covers almost all areas of activities.[72, 73]

3. As regards the objectives, one may compare the previous conventions which simply regulated the utilization of waters – mainly by economic developments or infra-structures which were taken into consideration or authorised – with the predominant objective today – the environmental protection of waters and ecosystems. This also signifies that these environmental media are thus perceived as a 'good'.[74] This is to say, they are conceived as a value in and of themselves, independent of the utilizations and profit that they may constitute for people. Thus, their long-term preservation and protection become the very condition of the uses or utilizations of waters. Simultaneously, a prevision of a general development exists in the new regime whose specific forms of water utilisation hereafter must be legitimised. This is achieved by requiring that these water uses comply with standards and criteria of (environmental) sustainability.[75] The normative treatment of environmental or quality issues[76] precedes that of quantitative matters and corresponding rights of use.[77] Clearly, this is an ordering which symbolizes the relative importance logically accorded to each of these areas of normative concern.

4. The time scale to which the new Convention refers to is also different: while the previous Conventions were simply focused on (the works of) a near future and the rules regarding 'waterflows' merely dealt, indiscriminately, with average or normal situations,[78] the new Convention attempts to promote sustainability, a goal which only a longer period of time may incorporate. To this end, it differentiates and regulates both normal[79] and extreme situations.[80] This new outlook may be explained by the horizon of the new regime which is not restrained by present problems

---

[72] Malin Falkenmark and G. Lindh, *Water for a Starving World*, Boulder, Colorado, 1976 and L. Veiga da Cunha *et al.*, *Management and Law for Water Resources*, Fort Collins, Colorado, 1977 and, in the social sciences realm, Evan Vlachos, 'Transnationale Resources and Hydrodiplomacy', *in* Luso-American Foundation, *Shared Water Systems and Transboundary Issues with Special Emphasis on the Iberian Peninsula*, Lisbon, 2000, 43–65.

[73] Namely, the already mentioned articles 4 ,§2 and 10. See, equally, in comparison, article 18 of the Danube Convention and articles 5 common to the Meuse and Scheldt Agreements.

[74] In a similar sense, Jutta Brunnée and Stephen J. Toope, 'Environmental Security and Freshwater Resources: Ecosystem Regime Building', 26, *AJIL*, 91 (1997).

[75] Apart from referring to Community ones, the Convention sets its own in Annex II.

[76] See the title of the Convention, article 2 and articles 13 and 14.

[77] See the title of the Convention, article 2 and articles 15 and 16.

[78] Or at least ignored the problem of physical variations.

[79] Part III of the Convention and §2 of articles 2 to 5 of the Additional Protocol.

[80] Part IV of the Convention and §3 of articles 2 to 5 of the Additional Protocol.

and generations, for which it, nonetheless, establishes hard rules.[81] Rather, it also encompasses any problematic issues which may follow as well as the interests of future generations.[82] Hence the attention devoted to all the subject-matters related to the problem of risks associated with waters.[83] It is true that this second dimension of the future that is envisaged or the risks to be avoided is expressed in a less persuasive manner at the level of the actions or measures which are immediately regulated.[84] Nevertheless, it already finds important expression in the definition of the procedures which have to be followed[85] as well as the instruments to be used.[86] In addition, it occasionally even co-involves the establishment of strict deadlines for the performance of such actions.[87]

5.   The list of issues and responsibilities or areas of cooperation is now much broader.[88] Moreover it demonstrates a concern with integration as well as the coherence of the various actions of management. This attention is rooted in the desire to achieve an integrated management of the waters, in conformity with the recommendations of Agenda 21. In addition, it reveals a holistic vision of the problem of management.[89] Hence, one may note:

5.1.   Besides the quantitative questions, and those of the 'sharing of waters', which still figure in this newer regime (as could be expected in a region of Europe in which these problems have particular relevance, in great measure due to the seasonal and geographical variabilities of rainfall), there are other issues which, tellingly, even precede and condition them. More specifically, the new regime reveals a great concern with such environmental questions as the ones of:

a)   the protection of the waters[90] and associated ecosystems,

---

[81]   For instance, the whole waterflows regime in the Additional Protocol.

[82]   This is already encompassed in the very concept of sustainability. However, article 2, §2 which binds the Parties to abide by the principles and rules of International and Community Laws also has this implication.

[83]   Such as the rules on floods, substances which are harmful to human health, the security of infrastructures and impacts assessments.

[84]   This is certainly the case with the obligation to take measures for the rationalisation, efficient use and conservation of water resources set out in articles 10, §1, e) and 15, §3.

[85]   Article 4, §2 and articles 5 to 9.

[86]   The management plans or the programs of measures, for instance.

[87]   See, for instance, articles 13, §3, 16, §5, 18, §7, 19, §8, 24.

[88]   Articles 4, §2 and 10.

[89]   Even if not in conceptually explicit terms, one may say that this perspective already transpires in the Preamble.

[90]   It is by no coincidence that the Convention always uses the concept of 'waters' when it refers to the measures of protection precisely in order to connote their worth and value in their natural condition. In contrast, it prefers the term 'water resources' when it addresses questions of utilization for the benefit of Man. See also '*supra*' footnotes 28, and 53.

whether surface, groundwaters, estuarine or marine waters.[91]

b) pollution prevention and control,[92] for which the Convention not only foresees a wide range of impact assessments[93] but also institutes or assumes the institution of parametric values or standards of quality and emission limits[94] as well as a program of priority fighting against certain more hazardous substances.[95]

c) transboundary impacts, which, apart from requiring assessment, even need to be prevented[96] (article 9).

5.2. There are subsequently[97] quantitative issues – those of sharing the benefits enabled by the waters- in need of legal regulation. Their treatment is conditioned by the principle of equitable utilization, but also, and increasingly, by all of those emerging principles of a more environmental sensitivity – prevention, precaution, sustainability, participation, cooperation. The Parties succeeded in defining a regime of waterflows involving guarantees of flows to the downstream country (almost always Portugal), differentiated according to normal or extreme hydrological situations.[98] In devising it, the following points, in particular, were taken into account:

a) the already existing exploitations whose viability and continued operation are safeguarded;[99]

b) and whose structures are even relied upon to contribute to the compliance with the agreed flows (for utilization or ecosystemic purposes);[100]

c) the water available in diverse time horizons;[101]

d) the foreseeable uses;[102]

---

[91] Article 13, principally.

[92] Article 14.

[93] Article 9 and the whole Annex II. These impact assessments concern not only projects or ongoing activities (many of which are detailed in an elaborate fashion in Annex II) but also plans and programmes (strategic impact assessment; §1). In addition, they may occur on a continuous basis (§4).

[94] Article 13, §1 a) and 14, §1, in conjunction with Annex I, 8 and Annex II.

[95] See Annex I, 8.

[96] See, apart from the 5th preambular paragraph, articles 2, §2, 9 and the entire Annex I.

[97] In effect, these issues are only considered afterwards. In the obviously deliberate economy or systematics of the Convention, this ordering should be taken as quite telling.

[98] Apart from articles 16 and 19 of the main body of the Convention, see, for instance, article 4, §§ 2 and 3 for the Tagus River.

[99] See article 1, §1 c) and d) of the Additional Protocol.

[100] See, for instance, article 1, §1 c) and d) of the Additional Protocol.

[101] For instance, in the case of the Tagus river basin, article 4, §§ 2, 3 and 4 of the Additional Protocol.

[102] Namely article 1,§1 b) and c) of the Additional Protocol.

e) the environmental needs – those that are known or simply estimated.[103]

Moreover, the water regime has to respect the environmental perspective which translates into the requirement that the agreed waterflows as well as the utilizations thereby rendered viable prove to be in rigorous conformity with or are instrumental to the compliance with environmental objectives. For instance, article 16, §1 illustrates that this 'sharing of waters' purports to achieve the good status of the waters and article 15, § 1 shows that the utilizations must be sustainable.

5.3. Another area of management with functional connections as much with the 'environmental' objective of the protection of waters as with that of sustainable utilization of the waters is that of the rationality, efficiency and economy of the uses. Article 10, §1e) prescribes that voluntaristic actions be carried out ('to promote the rationality and economy of the uses'). In particular, the definition of more specific common objectives is expected. This goal should be obtained through the coordination of management plans and programmes of measures[104] as well as the exchange of information on experiences and perspectives on the matter.[105]

5.4. Further, the management of emergencies – either caused by Man or resulting from natural phenomena – constitutes another dimension of the new regime.[106] This element denotes the present understanding of the management of waters as a 'continuum' which is tied not only to situations of normalcy but also to their exceptions and draws attention to the question of risks posed by water.

This management of emergencies is to be carried out in coordination between the two States and applies not only to emergencies currently occurring[107] but also to their prevention.[108] This goal justifies that coordinated actions between the Parties are also foreseen in the areas of:

---

[103] Article 6, §2 of the Additional Protocol. Naturally, this emerging concern is set against considerable lack of knowledge which the Parties have to progressively overcome. This is precisely one of the principal reasons explaining the provisional character of the present waterflows regime (article 16, §5). The ongoing studies aimed at the national basin plans (see *infra* III.3.3) represent an excellent opportunity for reducing the present ignorance on the ecological processes associated with the waters of the rivers and for determining scientifically-based water requirements to sustain these processes. This also corresponds to the expectations of the Water Framework Directive according to its norms regarding these instruments.
[104] Still article 10, §1e), '*in fine*'.
[105] Article 15, §3.
[106] Article 10, § , f), g), h) and Part IV.
[107] For instance, article 11, §§ 1 and 2 and article 12, §2.
[108] For instance, article 11, §§ 1 and 2 and article 12, §1.

a) droughts and water shortages (articles 10, §1 f), 11 and 17);

b) floods (articles 10, §1 f), 11 and 18);

c) incidents of accidental pollution (articles 10 ,§ 1 g), 11 and 19); and

d) safety of infrastructures (articles 10, §1 h), 11 and 12).

5.5. Moreover, in order to render all of this feasible, it is not surprising that a system of control and evaluation of the qualitative and quantitative state of the waters is envisaged and that actions of cooperation ensuring the fulfilment of this aim are foreseen.[109] This monitoring system[110] is also conceived as a mechanism by which the impacts of projects 'ex post' (i.e., once erected and functioning, as advocated by the International Court of Justice in the Gabcikovo-Nagymaros Case[111]) may be evaluated . It enables the Parties to make informed decisions that are required in order to satisfy the aforementioned responsibilities.

5.6. Good management depends increasingly on more than immediate and routine information though. Rather, it is presently more and more dependent on profound knowledge.[112] This knowledge must be based on essential or functionally oriented studies which indicate actions whose consequences are only measured in the future as well as on technologies which better enable the securing of such environmental objectives. This need is implicitly acknowledged by the Parties when they also place themselves under the obligation to cooperate in the field of Research and Development (article 9 and article 10, §1 q)). On the other hand, the Parties also demonstrate their rejection of a view of this substantive program which would reduce it to good intentions. Instead, they make a clear and resolute choice in favour of a living law – which is to say a law that is genuinely implemented or a 'law in action'. To this end, they integrate the concern of the complete fulfilment of the Convention (article 10, §1 l)) with that of its implementation, compliance with and efficacy of the system (article 10, §1 m)) as specific areas of

---

[109] Article 10, §1 i), as well as article 9, §4, to name just two norms.

[110] For instance, article 5, § 1and 4 and article 15, §4.

[111] Case Concerning the Gabcikovo-Nagymaros Project (Hungary V. Slovakia), (Judgement of 25 September 1997), 37 *ILM* 162 (1998), para. 112. On it, see Malgosia Fiztmaurice, 'Environmental Protection and the International Court of Justice', *in* V. Lowe and M. Fitzmaurice (eds.), *Essays in Honour of Sir Robert Jennings*, 1996, 308–315; as well as several articles on the topic in *YBIEL*, 1997, vol. 8 and *LJIL*, 1998.

[112] Apart from being a general problem in all matters related to the environment and its processes and balances, it is also a problem specifically experienced in the Iberian Peninsula in relation to its water resources. This is clearly denoted by the last preambular paragraph of the Convention.

cooperation between the Parties. This strategy constitutes an original solution in the Comparative Law in the field.[113]

6. Good management does not only entail the identification of the areas of interdependent action in which one must operate. Nor does it only involve the clarification of the material solutions or criteria for such problems. Indeed, this would be an inacceptable simplification because the pursuit of sustainable development is not a case of binary decisions to be taken in single steps in time. Rather, it is a continuous process of progressive approximation toward this kind of (environmental and developmental) justice. Therefore, it also entails the realistic definition of the procedures of dynamic implementation of such a regime.[114] In this light, the consideration given by the two Parties to the procedural question constitutes an unquestionable sign of the genuineness and determination in pursuing a modern form of management and dealing with the real existing problems.

6.1. This attention to the question of procedure was expressed primarily at the bilateral level, by foreseeing the following:

   a) apart from a general and repeated reference to a generic obligation of cooperation, which simultaneously also stands as one of the main objectives of the new regime;[115]

   b) a very broad (first) specific obligation of exchange of information between the Parties (articles 5, 8, §§1 and 2, 10, §4, 11, 12, §2, and Annex I);

   c) the provision of information by the Parties to the Commission itself (article 7);

   d) notification of certain more environmentally-sensitive projects, capable of producing impacts (article 8, §1);

   e) consultations on delicate matters, such as situations which involve foreseeable impacts (articles 8 and 9);

---

[113] As can be demonstrated by a comparison with analoguous dispositions on responsibilities in several Conventions. See, however, article 18, §5 of the 1994 Danube Convention and article 5, e) of the 1995 Meuse and Scheldt Agreements.

[114] The importance of this dimension of Water Law had already been duly stressed by Charles Bourne. See his articles collected in P. Wouters (ed.), *International Water Law. Selected Writings of Professor Charles B. Bourne*, London, 1997, especially Part III.

[115] See, for instance, apart from the title of the Convention, the letter and contents of article 2, and especially §1, the heading of article 4 (which states the objectives and the principal mechanism of cooperation), as well as article 10 which is the key norm that discriminates the bulk of measures of cooperation between the Parties not yet established in the preceding articles. Furthermore, even if no explicit reference to cooperation is normally made, all the other obligations – of means or result – to whose fulfilment the Parties have to act jointly or in a co-ordinated manner are also eloquent and constitute numerous examples of this general duty to cooperate. The relationship in this Convention between the general obligation and the specific duties recalls the relation between the obligation in article 8 and those of the articles corresponding to Part III in the United Nations Convention.

    f) transboundary impact assessments (article 9);

    g) coordination of such fundamental management instruments of each State as management plans and programs of measures.[116]

6.2. However, it is additionally important to note that this response to the procedural question was accomplished at a multilateral level, through a process founded on the relationship and communication with others (or, to cite Habermas, the 'inclusion of the other'[117]) thereby proving the resolve of the Parties to demonstrate their condition of 'open societies'[118] as well as their recognition of the advantages of such a condition and relationship in the pursuit of environmental values and sustainability. The poles of this multilateral dialogue are as follows:

    a) Not only the 'supra-state' 'other' – such as International Organisations- which also deal with management problems or have competing responsibilities in this area (article 10, §4 and article 25);

    b) But also the 'infra-state' 'other', such as, the 'anonymous' 'common man', who most directly experiences these problems. However, it encompasses NGOs as well, since the functions of this latter group also place them in immediate contact with these questions enabling them (if not even putting them in an advantageous position) to validly interact with the public authorities in the managerial procedure. Further, their inputs (and, occasionally, those of the leading elites or epistemic communities,[119] as well) are of importance both to the decision-making and the control ('watchdog' function) of the results thereof. To this end, the Parties promised to give the public (a notion, in which all these infra-state stakeholders can be integrated) very broad information 'on the matters which are the object of the Convention' (article 6). In this way, the participation of the public – which

---

[116] This procedure is accompanied, in the case of impacts, and accredited by the suspension of the planned measures or renewal or enlargement of ongoing activities (article 8, §6).

[117] See Jürgen Habermas, *Die Einbeziehung des Anderen. Studien zur politischen Theorie*, Frankfurt am Main, 1996, Surkamp.

[118] *I.e.*, tendentially embracing all human beings or participants, as in the distinction between 'open' and 'closed societies' drawn by the French philosopher H. Bergson, in 1932, *in Les Deux Sources de la morale et de la religion*, Paris, 1982, 283–307.

[119] On these, their influence, leadership and relevance, particularly in some processes, see Peter M. Haas, 'Do Regimes Matter? Epistemic Communities and Mediterranean Pollution Control', 43, *International Organization*, 377 (1989); Oran R. Young, 'The politics of international regime formation: managing natural resources and the environment', 48, *International Organization*, 349, 355 (1989); Oran Young and Gail Osherenko, *Polar Politics: Creating International Environmental Regimes*, 245 (1993).

seems to be unrestrictedly understood or 'defined'[120] – is, at least, rendered viable.

7. As it is important to note, a management model does not only depend on its 'quid' or contents (the question dealt with under 5.). Nor does it depend simply on its 'quomodo' or methods of its reinvention and fulfillment (the problem just addressed under 6.). Rather, a management model is also a function of the 'quiddam' or agent responsible for its implementation and realization.

   Without doubt, the Parties also considered the preceeding practice when addressing this topic. They first acknowledged its worthiness by integrating it in the present regime of the Convention in every solution which would not run counter to the specific rules of the Convention (article 27). However, they also simultaneously departed from it, indicating that the former practice could and even should be improved (article 29). Specifically, they agreed to create an institutional system[121] essentially guided by the fulfilment of the proclaimed 'desiderata' in two fundamental types of situations which are conceptually and normatively differentiated on the basis of the notions of 'questions' (article 22, §4) and 'disputes'(article 26, §1):

   (a) those of 'common', 'recurrent' or daily' problems, even if of an exceptional nature ('questions');

   (b) those of a true conflictive nature ('disputes').

   7.1. With respect to the former, the mechanism instituted is of a more generic nature and application. It appears to synthesize the past experience of management from the Conventions of the 1960's, the (good) experience of the negotiation of the Convention adopted in 1998 as well as adds several new elements appropriate for the more complex ambitions of the new regime. Thus, the institutional setting is composed of two levels corresponding to different organs:

   a) the top level, organized in the Conference of the Parties,[122] is composed essentially of political leaders.[123] The Conference meets when it is deemed convenient[124] in order to evaluate the cooperation, define new directions and, if necessary, overcome obstacles;[125]

---

[120] See the very wide and encompassing formulation of §1 of article 6. On the notions which may have been determinant in helping to find a correct answer to this end, yet less adroitely represented in the Convention, see, already after the adoption of the Convention, Jonas Ebbeson, 'The Notion of Public Participation in International Environmental Law', *YBIEL*, 1997, vol. 8, 51–97; Economic Commission for Europe, *The Aarhus Convention: An Implementation Guide*, New York and Geneva, 2000.

[121] Mainly article 4§2 and Part V.

[122] Article 21.

[123] Article 21, §1.

[124] Article 21, §2.

[125] Article 21, §3.

b) the ordinary level – instituted in the organ of the 'Commission for the Implementation and the Development of the Convention' (hereafter, Commission; according to the Convention, this organ succeeds to the former Commission of International Rivers[126]) – is comprised of national delegations of a more technocratic nature[127] which encompass diplomats, technicians and jurists.[128] These individuals have the collective responsibility of defining the concrete means of implementing the conventional regime[129] and even proposing to the Parties forms of developing it.[130]

Beyond the definition of the fundamental conditions of its work – composition,[131] responsibilities and powers,[132] essential rules of functioning,[133] – the Convention also confers upon the Commission powers of self-regulation (article 23, §6).

7.2. With regard to this latter level, of a rather contentious nature, the Convention points to a specific mechanism. It may act in two phases – pre-contentious[134] and contentious – and has a mixed diplomatic and jurisdictional nature. It may work according to various forms or involving different instances. These forms or instances are as follows:

a) the Commission, which article 22, §4 qualifies as 'the privileged organ of resolution of questions regarding the interpretation and application of the Convention';

b) (still in what may be termed the pre-contentious phase) the Conference which can meet to 'resolve those questions for which no agreement was reached in the heart of the Commission' (article 21, §3);

c) (already in what we may call the contentious phase) negotiation between the Parties or the utilization of any other diplomatic method of settlement of disputes (article 26, §1). It appears that the instances in which this negotiation should take place may be the Commission and/or the Conference, although, in view of the

---

[126] Article 1, §1 h) and 22, §5.

[127] Thus the recommendations of *functionalism* are followed according to which a certain division of functions should exist and these problems gain in being removed from the more politicized scene, at least in a prior moment, so that political intervention may concentrate on finding solutions to deadlocks.

[128] Article 21, §1.

[129] Article 21, §2.

[130] Article 21, §3.

[131] Article 22, §1.

[132] Article 22, §§ 2 to 5 and article 23, §§ 4 and 5.

[133] Article 23, §§ 1 to 5.

[134] Implicit is a clear preference for a non-confrontational approach.

           comprehensiveness of the reference to 'Parties', it also seems
           possible to conceive other interpretative solutions;

    d) if the legal dispute has a 'predominantly technical character'
        and the Parties agree upon this, they should resort to a
        commission of inquiry (article 26, §2);[135]

    e) once 'one year has passed' without a solution to the legal dispute
        having been found (article 26, §3), the appeal to a court of
        arbitration[136] whose composition and mode of functioning are
        defined by the Convention.[137]

2.2 Significance: Path to a new paradigm of management of Luso-Spanish waters?

The meaning of the new normative message is manifestly diverse from that of the Conventions which preceded the one of 1998 in the regulation of Luso-Spanish relations. It may be summarized in three fundamental options: environmental friendliness, relational friendliness and legal friendliness about which it seems important to note the following:

2.2.1 Environmental friendliness

Having been one of the aims always presented by Portugal, this option is clear and evident throughout the entire regime: from the definition of the object[138] to the enunciation of the objectives.[139] More specifically, it is apparent in the integration of the traditional vector of (economic, growth-oriented) water utilizations with the more modern one of the protection of the environment and even subordinating those uses to a general aim of (environmental) sustainable development. Further, it is incorporated in the list of the subject-matters or areas of cooperation included in the model of management.[140] Within this model, the primary domains of the protection of waters and ecosystems[141] and the utilizations of the waters,[142] find themselves powerfully conditioned by this vector. This contingency is symptomatically demonstrated by the use of the qualification 'sustainable' when the Convention refers to the

---

[135] See, similarly, article 3, §7 of the Espoo Convention.
[136] Article 26, §4.
[137] Article 26, §§ 4 to 8.
[138] Article 2.
[139] Article 4, §1.
[140] Article 4, §2 and article 10.
[141] Article 4, §1, article 10, §1, a), b) and c), articles 13 and 14.
[142] Article 4, §1, article 10, §1, d) and e), articles 15 and 16.

utilizations envisaged. Moreover, it is also reflected in the procedures. Indeed, one immediately notes the consecration of a broad mechanism of impact assessments[143] or the systems of communication, alert and emergency which also take into account the risks for the environment.[144] This is without mentioning the obligations of reporting[145] and publicity.[146] The same can be said of the specific material obligations and of instruments such as the water quality standards or objectives and emission limits,[147] best available techniques and best environmental practices[148] normally associated with this endeavour and environmental concern.[149] Finally, the same underlying philosophy is also present in the principles with which the management is supposed to comply: the principles of equitable and sustainable utilization and participation,[150] the precautionary principle,[151] the principle of prevention[152] and the (procedural) principles of exchange of[153] and access to information and public participation.[154, 155] Although not named, they are clearly implicit in this regime and result from the remissions to other juridical orders which are held as a model of reference (article 2, §2).

Hence, it becomes clear that this normative program does not necessarily correspond to a ecosystemic,[156] even perfect, absolute, or 'radical' environmental protection[157] – which is to say, one which would involve some general

---

[143] Article 9.

[144] Article 11, §2, '*in fine*'.

[145] Article 7, §2.

[146] Article 6, §3, in conjunction with article 5.

[147] They are foreseen, for instance, in article 14.

[148] They are foreseen, for instance, in Annex I.

[149] On these instruments, A. Kiss and D. Shelton, *Manual of European Environmental Law*, Cambridge, 1994, 234–239.

[150] It may be detected in articles 15 and 16, especially §1 and in the Additional Protocol, namely article 1, §1, as well as in the Annex to the Additional Protocol.

[151] See, in different ways, articles 5, 7, 9, 10, 13 and 14.

[152] For instance, in articles 13 and 14.

[153] Article 5.

[154] Article 6.

[155] On these principles, in general, see Philippe Sands, *Principles of International Environmental Law. Frameworks, standards and implementation*, vol. I, Manchester and New York, 1995, 194–196, 198–213, 222–230.

[156] Powerfully advocating an ecosystemic orientation, Jutta Brunnée and Stephen Toope, 'Environmental Security and Freshwater Resources: A Case for International Ecosystem Law', 5, *YBIEL*, 41 (1994).

[157] We are thinking of theories such as those of deep ecology or ecocentrism (Arne Naess being the most representative name of this movement; a milder trend within this movement is represented by such names as Robyn Eckersley and Dave Foreman), social ecology or eco-anarchism (Murray Bookchin), ecological post-modernism (J. Cheney), eco-socialism or socialist-ecologism or red-greenism, eco-feminism (Carlassare, Cuomo, Salleh, Vanda Shiva). These radical environmental theories have in common the contention that green incremental change is not sufficient and to a certain extent still involves a 'business as usual stance'. On this debate, see B. Goodwin, *Green Political Theory*, Cambridge, 1992; C.

impediment, in general, to utilizations of water or utilizations of waters affecting the ecosystems which waters sustain. In the same way, this normative program also does not demand the re-naturalization of the rivers[158] or the return to a pristine state of environmental conditions which is probably as much idealistic as non-existent in its equation with times previous to the human colonization and mobilization of Nature. Nevertheless, this program is certainly one of a demanding environmental protection. This is to say, one which, in the name of 'good status' of the waters – a goal of the Convention[159] equivalent to the concept,[160] then emerging in the European Law through the discussions of the proposed Water Framework Directive[161] – could, in fact, result in the imposition of either abstentions or prohibitions to certain projected utilizations and actions. As it also justifies voluntaristic and 'positive' measures, aimed at reversing an historical process of degradation of the waters, in particular, and of the environment, in general.

2.2.2 *Relational friendliness*

2.2.2.1 Plural relationships

The intention is unequivocal. The previous model was one of intermittent, sporadic relations that were based on a sentiment of self-sufficiency of the State Parties which was practised in reality.[162] Today, one is prepared for the contrary – a course of almost constant, even close or intimate relations of cooperation. In fact, these cooperative relations are required at multiple levels.

First, close ties must exist between the two riparian States. This relationship is imposed, from the start, because of the nature of the areas and matters of

---

cont.

    Merchant, *Radical Ecology: The Search for a Livable World*, 1992; R. Eckersley, *Environmentalism and Political Theory: Toward an Ecocentric Approach*, London, 1992; A . Dobson, *Green Political Thought*, 2nd. ed., London and New York, 1995; and the good summary by Timothy Doyle and Doug McEachern, *Environment and Politics*, London and New York, 1998, 36–54.

[158] In this more demanding sense, see the new Rhine Convention. Text *in* COM (1999) 51 *final*, February 5 1999; it revokes the 1963 Agreement on the International Commission for the Protection of the Rhine Against Pollution, the 1967 Additional Agreement and the 1976 Convention on the Protection of the Rhine Against Chemical Pollution.

[159] For instance, in article 13§2, a) and b).

[160] It is now consecrated in article 4 of the Water Framework Directive.

[161] See our 'Novos Rumos do Direito Comunitário da Água: a caminho de uma revolução (tranquila)?. Primeiras reflexões sobre a Proposta de 'Directiva que estabelece um quadro para a acção da Comunidade no domínio da Política da Água' (New Directions in Community Law of Water: the Path to a (quiet) Revolution?. Initial Reflections on the Proposal of the 'Directive establishing a Framework of Community Action in the Area of Water Politics'), *Revista do CEDOUA*, 1998, 1, 11–35, with a summary in English.

[162] As we have seen above 203, 'proudly alone' was the maxim of the time in Portugal.

cooperation as well as the objectives which are to be pursued. It is also demanded and facilitated by the established procedures which are equally intended to expediate the actual fulfilment of these intentions.

Second, cooperative relations are also necessary to ensure a dynamic Commission instituted by the 1998 Convention and the interconnection between the two delegations.[163]

Third, close ties are required with the public and any stakeholder. With the increasing concern with their environment and compatible models of development, they are equally expected to contribute to the realization of the Convention's objectives. In fact, it is of vital importance to the very health of this complex regime that the public becomes an active participant. This participation should not only take place at the stage of decision-making but also during the implementation of the conventional rules and the Commission's decisions. It must have certainly been with this hope in mind that the Parties bound themselves to furnish relevant information (article 6) and provide it to the public. This task can be accomplished through the usual communicational process between the public and the national environmental administration within the domestic system.[164] However, this form of dialogue should not impede the Commission from instituting similar discussions between the public and the Commission itself.

Further, cooperative relations must also occur at the international level. International organizations (e.g. the European Community or the United Nations Economic Commission for Europe) have already demonstrated that they share the idea that the global regional environment (that of Europe[165]) depends on or is a function of the local environments (in this case, the Portuguese-Spanish one). In parallel, the Parties acknowledged the importance of the International Organisations' contributions by admitting (in article 10, §4) that information should be provided to these organisations and by foreseeing (in article 25) a mechanism of mutual consultations.

[163] Furthermore, a possibility exists that the Commission may comprehend other elements in its own composition apart from State officials. This is a problem to be solved by the Statute or even future deliberations on the composition of the subsidiary organs. In our view, it would seem appropriate, particularly for the working groups foreseen by article 22, §1, to leave the door open to special competencies of the civil society (experts) and particular stakeholders (such as representatives of NGOs and those of the environment or of consumers as well as of economic organizations).

[164] See the assessment made in the mid–90's in Portugal and Spain, respectively by Adília Lopes and José Cunhal Sendim and Fe Sanchis Moreno, *in* Ralph E. Hallo (ed.), *Access to Environmental Information in Europe. The Implementation and Implications of Directive 90/313/EEC*, London, 1996, 215–223 and 225–248.

[165] For instance, one may remember the 'Environment for Europe' process.

2.2.2.2 Polygonal[166] dialogue in an open society

Hence, one notes the reinforcement of the material model of (environmental-friendly) integrated management which was outlined by the substantial norms discussed above. This process occurs on the subjective-institutional level as well, given that it is also a question of integrated management. However, it is now an issue of the integration of all of the relevant and contributing actors in what constitutes a polygonal process of dialogue, balancing the composition of the multifarious stakeholders and interests which are present (public and private, State and non-State), as well as the values that are shared. It may even be the case of practical application of the principle of subsidiarity as well, although this suggestion will have to be confirmed by future rules and the practice which is followed.

2.2.2.3 The solution to the question of the model of institutional cooperation: cooperative management

The particular modality of cooperation between the States or the contents and orientation of this particular inter-State institutional model is equally clarified: the Parties chose what may be termed a solution of cooperative management. Indeed, in the face of the two options equated by science and Comparative Law,[167] it becomes clear that the Parties did not intend to follow any 'supra-national' or unitary path which the political-administrative traditions of the two peoples do not favour. Hence, they did not propose an institutional solution of true joint management. As shown by the first sentence of article 3, §3 of the Water Framework Directive, this strategy would require, for instance, that the two States collectively devise a joint or common plan for the whole basins of reference. Instead, the Convention clearly chooses a mechanism of coordination of the actions, measures, plans and programmes of the two administrations – however extensive and intensive they may be. It is precisely on this coordinated basis that the aforementioned objectives, principles, solutions and processes shall be pursued and the coherence or substantial homogeneity of the final result

---

[166] We have borrowed the expression from a great Portuguese juspublicist and pioneer of environmental law studies in Portugal as well as epigon of a school of thought, J.J. Gomes Canotilho, 'A responsabilidade por danos ambientais – Aproximação juspublicística', *in* INA, *Direito do Ambiente*, 1994, 397–409.

[167] See Lucius Caflisch, 'Règles générales du droit des cours d'eau internationaux', *RCADI*, vol. VII, 1989, Stephen McCaffrey, 'Transboundary Water Resources', *in* United Nations – Department for Development Support and Management, *Transboundary Water Resources*, Ad Hoc Expert Group Meeting on Strategic Issues Concerning Transboundary Water Resources, New York, 14 May 1996, WA/SEM. 97, Annex I and our own 'The Future of International Water Law', in Luso-American Foundation, *Shared Water Systems and Transboundary Issues with special emphasis on the Iberian Peninsula*, Lisbon, 2000, 172–174.

guaranteed. This strategy signifies that this complex normative and managerial programme must be accomplished without any loss to the relative autonomy of the Parties – another value in the political culture and history of these two countries. Further, this autonomy must be strictly respected, even while they are (appreciably) united within the Commission. This solution of a cooperative institutional model constitutes one of conjunction and coordination of two independent entities in the management of shared basins. Clearly, it is in line with the other strategy that the above-mentioned article 3, §3 of the Water Framework Directive equally admits, although this time in the last sentence of the rule.

2.3 Legal friendliness

The friendliness towards the legal order and 'vis-à-vis' its coherence[168], [169] is a final strategic option of the new regime. It was initially revealed in the negotiations in which the invocation of juridical-normative models occurred with considerable frequency. It is presently evident in the Convention itself on numerous levels. For instance:

3.1. when it adopts a juridical form and style;
3.2. when it incorporates concepts or solutions that recall – if not actually import – elements from other juridical instruments which are more or less directly acknowledged. This strategy is clearly illustrated by the central concept of the 'good status of the waters'[170] which was derived from the Water Framework Directive, then still under negotiation in the competent Community organs;
3.3. when, in whatever form, it recalls (even in anticipation) other juridical instruments.[171] An example would be those cases in which the solutions of the Convention recall those of other treaties or 'instruments-peers'[172]

---

[168] How else can it claim to be an *order*?.
[169] First signs of attention to this theme are discernible in André Nollkaemper, *The Legal Regime for Transboundary Water Pollution: Between Discretion and Constraint*, Dordrecht, 1993, 307–314.
[170] For instance, article 3, §2 claims that 'the Convention applies to the activities aimed at the promotion and protection of the good status of the waters of these hydrographic basins and to the activities of utilization of the water resources (...)'. In addition, article 4, §1 says that 'The Parties coordinate the actions of promotion and protection of the good status of the superficial and underground waters (...)'.
[171] Either centered on similar objects or having objects just touching the one of the 1998 Convention; of a Water Law content or of either a structural content – access to information – or of another sector of International Law – Law of the Sea, for instance; representative of true International Law or of other juridical orders, such as the domestic or Community ones.
[172] *I.e.*, appertaining to a similar local or sub-regional level.

(such as the 1994 Danube Convention,[173] the 1994 Meuse Convention,[174] the 1994 Scheldt Convention,[175] the 1998 Oder Convention,[176] the new 1999 Rhine Convention[177]) or ('supra') inspirations[178] (such as the New York United Nations Convention, the Washington Rules on Land Based Pollution, but especially the 1992 Helsinki Convention on the Protection and Use of Transboundary Watercourses and International Lakes, the 1991 Espoo Convention on Environmental Impact Assessment in a Transboundary Context, the 1992 Helsinki Convention on the Transboundary Effects of Industrial Accidents, the 1998 Aarhus Convention on Access to Information, Public Participation in Decision-Making and Access to Justice in Environmental Matters,[179] the London Protocol on Water and Health to the 1992 Helsinki Convention,[180] the OSPAR Convention, the European Directives – principally those of the second generation such as the Urban Waste Water Treatment Directive,[181] the Directive concerning the protection of waters against pollution caused by nitrates from agricultural sources[182] and the so-called IPPC Directive[183] and, above all, the Water Framework Directive[184]);

3.4. when it refers to other juridical systems (international, European, Community or domestic laws) and particularly when it establishes that they shall constitute the hermeneutic parameter for the interpretation of rules[185] and the source of elements in order to integrate 'lacunae';[186]

3.5. when it shows particular attention, in the solutions devised, to the principles which the new Water Law embraced[187] when it adopted an

---

[173] Text reprinted *in* Patricia Wouters and Serguei Vinogradov, *Transnational Water Projects: Risks and Opportunities*, Dundee, 1997.

[174] *Idem.*

[175] *Ibidem.*

[176] Text *in* COM (1998), 528 *final*, September 16 1998.

[177] Text *in* COM (1999) 51 *final*, February 5 1999.

[178] Thus classified because they appertain, instead, either to the global or regional level.

[179] UNEcosoc ECE/CEP/ 43 (21 April 1998).

[180] See UN Doc. MP.WAT/AC.1/1998/14.

[181] Directive 91/271, *OJ* 1991, nº L 135/40.

[182] Directive 91/676, *OJ* 1991, nº L 375/1.

[183] Integrated Pollution Prevention and Control: Directive 96/61, *OJ* L 257, 10 October 1996. On this Directive, see Chris Backes and Gerritt Betlem (eds.), *Integrated Pollution Prevention and Control. The EC Directive from a Comparative Legal and Economic Perspective*, The Hague, 1999.

[184] Directive 2000/60.

[185] See article 2, §2.

[186] See article 3, §2.

[187] See 3rd preambular paragraph and article 3, §2.

environmental perspective.[188] Or, more broadly, when it converged with other dimensions of the modern 'post-ontological'[189] international legal order;[190]

3.6. when it organizes the normative handling of the matters, which are addressed in a systematic and coherent way.

Coherence is, in fact, a key word in the necessary understanding of this new regime.

First, that coherence which exists between the diverse normative texts on which the 1998 convention system is constructed. This cohesion may be seen as the result of an 'internal linkage' or 'internal articulation' between different instruments.[191] It may be direct – i.e. between the main body of the Convention, the Additional Protocol and the Annexes to both the Convention and the Additional Protocol – or indirect – through the reference to the 'regime of the Conventions of 1964 and 1968' which appears, for instance, in articles 1, §1 g and 16, §1 and through which the previous Conventions are also to be applied in what still remains valid,[192] as well as the Additional Protocols to the 1964 and 1968 Conventions and the decisions of the former Commission of International Rivers.[193] Finally, this concern with normative coherence is also the key to understanding the references to the International and European orders,[194] as well as the domestic legal ones.[195] This aspect may be referred to as the Convention's 'external linkage'. Thus, the Convention is presented as a normative 'bridge' in a complex, plural and open system of

---

[188] This convergence of the traditionally separate bodies of Law governing the uses of international waters and the protection of the Environment is, in our view, one of the most interesting developments of the present phase of International Water Law and one which seems to have powerfully inspired the general orientation of the negotiations and eventually the text finally adopted. This is particularly well illustrated by article 3 ,§ 2 with its openness to 'principles and norms of applicable International and Community Law' in the pursuit of the cooperation prescribed in the previous paragraph of the article.

[189] This excellent expression is taken from Thomas Franck in his seminal *Fairness in International Law and Institutions*, Oxford, 1995, p.7.

[190] For instance documented in the insistence on the protection of ecosystems, on a preventive instead of a remedy-oriented policy, on sustainability and on international cooperation and participation of the public which are unquestionably recurrent themes in the contemporary international legal order.

[191] And the Convention is, in fact, a *framework-Convention*, as its article 2, §1 actually denotes.

[192] More generally, article 27, §2.

[193] Thus, the Convention 'nests' or is constructed on this regime of the 1960's which, in this sense, serves as the Convention's normative foundation or patrimony.

[194] For instance, article 2, §2 and article 3,§2, but also articles 10, §3, 13, §§1, 2 c) and 3, 14, §1 (the references to Community Law, as illustrated by these three last examples of relevant articles are understandably more recurrent in all measures concerning the protection of the quality of waters).

[195] For instance, articles 5, §2, 6, §2, 10, §2, 14, §2.

Law. More specifically, it constitutes a bridge to other normative times, to other normative spaces and between different types of Law.

Second, coherence and coordination are also pursued in the implementation of the whole. This objective is certainly one of the reasons underlying the empowerment of the Commission to autonomously – as guardian of the regime –, make (binding) applicative deliberations.[196] Additionally, it also explains the focus on compliance with and development or incremental expansion of the conventional regime.[197] Further, it is from this angle that one should understand the demand for coordination of such national applicative instruments, 'par excellence', but which also have an international outlook when dealing with international basins. Examples of these crucial applicative instruments as foreseen by the Convention – for instance in articles 10, §2 and 13, §2 (which once again parallel what later became the solution of the Water Framework Directive) – would be the management plans and programs of measures. Finally, this perspective also sheds light – on a symbolic level which should not be disdained – on the recourse to the key notion of 'regime'. This term is used precisely to connote the unitary overarching result of all of these relevant pieces of the 'jigsaw' puzzle or normative building blocks from which a true normative system should result.[198] Hence, the Convention does not only defend substantive normative (environmental) managerial integration, accompanied by subjective, institutional and procedural integration. It (as well as the whole regime which is centered upon it) also reveals the belief in the integration of the legal instruments or 'corpus iuris' which are deemed relevant. No doubt, to this ambitious and complex end, the normative principles which the Parties venerate have a fundamental role to play – possibly even a decisive one – as a kind of normative 'cement' to such a Gaudí-like normative architecture.

---

[196] Article 22, §§ 4 and 5.

[197] Article 10 §1, l) and m).

[198] On the lessons of regime theory and its normative implications, see Robert O Keohane, 'The Demand for International Regimes', 36, *International Organization*, 325, 338–339 (1982); Stephen Krasner, 'Structural Causes and Regime Consequences: Regimes as Intervening Variables', *in* Stephen Krasner (ed.), *International Regimes*, 1983; Oran R. Young, *International Cooperation: Building Regimes for Natural Resources and the Environment*, 1989.

III

3. Guaranteed success? – The question of implementation

Clearly, this positive presentation transmits optimism in the readiness of this regime to extract the lessons learned from past experience as well as its resolve in facing both the problems of the present and those of the foreseeable future. However, can we assume that the battle has already been won and that we are left simply to bask in the obtained laurels?

The answer must naturally be a resounding 'No!'. On the contrary, in view of the nature and dimension of the challenge ahead – sustainability –, it is important to stress that, to a certain extent, the problems have only just begun. Indeed, one needs to ensure that the regime will be put into practice and become effective part and parcel of the life of the two Parties. In fact, an enormous task still lies ahead. Particularly given the difficulties in the implementation of the Conventions of the 1960's, it would not seem incorrect to expect that the application of the 1998 Convention will be even more problematic, especially because of its greater complexities. Realistically, not much has changed in the present except for the normative conditions. The negotiation process of the Convention certainly served as a learning curve for the integration of expectations, concepts and objectives and the establishment of a common 'hard law' normative playing ground. However, the apparent convergence of two approaches which 'ab initio' began as reasonably diverse will have to be tested against the practice that is yet to come. Clearly, the mere adoption of the Convention – however important, particularly as a means of stabilizing expectations and behaviours or of reducing the complexities of life[199] – is not a substitute for the task of its actual implementation which takes place in dialogue with real life and its ever changing circumstances.

It is understood that in the near future all these rules will have to be put to the test. Amongst foreseeable validations, the following seem to be of a more pressing nature:

1. the test of the creation of the Commission;
2. the test of the developments to be (immediately) carried out;
3. the test of the national plans;
4. the test of (the reform of) the institutions and processes;
5. the test of accompanying the evolution of the 'enveloping' Law;
6. the test of the public.

---

[199] Niklas Luhmann, *Soziale Systeme. Grundriss einer allgemeinen Theorie*, Frankfurt am Main, 1984.

3.1 *The test of the creation of the Commission*

This challenge deals not only with the actual creation of the Commission which was created on the 17th January 2000 (with the first two meetings having already taken place). It also refers to the beginnings of an institution from which there were great expectations in its ability to be autonomous, responsible, and functionally suited to deal with the magnitude of the task. Therefore, the Contracting Parties must refrain from turning the Commission into an empty shell by ceding to the possible temptation of corrupting and/or diminishing its complex and yet holistic, integrated and, as such, also balanced normative programme. Furthermore, the Parties should ensure the enabling political conditions. For instance, they should provide an adequate domestic legal framework and supportive actions. Particularly, in view of the probable difficulties arising from a new body, the Parties should be prepared to provide backing. Finally, they should also assure that the members of the delegations are carefully selected. Ideally, these members should be chosen on the basis of representation of the vast array of interests involved as well as personal competence in order to contribute to the prestige and usefulness of this international institution.

The adoption of a Statute capable of resolving some of the outstanding issues could be considered as a fundamental step in the proposed direction. This legal document could address such questions as the dialogue with the public and the means by which its participation could be assured. Additionally, it could deal with the issue of a functional organics which is capable of dealing with the defined responsibilities entrusted to the Commission. Subsequently, the rapid launching of the defined authorities should be carried out. In all probability, some working groups[200] would be created before others. In any circumstance, even if some of the expressions of the Commission were developed on a more 'ad hoc' basis and others only sometime in the future, one should never lose sight of the intimate correlation of all the corresponding matters which are part of the regime[201] when establishing this institutional edifice.

---

[200] This type of subsidiary organs of the Commission is foreseen, along with sub-commissions, in article 22, §1.

[201] Indeed, apart from the clearer '*quid pro quo*'-tit-for-tat-reciprocity which presided over the solution found for the quantitative problem, there is a more diffuse reciprocity underlying the other solutions of the Convention. It underlies, for instance, the listing of the areas of cooperation between the Parties. On this dual kind of reciprocity and its role, see Robert O. Keohane, 'Reciprocity in International Relations', 40, *International Organization*, 1 (1986).

3.2 *The test of the developments*

The question of the flows which are granted and the developments based thereupon was one of the most difficult issues which the negotiations had to resolve. In fact, the records of these meetings indicate that all the other normative solutions which had been found in the interim were 'held ransom', during the final stages of the process, until a solution for this more contentious matter could be discovered.

Therefore, one cannot expect that the Convention – as a whole or in its integrity – will be able to 'come alive' and, as is also desired, be applied in a 'healthy' manner if the Parties forget, or try to unilaterally maximize or re-define the balance between their developments during the 7-year period in which the Convention and its regime of flows are to come in force. This time frame is clearly conceived as a trial period for the re-adoption of the fundamental deal or its necessary renewal. Moreover, this is true not only in this particular domain in which a solution was barely found. Rather, it is also true for the more global balance between the solution found for this particular quantitative question and the others which are also part and parcel of the new Convention.[202]

In any case, some of the few developments already projected for the immediate future (unfortunately, in part, with a reasonable degree of vagueness), take on the role of a fundamental test-case. Among these, the Alqueva Dam project is the most striking example. This is true in terms of magnitude, expectations and importance for Portuguese development. However, it is equally true with respect to its possible contribution for the resolution of the environmental problems of the shared Low Guadiana, and particularly for the social and environmental sensibility,[203] and the historical 'doubts' which have surrounded it. Its progressive realisation without obstacles or delays will be a positive sign that the Parties have genuinely identified themselves with the regime in all its implications and balanced integrity, that they are really willing to carry it out.

---

[202] Indeed one of the main contributions of this Convention, in terms of Comparative Law, may be the bringing together of the 'traditional' questions of quantity and the modern concerns with quality and the environment in a binding international instrument (sometimes even in a detailed (quantified) manner). Therefore, it may be interesting to test this hypothesis of the *usefulness* of the Convention's *experience* for instance against such deservedly prestigious conventional instruments as the 1994 Danube Convention. The difference may naturally be attributed to the fact that this later document did not have to deal with what may not be such a pressing problem in the diverse conditions of the water situation of Central Europe. However, this ackowledgement only underlines the usefulness of this Luso-Spanish conventional *exercise* for the characteristic concerns of all those other numerous regions in which water is far from abundant and problems of inter-seasonal, inter-annual, and spatial distribution along with (mounting) quality problems equally matter.

[203] These were experienced both in Portugal and in Spain.

3.3 *The test of the national plans*

As previously mentioned, there must also be a sense of an 'intimate' method of cooperation in the pursuit of national policies. In the soon-to-sound 'first hour of planning' into which both States will fortunately enter at approximately the same time (the National Water Plan of each State is anticipated at the end of 2001 and the basin by basin plans should be ready soon afterward) and in which intentions will begin to be put into practice, three tests have appeared. They are as follows:

   a. the test of co-ordinating perspectives and warranting the fluidity of communication;
   b. the test of integrating the limits and prescriptions defined in the Convention;
   c. the test of harmonising the results.

In light of the progress which has already been recorded, it would seem safe to affirm that the first objective was exemplarily met. Indeed, the two Parties exchanged all relevant documents in order to assess the evolution of the ideas. With regard to the second test, it appears to be proceeding in the right direction as well, at least at the national level. A notable consequence of this second task is that Spain has distanced itself from (or simply not insisted upon) the possibility of huge diversions from the Douro to the South of the Peninsula – a project which had greatly concerned Portugal and constituted one of the principal catalysts for the negotiation of the 1998 Convention.[204] Finally, positive indications also exist with respect to the adoption of the third test. They will be confirmed by the studies and documents which are still being prepared. Indeed, there should be no illusion of the existence of another 'continuum' in order that the normative message of the Convention is fulfilled/realized. In other words, not only is there the horizontal one – of the Convention 'propriu sensu' and its other linked conventional instruments as well as the denser applicative resolutions of the Commission – but also the vertical one – of the Convention and the instruments of the domestic orders which, in the very terms of the Convention, are supposed to develop some of its concepts or solutions. Hence, a rule of instrumental subsidiarity or practical monism is also expected to be followed.

---

[204] See *supra* 205.

3.4 *The test of the institutions and the processes*

Even more difficult than the creation of new institutions, developments or instruments is the task of reforming the already existing entities and making the old processes act in a new manner.

In the face of this necessity, it is admissible to promote – as the Portuguese government announced – legal reforms in order to normatively adjust the means to the new bilateral framework, results and solutions. Furthermore, these reforms may also be useful, even if not strictly necessary, as 'shock therapy'. Said differently, they may act as a warning 'sign' to the actors who are satisfied with the 'status quo' or as a catalyst to elicit or to stimulate new resolves, means or dynamics. However, it is questionable whether the issue would not be more adequately set on the administrative level within which it would seem important to promote a new 'ethos' of efficiency, responsibility,[205] transparency and close relationship with the public. In view of the past, similar needs may be expected to exist in Spain.

What can assuredly be assumed is that the task will not be easy. Clearly, patience is required since changes will not occur (or at least be visible) for several years.

3.5 *The test of accompanying the evolution of the 'enveloping' law*

The Convention and its negotiation clearly benefited from the advances made in the last decade in the most diverse international 'fora' in which International Water Law has been the object of discussions and has suffered adaptations. This has certainly been the case in the United Nations during the discussions leading to the New York Convention.[206], [207] It is also illustrated in the framework of the UNECE, especially in the discussions leading to the two Helsinki Conventions, the Espoo Convention, the Aarhus Convention and the London Protocol. Finally, it seems equally appropriate to remember the

---

[205] In this sense, Hans Jonas, *Das Prinzip Verantwortung. Versuch einer Ethik für die Technische Zivilisation*, Frankfurt am Main, 1979.

[206] See *supra* footnote as well as Tobias Nussbaum, 'Report on the Working Group to Elaborate a Convention on International Watercourses', *RECIEL*, 1997, vol. 6, nº 1, 47–53.

[207] See equally the assessments of the Convention itself made in recent works by Patricia Wouters; Malgosia Fitzmaurice; Ellen Hey; Jutta Bunnée. It may also be of interest to remember the way the ICJ referred to it in the Gabcikovo-Nagymaros Project Case, even considering that it had acquired customary law status. Apparently this perspective is condoned by the 2000 SADC Revised Protocol on Shared Watercourses (see its Preamble).

process of adoption of the so-called 'second generation Directives' and the Water Framework Directive[208] in the European Community.

Nonetheless, it is hoped that the regime will still be enriched by other developments in this ongoing restructuring of the Law (for instance, in the ongoing discussions on the Law of liability for harm to the environment[209] [210] – still a toothless tiger). For this reason, it is important to continue to closely observe this process of Law-reconstruction. Despite its limited resources, Portugal has proven its capacity to do so, particularly during the difficult negotiations on the United Nations (Framework) Convention on the Law of the Non-Navigational Uses of International Watercourses[211] and the Water Framework Directive.[212] Equally, it also actively accompanied the first Meetings of the Parties of both the UNECE Helsinki Convention and the UNECE Espoo Convention. Further, it has been committed to strengthening the so-called OSPAR regime as well.[213] Finally, one should also recall its intervention in the Case C-36/98 before the European Court of Justice. It cannot lose heart now. On the contrary, it must make every effort to contribute to it. Similarly, it should attempt to involve Spain, establish a common ground with this State or at least stimulate Spanish interest in the process. It seems reasonable to venture that Spain has more benefits to reap than risks in working together with Portugal in the process. Nonetheless, the (continuing?) Spanish temptation to insist upon the quantitative 'necessity' – despite the progression at the regional level toward the integration of the

---

[208] We recently tried to assess the progress represented by these developments *in* 'The Future of International Water Law', Luso-American Foundation, *Shared Water Systems and Trans-boundary Issues with special emphasis on the Iberian Peninsula*, Lisbon, 2000, 149–216. See, in the same volume, at 79–148, Joseph Delappenna's contribution, 'The Costumary International Law of Internationally Shared Fresh Waters' which, as the title indicates, is more centered on the question of customary law.

[209] Apart from the Lugano Convention, see the ongoing discussion, at the Community level, of a possible Directive on the topic as well as the promises made by the Community's institutions in several recent documents (the 2000 White Paper on the topic and the Strategy in favour of Sustainable Development – COM (2001), 264 final, of May 15 2001, p 13– and the Sixth Community Action Plan.

[210] These developments at the European regional level do not obnubilate the most important ones currently in course at the global level, in the framework of the International Law Commission's, on the topic of Principles of Responsibility. See lately Rao's Report.

[211] See, in particular, the Comments sent at the request of the Secretary-General in 1996 (copy of the original document on file with the Author).

[212] This 'hard law' movement is paralleled by other important discernible 'revisions' of the legal patrimony in the sector put forward by the doctrine –mainly oriented, in general, to the discussions on the 'greening' of this body of Law- especially in the framework of expert associations such as the Institut de Droit International and the Water Resources Committee of the International Law Association (on this last one, see its website *www.ila-hq.org* and Joseph Dellapenna's article in this volume).

[213] As its Presidency in the Sintra meeting in 1998 seems to prove.

quantitative concern within a predominantly quality-environment-oriented philosophy[214] – can only deserve special attention.

Furthermore, a special effort should be made to improve the application of the ambitious regime of the EU Water Framework Directive. This is particularly true because it would not seem incorrect to expect gains resulting from the synergies between the process for the application of the Convention and the process of implementing the Water Framework Directive. One of the principal advantages would be that most of the obligations and objectives as well as the actions required to fulfil them will be envisaged as 'national' or communitarian issues, and not international. The Commission should have a special role to play in this regard.

3.6 The test of the public

The test of the public may be classified on two levels:

On the one hand, the national administrations and the Commission face the challenge of being open to the public. This openness is essential in order that the public is able to carry out its task of provider of inputs (information, ideas) to the decision-making process (the systemic communities having a privileged function, in this regard) and of 'watchdog' over the implementation[215] of the whole regime resulting from the conventional acts and the resolutions of the Commission. The participation of the public as well as its scrutiny and pressure are fundamental in obligating the authorities to fully carry out their responsibilities with rigour and professionalism. To this end, it is to be hoped that the Statute of the Commission shall contribute additional normative ideas rather than simply confirming the obligation of providing information already set out in the Convention (article 6). In the same light, it could, for instance, devise means and instances through which the public and the Commission might easily come together and efficiently communicate.

On the other hand, the public has another role to play. This additional task is usually not mentioned as often but, in our view, is equally important, particularly in the present context and circumstances. Indeed, the public must act in the vest of users and consumers as well as of simple citizens. The broad encompassing and ambitious programme of protection and sustainable development of the waters of the Luso-Spanish basins likely cannot be carried out without strong support or consensus from the public. Therefore, the public should know how to present its views and information. However, it also seems equally important that it share in the financial and economic costs – sometimes

---

[214] See, for instance, an illustration of this trend in article 4 of the Water Framework Directive.

[215] On this function, see W. Lang, H. Neuhold and K. Zemanek (eds.), *Environmental Protection and International Law*, London, 1993, 229.

of a large scale – necessarily implied in this qualitative leap forwards. Once again, the question of cooperation among all the actors through the enhancement of the communicative process – presently on this more informal and diffuse level – seems to be of vital relevance. Furthermore, the equally important value of the legitimacy of the entire process – this is to say the consensus and acceptance of the probable sacrifices involved in this venture – would hence also be assured, as is inevitably desirable. Indeed, it may even be (one of) the most decisive condition(s) for the hopeful success of the task of implementing the Convention and reaching a lasting protection and the sustainable development of the waters of Portugal and Spain.

4. Conclusion

4.1 How can (the two) Sysiphus be assisted?

In face of the challenges ahead – their number, relationship and magnitude – there should be no doubt that the task of implementing the Convention, even if an overall positive judgement of this instrument may be warranted, shall certainly not be an easy one. Furthermore, it shall be a continuous task that protracts in time. As with the Sysiphus of Camus[216] in its long and never-ending march to the top of the mountain while carrying the enormous, heavy rock (the rock of the sustainable imperative, in our case), the implementation of the Convention will undoubtedly also be plagued by moments of despair as well as setbacks and retrogressions. To complicate matters, there are at least two Sysiphus in the Luso-Spanish context. Despite the fact that their individual pace and motivation should be parallel, these two States come to the task with different traditions and approaches. In light of these caveats, it would seem appropriate to ponder a final general condition (for the success) of the ascension. In our view, the tonic for the inevitable moments of discouragement – this is to say the incentive to progress – resides in a clear and constant remembrance of the principles already implicit in the Convention and governing the task of management and to whose constant enrichment the Convention is always dynamically open, in particular through the reference to (and progress of) the International and Community juridical orders.[217] Indeed, the principles of environmental friendliness, as well as those of relationship-participation-cooperation-friendliness and also the ones promoting the Convention's Law-coherence-friendliness appear to us to constitute an effective orientating compass in disheartening times, particularly when

---

[216] A. Camus, *Le Mythe de Sisyphe*, Paris, 1960.
[217] Article 2, §2.

combined with the understanding that the regime is the result of a process, constantly 'in fieri', of the balanced integration of all substantive elements considered and the contributions of all stakeholders. As the Spanish poet António Machado once proclaimed, 'the path is made by walking' ('caminante no hay camino, se hace camino al andar'). The continued remembrance of these principles should sooth the pains of the path while simultaneously giving soul to the walking. Indeed, as Fernando Pessoa – another poet (Portuguese this time) – observed, 'everything is worthy when the soul is not small' ('tudo vale a pena quando a alma não é pequena').

MALGOSIA FITZMAURICE

Finnish–Swedish Frontier River Commission – An Effective Water Co-operation

This paper will examine the structure and the competence of the Finnish-Swedish Frontier River Commission (the 'FSFRC') as an example of the close and very successful co-operation between the two States, based on the approximation of national laws. This essay will also prove that the Agreement establishing this Commission has incorporated, already as early as 1971, the contemporary principles of water co-operation that were first incorporated in 1966 Helsinki Rules on the Uses of the Waters of International Water Basin, and later found their expression in the 1997 United Nations Convention on Non-Navigable Uses of International Watercourses.[1]

---

[1] The Helsinki Rules on the Uses of the Waters of International Rivers adopted by the International Law Association at the fifty-second conference held at Helsinki in 1966. Report of the Committee on the rules of the waters of International Rivers; Convention on the Law of the Non-Navigational Uses of International Watercourses, 36 *I.L.M.* 713–720 (1997), signed on 21 May 1997, not yet in force; Agreement between Finland and Sweden concerning Frontier Waters, 15 December 1971; entered into force 1 January 1972.

M. Fitzmaurice and M. Szuniewicz (eds.), Exploitation of Natural Resources in the 21st Century, 235–246.
© *2003 Kluwer Law International. Printed in Great Britain.*

1. The main contemporary principles governing the watercourse co-operation

The contemporary principles that govern the water co-operation are incorporated into the 1997 Convention.[2] The Convention includes several substantive and procedural principles. The most important substantive principles are contained in Articles 5-7 of the Convention, i.e., equitable utilisation (Article 5), factors relevant to equitable and reasonable utilisation (Article 6) and obligation not to cause significant harm (Article 7). The principle of equitable utilisation is without doubt the governing principle of the non-navigational uses of international watercourses.[3] It may be said that this principle has entered into the body of international customary law. It was for the first time conceptualised by the International Court of Justice in the *River Oder* case.[4] The Court said as follows:

> '[t]he community of interests in a navigable river becomes the basis of a common legal right, the essential features of which are the perfect equality of all riparian States in the user of the whole course of the river and the exclusion of any preferential privilege of any riparian State in relation to the others.'

This principle of the community of interests has found its continuation and further development in the principle of equitable utilisation. It was confirmed by the International Court of Justice in the *Gabcikovo- Nagymaros* case.[5] The Court said as follows:

> '[m]odern development of international law has strengthened this principle for non-navigational uses of international watercourses as well, as evidences by the

---

[2]   On the Convention see foe example, S. McCaffrey, *The Law of International Watercourses, Non-Navigational Uses*, Oxford University Press, (2001); M. Fitzmaurice, 'Convention on the Law of the Non-Navigational Uses of International Watercourses', *LJIL*, vol. 10 (1997), 501–508.

[3]   Article 5: '1. Watercourse States shall in their respective territories utilise an international watercourse in an equitable and reasonable manner. In particular, an international watercourse shall be used and developed by watercourse States with a view of attaining optimal and sustainable uiltisation thereof and benefits therefrom, taking into account the interests of the watercourse States concerned, consistent with the adequate protection of the watercourse. 2. Watercourse States shall participate in the use, development and protection of an international watercourse in an equitable and reasonable manner. Such participation includes both the right to untilise the watercourse and the duty to cooperate in the protection and development thereof, as provided in the preset Convebtion.'

[4]   *Territorial Jurisdiction of the International Commission of the River Oder, Judgement No. 16, 1929, P.C.I.J., Series A, No. 23, 27).*

adoption of the Convention of 21 May 1997 on the law of Non-Navigational Uses of International Watercourses by the United Nations General Assembly'.[6]

According to McCaffrey, the principle of equitable utilisation should be understood as a dynamic process, 'which depends heavily upon active cooperation between states sharing freshwater resources.'[7] The second of the fundamental principles is the principle of 'no-harm', or more precisely the principle of 'no significant harm.' The difficult relationship between these two principles, was resolved according to the primacy of the principle of the equitable utilisation. This principle derives from the obligation codified in general law and expressed in the maxim *sic utero tuo*. This principle is not absolute, but is mitigated by several factors; the harm must be significant; the obligation must be one of due diligence character; the harm must be unreasonable. As to the relationship between the principles of equitable utilisation and no-harm, this author observes that significant harm may have to be tolerated in order to achieve an overall regime of equitable utilisation. Therefore, harm is treated as one of the factors of equitable utilisation. The 1997 Convention introduced an obligation to protect international watercourses (Article 20),[8] a duty that was not traditionally included into the law of international watercourses. It may be described as an 'emerging duty,' which is based on the principle of due diligence.[9] It is worth mentioning that the 1966 Helsinki Rules, contained in Chapter 3 only the prohibition of pollution. However, the 1997 Convention, introduced the broader duty of protection, preservation and management of the environment, of which the prevention of pollution is one of the elements. The wider approach adopted by the Convention no doubt reflects the general development of environmental law.

The Convention, finally contains the cluster of procedural obligations that according to McCaffrey are necessary to implement the fundamental principle of equitable utilisation. First of all, Article 8 of the Convention, introduces the general duty to cooperate.[10] Other obligations include the obligation of prior notification and related obligations; the obligation to consult with other riparian States; the obligation to exchange data and information on regular basis.

---

[5] *Gabcikovo-Nagymaors Project*, (Hungary/ Slovakia), *I.C.J. Reports*, (1997), paragraphs 85 and 147.

[6] Paragraph 85; see also McCaffrey, note 2, 164.

[7] McCaffrey, note 2, 345.

[8] Article 20: '[w]atercourse States, shall, individually and, where appropriate, jointly, protect and preserve ecosystems of international watercourses.'

[9] McCaffery, note 2.

[10] Article 8: '[w]atercourse Stats shall cooperate on the basis of sovereign equality of, territorial integrity, mutual benefit and good faith in order to attain optimal utilisation and adequate protection of an international watercourse. 2. In determining the manner of such cooperation, watercourse States may consider the establishment of joint mechanism or commissions, as deemed necessary by them, to facilitate cooperation on relevant measures and procedures in the light of experience gained through cooperation in existing joint mechanism and commissions in various regions.'

At this stage the structure and the legal functions of the FSFRC will be assessed.

2. Effective water resource co-operation – the Nordic states

The system of water utilisation which appears to be very efficient and successful and which would be used as an example for other states is that of Nordic states: Norway, Finland and Sweden. The system of water administration in those states has overcome political difficulties and resulted in the setting up of an efficient water management which also involves, in certain areas participation of Russia. Between themselves, the Nordic states, in particular Norway and Sweden have to a great extent unified their legal systems. The systems of courts is very similar, and this is especially visible in the field of water and environmental control. Having created a compatible legal regime, it has become feasible to establish an effective global water management. Finland, Sweden and Norway share vast watercourse in Lapland. The degree of co-operation between the three Nordic states in their institutional arrangement varies. The closest co-operation is undoubtedly between Finland and Sweden and that culminated in the creation of the Finnish-Swedish Frontier River Commission which is vested with great powers (see below).

The Finnish-Norwegian Frontier River Commission, established in 1980 exercises much lesser powers. An interesting feature of the above Commissions is that they regulate the whole of the quantitative and qualitative aspects of the protection of water resources and regulate hydraulic development and the water supply.

Watercourse co-operation between Nordic states has had a long history. As an example of an earlier water treaty, one may cite the Convention between Norway and Sweden on Certain Questions Relating to the Law on Watercourses concluded in 1929.[11] That treaty regulated the whole basin of the river Klaräven. It applied to all watercourses which form or cross the frontier between Norway and Sweden, in particular the river Trysil and regulated water management as an integrated whole, having had its system of administration of waters based on their 'basin or hydrological' approach to watercourse management. This form of regulation represents a community of interest approach which goes beyond the allocation of equitable rights,

---

[11] *United Nations Treaty Series, vol. 120,* paras. 551–554.

however, and opens up the possibility of integrated development and international regulation of the watercourse environment.[12]

The above-cited approach usually presupposes the establishment of a joint body – the river commission – which has vested in it powers to implement and equitably administer the basin area. The creation of a river commission is not, however, an invariable rule. In the practice of the Nordic states many water treaties did not establish any joint body.

The treaties which belong to the second category, i.e. treaties which establish a special body may be divided into two categories:

a) those which set up bodies which are established for a special purpose – examples of which are mostly found in relations between Nordic states and Russia; and

b) those which set up bodies the scope of which jurisdiction is very extensive, relating to all aspects of the regulation of co-operation concerning the frontier rivers and their basins.

There are three Commissions of the second type in the Nordic states: the Finnish-Russian Joint Commission on the Utilisation of Frontier Rivers;[13] the Finnish-Swedish Frontier Rivers Commissions; and the Finnish-Norwegian Commission on Border Rivers.[14]

These Commissions have very extensive functions. In general, they regulate watercourse activities in their entirety. Their tasks encompass, for example, quantitative and qualitative protection of water resources, water supply regulation of watercourses, hydraulic development, flood prevention, hydro-power production, fisheries and navigation, monitoring and control of water quality, pollution prevention, construction and conservation of waterways.

The Commissions may have in practice even broader scope of geographical jurisdiction then provided for in agreements. For example, the Finish-Norwegian Commission surveys areas beyond those expressly indicated in the agreement, but in which activities may have an unfavourable effect on the transboundary waters. Another feature of these Commissions is that their activities are linked with other Commissions. It must be mentioned as well that observers from third countries which have interest in the region are invited to participate in the

---

[12] P. Birnie and A. Boyle *International Law of the Environment*, Oxford University Press (2002), p. 304, 222.

[13] Agreement between Republic of Finland and the Union of Soviet Socialist Republics concerning frontier.

[14] Agreement on the Finnish-Norwegian Commission on Boundary Watercourses. This Commission relates to the following watercourses: Näätämo, Pasvik and Tana. The river basin encompasses all surface waters which cross the frontiers between two states. The agreement was signed on 5 March 1980 in Helsinki and entered into force on 29 April 1980. 1987 SOPS 16 198; amendment to para. 2 signed on 5 June 1987 and entered into force on 15 June 1987.

meetings of the commissions. For example, a Russian representative is invited to the meetings of the Finnish-Norwegian Commission.

The Finnish-Swedish Frontier Rivers Commission (hereinafter the 'FSFRC' or the 'Commission') is a unique body as regards its powers and functions. The scope of its functions is very broad and due to its unusual features it deserves some more detailed presentation. The Commission, as stated above, was set up between Finland and Sweden to manage the watercourse system which constitutes the border and stretches on the both sides of it.

The total geographical area of the FSFRC is enormous. It covers about 75.000 square kilometres. It comprises of huge water systems which consist of main rivers together with tributaries, lakes etc. Thus in global terms the jurisdiction of the Commission extends from the northern part of the Baltic Sea almost up to the Norwegian coast of the Atlantic.

The FSFRC consists of six members who are appointed for an unspecified period of time – three appointed by each government.

The scope of functions of the Commission is vast: it includes virtually all matters both judicial and administrative, which may affect the use and the development of the watercourses, including matters relating to construction, to the regulation of water flow, to fishing and to the protection of the watercourses from pollution. In each and every area of its functioning, the Commission exercises great powers. For example, in pollution prevention, it can set extent of discharge limits which may cause detrimental silting, and injurious change in the quality of water, damage to fish stocks, danger to human health etc.

The pollution prevention encompasses the rules governing the use of: land, buildings, installation in the water area if it influences water quality.

All the uses which affect the quality of water and living resources are subject to permits granted by the Commission. The Commission may, if it deems necessary on account of the nature and effects of the activity, examine the question of the permissibility of such an activity and the conditions by which it should be governed, having regard to public interest.

The Commission may prohibit any activity or to request the person who conducts or intends to conduct such activity to take precautionary measures. For example, the protection of the environment in the FSFRC area is of paramount importance since a large complex of metal industries is located close to the mouth of the river Thorne on the Finnish side of the river. The commission issued very detailed set of regulations concerning the disposal of waste from these industries.

The most interesting is the legal nature of the Commission's activities. It acts not only as an international organisation but also as a national court for both states in matters under its jurisdiction. The Commission acts both as licensing board and as water court,[15] these being types of courts known to the

---

[15] Water courts were abolished in Finland as of 1 March 2000 and replaced by regional

legal systems in both countries. In general, licensing boards in each country grant permits on application from anyone performing activities, and may grant a permit for an activity after an examination carried out under the relevant national laws.

Water courts (at present environmental courts) have general jurisdiction over activities relating to rivers, lakes and other water recourses. An example, of such an activity is the erection of water constructions. These national courts combine judicial, administrative and supervisory powers. The unique feature of the Commission is that it replaces them within its jurisdictional area, where it exercises exactly the same powers – i.e., including judicial functions, administrative and supervisory functions.

Also applicable law singles out the character of this Commission as absolutely special. Although created on the basis of international law (by an agreement), and applying to some extent international law, i.e., provisions of the agreement, the Commission is not itself a classical international organisation in the sense of one which applies the norms of international law between the states, or whose decisions are intended to be enforceable through the application of international law.

The FSRFC, is rather, an embodiment of the merging of certain international and municipal powers of the two states which were previously administered by each state separately over its own territory, through its relevant judicial and administrative bodies, but which now are administered by the single common body, the Commission, over the whole area which comprises of the parts of the territories of two states.

The decision-making by the Commission is primarily based on the Agreement, but (this feature also singles out this Commission from the other river commissions) when the Agreement is silent on the matter, and does not contain provisions to the contrary, the law prevailing in each state is to be applied. Interpretation of the provisions contained in Chapter 1 gives an indication

cont.

environmental permit authorities. In Sweden, the environmental code entered into force as of 1 January 1999 and a new system of environmental courts was established, replacing water courts. There are regional environmental courts established as the district courts, similar to the National Licensing Board for Environmental Protection. The regional courts act as appellate courts for decisions of state authorities in environmental questions. The decisions of municipal boards may be appealed the County Administrative Board and only thereafter to environmental courts. The judgements and decisions of the regional environmental courts may be appealed to the Environmental Court of Appeal that is linked to the Svea Court of Appeal. Reviews by that court, however, are subject to leave to appeal being granted where the regional environmental court was not of the first instance in the matter. The Environmental Court of Appeal is the final instance in cases and matters that were initially adjudicated by municipalities or administrative authorities. Judgements and decisions of the Environmental Court of Appeal that are eligible for appeal, shall be appealed to the Supreme Court (information from VINGE, The Environmental Code).

on the scope of municipal law applicable. This includes: judgements of courts; ancient custom or other forms of special title.

Apart from this general indication as to the type of municipal law applicable by the Commission, the Agreement includes as well specific instances of particular application. For example, Chapter 6 (Protection against Water Pollution), provides in Article 2 that

'[i]n addition to those of this Chapter, the provisions of the legislation concerning health, construction and nature conservancy of the state's special protective legislation against specific types of water pollution protection shall apply'.

Payment of compensation is yet another example of the particular applicability of municipal law. Another interesting characteristics of this Commission is the very limited involvement of two governments in discharging of its functions. In fact, the main principle which underlies its work is its complete independence. Only a careful analysis of the Agreement indicates that in certain (very few) instances there is provision for the governmental involvement. Involvement of the governments is provided for in three cases:

(a) the Commission itself, if it deems it necessary, at its own discretion may submit question concerning permissibility of a potentially polluting activity to the examination of two governments;

(b) the Commission is required to submit questions concerning water related construction projects which have a particular importance for the population; and

(c) finally, the two governments may retain the right to have questions related to both water construction and pollution submitted for them for examination. In both instances, the Agreement provides that such submission will only take place if the governments' reservations are notified to the Commission before it has itself reached a decision.

Although the Commission was set up in 1972, it embodies certain modern principles of international water law. The Agreement undoubtedly promotes the principle of 'equitable utilisation'. Article 3 of Chapter 1 provides as follows:

'[i]n the light the considerations set out in detail in this agreement, the waters covered by the agreement shall be used in such a manner the both countries derive benefit from the frontier watercourse and the interests of this frontier areas are promoted as effectively as possible'.

The agreement also adheres to the principle of equitable participation. Since in Article 3 of Chapter 1 it further provides that:

'[p]articular importance shall be accorded to the interests of nature conservancy; the greatest possible attention shall be given to the preservation of fish stocks and the prevention of water pollution'.

The balance of interest principle which plays an important role in environmental law, and in particular in assessing the extent of damage, is also expressed in the Agreement. The formulation, however, which refers to the fundamental principles governing the co-operation of the parties under this agreement is moulded in accordance with the underlying nature of the Commission. It relates to potential conflicts and to the balancing of interests between all interested parties, by the states themselves or individuals, rather than the balancing only of international interests of the states in a more general way. An example of this may be found in Article 4, Chapter 1 of the Agreement which states as follows:

'[i]n cases involving a number of different projects which affect the same waters or for some other reason cannot be carried out concurrently, preference is given to the project which may be assumed to be of greatest public and private benefit. Conflicting interests shall in so far as possible, be adjusted in such a way that each may be satisfied without substantial injury to others'.

This general principle of balancing of interests is further developed in articles pertaining to particular areas of activities. For example, Article 2, Chapter 3, provides that:

'[h]ydraulic construction works shall be carried put in such a way that their purpose is achieved without unreasonable cost and with the least possible damage and inconvenience to other interests in either State. Due regard shall be given to proposed future projects that may be affected by that installation'.

The same principle was embodied in part in Article 3 of the same Chapter where it says:

'[w]here any person would suffer damage or inconvenience as a result of hydraulic construction work., the work shall be carried out only if they can be shown to bring public or private benefits that substantially outweighs the inconvenience'.

Similar concepts are to be found in Chapter 6 which covers protection against water pollution. Article 6 provides that a person who conducts or intends to conduct a polluting activity must take protective measures, endure such restrictions on such activity and observe such precautions as may be reasonably required to prevent or remedy a harm; and it further provides that this type of obligation is to be judged on the basis of what is technically feasible for this type of activity concerned and in the light of both public and private interests.

This article is the embodiment of both the Helsinki Rules (Article V) and Article 6 of the 1997 Convention which states as follows: ('[t]he weight to be given to each factor is to be determined by its importance in comparison with that of other relevant factors. In determining what is a reasonable and equitable use, all relevant factors are to be considered together and a conclusion reached on the basis of the whole').

Thus the balancing of mutual environmental interests is also the nature of equitable utilisation. The nature of balanced solution may be summarised in the words of Lammers who said that it requires observation of the relationship between the nature of the area which may be exposed to pollution and the significance of the pollution, on one hand, and the usefulness of the activity and the cost of protective measures which may be required on the other.[16] The embodiment of these concepts of balancing of interests provides a striking example of the extent to which the Agreement envisages the merging of interests of two states.

Another example is that of hydraulic construction in relation to which Article 3 Chapter 3 provides as follows:

> '[w]here the construction would result in substantial deterioration in living conditions of the population or cause a permanent change in natural conditions such as might entail substantially diminished comfort for people living in the vicinity or a significant nature conservancy loss or where significant public interest would be otherwise prejudiced, the construction shall be permitted only if it is of a particular importance for the economy or the locality or from some public stand point'.

It is quite striking that in this formulation, references are made, for example, to the population in general, not to population of one of the parties to the Agreement. Likewise, in the balancing of public against private interests, the Agreement does not differentiate between the interests of one or the other of the state parties. The differentiation is indeed expressly prohibited by the Agreement. In Article 4 of the same Chapter it says as follows:

> '[i]n deciding whether projected construction is to be carried out, conditions in both states shall be given equal weight'.

The balancing of interests clearly envisages the possibility of harm being allowed to some extent to certain interest, possibly even significant harm if it can be justified by the benefit derived by other interests. Article 7 (2) of Chapter 6 says:

---

[16] J. Lammers *Pollution of International Watercourses*, Martinus Nijhoff Publishers (1984), 66.

'[w]hen the anticipated inconvenience entails a substantial deterioration in living conditions for a large number or people of significant loss from the standpoint of nature conservancy or any other substantial damage to the public interest, the operation may not be carried out'.

These considerations bring us to the question of treatment of duty not to cause significant harm as embodied in the Agreement. It includes many references concerning harm and compensation, not only in the field of pollution control but also in the fields of water construction and of the regulation of diversion of water. The particular character of the Commission conditions also an application of certain international principles in the context of its work. In particular, the concept of one state doing, or allowing doing of, damage to the other state is alien to the structure of the Commission. Rather, what is covered is a joint regulation by the FSFRC of anyone, be it one of the states or a private party, causing harm to the Commission's area as such, regardless of the side of the border on which the harm originates or is suffered. The way the question of harm is treated in the Agreement, derives directly from the concept adopted by the two governments which is rather that of an individual's than that of the state's participation. Thus, the degree of permissible harm, the balancing of interests and the question of compensation are conditioned by the public versus private requirements.

Taking into consideration such a great degree of human interest, human health and well being Article 10 paragraph 2 of the 1997 Convention states:

'[i]n the event of a conflict between uses of an international watercourse, it shall be resolved with reference to articles 5 and 7 with a special regard being given to the requirement of vital human needs'.

In conclusion, it may be said that the Commission is a very special body- unique within the system of the other river Commissions. Its specific features are the reflection of the great proximity of legal and administrative systems in Finland and Sweden. The premise on which the Commission has been set up embodies a particular and somewhat different approach to the concept of state sovereignty by the two states. The establishment of an international body fulfilling the functions both of a court and on an administrative organ in both states, to the exclusion of national courts and national administrative organs, can only be possible where the judicial systems, organisation of justice and existing law are as close as they are in both states, The legal proximity allowed the solution which may be loosely called 'merged sovereignty'.

This aspect of the FSFRC was stressed by Lammers who said as follows: '. . . an extraordinary machinery whereby they [the two states] have eliminated many of the defects attaching to the domestic or intergovernmental approach'.[17] The same author lists other advantages of the solution adopted

---

[17]   *Ibid*, 67.

in the Agreement. This solution enables the Commission to work smoothly and efficiently, the most important achievement being the FSFRC's broad jurisdiction in cases concerning transboundary pollution, where, whether, it is acting as a court of a country where the damage occurs, or of the country of origin of the damage, there is only one competent body – that of the Commission.

DANIEL OWEN[1]

Legal and Institutional Aspects of Management Arrangements for Shared Stocks of Marine Fish

1. Introduction

The purpose of this chapter is to identify current and potential practice by States with regard to the management of shared stocks of marine fish, through an analysis of existing fisheries management arrangements. The chapter draws upon work done by the author for the Food and Agriculture Organization of the United Nations ('FAO') and submitted to the FAO in May 2001.[2]

---

[1] Barrister, Fenners Chambers, 3 Madingley Road, Cambridge, CB3 0EE, England, UK (e-mail: daniel.owen@fennerschambers.co.uk).
[2] The material presented in this chapter has not been updated since May 2001. For the specific purpose of publication in this book, and with the kind permission of the Food and Agriculture Organization of the United Nations, copyright of the material in this chapter rests with the author. The author in turn gives permission to Kluwer Law International to publish the said material, in print and electronic format, in this book.

For the purposes of this chapter, the term 'shared stock' means a single fish stock occurring in the waters of two or more neighbouring coastal States (whether adjacent or opposite neighbours), but not ranging onto the high seas. Thus for current purposes, the term 'shared stock' does not include highly migratory stocks ranging onto the high sea or stocks straddling onto the high seas. Likewise, it does not include stocks of the highly migratory species listed in Annex I to the 1982 United Nations Convention on the Law of the Sea (the LOSC).[3] The term 'waters of a coastal State' is used here to refer to that State's internal waters and territorial sea and its exclusive economic zone or exclusive fishing zone.

Caddy[4] states that:

'we use a global GIS (Geographical Information System) database ... to estimate that at least 500 contiguous maritime boundaries exist between the [exclusive economic zones] of contiguous pairs of mainland States. Even assuming that a modest number of 2-3 important transboundary [fisheries] resources for each of these would benefit from joint management, a total of the order of some 1000-1500 actual or potential shared resource-bilateral boundary issues may exist with respect to more or less important marine [fisheries] resources'.

Joint management of shared stocks is promoted through Article 63(1) of the LOSC. That provision, in relation to a stock (or stocks of associated species) occurring within the exclusive economic zones of two or more coastal States, requires those States to 'seek ... to agree' upon measures to, *inter alia*, ensure the stock's conservation and development.[5]

---

[3]   This limitation on the definition of 'shared stock' is, as noted, adopted for the purposes of this chapter. The limitation is adopted for the sake of simplicity, i.e. to allow a focus on stocks shared between neighbours rather than additionally entering into the realm of (a) duties imposed by the 1995 United Nations Fish Stocks Agreement (see footnote 10) in respect of stocks that use both coastal State waters and the high seas and (b) duties imposed by the LOSC in respect of highly migratory species (see Article 64 of the LOSC).

[4]   J.F. Caddy, 'Establishing a Consultative Mechanism or Arrangement for Managing Shared Stocks Within the Jurisdiction of Contiguous States', 92 in D.A. Hancock (ed.), *Joint Workshop Proceedings – Taking Stock: Defining and Managing Shared Resources, Darwin 15–16 July 1997* (Australian Society for Fish Biology, Sydney, 1998)

[5]   Article 63(1) of the LOSC reads as follows: 'Where the same stock or stocks of associated species occur within the exclusive economic zones of two or more coastal States, these States shall seek, either directly or through appropriate subregional or regional organizations, to agree upon the measures necessary to coordinate and ensure the conservation and development of such stocks without prejudice to the other provisions of this Part.'

However, Burke[6] states that '[t]he substantive obligation imposed by Article 63(1) cannot fairly be described as awesome, imposing, or, even, perhaps, very consequential'. Churchill and Lowe[7] observe that '[n]othing further is said ... [in Article 63(1)] ... about management objectives or allocation of the catch among interested States, which are the kinds of things that the States concerned need to agree on if there is to be effective management of shared stocks'.

Overall, Churchill and Lowe[8] conclude that 'there still exist many shared stocks for which no cooperative arrangements have yet been agreed by the States concerned'. In contrast, joint management of straddling stocks and highly migratory species and stocks is promoted not just through the LOSC[9] but also through the 1995 United Nations Fish Stocks Agreement[10] and an increasing number of regional fisheries management organisations.

This chapter will analyse 39 arrangements (see Annex) relevant to the management of shared stocks.[11] For the purposes of this chapter, the term 'arrangement' means the actual underlying instrument (i.e. treaty, memorandum of understanding etc.). The arrangements have been chosen on the basis that (a) they are arrangements for the management of shared stocks or (b) the management approach they provide for is potentially applicable to shared stocks. Thus the emphasis is primarily on identifying the types of approach that these arrangements do bring or can bring to the management of shared stocks, rather than on analysing each arrangement independently and in full.

---

[6] W.T. Burke, 'Annex 1 – 1982 Convention on the Law of the Sea Provisions on Conditions of Access to Fisheries Subject to National Jurisdiction' in FAO, *Report of the Expert Consultation on the Conditions of Access to the Fish Resources of the Exclusive Economic Zones, Rome, 11–15 April 1983: A Preparatory Meeting for the FAO World Conference on Fisheries Management and Development*, FAO Fish. Rep. 293 (FAO, Rome, 1983)

[7] R.R. Churchill and A.V. Lowe, *The Law of the Sea* (3rd edn, Manchester University Press, Manchester, 1999), 294

[8] *Ibid*, 296

[9] See Article 63(2) (regarding straddling stocks) and Article 64 (regarding highly migratory species).

[10] Full name: 1995 United Nations Agreement for the Implementation of the Provisions of the United Nations Convention on the Law of the Sea of 10 December 1982 relating to the Conservation and Management of Straddling Fish Stocks and Highly Migratory Fish Stocks.

[11] With reference to the Annex: The Mediterranean Agreement is not yet in force. Is it not known whether the following arrangements are yet in force: Japan/China Agreement; Norway/Russia 1976 Agreement; Loophole Agreement; Colombia/Costa Rica Treaty; SRFC Access Convention; SRFC Hot Pursuit Convention; Mauritania/Senegal Convention. Regarding the Trinidad and Tobago/Venezuela Agreement (adopted in 1985), Churchill (in R.R. Churchill, 'Fisheries Issues in Maritime Boundary Delimitation' [1993] *Marine Policy* 44, 47) states that: 'In 1990 a comprehensive maritime boundary was established between Venezuela and Trinidad and Tobago. The agreement establishing this boundary makes no reference to the previous fisheries arrangements, so it is assumed that they have lapsed.'

For the purposes of this chapter, the term 'conservation and management' is used to refer to measures, including laws and regulations, that specify the manner in which harvesting is to be effected (e.g. regulations on catch or effort limits (including allocation), mesh sizes, gear types, fishing zones). In contrast, the term 'monitoring, control and surveillance' ('MCS') is used here to refer to measures, again including laws and regulations, aimed at ensuring compliance with conservation and management measures. Finally, the term 'enforcement' as used here refers to the procedures that follow after detection of infringements of conservation and management measures or indeed infringements of MCS measures.

The work done for FAO upon which this chapter draws includes an extensive annex containing a summary of each of the 39 arrangements under consideration. Each summary uses standardised headings, and the analysis in this chapter is based largely on those summaries. The 39 arrangements have been selected from a larger pool, discovered by a literature search, an internet search and informal enquiries. It should be emphasised that the analysis that follows is based on the various arrangements as they appear on paper (supplemented by internal rules where known, and exceptionally by commentaries from the literature or feedback from individuals).

2.   Nature of arrangement

2.1 Comparative analysis

With three exceptions, each of the arrangements is a treaty. The three exceptions are:

(a) Argentina/UK Joint Statement;
(b) Australia/Indonesia MOU; and
(c) the Agreed Records of the Mackerel System and of the Herring System.

2.2 Commentary

2.2.1 Joint statements

Joint statements may be helpful in cases of political sensitivity, where a treaty would be seen as politically unacceptable by one or more parties. (Indeed, the Argentina/UK Joint Statement is not signed.) They can provide a political impetus, yet can be abandoned at short notice. The inherently transient nature of management regimes under joint statements may not inspire confidence in fishery managers. However, this impact may potentially be mitigated by a track record of meetings and collaboration under the joint statement. (For example, since 1990 there have been 18 regular meetings and at least one *ad hoc* meeting under the Argentina/UK Joint Statement.)

2.2.2 *Memoranda of understanding*

Memoranda of Understanding constitute a flexible type of instrument. However, situations may arise where one party considers the instrument to be binding, while the other does not. The wording used is therefore of critical importance.[12] When considered as non-binding instruments, they permit use of imperative language (with the political message that that carries) without the binding impact that such language would have if contained in a treaty. The Australia/Indonesia MOU provides for a fisheries surveillance and enforcement 'arrangement' and a fisheries line, but both are stated to be 'provisional'. The provisional nature of the regime, set against a background of ongoing negotiations,[13] was presumably a factor dictating the choice of instrument in that case.

2.2.3 *Agreed Records of the Mackerel System and of the Herring System*

The first page of each of the two Agreed Records in the Mackerel System states that '[t]he Heads of Delegation agreed to recommend to their respective authorities the arrangements for the management of mackerel for [the year concerned] as set out in the Annexes to this Agreed Record'. The first page of each of the Agreed Records in the Herring System for 2000 and 2001 contain equivalent wording for herring. This suggests that the measures in the annexes are not binding until agreed by the 'respective authorities'. As such, the exact nature of the Agreed Records relating to

---

[12] For further information on memoranda of understanding, see: A. Aust, *Modern Treaty Law and Practice* (Cambridge University Press, Cambridge, 2000), 26–46.

[13] Article 6 of the Australia/Indonesia MOU states that: 'In relation to the delimitation negotiations between the two countries, it is expressly understood that this arrangement is provisional in nature, is without prejudice to the position of either Government in those negotiations and does not affect the limits of the 200 nautical mile zones established by either country or the exercise of fisheries jurisdiction by either country within such zones except as provided under this arrangement.'

mackerel in the northeast Atlantic and Norwegian spring-spawning herring is unclear.[14]

2.2.4 *Treaties*

Treaties are binding on their contracting parties and apply unless terminated, or suspended or withdrawn from. This brings certainty, which is both attractive to fisheries managers and creates a political impetus that may be lacking in non-binding, more transient instruments. Yet they are also flexible instruments. They can be broad frameworks or very specific technical instruments, applying for, say, just a year or much longer. Having said that, the effectiveness of a treaty of course depends on the political will of its contracting parties.

3. Scope

3.1 *A scope beyond fisheries*

3.1.1 *Comparative analysis*

Most of the arrangements relate to fisheries alone (or fisheries and aquaculture). There are ten exceptions [*River Plate Treaty; Torres Strait Treaty; Faroes/UK Agreement; the seven delimitation treaties relating to Central America and the Caribbean*].

The primary purpose of each of these latter ten treaties is to establish one or more maritime boundaries. Subjects covered by these treaties in addition to maritime boundary delimitation and fisheries include (depending on the treaty concerned): (a) navigation; (b) pollution; (c) research; (d) exploitation of transboundary or near-boundary mineral resources; (e) protection and preservation of the marine environment; (f) wrecks; and (g) protection of the traditional way of life and livelihood of traditional inhabitants.

---

[14] In contrast, the 1996 Protocol on the Conservation, Rational Utilization and Management of Norwegian Spring Spawning (Atlanto-Scandian) Herring in the Northeast Atlantic (part of the Herring System) appears to be a treaty. Many of its more general provisions endure beyond 1996. For more information on the Herring System and the Mackerel System see: R.R. Churchill, 'Managing Straddling Fish Stocks in the North East Atlantic: A Multiplicity of Instruments and Regime Linkages – But How Effective a Management?', Chapter 8 in O. S. Stokke (ed.), '*Governing High Seas Fisheries – The Interplay of Global and Regional Regimes*' (Oxford University Press, Oxford, 2001).

3.1.2 Commentary

In the interests of integrated management of the marine environment, there may be benefits in extending the scope of an arrangement between neighbours beyond fisheries to, for example, protection and preservation of the marine environment or marine scientific research. It may also be possible to extend the arrangement to cover management of shared offshore mineral resources. However, agreement over mineral resources is generally likely to provoke more national sensitivity than agreement over certain fish stocks; it would be unfortunate for agreement on shared stock management to be slowed down accordingly.

As noted above, ten of the arrangements under consideration address fisheries as part of a broader agenda. However, in practice, only two of these deal with fisheries in any detail [*Torres Strait Treaty; River Plate Treaty*]. The other eight (all of which are delimitation treaties) only deal with fisheries at the level of broad principles. This is perhaps attributable to their primary purpose being to find a political solution over a boundary, rather than to provide for the effective management of shared stocks.

3.2 References to 'shared stocks'

3.2.1 Comparative analysis

Four arrangements [*Australia/Indonesia Agreement; Pacific Salmon Treaty; Nauru Agreement; Mauritania/Senegal Convention*] refer to stocks that are 'shared' or 'common' between the parties. Language similar to that in Article 63(1) of the LOSC is used in two arrangements [*Australia/Indonesia Agreement; African Atlantic Convention*]. 11 other arrangements make more tangential references to shared stocks, and the remainder make no reference at all.

3.2.2 Commentary

The lack of reference to shared stocks in some cases is perhaps attributable to: (a) the negotiators of those arrangements not having shared stocks particularly in mind (e.g. Faroes/UK Agreement and Colombia/Jamaica Treaty (focus on delimitation), NEAFC Convention (focus on straddling stocks)); (b) an assumption by the negotiators that coordination because of the shared nature of the stocks was the primary purpose of the arrangement (e.g. Baltic Sea Convention, Herring System, River Plate Treaty (regarding the 'common fishing zone')); or (c) the arrangement in question being somehow subsidiary to an arrangement that does make reference to shared stocks.

In practice, where the management of shared stocks is clearly the purpose of the arrangement, it would indeed be preferable to refer to such stocks in, say, the preamble and the 'objectives' clause. Such references could then potentially assist in the event of problems of interpretation arising between the parties. One solution could be to use the terminology from Article 63(1) of the LOSC, adapted to include stocks shared between territorial seas if appropriate.

3.3 Provision for consultative mechanisms[15]

3.3.1 Comparative analysis

Broadly speaking, the term 'consultative mechanism' is used here to mean the institutional mechanism by which the parties to an arrangement are able to consult together and adopt measures regarding the management of shared stocks. Nine of the arrangements clearly have as their main feature the establishment of a formal consultative mechanism [*Argentina/UK Joint Statement; NEAFC Convention; Norway/Russia 1975 Agreement; Baltic Sea Convention; Mediterranean Agreement; Gulf Agreement; Pacific Salmon Treaty; FFA Convention; Lake Victoria Convention*].

19 further arrangements do provide for a consultative mechanism, but more as a secondary feature rather than as their main feature. The typical structure of the instrument in these cases is (a) several provisions establishing duties for the parties, some requiring cooperation and some not, and then (b) a provision on a consultative mechanism. That provision can vary from, say, a power to 'call for consultations' [*Faroes/UK Agreement*] to a duty to establish a commission.

In respect of two further arrangements, the consultations between the parties happen simply at the desire of the parties to meet annually [*Herring System; Mackerel System*]; there is no provision in the arrangement itself for such meetings. In a further two arrangements [*SRFC Access Convention; SRFC Hot Pursuit Convention*], the parties meet anyway through a pre-existing mechanism. The remaining seven arrangements do not provide for any fisheries consultative mechanism at all.

---

[15] The term 'consultative mechanism' is adopted from: J.F. Caddy, 'Establishing a Consultative Mechanism or Arrangement for Managing Shared Stocks Within the Jurisdiction of Contiguous States', 92 in D.A. Hancock (ed.), *Joint Workshop Proceedings – Taking Stock: Defining and Managing Shared Resources, Darwin 15–16 July 1997* (Australian Society for Fish Biology, Sydney, 1998).

3.3.2 Commentary

The difference between the arrangements establishing a commission or equivalent as a main feature and those establishing such a mechanism as a secondary feature may be described as follows. The former have fewer provisions aimed at the parties as individuals but more on the parties acting collectively through the commission. The latter have several provisions aimed at the parties as individuals, including, *inter alia*, on cooperation, and then use the provisions on the commission to (a) effect some or all of this cooperation, or (b) specify some of it in more detail, or (c) focus on one specific area of cooperation. At least in this last instance, the difference is not simply stylistic. Two States may wish to cooperate generally on fisheries through a treaty, but may also wish to reserve one geographic area or stock for attention through a specialised commission. In that case, an arrangement establishing such a commission only as a secondary feature may be more appropriate.

Of the seven arrangements not providing for any consultative mechanism at all, six are delimitation treaties in Central America/Caribbean. These six all include provisions on cooperation on fisheries, and so it is unclear why consultative mechanisms are not in turn provided for. This is particularly the case for the Colombia/Dominican Republic Agreement, which goes so far as to establish a 'zone of scientific research and common fishing exploitation'. The seventh arrangement not providing for any consultative mechanism is the Loophole Agreement. The parties are Iceland, Norway and the Russian Federation; a consultative mechanism may have been omitted for political reasons.

3.4 Species covered

3.4.1 Comparative analysis

There are three cases of single-species arrangements [*Herring System; Mackerel System; Halibut Convention*]. Some arrangements put particular weight on certain types of fishery (notably the South Pacific arrangements which, expressly or impliedly, focus on highly migratory species). Most of the remainder cover all fisheries in the area concerned. Examples of arrangements expressly excluding species are the River Plate Treaty, the NEAFC Convention, and the Norway/Russia 1978 Agreement. The first of these expressly excludes 'capture of aquatic mammals' from the scope of the fishing chapter of the treaty. The second excludes from its scope 'sea mammals, sedentary species ... and, in so far as they are dealt with by other international agreements, highly migratory species and anadromous stocks'. Regarding the third arrangement, Hey[16] relates that 'the agreement applies to all fisheries . . . except Atlantic-Scandinavian herring which is to be regulated by a separate agreement'.

3.4.2 *Commentary*

Where different groupings of States are relevant depending on the stock (e.g. the five-participant Herring System compared to the three-participant Mackerel System), or where the institutional machinery required is fundamentally different from one stock to another, a species-specific arrangement may be appropriate. However, in other cases a more general arrangement may be appropriate, though its consultative mechanism would potentially need to be sufficiently flexible to deal with a variety of stocks (ranging from, say, small pelagics to demersal species). In these more general agreements, exclusions are a matter for the parties. However, it may well be appropriate to exclude stocks already under the competence of other arrangements to which the States concerned are parties.

An arrangement's scope, in terms of the species it covers, may in part be dictated by the political situation. For example, States working together for the first time in the context of conservation and management measures might be unwilling to create a framework arrangement for management of shared stocks in general, but might be happier to start with an arrangement expressly limited to a named species. Satisfactory progress with regard to that species might then lead to new arrangements for further species or to the drafting of a general framework arrangement.

3.5 *Access rights*

3.5.1 *Comparative analysis*

The main thrust of several arrangements is access rights. In some cases, these may be given among the parties, whether reciprocal or one-way [*Japan/China Agreement; Japan/Korea Agreement; Norway/Russia 1976 Agreement; Loophole Agreement; Trinidad and Tobago/Venezuela Agreement*]. In other cases the main motivation for the arrangement is cooperation by the parties with regard to access by distant water fishing States [*Nauru Agreement; Niue Treaty; Micronesia Arrangement; SRFC Access Convention; SRFC Hot Pursuit Convention*].

---

[16] E. Hey, *The Regime for the Exploitation of Transboundary Marine Fisheries Resources* (Martinus Nijhoff, Dordrecht, 1989), 170.

3.5.2 Commentary

If the politics of the situation permit, there may be scope for reciprocal or one-way access among the States involved in any cooperation arrangement. However, if such access is to be an element in cooperation over shared stocks, rather than simply a tool for political cooperation or raising of revenue, it should be carefully integrated into any cooperation arrangement. The details of integration will of course depend on the degree of cooperation that the States have in mind, though there is scope for integration at the levels of conservation and management, MCS and enforcement.

Beyond reciprocal or one-way access by vessels flying the flag of a party to a cooperation arrangement, there is also the question of access by vessels of third parties. Arrangements from the South Pacific demonstrate the scope for cooperation between neighbouring coastal States with regard to such access. Though the South Pacific arrangements in practice relate to highly migratory species, notably tuna, elements of these arrangements could equally be applied to cooperation in respect of other shared stocks being fished by third party vessels.

3.6 No provision for conservation and management

3.6.1 Comparative analysis

Six of the arrangements do not provide expressly for cooperation on the establishment of conservation and management measures [*Australia/Indonesia MOU; Canada/US Enforcement Agreement; Nauru Agreement; Niue Treaty; Micronesia Arrangement; SRFC Hot Pursuit Convention*]. Instead, they provide expressly for cooperation on MCS and/or enforcement.

However, with two exceptions [*Australia/Indonesia MOU; Canada/US Enforcement Agreement*], these arrangements relate to a pre-existing treaty. Thus the Nauru Agreement, Niue Treaty and Micronesia Arrangement can all be related to the FFA Convention, and the SRFC Hot Pursuit Convention can be related to the convention establishing the SRFC.

3.6.2 Commentary

An arrangement dealing specifically with MCS and/or enforcement may well be appropriate if cooperation over conservation and management has already been dealt with in an earlier instrument or there is no scope for political agreement on conservation and management cooperation.

3.7 Conservation and management only

3.7.1 Comparative analysis

Three arrangements fail to provide for meaningful cooperation on MCS and/ or enforcement, yet have strong provisions on conservation and management cooperation [*Black Sea Convention; Pacific Salmon Treaty; Lake Victoria Convention*].

3.7.2 Commentary

In the cases of the Black Sea Convention and the Lake Victoria Convention, the omission of cooperation on MCS and/or enforcement is indeed a shortfall.[17] In the former case it is perhaps explainable only in terms of the politics among the three parties at the time (i.e. Bulgaria, Romania, and the then USSR); in the latter case, the reason is unclear. The Pacific Salmon Treaty's strong and highly detailed focus on conservation and management and enhancement is not a logical justification for its omission of cooperation on MCS and/or enforcement. As conjecture, in view of the nature of salmon politics between the two parties (i.e. Canada and the United States), perhaps such cooperation has been seen as a bridge too far. However, cooperation on enforcement is now provided by the Canada/US Enforcement Agreement, which in principle applies to all fisheries (and was in force before the 1999 Agreement regarding Pacific salmon was negotiated).

4. Provision for harmonisation

4.1 Comparative analysis

The term 'harmonisation' is frequently used in the fisheries management literature, but seldom defined. The terms 'harmonise', 'harmonisation' or 'harmonising' are also used in some of the arrangements [*Herring System (1996 Protocol); Norway/Russia 1976 Agreement; Trinidad and Tobago/Venezuela Agreement; African Atlantic Convention*], again without definition.

In this chapter, harmonised measures will be taken as meaning compatible measures, i.e. measures that fit well together for the purpose of achieving the

---

[17] Regarding the Black Sea Convention see: A.E. Reynolds, 'The Varna Convention: A Regional Response to Fisheries Conservation and Management' [1987] *International Journal of Estuarine and Coastal Law* 154, 167–168.

desired fisheries management objective. Thus although harmonisation derives from cooperation, not all cooperation leads to harmonisation. In the following analysis, the focus will be on harmonised conservation and management measures within the zone under consideration. Thus harmonisation in the context of research and stock assessment, MCS, enforcement or a matter other than fisheries has not been addressed here.

The arrangements have been analysed for evidence that the parties have wished to place themselves under a duty in respect of harmonisation. The method used has been to look for: (a) provision for a primary consultative mechanism that can adopt binding measures; (b) provision for quantitative conservation and management measures; or (c) use of appropriate words (such as harmonisation, unification, coordination, complementarity, compatibility, uniformity). The analysis has excluded (a) bare cooperation or collaboration, (b) information exchange and (c) primary consultative mechanisms adopting only non-binding measures, on the assumption that none of these would at face value be sufficiently likely to lead to harmonisation.

Express references to harmonisation of legislation are found in only two arrangements. Thus the River Plate Treaty refers to the promotion of studies and presentation of projects on the 'unification of the laws of the two Parties ...', and the Netherlands/Venezuela Treaty refers to agreement by the parties to 'coordinate their respective legislation and regulations ...'. In contrast, express references to harmonisation of regimes, policies or measures are found in 14 arrangements.

In 11 of these 16 arrangements, a duty on the parties as individuals is involved. In nine instances, the duty is not to harmonise *per se* but, *inter alia*, to 'seek to develop' [*Australian/Indonesia Agreement*], 'endeavour to' [*African Atlantic Convention*], 'initiate work to' [*Herring System (1996 Protocol)*], 'cooperate ... with a view to' [*Norway/Russia 1976 Agreement*] or 'support the broadest international cooperation in order to' [*Colombia/Costa Rica Treaty*]. In some instances, the objective of harmonisation is qualified. Thus the parties simply agree to 'coordinate as much as possible' [*Colombia/ Dominican Republic Agreement*], or 'coordinate ... insofar as possible' [*Netherlands/Venezuela Treaty*].

Eight arrangements provide for primary consultative mechanisms that can in turn adopt measures that are binding [*Japan/China Agreement (on specified matters); Japan/Korea Agreement (on specified matters); NEAFC Convention; Baltic Sea Convention; Mediterranean Agreement; Black Sea Convention; Gulf Agreement; Lake Victoria Convention (on the basis that the Council's measures are adopted by ministers)*] (see also section 9 below). Two arrangements require the parties to implement specified quantitative conservation and management measures [*Black Sea Convention; SRFC Access Convention*] and a further six arrangements set allocation tonnages or percentages [*Torres Strait Treaty; Herring System; Mackerel System; Norway/Russia 1978 Agreement; Halibut Convention; Pacific Salmon Treaty*].

4.2 Commentary

Harmonisation of conservation and management measures, in the sense defined above, is a reasonable goal for any arrangement aiming to achieve cooperation on conservation and management. It adds a level of sophistication to bare cooperation or collaboration. As a minimum, it could be provided for in an arrangement in terms of a duty to try to harmonise or a duty to harmonise as much as possible. Such wording may be more acceptable to States that feel uneasy with the whole notion of cooperation on conservation and management measures.

To take a step further than simply creating such a duty, the arrangements analysed above show that there are two main options: (a) to provide for a primary consultative mechanism that can in turn adopt binding measures; and/or (b) to provide for quantitative conservation and management measures in the arrangement. In a multilateral situation using majority voting, the first of these may be acceptable if there is a suitable objection procedure (see section 9 below). The second of the options may create inflexibility; for improved flexibility, it might be more appropriate for matters such as mesh size to be established and amended instead by the consultative mechanism.

Allocation is a particularly tough political hurdle to cross. In general, allocation is made on the basis of specified criteria. Examples of such criteria include zonal attachment, historical catch records and conservation efforts. However, States may be reluctant to lock themselves into a formula that may be based on unreliable statistics or may prove difficult to alter if the circumstances change. Admittedly, agreement over allocation is a very useful foundation for cooperation. But cooperation is not impossible without it. In view of the potential difficulties in agreeing allocation, failure to provide for quantified allocations in an arrangement should not be seen as a reason for not proceeding with cooperation on conservation and management in other directions.

5. Arrangements with a maritime boundary delimitation aspect

5.1 Comparative analysis

5.1.1 Arrangements establishing one or more maritime boundaries

12 of the arrangements establish one or more maritime boundaries, including a fisheries jurisdiction boundary, between the parties. One of these [*Australia/ Indonesia MOU*] establishes only a 'provisional fisheries line'. Seven of the 12

arrangements [*River Plate Treaty; Torres Strait Treaty; Japan/Korea Agreement; Faroes/UK Agreement; Colombia/Jamaica Treaty; Colombia/Dominican Republic Agreement; Colombia/Ecuador Agreement*] in turn establish a special zone in relation to the fisheries jurisdiction boundary. Within the special zone, a particular fisheries regime is applied (e.g. see sections 11 and 12 below). In some of these seven cases, the special zone is a negotiated response to uncertainty over part of the maritime boundary between the parties.

5.1.2 *Other arrangements, identifying zones as yet undelimited between the parties*

Five arrangements [*Argentina/UK Joint Statement; Japan/China Agreement; Norway/Russia 1978 Agreement; Halibut Convention; Trinidad and Tobago/Venezuela Agreement*], though not delimiting any maritime boundary between the parties, identify special zones that are to some extent as yet undelimited between the parties and then proceed to apply specified fisheries regimes to these zones.

5.1.3 *Some remaining arrangements where maritime boundaries are undelimited*

At least two arrangements [*Australia/Indonesia Agreement; Canada/US Enforcement Agreement*], by virtue of their broad geographical scope, apply to areas where maritime boundaries are as yet undelimited between the parties. However neither arrangement provides for solutions, such as special zones, in relation to these types of area (though the Australia/Indonesia Agreement does refer to the 'provisional fisheries surveillance and enforcement line' established by the Australia/Indonesia MOU).

5.2 *Commentary*

Any lack of certainty in relation to the delimitation of maritime boundaries between potentially cooperating States may have implications for the management regimes for shared stocks. If two neighbouring States wish to commence cooperation over a shared stock, those States may need to pay more attention to boundary regions that may previously have been 'overlooked' from the point of view of delimitation.

To facilitate this, the uncertain status of these waters can either be clarified by (a) the delimitation of the entire boundary in all respects, (b) the delimitation of the fisheries jurisdiction boundary, whether on a permanent or provisional basis, or (c) the establishment of a special zone in which a specified fisheries regime can in turn be applied as part of the overall cooperation effort.

As noted above, several of the arrangements under consideration provide for a special zone in the face of uncertainty about the boundary. However, depending on the arrangement, it is open for debate whether the intention behind establishing such a zone was genuinely to improve management of shared stocks or was principally to assist in reaching overall settlement over delimitation of a boundary. The scope of this chapter does not permit an empirical analysis to assess the success or otherwise of special zones regarding stock management.

It is also notable that none of the arrangements creating a special zone has more than two parties. In most cases, this result derives from the fact that the main purpose of the arrangement is either to establish a maritime boundary or to manage an area where a boundary is unclear. By their nature, such arrangements will tend to involve only two parties.

There is, however, no reason in principle why an arrangement involving more than two parties could not, as part of its purpose, establish boundary-specific solutions. In practice though, the two States concerned might well prefer either to settle their boundary-specific concerns before commencing negotiations involving other parties.

6. Geographical scope

6.1 Comparative analysis

6.1.1 Geographical scope relevant to boundary delimitation or undelimited zone issues

Those arrangements establishing one or more maritime boundaries (see section 5 above) first define the position of the boundary. The location of any special zone established in relation to the fisheries jurisdiction boundary is then also defined. For example, the River Plate Treaty defines its 'common fishing zone' in terms of circumferential arcs of a given radius with centres at specified points, while the Faroes/UK Agreement defines the boundary of its 'Special Area' using coordinates in a schedule.

Where this zone is simply superimposed on the established boundary such that the boundary remains in place in the background (e.g. Colombia/ Dominican Republic Agreement's 'zone of scientific research and common fishing exploitation'), the arrangement can usually proceed by referring to each party's waters within that zone. However, where the zone is a solution to some uncertainty over the boundary such that there is no boundary in place in the background (e.g. the Faroes/UK Agreement 'Special Area'), the arrangement will refer to the zone by its name but will obviously avoid references to the parties' waters within that zone.

6.1.2 *Geographical scope in all other cases*

Several arrangements use a clause to define their scope in terms of geographic features (including seas), or coordinates, or lines of latitude/longitude, or a combination of these [*NEAFC Convention; Baltic Sea Convention; Mediterranean Agreement; Gulf Agreement*]. A shorthand is then used to refer to this zone. The NEAFC and Baltic Sea Conventions refer to 'the Convention area', the Mediterranean Agreement and African Atlantic Convention refer to 'the Region', and the Gulf Agreement refers to 'the Area'. The Norway/Russia 1975 Agreement cross-refers to 'the area covered by the North-East Atlantic Fisheries Convention . . .'.

Several arrangements use a clause to define their scope as being the parties' waters or a specified part of these waters [*Japan/China Agreement; Japan/Korea Agreement; Halibut Convention; Micronesia Arrangement*]. The Micronesia Arrangement then uses the shorthand of 'Arrangement Area' to refer to these waters. In other arrangements, although it is evident that the arrangement is restricted in scope to the parties' waters, this is not stated in any scope clause [*Pacific Salmon Treaty; FFA Convention; Nauru Agreement; Niue Treaty; SRFC Access Convention; SRFC Hot Pursuit Convention; Mauritania/Senegal Convention*]. One arrangement [*African Atlantic Convention*] takes a hybrid approach between referring to geographic and jurisdictional features, by referring to the area comprising specified States.

In some cases, the majority of the provisions apply to the parties' waters but there are also provisions applicable further afield (e.g. Herring System; Mackerel System; Norway/Russia 1976 Agreement; see also Loophole Agreement). The Black Sea Convention refers to 'the fishery resources of the Black Sea'. However, in that its parties consist of only three States (i.e. Bulgaria, Romania, and the then USSR), the geographical scope is to be implied as the waters of the parties and any waters beyond to the extent that actions there do not prejudice the legitimate rights of non-parties.

6.1.3 *Exclusions*

Some arrangements in both of the above categories expressly exclude application to certain specified waters. The Baltic Sea Convention and the Gulf Agreement exclude application to the parties' internal waters. Some arrangements, notably those relating to access rights, expressly or impliedly exclude application to the waters landwards of the parties' 12 nautical mile limits [*Japan/China Agreement; Japan/Korea Agreement; Norway/Russia 1976 Agreement; Loophole Agreement; Nauru Agreement; Micronesia Arrangement; River Plate Treaty (regarding landward limits of the 'common fishing zone')*].

The Micronesia Arrangement applies to the exclusive economic or fisheries zones of the parties, with the exception of an area defined in the annex of the arrangement. The Japan/China Agreement excludes two specified zones delimited by lines of latitude and longitude, respectively; Park Hee Kwon suggests that one of these exclusions is due to the presence of politically sensitive islands.[18] The NEAFC Convention operates a two pillar system, whereby (a) overall the convention applies to the area defined in the scope clause (consisting of coastal States' waters and high seas) and then (b) coastal States' waters are subject to qualified exclusion in several respects. The Mediterranean Agreement requires States, when accepting the agreement, to 'state explicitly to which territories their participation shall extend'.

6.2 Commentary

Applying the definition of the term 'shared stock' adopted at the beginning of this chapter, cooperating coastal States may legitimately confine the scope of the cooperative arrangement to their waters. Subject to agreement, the States obviously have discretion over which areas are excluded (for example internal waters or territorial waters). There is scope for flexibility here. For example, internal waters could be included for the purpose of, say, the geographical scope of the total allowable catch but then excluded with regard to access by certain categories of vessel.

In the examples analysed in this chapter, the geographical scope of the arrangement has been defined either directly by reference to geographic features, coordinates or lines of latitude/longitude, or indirectly by reference to zones of jurisdiction. Reference to features, coordinates or lines has been used by those arrangements relating to specific seas (i.e. the Baltic, Mediterranean and Gulf) or by the NEAFC Convention which covers, *inter alia*, a portion of the high seas and so needs such reference points. Where there is no specific sea or area of high seas involved, definition of the scope by reference to zones of jurisdiction may well be appropriate. The approach adopted by the African Atlantic Convention of referring to the area comprising specified States is confusing in that it is not immediately clear how much of a State's waters are included; matters only become clearer by inference from some later provisions in that treaty.

When the parties to an arrangement create a special zone in response to some uncertainty over a maritime boundary, the general tendency is to define the location of that zone. The alternative is to refer to the zone simply as, say, 'boundary waters'; however, this simple drafting solution may well bring problems of interpretation later. The special zone is normally given a name both for ease of reference and to avoid the need to refer to the parties' respective waters in that context.

[18] Park Hee Kwon, *The Law of the Sea and Northeast Asia: A Challenge for Cooperation* (Kluwer Law International, The Hague, 2000), 53

7. Consultative mechanism in relation to fisheries aspects

7.1 Types of consultative mechanism[19]

7.1.1 Comparative analysis

Seven arrangements do not appear to have any consultative mechanism at all, either directly or indirectly. Six of these are delimitation treaties in Central America/Caribbean; the other is the Loophole Agreement. These arrangements have all been mentioned in section 3.3.2 above.

Five of the arrangements [*Australia/Indonesia MOU; Australia/Indonesia Agreement; Faroes/UK Agreement; Canada/US Enforcement Agreement; Niue Treaty*] provide only for consultations. Two of the arrangements [*Herring System; Mackerel System*] do not expressly provide for any consultative mechanism; instead, the fact that in each case the parties decide to meet on an annual basis is the way that the necessary consultations occur. Two of the arrangements [*SRFC Access Convention; SRFC Hot Pursuit Convention*] involve the members of the SRFC (Sub-Regional Fisheries Commission).[20] Though neither of these arrangements expressly provides for a consultative mechanism, in each case the parties may resort to the SRFC mechanism itself.

The remaining arrangements expressly provide for more formal consultative mechanisms, under the name of 'commission', 'council', 'committee', 'annual meeting' or 'conference'.

7.1.2 Commentary

In the case of the five arrangements providing only for consultations [*Australia/ Indonesia MOU; Australia/Indonesia Agreement; Faroes/UK Agreement; Canada/US Enforcement Agreement; Niue Treaty*], the intention was evidently not to create any kind of firm institutional structure but nonetheless to leave a consultative channel available if necessary. Such a system may be appropriate where there is less of a need for routine cooperation, but where urgent issues may nonetheless arise.

However, in that sense the lack of any kind of commission for the Australia/ Indonesia Agreement or for the Niue Treaty is surprising. After all, the former arrangement states that '[t]he Parties shall seek to develop complementary

---

[19] This chapter does not address consultative mechanisms established for dispute resolution purposes.

[20] Also known as the CSRP (Commission Sous-Régionale des Pêches).

regimes for the conservation, management and optimum utilisation of shared stocks, straddling stocks and highly migratory species', and the latter arrangement states that '[t]he Parties shall cooperate to develop regionally agreed procedures for the conduct of fisheries surveillance and law enforcement'.

The two arrangements that simply rely on the parties deciding to meet on an annual basis [*Herring System; Mackerel System*] may appear precarious. However, arguably, the main reason that the parties continue to meet on an annual basis is that in each case they wish to prepare their joint position prior to the annual meeting of the North-East Atlantic Fisheries Commission (NEAFC). That way, they achieve a coordinated quantitative stance against the non-coastal State parties desiring access to the straddling stocks concerned. Thus what at first sight may appear to be rather fragile arrangements are in fact more robust because of the linkage with the NEAFC Convention.

Assuming a need for regular meetings, and in the absence of an external force driving the need for such meetings, a commission or equivalent, with its mandate and timetable provided for in the arrangement, may be an appropriate solution. It is for the parties to decide whether the principal consultative mechanism is, say, a council of ministers or a commission of officials. The exact name given to the mechanism may be irrelevant so long as the desired functional elements are provided for and the name does not conflict with these elements.

7.2 Internal rules

7.2.1 Comparative analysis

In arrangements establishing formal consultative mechanisms, the practice is generally for the arrangements themselves to establish the key principles relating to that mechanism. They then omit more detailed internal rules and instead provide for the consultative mechanism to draft its own.

In the arrangements analysed, this approach is generally only used in the arrangements creating 'commissions' *per se*. However, there are three exceptions [*FFA Convention; Micronesia Arrangement; Lake Victoria Convention*], and five arrangements creating 'commissions' contain no such provision [*Argentina/UK Joint Statement; Norway/Russia 1975 Agreement; Halibut Convention; Colombia/Jamaica Treaty; Trinidad and Tobago/Venezuela Agreement*]. Rules of procedure do in fact exist for the commission established under at least one of these five arrangements [*Halibut Convention*]; it may be that the commissions established under the other four arrangements mentioned also have their own rules despite lack of a provision in the arrangement itself.

7.2.2 *Commentary*

The need for rules of procedure and financial rules depends in part on the degree to which such matters have already been covered in the arrangement. However, in most cases the arrangement itself is unlikely to cover the necessary procedures and financial issues in sufficient detail.

Various models for internal rules exist. As well as regulating the primary consultative mechanism, such rules can also be used to provide for the mandate of subsidiary bodies (see section 8 below). As such, they can contribute to the legal framework in place for the management of the shared stocks in question, but avoid the need for too much prescription in the arrangement itself.

7.3 *Secretariats*

7.3.1 *Comparative analysis*

Again, it is generally only the 'commissions' *per se* that have their own secretariats. However, there are three exceptions [*FFA Convention; Lake Victoria Convention; African Atlantic Convention*], and five of the treaties establishing commissions have no express provision for a secretariat [*Argentina/UK Joint Statement; Norway/Russia 1975 Agreement; Black Sea Convention; Colombia/Jamaica Treaty; Trinidad and Tobago/Venezuela Agreement*]. Of the 13 bilateral arrangements with a formal consultative mechanism, only three expressly provide for a secretariat [*River Plate Treaty; Halibut Convention; Pacific Salmon Treaty*]. The terminology for 'secretariat' varies, including also headquarters [*River Plate Treaty*] and references to an office (or seat), director (or executive secretary) and staff [*NEAFC Convention; Baltic Sea Convention; Halibut Convention; Pacific Salmon Treaty*].

7.3.2 *Commentary*

Whether or not a secretariat is appropriate depends, *inter alia*, on the work programme of the consultative mechanism. For an arrangement with a large number of parties and/or an active coordination function, a secretariat may well be appropriate for facilitating such coordination (e.g. in terms of administering meetings, including those of subsidiary bodies, or other initiatives such as research programmes). An arrangement with just two parties may well justify a secretariat if its work programme merits it. This would explain the difference between, say, the Argentina/ UK Joint Statement (no secretariat) and the Pacific Salmon Treaty (secretariat). However, though secretariats may be a good idea in theory, they inevitably having running costs. If money is not available for secretariat funding, it may be more appropriate to aim for a realistic work programme that can be administered instead by, say, the government offices of the parties.

7.4 Meeting frequency

7.4.1 Comparative analysis

Meeting frequency is of course variable, ranging from 'as necessary' [*Australia/ Indonesia MOU; Torres Strait Treaty; Canada/US Enforcement Agreement*] to at least twice a year [*Argentina/UK Joint Statement; Trinidad and Tobago/Venezuela Agreement*] to once ever two years [*Lake Victoria Convention; African Atlantic Convention*]. The norm, however, is annual meetings. With one exception, the multilateral arrangements do not specify the quorum required to constitute a valid meeting. The exception is the Lake Victoria Convention, which specifies that no meeting of either the 'Council of Ministers', the 'Policy Steering Committee' or the 'Executive Committee' is to take place unless all three parties are present.

7.4.2 Commentary

The most appropriate frequency for meetings depends, *inter alia*, on the work programme, the desired responsiveness of the arrangement, and the funding available. The first two of these factors will in part be determined by the stocks and fisheries covered. In general, meetings held at least annually may be desirable for effective management of shared stocks. One solution may be to opt for annual meetings but provide scope for additional special meetings (see section 7.5 below). Regular meetings, rather than ones 'as necessary', allow for both forward planning and coordination with regular meetings in other relevant forums (e.g. the annual Mackerel System meeting timed to be just prior to annual meeting of the North-East Atlantic Fisheries Commission). With respect to quorums in multilateral arrangements, some arrangements specify the quorum required for a vote, rather than specifying the quorum required for a meeting.

7.5 Special meetings

7.5.1 Comparative analysis

Of the arrangements setting frequencies for their regular meetings, almost all provide for special meetings as an option. The pre-conditions for such meetings are very variable. Of the bilateral arrangements, the trigger may be (a) agreement by both parties [*Japan/China Agreement; Japan/Korea Agreement*], (b) a request of either party [*River Plate Treaty; Pacific Salmon Treaty; Trinidad and Tobago/Venezuela Agreement; Mauritania/Senegal Convention*], or (c) as the Commission determines necessary [*Halibut Convention*]. Of the multilateral arrangements, the number of parties that must be in agreement for a special meeting to occur varies. Two arrangements require at least three requesting parties [*Nauru Agreement; Micronesia Arrangement – seven parties*]. Two others require at least four requesting parties [*NEAFC Convention – six parties; FFA Convention – 16 parties*]. Three require the request of the majority [*Mediterranean Agreement; Gulf Agreement; African Atlantic Convention*].

7.5.2 Commentary

One disadvantage of a provision for special meetings is the risk that it may be abused by parties with strong vested interests. However, with multi-lateral arrangements there is scope for introducing procedural safeguards to minimise this risk. Where there is a requirement for a minimum number of supporting States, there appears to be no fixed practice based on percentages: in four arrangements with six to 16 contracting parties, the requisite minimum number of requesting parties hovers around three or four.

7.6 Delegations

7.6.1 Comparative analysis

Many arrangements provide for a specified maximum number of delegates, in turn referred to as 'delegates', 'members', 'representatives', 'commissioners' or 'ministers'. Typically, the arrangements allocate a delegation size of two to each party.

However, in general, this maximum number may be accompanied by an unspecified number of experts and advisers and sometimes by alternates. Two arrangements specify the categories from which the delegates are to be drawn

[*Torres Strait Treaty; Mauritania/Senegal Convention*]. One sets rules for accompanying delegates depending on whether the meeting is an open meeting or an executive meeting [*Pacific Salmon Treaty (see internal rules)*]. One places a duty on each party to try to ensure that the minister is accompanied by heads of specified government departments [*Lake Victoria Convention*].

7.6.2 Commentary

To give the work of any consultative mechanism credibility in the eyes of environmental and industry organisations, the latter bodies need access to, and some degree of influence over, the decision-making process. Though this may be done by giving such bodies observer status or an involvement in subsidiary bodies, an alternative is to involve them in the parties' delegations in some respect. In terms of industry, this is provided for by the Mauritania/Senegal Convention. It is possible that other arrangements do so through their rules of procedure.

8.   Subsidiary bodies[21]

8.1 Comparative analysis

23 of the 39 arrangements either do not provide for a power or duty to create subsidiary bodies or have not, to the author's knowledge, given rise to such bodies. Of the remaining arrangements, almost all provide a power or duty to the primary consultative mechanism to establish subsidiary bodies. However, in three arrangements there is no such provision, and yet subsidiary bodies nevertheless have been created [*Argentina/UK Joint Statement; Norway/Russia 1975 Agreement; Halibut Convention*].

There are two main types of subsidiary body. One type deals with administrative matters (e.g. NEAFC Convention: Finance and Administration Committee and Ad Hoc Working Group on Computerisation of the Secretariat); the other type addresses substantive aspects of coordination on research and stock assessment, conservation and management, MCS or enforcement. Bodies in the latter category are typically arranged in a hierarchical manner (e.g. Lake Victoria Convention: the 'Fisheries Management Committee' reporting to the

---

[21]   This chapter does not address subsidiary bodies established for dispute resolution purposes.

'Executive Committee', reporting to the 'Policy Steering Committee', reporting to the 'Council of Ministers').

With a few exceptions [*Herring System; Pacific Salmon Treaty; Lake Victoria Convention; African Atlantic Convention*], the arrangement itself does not specify the names of the subsidiary bodies to be created. There appears to be no relationship between the number of subsidiary bodies actually established under an arrangement and the number of parties to that arrangement.

8.2 Commentary

One reason why an arrangement may have no subsidiary bodies is that it has no primary consultative mechanism. However, of the 23 arrangements mentioned above, only seven have no such primary body [*six of the seven Central American/Caribbean boundary arrangements; Loophole Agreement*]. The remainder (16) have a primary consultative mechanism, either directly or indirectly. Six of these 16 arrangements do not provide expressly for cooperation on the establishment of conservation and management measures (see section 3.6 above) [*Australia/Indonesia MOU; Canada/US Enforcement Agreement; Nauru Agreement; Niue Treaty; Micronesia Arrangement; SRFC Hot Pursuit Convention*]. However, there is no reason in principle why such arrangements should not have subsidiary bodies.

Four of the 16 have consultations alone as their primary consultative mechanism [*Australia/Indonesia MOU; Faroes/UK Agreement; Canada/US Enforcement Agreement; Niue Treaty*]. However, again, there is no reason in principle why consultations should not be able to spawn subsidiary bodies.[22] In general, then, it is hard to explain why in principle any of the 16 arrangements should not either provide for or otherwise have subsidiary bodies.

The answer must lie partly in that the number and type of subsidiary bodies is dictated by the circumstances surrounding the consultative mechanism. Turning now to the arrangements that do provide for a power or duty to create subsidiary bodies (or where the author is otherwise aware of any such bodies), some patterns can be seen.

Of the three arrangements with subsidiary bodies on administrative matters [*NEAFC Convention; Baltic Sea Convention; Pacific Salmon Treaty*], all have a secretariat. Secretariats create the need for administrative and financial oversight by the parties, and one means of exercising that oversight is to create a subsidiary body with an administrative brief. Secretariats may also need attention by the parties for other reasons associated with their function (e.g.

---

[22] The Australia/Indonesia Agreement, which provides for consultations between the parties, also provides for 'the convening of technical meetings on marine areas or stocks of special interest to both Parties . . .'.

NEAFC Convention: Ad Hoc Working Group on Computerisation of the Secretariat). However, some arrangements have a secretariat yet appear not to have a subsidiary body on administrative matters amongst their other bodies (e.g. Mediterranean Agreement; Halibut Convention) suggesting some other means for oversight of the secretariat may exist.

Regarding subsidiary bodies relating to substantive aspects of cooperation, the number needed will be determined in part by the scope of the cooperation, the arrangement's political or geographical complexity, and the funding available. The Pacific Salmon Treaty is one of the most politically and geographically complex arrangements, and this complexity is reflected not only by the detail of the arrangement's provisions but also its highly evolved system of subsidiary bodies.

The degree to which a subsidiary body with a stock assessment or science remit is required will depend in part on whether or not the arrangement uses the services of a science secretariat. For example, the North-East Atlantic Fisheries Commission (NEAFC) uses the services of the International Council for the Exploration of the Sea (ICES). This is illustrated by the fact that its suite of subsidiary bodies includes an informal group to prepare NEAFC's request for scientific advice from ICES. The whole question of reliance on science secretariats as opposed to relying on the parties to the arrangement is addressed by Ward *et al.*[23] and will not be further discussed here.

Subsidiary bodies may also be an effective means of integrating the fishing industry or environmental groups into the cooperative regime. In the case of the Halibut Convention, the primary consultative mechanism is the International Pacific Halibut Commission. The Conference Board represents Canadian and United States commercial and sport halibut fishermen, designated by union and vessel owner organisations. The Processor Advisory Group ('PAG') represents halibut processors. At the Commission's annual meetings, the Commission's staff make presentations on stock status, seasons etc. to the Board and the PAG, plus the Commissioners. Each of the Board and the PAG then meets over several days and in turn delivers an independent report to the Commissioners on the staff's presentations. The industry therefore has a strong and integrated role in the regime, through the means of subsidiary bodies.

Four of the arrangements [*Torres Strait Treaty; NEAFC Convention; Norway/ Russia 1975 Agreement; Baltic Sea Convention*] have subsidiary bodies specialising in MCS and/or enforcement issues. In general, the numbers of subsidiary bodies with this specialisation are likely to increase in response to increased awareness of illegal, unreported and unregulated (IUU) fishing and the growth of ideas for combating this threat.

The previous point illustrates that subsidiary bodies provide one mechanism by which the arrangement may respond to current issues. Thus if, say, IUU

---

[23] P. Ward, R. Kearney and N. Tsirbas, 'Science Arrangements for the Regional Management of Tuna Fisheries' [2000] *Marine Policy* 93.

fishing becomes a threat to the sustainability of the stock concerned, a subsidiary body may be convened to suggest solutions for the duration of the threat. If the threat disappears, the body may be disbanded. This need for responsiveness means that in cases where the arrangement itself specifies the names of the subsidiary bodies to be established [*Pacific Salmon Treaty; Lake Victoria Convention*], it is preferable not to overly limit the discretion of the primary consultative mechanism with regard to those other bodies that it may additionally create.

Finally, some of the issues already discussed above in sections 7.2-7.6 regarding the primary consultative mechanism also apply to subsidiary bodies. Internal rules, meeting frequencies, special meetings, delegations (and decision-making) are all factors that potentially need to be addressed regarding subsidiary bodies.

9. Decision-making mechanism of primary consultative mechanism

The analysis here will be restricted to decision-making in respect of conservation and management measures; as such it covers only 20 of the arrangements.

9.1 Comparative analysis

Of the two-party arrangements under consideration, decision-making is by consensus. However, consensus decision-making is not confined to the two-party arrangements. Whether the measures are binding or merely advisory appears to bear no relationship to the number of parties. With one exception [*Lake Victoria Convention*], multilateral arrangements using majority voting to adopt binding measures have an objection procedure.

9.2 Commentary

Where the measures of a consultative mechanism are binding, it is in the interests of the parties to send delegations of sufficient competence. However, it is also logical that in such cases, any use of majority voting should be accompanied by an objection procedure. Such a system represents a balance between the potentially inhibitory influence of the need for consensus and the threat to sovereignty posed by majority voting with no objection procedure.

Where the measures of a consultative mechanism are merely advisory, it is assumed that one of the reasons for this restriction in the power of the mechanism is the politics of the situation. Thus in a politically sensitive situation, one area for compromise whilst retaining the concept of cooperation over shared stocks could be to agree to a consultative mechanism but not give it the power to adopt binding measures. In some instances, this may be the price to pay for at least some cooperation.

10. Approach to cooperation on research and stock assessment

A mandate may be given to the primary consultative mechanism to, *inter alia*:

(a) collect information on resources and fisheries from the parties [*Argentina/ UK Joint Statement; Baltic Sea Convention; FFA Convention*] or determine what information is to be received [*Black Sea Convention*];

(b) recommend the format in which such information is to be provided [*Argentina/UK Joint Statement*] or establish requirements for the collection of statistics [*NEAFC Convention; Halibut Convention*];

(c) analyse such information [*Baltic Sea Convention; FFA Convention*] or review the status of fisheries resources and fisheries [*Mediterranean Agreement; Gulf Agreement*];

(d) analyse the effect of conservation measures on fishery resources [*NEAFC Convention*];

(e) coordinate exchange of data [*NEAFC Convention; FFA Convention; Trinidad and Tobago/Venezuela Agreement*];

(f) propose scientific research work [*Mediterranean Agreement; Gulf Agreement*], including joint work [*Argentina/UK Joint Statement; River Plate Treaty*];

(g) coordinate scientific research work [*River Plate Treaty (via the secretariat – see internal rules); Black Sea Convention; Mediterranean Agreement; Gulf Agreement; Pacific Salmon Treaty*] including establishing procedures for joint work [*Colombia/Jamaica Treaty; Trinidad and Tobago/Venezuela Agreement*];

(h) conduct studies itself [*River Plate Treaty; Mediterranean Agreement; Gulf Agreement; Halibut Convention*].

If there is no duty on the primary consultative mechanism to collect relevant information from the parties, the arrangement may instead be phrased so as to place a duty on the parties to supply the mechanism with such information (e.g. Pacific Salmon Treaty; Lake Victoria Convention).

Sometimes, the number of research tasks allocated to the primary consultative mechanism is reduced because the mechanism relies on a science secretariat (e.g. reliance on the International Council for the Exploration of the Sea (ICES) is provided for by the NEAFC Convention, Herring System and Baltic Sea Convention). The North-East Atlantic Fisheries Commission has a Memorandum of Understanding with ICES. Ward *et al.*[24] have reviewed the use of science secretariats, and the issues will not be reiterated here. Alternatively, a scientific committee may be created as a subsidiary body to address the some or all of the research and assessment mandate allocated to the primary consultative mechanism (e.g. Argentina/UK Joint Statement; Pacific Salmon Treaty; Lake Victoria Convention). Rarely, the primary consultative mechanism has a mandate to conduct its own research cruises [*Halibut Convention*].

Even if there is a primary consultative mechanism in place, there may nonetheless be a duty addressed to the parties as individuals to:

(a) cooperate on scientific research [*Japan/China Agreement; Norway/Russia 1975 Agreement; Colombia/Jamaica Treaty; African Atlantic Convention; Mauritania/Senegal Convention (implemented by a protocol)*];
(b) exchange results of fisheries research [*Norway/Russia 1975 Agreement; Black Sea Convention; Trinidad and Tobago/Venezuela Agreement*];
(c) jointly undertake programmes of research under the procedure established by the commission [*Trinidad and Tobago/Venezuela Agreement*];
(d) exchange relevant information on fisheries resources [*Japan/Korea Agreement; Herring System (1996 Protocol); Norway/Russia 1975 Agreement; Black Sea Convention; Pacific Salmon Treaty; Trinidad and Tobago/Venezuela Agreement; African Atlantic Convention*].

Even if the primary consultative mechanism consists only of consultations there may still be a duty for the parties to: (a) facilitate cooperation on fisheries research; (b) exchange catch/effort data; and (c) exchange results of specified scientific research [*Australia/Indonesia Agreement*].

If there is no primary consultative mechanism of any form, there may be a duty on the parties to:

(a) provide each other with research results, jointly coordinate and undertake scientific research, and exchange catch information [*Colombia/Dominican Republic Agreement, regarding the 'zone of scientific research and common fishing exploitation'*];
(b) give each other 'the greatest possible facilities' for the purpose of developing activities to exploit and use the living resources of their respective maritime jurisdictional zones through, *inter alia*, cooperation on scientific research [*Colombia/Costa Rica Treaty; Colombia/Ecuador Agreement*];

---

[24] *Ibid.*

(c) promote, encourage and facilitate scientific research [*Netherlands/ Venezuela Treaty*].

One party may be under a duty to allow the other party to carry out research in its waters on specified matters of common interest and according to specified procedures [*River Plate Treaty; Pacific Salmon Treaty; Lake Victoria Convention*]. Some arrangements provide that they or their conservation and management measures are not to apply to research cruises [*Baltic Sea Convention; Halibut Convention*]. The African Atlantic Convention requires parties to: (a) encourage exchange of experience, twinning of institutions, and optimum use of vessels for research; and (b) to collaborate in the establishment of a data and information bank.

11. Approach to cooperation on conservation and management[25]

Many arrangements provide expressly for the primary consultative mechanism to adopt measures on conservation and management [*Argentina/UK Joint Statement; River Plate Treaty; Japan/China Agreement; Japan/Korea Agreement; NEAFC Convention; Norway/Russia 1976 Agreement; Norway/Russia 1978 Agreement; Baltic Sea Convention; Mediterranean Agreement; Black Sea Convention; Gulf Agreement; Halibut Convention; Pacific Salmon Treaty; Trinidad and Tobago/ Venezuela Agreement; Lake Victoria Convention*]. The measures adopted by the consultative mechanism may be binding on the parties, or merely advisory, depending on the arrangement concerned (see sections 4 & 9 above). Often, the arrangement will specify the types of conservation and management measure to be adopted by the consultative mechanism. Examples include:

(a) determination of total allowable catch (TAC) [*Baltic Sea Convention; Norway/Russia 1978 Agreement*];
(b) determination and allocation of TAC [*River Plate Treaty, regarding the 'common fishing zone'; NEAFC Convention; Mediterranean Agreement; Gulf Agreement; Halibut Convention, regarding 'Area 2'*];
(c) determination and allocation of allowable fishing effort [*NEAFC Convention; Mediterranean Agreement; Gulf Agreement*];
(d) determination of quota for the vessels of one party fishing in the waters of the other party [*Japan/China Agreement*];
(e) establishment of closed (or open) areas or seasons [*Japan/China*

---

[25] An analysis of the arrangements' references to harmonisation in the context of conservation and management measures has already been made in section 4 above and will not be repeated here.

Agreement; NEAFC Convention; Baltic Sea Convention; Mediterranean Agreement; Gulf Agreement; Halibut Convention; Trinidad and Tobago/ Venezuela Agreement];

(f) regulation of by-catch [*Halibut Convention*], fishing gear and appliances [*NEAFC Convention; Baltic Sea Convention; Mediterranean Agreement; Gulf Agreement; Halibut Convention; Trinidad and Tobago/Venezuela Agreement*], catching methods [*Baltic Sea Convention; Trinidad and Tobago/Venezuela Agreement*], and size limits of fish [*NEAFC Convention; Baltic Sea Convention; Mediterranean Agreement; Gulf Agreement; Halibut Convention; Trinidad and Tobago/Venezuela Agreement*];

(g) application of precautionary approach [*Mediterranean Agreement; Gulf Agreement*];

(h) amendment of quantitative conservation and management measures prescribed in the arrangement [*Black Sea Convention*].

However, some of the arrangements additionally include a catch-all provision. For example, the Baltic Sea Convention allows the primary consultative mechanism to additionally make recommendations on 'any other measures related to the conservation and rational exploitation of the living marine resources'. Some consultative mechanisms produce an annual set of their rules (e.g. Baltic Sea Convention; Halibut Convention). The consolidated 'Fishery Rules' issued by the International Baltic Sea Fishery Commission show that the consultative mechanism under the Baltic Sea Convention has additionally adopted measures regulating, *inter alia*, quota exchanges and quota transfers, by-catch, and discarding. The Agreed Records in the Herring System and Mackerel System show that the participants have adopted, *inter alia*, long-term management strategies.

Only rarely do arrangements include specified quantitative conservation and management measures. The Black Sea Convention establishes minimum landing sizes for certain species, and by-catch limits for under-sized fish. The SRFC Access Convention sets minimum mesh sizes for specified fisheries. Regarding allocation, one arrangement sets out very general principles on allocation criteria [*River Plate Treaty*], while others actually establish the allocation tonnages or percentages between the parties, to varying degrees [*Torres Strait Treaty; Herring System; Mackerel System; Norway/Russia 1978 Agreement; Halibut Convention; Pacific Salmon Treaty*]. In the Norway/Russia 1978 Agreement (regarding the 'provisional joint fishing zone'), allocations to third States are to be by agreement, and Hey[26] relates that 'fish caught by a vessel licensed by both parties shall be deducted in equal parts from the allocations made to each party'.

---

[26] E. Hey, *The Regime for the Exploitation of Transboundary Marine Fisheries Resources* (Martinus Nijhoff, Dordrecht, 1989), 170.

Often the consultative mechanism has a duty to collate information on the conservation and management measures being taken by the parties, or alternatively the parties have a duty to provide such information to the consultative mechanism. Some of the arrangements have subsidiary bodies specialising in conservation and management issues [*NEAFC Convention; Herring System; Baltic Sea Convention; Pacific Salmon Treaty; Lake Victoria Convention*]. Several arrangements (e.g. Halibut Convention) expressly allow parties to take stricter measures than those adopted by the consultative mechanism. At least one arrangement involves coordination between two of the three parties over to what extent they will allow fishing by the third party in their waters [*Loophole Agreement*].

The Torres Strait Treaty requires the parties to, where appropriate, negotiate subsidiary conservation and management arrangements for individual commercial fisheries in the 'Protected Zone'. There is a duty on the parties to enter into consultations if (a) one party considers that one of the 'Protected Zone' commercial fisheries should be subject to common conservation and management measures, or (b) one party has reasonable grounds for believing that exploitation of a 'Protected Zone' commercial fishery could cause serious damage to the marine environment or might endanger another species.

The Norway/Russia 1976 Agreement includes an agreement that neither party will fish for anadromous stocks beyond their respective fisheries jurisdictions. The Black Sea Convention likewise states that the parties are not to fish for *Acipenser nudiventris* for a specified period of years. At least two arrangements propose exchanges of fisheries managers to improve cooperation [*Australia/Indonesia Agreement; Pacific Salmon Treaty (through the 1999 Agreement)*].

12. Approach to cooperation on MCS and/or enforcement

In some cases, the primary consultative mechanism has an express function to adopt measures on MCS and/or enforcement (e.g. NEAFC Convention). In some other cases, this function is implied (e.g. Japan/Korea Agreement; Baltic Sea Convention; Mediterranean Agreement; Gulf Agreement). The measures adopted by the consultative mechanism may be binding on the parties or merely advisory, depending on the arrangement concerned (see sections 4 & 9 above).

Some arrangements have adopted so-called 'schemes' related to MCS and/or enforcement (e.g. the North-East Atlantic Fisheries Commission's two schemes, albeit that these relate to the activities of vessels on the high seas). Schemes directed at non-party vessels within the waters of the parties are potentially useful (even for bilateral coastal State arrangements). For example, the Herring System (1996 Protocol) requires parties to cooperate to deter activities of non-party vessels which undermine the effectiveness of agreed conservation and management measures; such cooperation could be initiated by drafting of a joint scheme of measures.

Four of the arrangements [*Torres Strait Treaty; NEAFC Convention; Norway/ Russia 1975 Agreement; Baltic Sea Convention*] have subsidiary bodies specialising in MCS and/or enforcement issues. The subsidiary body of this type established under the Norway/Russia 1975 Agreement in 1993 has been very active. Honneland[27] reports that measures developed through it have included, *inter alia*:

(a) the 'exchange of catch and landing data';
(b) the participation of inspectors from one party in inspections of that party's vessels in the ports of the other party;
(c) the 'elaboration of joint conversion factors' for fish products;
(d) the 'elaboration of joint routines for the closing and opening of fishing grounds';
(e) the establishment of 'joint seminars for enforcement officers'.

Practice varies on how fisheries laws and regulations may be enforced by the coastal State or the flag State. Some arrangements reassure that the party in whose waters the vessels of the other party are fishing has the power to ensure compliance (e.g. Japan/China Agreement; Japan/Korea Agreement; Norway/ Russia 1976 Agreement), and there may be express recognition that the flag State may not board or stop its vessels in the other party's waters [*Japan/Korea Agreement*]. The Halibut Convention states expressly that each party has the right to enforce the convention in all convention waters in respect of its own nationals and fishing vessels, but adds that each party also has the right to enforce the convention in its waters against vessels of either party.

The Torres Strait Treaty, regarding the 'Protected Zone', establishes a (qualified) general principle that corrective action 'in respect of offences or suspected offences against the fisheries laws or regulations of the Parties' is to be taken by 'the authorities of the Party whose nationality is borne by the vessel or person concerned ... and not by the Party in whose area of jurisdiction the offence or suspected offence occurs ...'. However, as a safeguard, the parties acknowledge that this principle 'should not be applied so as to frustrate the enforcement of fisheries laws or regulations or to enable offenders against those laws or regulations to go unpunished'. One arrangement [*Colombia/Ecuador Agreement*] creates a 'special zone' for the purpose of ensuring that the 'accidental presence' of 'local' fishermen of either

---

[27] See: G. Honneland, 'Enforcement Cooperation between Norway and Russia in the Barents Sea Fisheries' [2000] *Ocean Development and International Law* 249, 257–259

party in that zone should not be considered a violation of the maritime boundary.

Where a special zone has been established in an area where there is uncertainty over the maritime boundary, the arrangement usually provides for enforcement in that zone only by the party that is the vessel's flag State [*Japan/ China Agreement; Japan/Korea Agreement; Norway/Russia 1978 Agreement; Halibut Convention, regarding 'boundary regions'; Colombia/Jamaica Treaty*] or for enforcement only by the party that has issued the vessel's licence [*Faroes/UK Agreement*]. However, in these instances cooperation may be facilitated by, *inter alia*:

(a) provision for one party to call the other party's attention to breaches by its vessel of joint conservation and management measures [*Japan/China Agreement; Japan/Korea Agreement*] and a corresponding duty on the other party to take certain actions [*Japan/China Agreement; Japan/Korea Agreement; Colombia/Jamaica Treaty*] and to notify these [*Japan/China Agreement; Japan/Korea Agreement*];

(b) a duty to exchange information on catches and modes of fishing [*Japan/ Korea Agreement*] and on vessels [*Norway/Russia 1978 Agreement*];

(c) a requirement that neither party authorises third State fishing [*Halibut Convention*] or a requirement that such fishing must meet certain conditions [*Norway/Russia 1978 Agreement*];

(d) agreement for either party to take enforcement action against a vessel that is not licensed by either party [*Norway/Russia 1978 Agreement*] or against any third State vessel [*Halibut Convention*].

If there is no boundary in place (and no special zone), there may nonetheless be a duty to consult with a view to avoiding difficulties regarding the exercise of the parties' respective jurisdiction [*Australia/Indonesia MOU, regarding areas where the provisional line does not apply*].

In general, cooperation on MCS and/or enforcement is facilitated by, *inter alia*:

(a) a duty on each party to ensure compliance by its vessels with the other party's rules when fishing under authorisation in the other party's waters [*Australia/Indonesia Agreement; Japan/China Agreement; Japan/Korea Agreement; Norway/Russia 1976 Agreement; Loophole Agreement*], including making it an offence to breach the other party's rules [*Canada/US Enforcement Agreement; Torres Strait Treaty*] or placing other detailed enforcement duties on the vessel's party [*Micronesia Arrangement*];

(b) provision for one party to call the other party's attention to alleged breaches of the former's conservation and management measures by the latter's vessels, with certain follow-up expectations [*Micronesia Arrangement*];

(c) notification in the event of arrest, seizure, detention or other enforcement action by one party against the other party's vessels

[*Australia/Indonesia Agreement; Japan/China Agreement; Japan/Korea Agreement; Micronesia Arrangement*];

(d) express agreement on prompt release of vessels and crews upon posting of reasonable bond or other security [*Japan/China Agreement; Japan/Korea Agreement; Micronesia Arrangement*];

(e) a duty on each party to ensure compliance by its vessels with the consultative mechanism's conservation and management binding measures and to report back to the consultative mechanism on the control measures taken [*Baltic Sea Convention*], or a duty simply to enforce the fishery regime [*NEAFC Convention, Pacific Salmon Treaty*];

(f) coordination of laws and regulations on fishing registration and fishing licences [*Colombia/Ecuador Agreement*], or consultation and cooperation in the issue and endorsement of licences [*Torres Strait Treaty, regarding the 'Protected Zone'*];

(g) agreement to cooperate on inspection and enforcement [*Torres Strait Treaty*], inspection and control [*Herring System (1996 Protocol)*], or inspection and boarding [*Halibut Convention*];

(h) a duty on the parties to consult to ensure that laws and regulations on cooperation on inspection and enforcement are, as far as practicable, consistent between the parties [*Torres Strait Treaty*];

(i) a duty on one party to furnish witnesses or evidence under its control promptly to the authorities of the party having jurisdiction to conduct prosecutions [*Halibut Convention*];

(j) cooperation on extradition [*Niue Treaty*];

(k) establishment by the consultative mechanism of measures relating to logbooks [*Baltic Sea Convention (see consolidated 'Fishery Rules'); Halibut Convention (see 2000 'Pacific Halibut Fishery Regulations')*], catch reporting, gear stowage and marking of fishing gear [*Baltic Sea Convention (see consolidated 'Fishery Rules')*];

(l) exchange of information on MCS systems and technology [*Australia/Indonesia Agreement*];

(m) agreement to pool surveillance resources, or agreement for one party to extend its surveillance and enforcement activities to the waters of another party [*Niue Treaty*];

(n) port State control [*Loophole Agreement, Micronesia Arrangement*], e.g. bans on landings of illegal catches and denial of port access to vessels undertaking illegal fishing [*Loophole Agreement*];

(o) observer programmes [*Nauru Agreement; Micronesia Arrangement*];

(p) conditions for the licensing of third State vessels [*Torres Strait Treaty, regarding the 'Protected Zone'*] including standardisation of such conditions [*Nauru Agreement; Niue Treaty; Micronesia Arrangement; SRFC Access Convention*];

(q) information exchange on licensed third State vessels [*Mauritania/Senegal Convention, Protocol*], including nature of such information [*Niue Treaty*] and standardisation of procedures [*Nauru Agreement; Niue Treaty*];

(r) regional registers of vessels, including agreed eligibility and joint review of registered vessels [*Micronesia Arrangement*];

(s) agreed quantitative criteria for the ejection of a vessel from the waters covered by the arrangement [*SRFC Access Convention*];

(t) cooperation on hot pursuit [*SRFC Hot Pursuit Convention (including by additional protocol); Mauritania/Senegal Convention*];

(u) exchange of personnel [*Torres Strait Treaty; Mauritania/Senegal Convention, Protocol*].

13. Conclusion

Logic suggests that cooperation amongst neighbouring coastal States with respect to a shared stock is likely to lead to more effective management of that stock. Yet various hurdles potentially stand in the way of cooperation. These include: lack of political will; lack of trust between neighbours; lack of appreciation as to whether a particular stock is shared or not; poorly defined maritime boundaries; and lack of funding to carry out effective fisheries management.

However, it is hoped that this chapter has demonstrated that cooperation on management of shared stocks need not be an 'all or nothing' action. Instead, there is great scope for flexibility, whereby cooperating States may jointly chose to adopt as many or as few of the tools that are potentially available. Thus the amount of cooperation can be readily adapted to, *inter alia*, the nature of the political situation and the amount of funding that exists between the States in question. In practice, the arrangements under consideration here show that States may sometimes prefer to focus on conservation and management alone or on MCS and/or enforcement alone. However, the point is that effective management of shared stocks ideally requires cooperation on research and stock assessment, conservation and management, MCS and enforcement together, and that States should strive to go as far as possible in each of these areas.

Annex: The 39 arrangements under consideration

Each entry below lists the short name of the arrangement (adopted for the purposes of this chapter), the full name and the source of the text:

1. **Argentina/UK Joint Statement**
   Joint Statement on the Conservation of Fisheries, 1990
   [1991] *International Journal of Estuarine and Coastal Law* 146

2. **River Plate Treaty**
   Treaty of the La Plata River and its Maritime Limits, 1973 [*Argentina/Uruguay*]
   13 *International Legal Materials* 1974, 251-267

3. **Australia/Indonesia MOU**
   Memorandum of Understanding between the Government of the Republic of Indonesia and the Government of Australia Concerning the Implementation of a Provisional Fisheries Surveillance and Enforcement Arrangement, 1981
   J.I. Charney and L.M. Alexander (eds.), *International Maritime Boundaries* (Martinus Nijhoff, Dordrecht, 1993), 1238-1239

4. **Australia/Indonesia Agreement**
   Agreement between the Government of Australia and the Government of the Republic of Indonesia Relating to Cooperation in Fisheries, 1992
   < www.austlii.edu.au/au/other/dfat/treaties/1993/18.html > (last visited 02.06.02)

5. **Torres Strait Treaty**
   Treaty between Australia and the Independent State of Papua New Guinea concerning Sovereignty and Maritime Boundaries in the area between the two Countries, including the area known as Torres Strait, and Related Matters, 1978
   < www.austlii.edu.au/au/other/dfat/treaties/1985/4.html > (last visited 02.06.02)

6. **Japan/China Agreement**
   Agreement on Fisheries between Japan and the People's Republic of China, 1997
   Park Hee Kwon, *The Law of the Sea and Northeast Asia: A Challenge for Cooperation* (Kluwer Law International, The Hague, 2000), 208-215 (unofficial translation)

7. **Japan/Korea Agreement**
   Agreement on Fisheries between the Republic of Korea and Japan, 1998
   Park Hee Kwon, *The Law of the Sea and Northeast Asia: A Challenge for Cooperation* (Kluwer Law International, The Hague, 2000), 215-223 (unofficial translation)

8. **NEAFC Convention**
   Convention on Future Multilateral Cooperation in North-East Atlantic Fisheries, 1980
   < www.neafc.org/ > (last visited 02.06.02)
9. **Herring System**
   Protocol on the Conservation, Rational Utilization and Management of Norwegian Spring Spawning Herring (Atlanto-Scandian Herring) in the Northeast Atlantic, 1996 and Agreed Records 1997-2001
   < www.oceanlaw.net/texts/herring2.htm > (last visited 02.06.02), and hard copies supplied to the author of the Agreed Record of Conclusions of Fisheries Consultations on the Management of the Norwegian Spring-Spawning (Atlanto-Scandian) Herring Stock in the North-East Atlantic for each of 2000 and 2001
10. **Mackerel System**
    Agreed Record of Conclusions of Fisheries Consultations between the European Community, the Faroe Islands and Norway on the Management of Mackerel in the North-East Atlantic for 2000 and for 2001
    Hard copies supplied to the author
11. **Faroes/UK Agreement**
    Agreement between the Government of the Kingdom of Denmark together with the Home Government of the Faroe Islands, on the one hand, and the Government of the United Kingdom of Great Britain and Northern Ireland, on the other hand, relating to the Maritime Delimitation between the Faroe Islands and the United Kingdom, 1999
    [1999] *International Journal of Marine and Coastal Law* 551
12. **Norway/Russia 1975 Agreement**
    Agreement on Cooperation in the Fishing Industry, 1975
    United Nations Treaty Series, vol. 983, 8-9
13. **Norway/Russia 1976 Agreement**
    Agreement Concerning Mutual Relations in the Field of Fisheries, 1976
    United Nations Treaty Series, vol. 1157, 147–149
14. **Norway/Russia 1978 Agreement**
    Agreement on an Interim Practical Arrangement for Fishing in an Adjoining Area in the Barents Sea, 1978
    Text not seen, but commentary available in: (a) E. Hey, *The Regime for the Exploitation of Transboundary Marine Fisheries Resources* (Martinus Nijhoff, Dordrecht, 1989), 169-171 and (b) R.R. Churchill and G. Ulfstein, *Marine Management in Disputed Areas: The Case of the Barents Sea* (Routledge, London, 1992), 91-125
15. **Loophole Agreement**
    Agreement between the Government of Iceland, the Government of Norway and the Government of the Russian Federation Concerning Certain Aspects of Cooperation in the Area of Fisheries, 1999
    < www.oceanlaw.net/texts/barents.htm > (last visited 02.06.02)

16. **Baltic Sea Convention**
Convention on Fishing and Conservation of the Living Resources in the Baltic Sea and the Belts, 1973 (as amended)
< www.ibsfc.org/ > (last visited 02.06.02)

17. **Mediterranean Agreement**
Agreement for the Establishment of the General Fisheries Commission for the Mediterranean, 1997
< www.fao.org/Legal/default.htm > (last visited 02.06.02)

18. **Black Sea Convention**
Convention Concerning Fishing in the Black Sea, 1959
< www.oceanlaw.net/texts/blacksea.htm > (last visited 02.06.02)

19. **Gulf Agreement**
Agreement for the Establishment of the Regional Commission for Fisheries, 1999
< www.fao.org/fi/body/rfb/RECOFI/recofi_agreement_text.htm >
(last visited 02.06.02)

20. **Canada/US Enforcement Agreement**
Agreement Between the Government of the United States of America and the Government of Canada on Fisheries Enforcement, 1990
Hard copy supplied to the author

21. **Halibut Convention**
Convention for the Preservation of the Halibut Fishery of the Northern Pacific Ocean and Bering Sea, 1953 (as amended)
D.A. McCaughran and S.H. Hoag, 'The 1979 Protocol to the Convention and Related Legislation', *International Pacific Halibut Commission Technical Report No.26* (IPHC, Seattle, Washington, 1992), 15–21

22. **Pacific Salmon Treaty**
Treaty between the Government of Canada and the Government of the United States of America Concerning Pacific Salmon, 1985 (as amended), and Agreement between the Government of Canada and the Government of the United States of America, 1999
< www.psc.org/Treaty/TREATY.HTM > (last visited 02.06.02)

23. **FFA Convention**
South Pacific Forum Fisheries Agency Convention, 1979
< www.oceanlaw.net/texts/ffa.htm > (last visited 02.06.02)

24. **Nauru Agreement**
Nauru Agreement Concerning Cooperation in the Management of Fisheries of Common Interest, 1982
< www.oceanlaw.net/texts/nauru.htm > (last visited 02.06.02)

25. **Niue Treaty**
Niue Treaty on Cooperation in Fisheries Surveillance and Law Enforcement in the South Pacific Region, 1982
< www.oceanlaw.net/texts/niue.htm > (last visited 02.06.02)

26. **Micronesia Arrangement**
    Federated States of Micronesia Arrangement for Regional Fisheries
    Access, 1994
    < www.oceanlaw.net/texts/micronesia.htm > (last visited 02.06.02)

27. **Colombia/Jamaica Treaty**
    Maritime Delimitation Treaty between Jamaica and the Republic of
    Colombia, 1993
    J.I. Charney and L.M. Alexander (eds.), *International Maritime
    Boundaries* (Martinus Nijhoff, Dordrecht, 1998), 2200–2204

28. **Colombia/Dominican Republic Agreement**
    Agreement on the Delimitation of Marine and Submarine Areas and
    Maritime Cooperation between the Dominican Republic and the
    Republic of Colombia, 1978
    J.I. Charney and L.M. Alexander (eds.), *International Maritime
    Boundaries* (Martinus Nijhoff, Dordrecht, 1993), 488–490

29. **Colombia/Costa Rica Treaty**
    Treaty on Delimitation of Marine and Submarine Areas and Maritime
    Cooperation between the Republic of Colombia and the Republic of
    Costa Rica, 1977
    J.I. Charney and L.M. Alexander (eds.), *International Maritime
    Boundaries* (Martinus Nijhoff, Dordrecht, 1993), 474–476

30. **Colombia/Panama Treaty**
    Treaty on the Delimitation of Marine and Submarine Areas and
    Associated Matters Between the Republic of Panama and the Republic
    of Colombia, 1976
    J.I. Charney and L.M. Alexander (eds.), *International Maritime
    Boundaries* (Martinus Nijhoff, Dordrecht, 1993), 532–535

31. **Colombia/Ecuador Agreement**
    Agreement between the Government of Colombia and the Government
    of Ecuador Relating to the Maritime Boundary between Colombia and
    Ecuador, 1975
    J.I. Charney and L.M. Alexander (eds.), *International Maritime
    Boundaries* (Martinus Nijhoff, Dordrecht, 1993), 815–817

32. **Costa Rica/Panama Treaty**
    Treaty Concerning Delimitation of Marine Areas and Maritime
    Cooperation between the Republic of Costa Rica and the Republic of
    Panama, 1980
    J.I. Charney and L.M. Alexander (eds.), *International Maritime
    Boundaries* (Martinus Nijhoff, Dordrecht, 1993), 547–549

33. **Netherlands/Venezuela Treaty**
    Delimitation Treaty between the Kingdom of the Netherlands and the
    Republic of Venezuela, 1978
    J.I. Charney and L.M. Alexander (eds.), *International Maritime
    Boundaries* (Martinus Nijhoff, Dordrecht, 1993), 631–637

34. **Trinidad and Tobago/Venezuela Agreement**
    Fishing Agreement between the Government of the Republic of Trinidad and Tobago and the Government of the Republic of Venezuela, 1985
    [1987] *International Journal of Estuarine and Coastal Law* 101

35. **Lake Victoria Convention**
    Convention for the Establishment of the Lake Victoria Fisheries Organization, 1994 (as amended)
    < www.fao.org/fi/body/rfb/LVFO/lvfo_agreement_text.htm > (last visited 02.06.02)

36. **African Atlantic Convention**
    Regional Convention on Fisheries Cooperation Among African States Bordering the Atlantic Ocean, 1991
    < www.fao.org/fi/body/rfb/AAFC/aafc_convention_text.htm > (last visited 02.06.02)

37. **SRFC Access Convention**
    Convention Relative à la Détermination des Conditions d'Accès et d'Exploitation des Ressources Halieutiques au Large des Côtes des Etats Membres de la Commission Sous-Régionale des Pêches, 1993
    Hard copy supplied to the author

38. **SRFC Hot Pursuit Convention**
    Convention sur la Cooperation Sous-Régionale dans l'Exercise du Droit de Poursuite Maritime, 1993
    Hard copy supplied to the author

39. **Mauritania/Senegal Convention**
    Convention entre le Gouvernement de la République du Sénégal et le Gouvernement de la République Islamique de Mauritanie dans le domaine de la Pêche Maritime, 1999
    Hard copy supplied to the author

Participants

Professor Paulo Canelas de Castro has been a lecturer in International, Community and Environment and Water Law at the Faculty of Law, University of Coimbra since 1988, and has been Legal Counsel for the Ministry of the Environment, since 1996.

Professor Joseph W. Dellapenna is Professor of Law at Villanova University, in Villanova, Pennsylvania. He has taught at law schools in the United States and abroad for 27 years. In the course of his career he has practiced, taught and written about managing the water environment, both in the United States and internationally. He contributed nearly the whole of volume 1, part of volume 2, and part of volume 6 to the treatise *Waters and Water Rights*, the standard work on water law in the United States. He has served as a consultant on water management problems to the Directory-General of Natural Resources (Direçao-General dos Recursos Naturais) in Portugal and has consulted in the Middle East on problems of transboundary water management. He is completing a book on *Water in the Middle East: The Limits and Potential of Law*, and has written numerous articles on international water law as well as on other topics.

Dr Olufemi Elias works at the United Nations Compensation Commission in Geneva, Switzerland. Prior to that he was a lecturer at King's College, London.

Professor Malgosia Fitzmaurice LLB, LLM and PhD University of Warsaw: Her field of expertise is public international law with special interests in international environmental law and the law of treaties on which topics she has extensively published. In summer 2001 she delivered the Hague Academy lectures on 'The International Protection of the Environment.' Secretary of the International Law Association group on International Water Resources. Convenor of the Public International Law Group within the London University LLM.

Professor David Freestone has been the head of the Environmentally and Socially Sustainable Development (ESSD) and International Law Group in the Legal Department of the World Bank since May 1996. Prior to that he was Professor of International Law at the University of Hull, England, from where he holds the degree of LL.D. He has written widely on European and International Environmental Law and Law of the Sea. He is Editor in Chief of the International Environmental Law and Policy monograph series published by Kluwer Law International and is founder and Editor-in-Chief of the *International Journal of Marine and Coastal Law*.

Professor Gerhard Hafner studied law in Vienna and subsequently in the Hague and Moscow; since 1970 member of the Institute of international law and international relations of the Vienna University; Prof. of international law at the Vienna University; teaching activities at Bratislava, Stanford (USA) and Paris; 1993–1995 Head of the Division of General International Law in the Austrian Federal Ministry for foreign Affairs; Member of Head of Austrian delegations to international conferences; since 1 January 1997 Member of the UN-International Law Commission: associate Member of the Institut de Droit International.

Nigel Haigh retired as Director of the Institute for European Environmental Policy (IEEP) in 1998, but remains an Honorary Fellow. He studied engineering, practiced as a Chartered Patent Agent for ten years, and turned to the environmental field in 1972. He was Vice-President of the European Environmental Bureau (1975–1979), Chairman of the Green Alliance (1989–1998) and Board Member of the Environment Agency (1995–2000). He is now a member of the Management Board of the European Environment Agency (nominated by the European Parliament). He is an Honorary Research Fellow, Faculty of Laws, University College London and Visiting Research Fellow at Imperial College.

David Ong is a Senior Lecturer at the Department of Law, University of Essex, where he researches and teaches in Law of the Sea and International Environmental Law. He is also a Research Associate on the Joint Development Regimes project at the British Institute of International & Comparative Law. This project aims to publish a collection of the texts of bilateral joint development and transboundary unitisation agreements, along with commentary highlighting their main features and the provision of maps where these are available.

Professor Thomas Wälde has spent the last 30 years on international economic law, in particular natural resources and energy industries, international investment, negotiation, renegotiation and dispute settlement, financing and tax. After law practice and a research fellowship with the Institute for International Economic Law in Frankfurt, he worked for various UN agencies (Centre on Transnational Corporations, UNIDO, Natural Resources and Energy Division), until 1990 as the UN Interregional Adviser on International Investment Policy and Petroleum/Mineral Legislation. In this time, he designed, set up, arranged funding and managed advisory teams in virtually all developing countries on behalf of the World Bank, the UN and the EC dealing with legislative reform and large-scale natural resources/energy & infrastructure project negotiations. Throughout the 1980s, he was responsible for the completion of major natural resources investment contracts, in particular in Africa, Asia, Latin America and Eastern Europe. Advisory services included negotiation, renegotiations and conciliation/dispute settlement in natural resources and energy projects amounting to several billion US$.

Index

Aarhus Convention on Access to
Information, Public Participation
in Decision-Making and Access to
Justice in Environmental Matters,
222, 229
Abatement and prevention of
environmental damage, 78, 87, 89,
112
Africa, 13, 20, 93, 98, 165, 201, 291
African Atlantic Convention, 153,
158, 275, 276
Asian-African Legal Consultative
Committee, 168
Agenda 21, 1, 104, 130, 160, 208
Agriculture, 2, 3, 6, 28, 33, 194
Arab-Israeli Conflict, 162, 187
Arbitration, 24, 38, 43, 149, 160, 173, 216
arbitral tribunal, 30, 73,118, 150, 160,
173
Armed conflict, 56, 78, 84, 164
Arms trade, 43
Autonomy, see sovereignty

Baltic Sea Convention, 253, 254, 259,
263, 264, 267, 271, 272, 274, 275,
276, 277, 278, 279, 281, 285
BP, 42, 98, 107, 111

CEEC (Central and Eastern European
Countries), 21, 22, 23, 26, 38
Chernobyl, 37
Civil Society, 17,40, 41, 43, 44, 45, 49, 51,
103, 110, 201, 202, 219
Clean Development Mechanism, 28
Clean energy, 29, 31, 32,
Climate change, 13, 16, 19, 27, 28, 29, 32,
37, 39, 48, 50, 51, 95, 105, 106, 107,
110
Coal, 10, 16, 22, 30, 32, 37
Compensation, payment of 69, 71, 73, 74,
77, 242
Competition, 11, 15, 18, 21, 22, 23, 26,
31, 35, 40, 48, 51
Compliance mechanisms, 64, 66, 135,
205, 210, 279, 280, 281
Corruption, 25, 38, 42, 43, 49
anti-bribery, 44, 49
anti-corruption, 25, 39
Cotonou Agreement, 13, 17, 25, 43, 44,
46, 51
Customary law, 44, 59, 61, 62, 63, 80,
117, 118, 143–152, 153, 155–164,
167, 168, 169, 171, 175, 178, 179,
187, 188, 189, 190, 229, 230, 236

Danube Convention, 203, 207, 212, 222, 227
Democracy, 12, 15, 63
   democratic principles 25, 43
Developing countries, 15, 20, 26, 27, 28, 33, 38, 42, 43, 44, 45, 84, 95, 101, 104, 105, 107, 151, 291
Dispute resolution 146, 152, 265, 270
Dispute settlement mechanism, 33, 39, 49, 100, 119, 122, 125, 152, 291
Dumping, 30, 33, 34, 42
   anti-dumping, 30, 34, 46

EBRD (European Bank for Reconsruction and Development), 14, 15, 20, 52
Economic cooperation agreements, 24
Economic development, 6, 79, 83, 84, 113, 114, 168, 199,
Ecosystems, 55, 86, 103, 123, 132, 140, 178, 206, 207, 208, 218, 223, 237
Emissions trading, 16, 28, 29, 34, 37, 38, 39, 99, 111, 209, 217
Endangered species, 103
Energy, 2, 9, 10, 11, 13, 15, 16, 17, 19, 20, 21, 23, 24, 25, 27, 29, 31, 32, 33, 34, 35, 37, 39, 41, 42, 43, 45, 46, 47, 48, 49, 50, 51, 148, 291
Energy Charter Treaty, 13, 16, 17, 21, 23, 24, 33, 50,
Environmental degradation, 55, 86, 92, 105, 106, 134, 178, 218
Environmental protection, 2, 6, 55, 79, 81, 83, 88, 113, 114–119, 141, 202, 204, 211, 217, 218
Espoo Convention on Environmental Impact Assessment in a Transboundary Context, 203, 216, 222, 229, 230
European Community/European Union
   accession countries, 11, 12, 16, 21, 22, 23, 24, 26, 27, 33, 34, 40, 50, 52, 195
   association agreements, 24, 25, 26
Europe agreements, 26, 27, 33, 34, 38, 43, 50,
European Environment Agency, 3, 193
Exclusive Economic Zones, 116, 137, 138, 248, 263

Finland, 111, 235, 238, 239, 240, 245
Finnish-Norwegian Frontier River Comission, 238, 239, 240
Finnish-Russian Joint Commission on the Utilisation of Frontier Rivers, 239
Finnish-Swedish Frontier River Comission, 235, 238, 239, 240
fisheries, 3, 33, 123, 134, 239, 247, 248, 249, 251, 252, 253, 254, 255, 256, 258, 259, 260, 261, 262, 263, 265, 266, 268, 274, 275, 277, 278, 279, 282
Forest Alliance, 92, 103
Freshwater, 86, 154, 206, 237

Gabcikovo-Nagymaros case, 81, 145, 211, 229, 237
GATS, 38
GATT, 16, 25, 30, 33, 34, 35, 36, 38, 39, 40, 46
Global warming, 16, 28
Good Governance, 9, 12, 16, 17, 20, 26, 43, 44, 49
Greenhouse gases, 7, 110
Groundwater, 73, 86, 153, 163, 164, 165, 166, 167, 168

Habitats, 98
Hazardous waste, 30, 209
Human rights, 9, 12,15, 17, 25, 41, 42, 43, 80, 148, 168
   violations, 42, 44
Hydrocarbons, 116, 118, 119, 120, 127, 132, 134, 136, 138, 141

IBRD (International Bank for Reconstruction and Development), 91, 92, 93, 96, 99, 100, 106, 110
Inspectors, 100, 124, 125, 137, 279
International Atomic Energy Agency, 148
International Energy Agency, 51,198
Investment, 10, 13, 15, 16, 17, 19, 22, 23, 24, 25, 27, 38, 42, 43, 44, 46, 47, 50, 52, 58, 96, 98, 107, 108, 112, 149, 291
Investors, 14, 23, 24, 38
IPPC, 4, 5, 222

Iraq, 46, 47, 68, 69, 70, 71, 72, 73, 74, 75, 76, 77, 79, 82, 83, 84, 86, 87, 89, 122, 188

Irrigation, 86, 155, 194, 197, 201

Israeli-Palestinian conflict, 162, 186, 187

Kyoto Protocol, 7, 13, 21, 27, 28, 29, 37, 38, 39, 92, 107, 110, 111

Landfill, 7

Lending, 15, 94, 112

Libya, 13, 46, 47, 48, 49, 149, 151

Lome Conventions, 13, 25

Maritime boundaries 116, 117, 118, 121, 126, 129, 131, 133, 135, 138, 148, 152, 249, 252, 260, 261, 262,

Migratory species, 248, 249, 255, 257, 266,

Mining, 30, 129, 130

Multinational companies, 14, 40, 41, 42, 44, 47,48, 108, 122, 126, 134, 136

Multilateral environmental agreements, 16, 19, 35, 107, 124

NAFTA, 30, 31, 35

Non-renewable natural resources, 80

Non-state actors, 14, 15, 16, 18, 26, 40–43,47–49, 51, 62, 64, 65, 80, 92, 100, 103, 105, 147, 148, 213, 219

Norway, 11, 38, 111, 124, 125, 136, 139, 140, 148, 157, 173, 238, 249, 254, 255, 256, 258, 259, 261, 263, 266, 267, 270, 272, 275, 276, 277, 278, 279, 280, 284

Nuclear energy, 28, 35

Nuclear safety, 19, 37, 50

Nuclear power plants, 22, 27, 32, 35, 37, 38, 31,

OECD, 14, 15, 17, 25, 41, 44, 49, 52, 181

OPEC, 15, 29, 50, 51, 52

Ozone depletion, 7, 105, 106, 107, 108

Petroleum products, 29, 30, 38, 44, 46, 70, 121, 123, 125, 126, 128, 129, 130, 131, 132, 134, 136, 137, 138, 139, 140

Phare Programme, 21, 24, 27

Pollutants, 86

Pollution, 4, 5, 7, 19, 29, 71, 86, 88, 95, 111, 121, 122, 123, 124, 125, 127, 128, 130, 132, 134, 137, 138, 139, 140, 152, 162, 164, 168, 173, 174, 175, 178, 182, 183, 206, 209, 211, 222, 237, 239, 240, 242, 243, 244, 245, 246, 252

Poverty policies, 15, 45, 94, 95

Portugal, 25, 148, 158, 192, 193, 194, 195, 196, 197, 198, 199, 200, 201, 202, 203, 205, 209, 216, 218, 219, 220, 227, 228, 230, 232, 289

Prevention of environmental damage, 4, 59, 60, 78, 109, 112, 121, 137, 175, 182, 202, 203, 206, 209, 210, 217, 240, 243

Procurement, 11, 20, 21, 30, 39

Protected, 103, 109, 278, 279

Public-opinion, 41, 43

Quality standards, 32, 33, 86, 139, 154, 199, 202, 203, 206, 207, 209, 217, 223, 227, 231, 239, 240

Reciprocity principle, 31, 32, 33, 39, 43, 64, 226

Refugees, 71, 86

Regional, 10, 11, 12, 17, 39, 99, 106, 170, 219, 240, 241, 248, 249, 265 282, 285, 286, 287

Regional development, 99, 1056,

Remedies, 39, 83, 88,137, 138, 223

Renewable energy, 21, 25, 28, 31, 80, 110

Rio Declaration on Environment and Development, 55, 56, 80, 84, 103, 104, 105, 107, 110, 113, 155, 156, 158, 161, 165, 185, 189, 204

River Oder, 159, 160, 222, 236

Rivers, 86, 144, 154, 155, 156, 157, 159, 161, 168, 171, 175, 188, 193, 196, 197, 198, 199, 200, 201, 206, 210, 239, 240, 241

Safeguard policies, 92, 95, 96, 98, 99

Sanctions, 13, 35, 36, 38, 40, 43, 44, 45, 46, 47, 48, 49, 51, 146, 152

Settlement, see dispute

Shrimp-turtle dispute, 34, 35, 36,
Sovereignty, 9, 37, 44, 45, 46, 49, 57, 118, 119, 120, 124, 127, 145, 154, 155, 156, 157, 159, 160, 161, 162, 163, 170, 177, 199, 245, 273, 283
Spain, 6, 13, 25, 122, 140, 158, 159, 192, 193, 194, 195, 196, 197, 198, 200, 201, 202, 203, 205, 219, 227, 228, 229, 230, 232
Subsidies, 30, 39
Sustainable development, 1, 2, 3, 5, 7, 16, 21, 43, 53, 54, 55, 56, 57, 59, 60, 61, 63, 64, 65, 67, 76, 79, 80, 81, 82, 83, 85, 87, 89, 91, 92, 93, 94, 95, 97, 99, 101, 103, 105, 107, 109, 110, 111, 112, 113, 117, 130, 185, 189, 190, 192, 193, 194, 204, 205, 230, 290
Sweden, 4, 111, 157, 235, 238, 240, 241, 245
Swedish, 2, 3, 237, 239, 241, 243, 245

Tariffs, 30, 37, 46
Taxes, 15, 28, 29, 30, 31, 32, 47, 50, 51, 128, 139, 291
Technology, 11, 27, 38, 107, 108, 111, 120, 121, 281
Trade, 11, 12, 15, 16, 17, 19, 23, 24, 25, 26, 27, 29, 30, 31, 32, 33, 34, 35, 36, 38, 39, 40, 43, 44, 45, 46, 47, 50, 77, 147
  non-tariff trade barriers, 30
  energy trade, 12, 15, 17, 29, 32, 33, 34
Transboundary pollution, 7, 114, 178, 246
Transboundary unitisation agreement, 125
Treaty, 1, 2, 3, 4, 5, 7, 13, 16, 17, 18, 19, 21, 23, 24, 33, 43, 50, 51, 61, 82, 96, 114, 124, 128, 129, 130, 131, 135, 137, 138, 145, 149, 150, 156, 157, 158, 160, 162, 165, 166, 173, 181, 195, 196, 198, 199, 238, 249, 251,

252, 253, 254, 255, 256, 257, 258, 259, 260, 261, 262, 263, 265, 266, 267, 268, 269, 270, 271, 272, 273, 274, 275, 276, 277, 278, 279, 280, 281, 282, 283, 284, 285, 286
Tribunals, 44, 74, 80, 81, 149, 160
Tuna-dolphin cases, 34, 35, 36

UN/United Nations, 14, 15, 20, 56, 70, 75, 100, 104, 147, 150, 151, 161, 162, 166, 177, 188, 189, 247, 291
UN/United Nations Charter, 44, 46, 68, 147, 151
UN/United Nations Compensation Commission, 67, 68, 69, 70, 73, 289
UN/United Nations Security Council, 44, 46, 68, 69, 147, 151
UNCED, 113, 160
UNCLOS, 130, 139
UNDP, 71, 104, 105, 106, 107
UNECE, 203, 229, 230
UNEP, 79, 99, 104, 105, 106, 107, 108, 139
UNFCCC, 104, 107, 110, 111
UNIDO, 99, 106, 107, 291

War, 10, 23, 41, 67, 69, 71, 73, 75, 77, 79, 81, 83, 85, 87, 89, 148, 165, 199
Waste, 30, 86, 111, 240
  waste management, 4, 120
  waste disposal, 31, 121
  waste water, 222
Watercourses, 58, 154, 157, 159, 162, 163, 167, 171, 172, 175, 176, 178, 179, 180, 181, 182, 184, 186, 236, 237, 238, 239, 240, 242, 245
Wetlands, 73, 86
Wildlife, 41, 132
World Bank 14, 15, 20, 41, 43, 44, 91–112, 290, 291
WTO, 14, 15, 17, 30, 34, 35, 36, 37, 38, 39, 41, 49, 51

International Energy and Resources Law and Policy Series

Other titles in this series:

1. *European Community Energy Law – Selected topics*, D. MacDougall & T.W. Wälde (eds.)
2. *Insurance and Legal Issues in the Oil Industry*, D.D. Peng (ed.) (ISBN 1-85333-79-X)
3. *Natural Gas in the Internal Market*, E.J. Mestmácker (ed.) (ISBN 1-85333-795-1)
4. *Minerals Investment under the Shari'a Law*, W.M.H. El-Malik (ISBN 1-85333-907-5)
5. *International Oil and Gas Investment*, T.W. Wälde & G.K. Ndi (eds.) (ISBN 1-85333-963-6)
6. *An Introduction to the Regulation of the Petroleum Industry*, B.G. Taverne (ISBN 1-85966-081-9)
7. *Taxation of Mineral Enterprises*, J. Otto (ed.) (ISBN 1-85966-105-X)
8. *International Petroleum Contracts*, Z. Gao (ed.) (ISBN 1-85966-103-3)
9. *Co-operative Agreements in the Extractive Petroleum Industry*, B.G. Taverne (ISBN 90-411-0926-9)
10. *The Energy Charter Treaty*, T.W. Wälde (ed.) (ISBN 90-411-0913-7)
11. *Environmental Regulation of Oil and Gas*, Z. Gao (ed.) (ISBN 90-411-0726-6)
12. *Liquefied Natural Gas Developing & Financing International Energy Projects*, G.B. Greenwald (ed.) (ISBN 90-411-9664-1)
13. *Negotiating Mining Agreements: Past, Present & Future Trends*, D. Barberis (ISBN 90-411-9673-0)
14. *Contemporary Developments in Nuclear Energy Law: Harmonising Legislation in CEEC/NIS*, Nathalie L.J.T. Horbach (ISBN 90-411-9719-2)
15. *Petroleum, Industry and Governments: An Introduction to Petroleum Regulation, Economics and Government Policies*, Bernard Taverne (ISBN 90-411-9747-8)
16. *The Promotion and Licensing of Petroleum Prospective Acreage*, Michael A.G. Bunter (ISBN 90-411-1712-1)
17. *Disused Offshore Installations and Pipelines: Towards "Sustainable Decommissioning"*, Morakinyo Adedayo Ayoade (ISBN 90-411-1739-3)

18. *Exploitation of Natural Resources in the 21st Century*, Malgosia Fitzmaurice & Milena Szuniewicz (eds.)
    (ISBN) 90-411-2063-7)
19. *Energy Policy and Regulation in the People's Republic of China*, Philip Andrews-Speed
    (ISBN 90-411-2233-8)
20. *Oil and Gas Law in Kazakhstan: National and International Perspectives*, Illias Bantekas, John Paterson & Maidan Suleimenov (eds.)
    (ISBN 90-411-2250-8)